Inside Maharishi's Ashram

A Personal Story

Rhoda Orme-Johnson

Oil painting of Maharishi by David Orme-Johnson, 2005, after a photo by Robert Oates, 1975.

Inside Maharishi's Ashram

A Personal Story

Rhoda Orme-Johnson

TM-Sidhi®, Yogic Flying®, Transcendental Meditation®, TM®, Maharishi AyurVeda®, Maharishi Vastu®, Science of Creative Intelligence®, Maharishi Yagya®, Amrit Kalash™, Age of Enlightenment Governor Training Course, AEGTC, Maharishi Gandharva Veda, Maharishi Jyotish, Maharishi Vedic Science, Maharishi Vedic University, Transcendental Meditation Teacher Training Course (TTC), and Vedic Science are protected trademarks and are used in the U.S. under license or with permission.

ISBN: 978-1540493699
Library of Congress Control Number: 2016920850

CreateSpace Independent Publishing Platform, North Charleston, SC

First edition, 2017
First printing, 2017

Cover painting: Oil painting by David Orme-Johnson, from a photo by Victor Raymond (c. 1975)
Cover and book design: Warren Simons and Janice Prescott

Contents

Preface

MANY YEARS HAVE PASSED since I have had any personal contact with Maharishi, and my memories are fading fast, but it seems important to try to recall and to relate what I saw, heard, and learned from him. I absorbed his knowledge as much by example as by direct teaching, and my contributions to his history may seem trivial and anecdotal to some, but I believe they show many facets of his activity and his methods that may be of interest to those who now admire him from great reaches of time and space.

I have included stories from my own personal history for the sake of my children, grandchildren, family, and friends. You may find them amusing, or may wish to skip over them. As you like. I am indebted to all of them for supporting my devotion to the Transcendental Meditation technique® (TM®) and for contributing to my life with Maharishi and the TM organization, or movement as we called it in those enthusiastic early days. I deeply appreciate their roles and sacrifices, especially those of my children, who had to do without us sometimes for months at a time, and who often wanted to be like other children and have what they had. And especially, I must thank my husband David for dragging me along, often reluctant, sometimes resentful, and always, I would eventually realize, for our greater good. He had the vision and knew he wanted to be with Maharishi from his first glimpse of him in *Life* magazine back in the 1960s. While he was looking forward, I was usually looking backward, toward my children, my abandoned homes, and my comforts, but I eventually adapted, stopped weeping, became cheerful, worked my hardest, and did my best. David's memoirs (in progress) will give a richer, fuller picture of our lives with Maharishi and the TM movement, but this is my angle on what happened, told in my often irreverent voice.

Full disclosure: I loved Maharishi from the beginning and knew on some deep level that he was the wisest, most generous, most exceptional being I would ever know. I was immediately "in the pocket," as he would say. Once I questioned him about special treatment he was awarding some people and not others. He was wooing some, it seems, for their own good, of course, while others didn't need special treatment; they were already "in the pocket." The new tree, he said, requires attention and has to be watered every day. The old tree doesn't require much attention and gives fruit year after year.

My friend Sheila once asked him about some of the strange birds that flocked around him. "I take whatever I can get," he said, "and I use them for whatever they are worth." That may sound selfish or heartless, but the truth was, if you offered to work for him or for the TM movement, which was really the same thing, or asked for his guidance, or even if you just put yourself in his way to give him a flower or ask him a question, he would spontaneously act for your evolution. He would give you something to do, or not do, something that would ultimately be best for you. There was one exception. If you asked for his advice and he gave it, but you couldn't accept it, because you wanted what you wanted so very badly, and you asked again and again, he would tell you, on the third attempt, what you wanted to hear. He would no longer stand between you and your karma, your just desserts coming to you from your past. Or if you asked him to bless something you had already done, he would nod. Too late to redirect your actions.

He was unfailingly polite and courteous and mindful of the needs and comforts of others, never brusque or rude. You have only to watch videos of him interacting with the crude and sometimes vicious reporters who questioned him to see this in action. And he had a wonderful sense of humor and ability to enjoy a joke or the moment or a sunrise or a child offering a flower. He was alive in the moment and aware that he was on display at all times, for everyone's good.

Over the years Maharishi changed the names of his organizations and its leaders' titles, and even gave familiar terms "Being" new labels (like "Constitution of the Universe"), and so kept the knowledge ever new and interesting. He also added new courses and programs on health (Maharishi AyurVeda®), building and city design and architecture (Maharishi Vastu®), Vedic astrology (Maharishi Jyotish), and music for world peace (Maharishi Gandharva Veda^SM). Why "Maharishi" in the titles? As he researched each area of Vedic knowledge, Maharishi gathered experts from all over India and southeast Asia to his side (or by phone). He searched the ancient texts and then structured each program to be optimally evolutionary and authentic, thus identifying and separating his unique programs from the multitude of other schools of thought and practices. I will use the terms and names appropriate for each historical period and grow into the current designations and trademarks as they come about. This is not an official publication of the TM organization. It is a personal memoir, and I hope to keep it true to the times in which we lived.

I am offering this flower to his memory, and more than that, to his eternal presence among us.

Part One:
From Shtetl to Ashram

Maharishi Mahesh Yogi at the course on the Science of Creative Intelligence® held at Humboldt State University, Arcata, California, 1971. Maharishi would slowly walk into the lecture hall and allow the meditators an opportunity to see him up close and offer him a flower in gratitude for the techniques and knowledge they were enjoying.

Sitting Before the Guru

THE TM MOVEMENT had taken over Humboldt State University in August 1971 while all the usual students and faculty were on vacation. About 1,700 mostly college-aged young people, practitioners of the Transcendental Meditation technique, were lodged in dormitories and filled the grand field house where Maharishi Mahesh Yogi would offer a one-month course on the Science of Creative Intelligence, the first course toward becoming a TM teacher. On a tall stage, so everyone could see, was a small sofa covered in white silk and a low table in front of it with a microphone and flowers. On that sofa sat Maharishi, an Indian monk. Video cameras were positioned to capture every word and gesture. In a special section right in front sat the elders and dignitaries of the movement, mostly those who had welcomed Maharishi on his first visits to the U.S. in 1958 and opened their homes and hearts to him, people like Mother Olson, who told her story in her memoir first published as *Hermit in the House*. They belonged to the first TM organization, founded in England, called the Spiritual Regeneration Movement (SRM).

There among that SRM group sat my husband David and I. He, because he had done one of the first research studies on TM and was invited to present it, and I, his wife. Our kids, Nate and Sara (almost 3 and 1), were with a babysitter. We had our notebooks in

15

front of us and our pens poised. We were disoriented and amazed. Maharishi talked about swinging between two infinities (I knew what that meant mathematically, but that wasn't what he meant), Being (what was that?) and God (who exactly was that?) and the Science of Creative Intelligence (what was that?), and David and I looked at each other and shrugged and wrote it all down. We would figure it out later.

Maharishi spoke with unfailing courtesy and gentleness, patiently explaining over and again to his materialist Western audience that there was a field of life, the most important field of life, that they had somehow missed learning about, and that mistake, that ignorance, was the source of all misery and suffering. How in the world had I, a Jewish girl with a degree in mathematics and philosophy from Vassar College, and with serious issues with God, ended up here, sitting in front of an Indian monk?

I was raised in an insular Jewish community in East Cleveland, Ohio, self-isolated from the surrounding population, while WWII and the Holocaust raged in Europe. My mother had been born in a *shtetl*, a small Jewish village in western Russia, and had come to Cleveland in 1923, knowing neither her age nor her birthdate. The usual American translation of her Yiddish name, Feiga, was Fanny, which meant *tuchas* to her new American friends. She changed her name to Fay, picked a birthdate and age, and became fluent in English without an accent, but was most comfortable among her own people, as was my father Nate, whose father Frank Bonovitz had traveled to Cleveland as an orphan with countrymen from Vilnius in Lithuania a generation earlier.

I was born in 1940, their first child, and we lived on E. 142 Street across the street from Robert Fulton Elementary School. My father's sister Dorothy and her family lived upstairs in our duplex. Ice was delivered by horse and cart and placed in our icebox in the kitchen. We wouldn't have a refrigerator for years. I remember a big celebration in the street when the war ended. Alan Mars, who lived up the street, was the first to have a television, and we all went to his house to watch Howdy Doody and the test pattern on a small black and white screen. I was nine that year. Family was all. Every Christmas Eve my uncle Moe (married to my father's eldest sister Betty) always took us kids to some kind of street fair and bought us big mesh stockings filled with little toys so we could share in the Christmas holiday. My mother celebrated Hannukah with us. My father smiled benignly on the whole thing, uninvolved. Every day was children's day, he said.

My father worked for my uncle Moe in his fish house, as we called the business. They fished Lake Erie, gutted and filleted the fish, and sold it to markets throughout the city. Later they would freeze it into little packages. Uncle Moe hired my Uncle Harry, my dad's older brother, and they were president and vice-president, and when my dad's time came to enter the work force he became, what?, the floor manager, the handyman, the personnel manager? I don't know. I do know he was awakened at night when the ice machine stopped spewing out ice and he had to go fix it before the fish rotted. He came home exhausted from long days in the cold and wet and being on his feet in rubber boots. When someone failed to show up on the filet line, he took their place. I followed him everywhere any chance I got because he only had Sunday off. Once he took me with him to the doctor to have his finger lanced from an infection he got from a fish bone on the line.

My dad wanted to go to the war, to be part of the general fever, but Aunt Betty wouldn't hear of it. She got Moe to have him excused because he was essential to producing food for the nation. He was not happy about that. Uncle Ben, one of my mother's brothers, got to go. Europe was no big deal, he assured my father, full of ruins and bombed out buildings and poverty and horror. He brought back a set of delicate, gold rimmed china for his wife. Who knows what miserable family had to sell it or abandon it or lost it to thieves. My sister Adele has it now. A lady up the street, it was whispered, had been recognized as one who had worked with the Germans in the camps and she was then shunned.

My father struggled to get out of the fish house. He tried being an upholsterer with Uncle Ben. Dorothy's husband Morrie had a small plumbing supplies business but already had a partner. Another of my mother's brothers was a butcher. One had a small grocery store. My dad tried to learn furniture repair, and soon hit on an idea. He wasn't very good at the trades but he could organize the workers and take care of furniture damage. Insurance companies would need an adjuster to assess fire damage and then find someone to repair it. My dad started Bonney Service Company and combined all those functions, making it easier for the insurance company to handle the loss. He tried to make a go of it, and couldn't at first earn enough to support the family and had to go back to the fish house. He tried again and it took off. When I was eleven we were able to move up to the Heights, Cleveland Heights, to a side-by-side duplex with my aunt Dorothy, again in a Jewish neighborhood, and a school full of Jewish kids. I helped with the business by entering the daily calls each night in a ledger.

I was a difficult child, with a temper, but usually laughing and cheerful. When I was five I had a little boyfriend down the street named David and we played together in a little pool. My mother panicked. She was afraid I would marry a non-Jew. (Prescient!) I wasn't taking to Judaism. I was made to go to Sunday school, but one day when the teacher was explaining about the Pharaoh and the 10 plagues of Egypt, I raised my little hand. Why, I asked, didn't God make Pharaoh nice? Why didn't God get the Jews out of slavery without killing all those children? What kind of God was this? My teacher couldn't answer. I told my parents I wasn't going back. My dad supported me. He usually humored my mother and her religious directives, but he insisted on his ham steak Sunday mornings and he let me prevail.

I read widely, especially the classics. My local library in the Heights had a shelf called Great Books. I read most of them, even though I was probably too young to understand them very well. I read away the long nights I spent babysitting as a teenager. I got into the literature of the disenfranchised. I read *Ramona* by Helen Hunt Jackson, the story about how the greedy Californians persecuted the Indians and Spanish and stole their lands and lives. I read Richard Wright's *Black Boy* and learned about racism right here and now. The world seemed so full of injustice. Where was my mother's God? What was He doing? I remember one late misty night when I was babysitting somewhere and had been reading some novel of misery and persecution. I was in a fever of righteousness. I wanted to talk to God. He was certainly not in that middle-class living room. I went outside and stood under the streetlights, shaking my fist and asking God where He was and why He wasn't doing a better job of it. Why was He allowing so much pain and suffering? What kind of creation was this!

In my late teens I became interested in other religions. What were they all about? I read novels about the disciples. I read books on Zoroastrianism and anything else on the religion shelves at the downtown library. Finally, I stumbled on Jean Paul Sartre and existentialism, and somewhere he said that *we* are totally responsible for our own selves and that man creates God, that *man* makes God in his own image, not the other way around. Aha, I thought, it is all a construct man can't live without. No One is responsible for this world. WE all are. Liberating, to be sure, but lonely, and without order or meaning. But truth is truth.

When I fell in love with my future husband David Orme-Johnson and brought him home to meet my parents, my mother was upset. She got down the encyclopedia and looked up Christianity. She didn't know any Christians, except maybe Kermit, who worked for my dad and refinished tables, and John Saah, who was probably not a Christian but a Muslim and did the carpet repair and who always gave us a tray of baklava and other sweets for Christmas that his wife had made.

Why couldn't you marry a Jew like you, she reproached me. But we are both atheists (David says he wasn't), I replied. Well, why can't you marry a Jewish atheist, she argued. Finally, I said, look, if you don't shape up, I'm not inviting you to the wedding. She gave up and wrote a letter to David. You are not the man of my dreams, she said, but I'll put you in my dreams. David, who knew that his family had the very same values and ideals, knew they would all love each other. His family lived in a Jewish neighborhood in El Paso, Texas; his first girlfriends were Jewish girls; and his family ate bagels and lox for their traditional Christmas breakfast before they opened their presents. And he was right. They all did love each other and were very comfortable together.

We got married in 1963 in my parents' living room by a Jewish lawyer (a Rabbi wouldn't do it unless we promised to raise the children Jewish). He was wearing sunglasses because he had an eye infection. My mother was satisfied. Unusual but it seems to have taken. We all lived happily ever after. And my brother married a *shiksa*. Poor mom. At least my sisters married Jews. Adele married a Jewish biophysicist, almost as good as a Jewish doctor! Mom was thrilled. And Linda married a Jew too, but after my mother had died. She was probably there anyway, standing close to the *chuppah* (the canopy over the bride and groom) and *kvelling* (feeling happy and proud).

So, how did I get to Humboldt? Why was I sitting in front of an Indian guru talking about God and infinity? It was TM's fault.

'Want to Enjoy Life More?'

DAVID FINISHED HIS COURSEWORK and dissertation for his PhD in psychology in 1968 at the University of Maryland in College Park. But he always wanted to be an artist, a painter and a sculptor. He had learned to weld in the family steel fabricating business in El Paso and he had turned our garage in Takoma Park, near the University, into a welding studio. He fashioned delicate flowers and large abstract pieces out of found objects and old washing machine sides. He experimented with glass glazing to color the metal. David turned his attention to art with the same dedication and purposefulness that has always characterized his activity. As a graduation present his parents took us and our baby Nate to Hawaii and we camped with them on three different islands. A company picked us up at each airport, took us to a camper, and we circled the islands, staying at beaches and beautiful parks. David got inspired by the many waterfalls and ponds of Hawaii and came back home interested in making fountains, and started in on that.

David's new fountains were made of colorful metal pieces and they started to sell. He was getting known and was beginning to pick up commissions. He had set psychology aside for the time being and was serious about making a career out of sculpture. The shop in El Paso would be the ideal studio for him. It was huge and

Nate on our front lawn enjoying the warm spring weather. The fountain behind him is a mother holding a baby in her arms. You can see the baby's legs. Her skirt was concrete plastered over lathing and David pressed flowers and other articles into the wet material to make the patterns and decorations. David also used pieces of old water conduits to form her hat and other parts. It sits in a little pond he dug and lined with concrete and has a pump recirculating the water.

had the best equipment, and there were pieces of steel lying around everywhere. We made the decision to start our lives over again at the ages of 27 and 28, so we put our house up for rent for a year, put Nate in the car seat between us and drove to El Paso so David could sculpt there. He made large realistic and abstract pieces, as well as fountains and birdbaths, and soon had his work in a gallery in the area of Kern Place near where his parents lived. His first show garnered good reviews in the newspapers and he was seriously off on his new career (go to www.Orme-Johnsonpaintings .com and click on sculptures to see a selection of his work from that period). I got a part-time job teaching English and world literature at nearby University of Texas at El Paso (UTEP). David's grandfather Percy McGhee had been the University architect for years and designed a number of building in the Tibetan style of Katmandu.

One day David saw a small handwritten note on a bulletin board near the corner drugstore in Kern Place, just a few doors up from his gallery. It said, "Want to enjoy life more? Lecture on Transcendental Meditation." David never reads signs or looks at bulletin boards, but he felt a force moving his head until his eyes rested on this little piece of paper. He quickly wrote down the information, checking it several times to make sure he had it right.

David had heard about TM from a high school buddy of his and when we visited Clint Lee in New York once from our Maryland home, we discovered that he had learned Transcendental Meditation, met Maharishi and the Beach Boys who were touring through, and was considering becoming a TM teacher himself. David thought that meditation had transformed the guy into a self-confident, more centered version of himself. Here was his chance to learn that technique. He couldn't locate a teacher so he tried a meditation technique my sister Adele had picked up on one of her India trips, but it didn't do much for him. We went to the TM introductory lecture at the college. A young fellow named Casey Coleman sat on a small stage and talked about all the wonderful benefits of the technique. I was not impressed. How would you know if you were doing it right? And who had proved that those benefits were real? David sensed something spiritual in the guy and signed up. Our friend Jean and I decided we would wait and see what happened to him.

David wasn't a student anymore so he would have to pay the adult rate, which was $75. It was a lot of money for us. I had to borrow money from his parents to buy groceries that week. He was adamant, we quarreled, he bought some very expensive flowers, a new white handkerchief, and several pieces of fruit. It seems there would be a brief ceremony of thanksgiving to the ancient tradition from which this meditation had come, and the student was supposed to contribute a few items. He drove off to a nearby motel where rooms had been rented, and there he learned the Transcendental Meditation technique and did his very first meditation.

That afternoon, after lunch, we took Nate to a neighborhood park to play on the swings, and I was totally surprised. David was different. Instead of being restless, uncomfortable, and anxious, as he usually was in public places, images of snipers aiming at him from nearby windows flashing through his mind, he was relaxed, happy, in the moment. What had happened? TM did that? I was ready! Sign me up!

In those days, there were only a few teachers, and they covered large territories. I would have to wait six months, until the following fall, before one would come back to El Paso. My life was very intense at that time. Over that six-month wait we had bought a house in Kern Place, adopted new baby Sara, rented out that house for the summer, and had driven across the country with baby Sara and Nate to Cleveland so David could renovate my mother's back porch. Then we drove on to Maryland in order to sell our house and furniture there. The fountain was too good to just abandon. David built a new pond and moved the mother and baby into the back yard of our friends Debby and Keith Fort. Later we inspired

Debby to learn TM and even later I taught Keith to meditate, enabling him to stop smoking and extending his life by several years at least. We packed what little we could take into our car and camper, drove across the country to El Paso, and moved back into our new but very empty house. It takes my breath away just to remember how busy and intense that time actually was.

Back in El Paso I resumed teaching a part-time load of English and literature courses at the University, preparing classes, grading papers, and learning enough Spanish so I could communicate with Mercedes, a young Mexican girl who crossed the border illegally and worked for us for six days a week, going home on Sundays. And I was mothering two kids, sewing curtains for all our many windows, and driving all over El Paso in the evenings shopping at garage sales for furniture, a better stove, beds, etc. I had gotten an MA in Comparative Literature and done all my course work for the PhD, so now I had to study for my doctoral comprehensives and find a dissertation topic, *in my spare time.* I was stretched to my limits and was often very irritable.

When he was not welding sculptures and building fountains David built bookcases and we made a dining table out of a red-wood picnic table. Steel sculptures were everywhere in our house. From working every day with heavy materials and an arc welder, he put on bulk and got a welding tan in the open area of his shirt below the mask. Every afternoon after coming home sooty and tired, he would shower and then withdraw into the bedroom for his twenty-minute meditation, leaving me to deal with the hungry children, the diapers, the dinner, the house, and grumpy me. I counted the minutes, resentfully.

Finally my turn came. My teacher Robert Winquist, a tall gangly young fellow, flew into El Paso. The meditator group welcomed him and set him up to stay and teach at a local motel. Robert recently told me that in a meeting with Maharishi, one of the TM teachers (initiators) asked him what they could do to help. Maharishi told them that the best thing they could do would be to initiate 1,000 people, thus paying back the tradition for the knowledge they had gotten. Robert immediately set off to tour the small towns and cities of the country teaching TM and within a year he had reached the goal of his first 1,000 initiates.

October 10, 1970. I had my fruits, flowers, new white handkerchief and course fee in hand. After performing the ceremony of gratitude, which was very charming, although the song was in a foreign language and I didn't understand a word of it, Robert sat me down and started the lesson. Following that day's personal instruction there were three days of checking: first night checking was the owner's manual, all the do's and don'ts and how to know if you were doing it correctly. Second night covered the whole theory and mechanics of getting deep rest and releasing stresses. Third night covered, among many other things, the goal of the whole process, Enlightenment.

I started doing my twenty minutes twice daily, before breakfast and dinner as instructed, and life changed dramatically. Instead of being exhausted, irritable, and brusque with the kids at the end of the day, I was reborn. I came out of meditation sweet, settled, rested, and revitalized. I could get through the rest of the day, the dinner, put the kids to bed and still have enough mind and energy to prepare my classes, grade my papers, and make it through the evening. Impressive! I didn't understand the theory, but the practical results were awesome.

What was happening in my meditation? Mostly thoughts and a lot of weeping and sometimes falling asleep. Weeping because the baby died (she hadn't) or Nate died (he hadn't) or David died (he hadn't either). Finally, I got it. My father had died about four years earlier and I was still shocked and miserable about it and I was grieving. After some time, the weeping stopped, and not only that, anger ebbed. Fears started to disappear. When I drove our old car I would imagine an accident up ahead that I would be entering into. That stopped. One day I was searching for something in the little corner medicine cabinet in our bathroom and I noticed a large generic dusty bottle of aspirins against the back wall. I was struck! I hadn't had a headache in months. I used to have them all the time. They had disappeared, the unused bottle had migrated to the back of the shelf, and I hadn't noticed.

We found ourselves in the middle of a lovely group of young meditators. There was Don Fenton, a student at UTEP, David Beaver, a short young fellow who had lived in Alaska, his friend Rick the Stick. There were the Rosell brothers, Tom, and his younger brother Mike, who wore overalls all the time with no shirt, and Leslie Addington, Tom's girlfriend, all of them students. There was a handsome young man named Mike Stammer who wanted to be a dancer, and his girlfriend of the time. The girl-friends changed but he always brought the new one in to learn TM. And there were long-time seasoned meditators Bill and Sue Liles. They were no longer students and lived outside of town up the valley in an adobe house. Most of them would eventually be-come TM teachers and/or work for the movement until marriage and family life took over.

We were the only ones with a real house in town. We were the oldest and most "grown up" of the group so our house became the place where the visiting TM teacher would often stay. They were heroic young people, these initiators, traveling around from place to place on a strenuous schedule to bring TM to remote areas of the U.S. I remember Steve Boggs, Michael and Elaine Yankaus, Gene Spiegel, Ed Fox, David Rosenkrantz. Some of us meditators would go to the airport to meet him or her and watch the people descending the stairs, and there, glowing with an inner light, beau-tiful in spite of anything external, would be the teacher. And we would also be recognized, maybe because we were standing there with a flower. Amazing! We went to every Intro lecture (I was still trying to make sense of it all), and afterwards we all went to Baskin-Robbins and ate ice cream, laughing and talking and not wanting the glow to end.

I was learning a whole new language. Karma meant whatever

one had earned, good or bad, as the result of past actions (this life or a past life). Past life? Reincarnation? Well, let me think about that. Support of nature. That meant that if what you were doing was good, that is, evolutionary for you or others or the planet, you got helped along by nature. Things were easier, more successful, more productive. If the opposite happened, you had to question whether that was the right direction or not, possibly not. Could I admit to forces outside myself that were guiding my actions, my thoughts? Perhaps. I would wait and see.

Residence Courses

We all went together to some residence courses in Abiquiu, in northern New Mexico, at a place called Ghost Ranch. Residence courses are like retreats, an opportunity for more meditation away from the responsibilities and demands of daily life. Nate and Sara stayed with the grandparents. If we had had cell phones, we would have turned them off or left them home. It was a long drive up from El Paso, maybe seven hours, but it was worth it. We stayed in little bungalows and met and ate in the bigger buildings. They taught us some yoga postures or asanas and a breathing exercise. At the time we were told that the asanas helped the body adjust as meditation healed it and released stresses, untangled snarls, and unknotted knots in the nervous system, physical and chemical, and who knows what else. Now there is a considerable body of research showing that these gentle and simple stretching postures are extremely beneficial on many levels. Then there were no journals, associations, etc. Now yoga is a household word. Everyone knows about it and does it. We were pioneers.

The breathing exercise we learned would, technically speaking, create partial pressures in the lungs, get rid of stale air, fill the lungs with fresh air, wake us up, make us livelier. We called it pranayama. You might hear of it these days as alternate breathing or some such thing, and research studies are showing many benefits.

I would have loved to have known about this research, and about research on TM (now over 700 studies). It would have given me more confidence. Instead, I listened and learned and waited to see what my personal experience would be, if it would corroborate the advertised benefits.

The best thing about the residence course was that we got to round!! Rounding meant doing extra meditations, along with the new things we had learned, morning and afternoon, and we watched video tapes of Maharishi in the late morning, afternoon, and evening. We went deeper and deeper inward. No responsibilities, no work, nothing, just meditation and knowledge. It was like a super meditation. We took "walk and talks" after each meal around the beautiful grounds with views of the mountains. We walked with our friends and ate with them, made new friends, all TMers, and laughed and laughed. Thanks to the deeper and more frequent meditations emotions would flit through our minds, we might feel a little tender and delicate for a while, or a little irritable as things settled down. We were told to stay on the program, follow the clock, not make any major decisions or give heed to any life-shattering realizations until we were back to our regular lives and could consider them with our intellects and experience. We hated to leave, but we could take home our new practices and add them to our meditation routine at home.

We told everyone we knew about meditation and many of those people came to learn, including David's parents. We helped with the TM instruction, taking people in and out of the meditation room, prepping their flowers and fruit, and we saw them transformed in a matter of days. They took on a glow, an inner light, which was hard to describe, but easy to see. I did a lot of the organizing, finding places to hold lectures and the instruction and the three days of checking that followed. As a faculty member I helped the students start a TM club at the University and, as a club, we could use rooms in the Student Union for these things.

I remember one young guy. He had lost a leg in Vietnam and

he was very bitter and depressed. He came to learn TM unshaven and dressed very sloppily. Driving home from his first meditation, he later told me, he found himself spontaneously laughing, something he hadn't done in a long, long time. Meditation had opened the door to his inner reservoir of bliss. He could live again.

First Psychophysiological Research Study on TM

David agreed to teach a couple of psychology courses at the University in the spring of 1971. We were thinking of going to a big, advanced TM course that summer in California and needed the money to fly out there and take the course, and teaching those courses would be easy for him. One was a course in experimental psychology, his field. A number of the meditators signed up for it because he was the teacher. Nature was organizing. He wanted to demonstrate how to do an experiment. Tom Rosell dug around in a closet and discovered an old GSR machine. Perfect. It would measure galvanic skin responses, like a lie-detector. If you were stressed, your hands would sweat and a sensor would pick that up. David got the machine working, hooked up a noise generator and headphones and blasted a loud tone in the students' ears and watched what happened.

David first did a pilot study with the four meditators in the class and four other students, and the differences were clear. The meditators "habituated" much more rapidly. This means they quickly adapted (after all, it was only a noise) and stopped stressing out. One non-meditating lady couldn't adapt at all, kept on stressing out, and finally walked out! And if you turned up the sensitivity of the machine, you could see that the non-meditators had lots of little stress responses all the time as stresses, real or imagined, came and went in their minds. The meditators had way fewer. You could measure how TM reduced stress. It was real. Meditation made you less reactive to stress. It was the first time anyone had ever shown what TM could do outside of meditation, in activity.

David added a few more subjects to make it a proper study. I was dragged in and blasted. I had the biggest stress response of anyone, but I adapted very rapidly. It was true. I am very sensitive to noise but very flexible. David sent the research paper to a major medical journal, *Psychosomatic Medicine*, the first ever mind-body journal, and they eventually accepted it and finally published a few years later. At this point there was only Keith Wallace's research on the physiological effects of meditation (lower breath rate, heart rate, etc.) just published in *Scientific American*.

David wrote to Jerry Jarvis, the head of the American TM movement, telling him about the research and its results. Jerry told Maharishi about it. Maharishi sent David a note on gold decorated stationary and in his own handwriting, "A Guru's Blessing." So thrilling! We were invited to come to the next one-month course in the Science of Creative Intelligence, to be held that summer in Arcata, California, and to present his research to the course and to the symposium as well as to invited Nobel Laureates and famous scientists and thinkers, like Buckminster Fuller (you can see what Buckminster Fuller says about meeting Maharishi at one of the symposia on You Tube). This SCI course was the prerequisite for the *Transcendental Meditation* Teacher Training Course (TTC)[SM]. Maybe we could become teachers of Transcendental Meditation. Things were moving very fast. Nature was in a hurry.

Our happy family standing outside the little townhome in Arcata at the SCI course. Nate is in his pajama top and shoulder brace. David still has his beard. That disappeared after he met Maharishi. There I am holding baby Sara with her blond halo of curls.

Back in the Classroom

WE PACKED UP THE KIDS and flew to California and then took a bus up to Arcata for the one-month course in the Science of Creative Intelligence, whatever that was. David Beaver was taking the course too. He had driven there from El Paso, and he loaned us his hippie truck (multi-colored with bells hanging inside it) to drive around in. He was staying in one of the dorms and eating on campus so he didn't need it and we did. We were put in a little townhome with a living area downstairs and two bedrooms upstairs, near the other "grownups." There was childcare offered, but we had to shop for food and cook our own meals. And do laundry and pick up and drop off the kids and get to all the meetings. One day Nate tumbled down the stairs and broke his collarbone. Off to the Emergency Room. He got a brace to hold his shoulders back while he healed and he had to wear his pajama top from then on, or something like it with buttons and sleeves. No tee shirts. We had to shop for clothes. It was difficult, challenging, but once it started we didn't have time to think. Just go from place to place and flop into bed at night.

The course began on August 8, 1971. At registration they made photo badges for us so we could get into the meetings and they gave us a large spiral notebook especially for the course. It had a gold cover and the picture of Maharishi from all the TM posters used in those days, a three-quarter view of him with long, dark hair. On top it said Jai Guru Dev, and below his picture it said:

Transcendental Meditation Teacher Training Course
Summer 1971
International Symposium on the Science of Creative Intelligence

This really got to me. The intention was clearly stated. We were on a course to become teachers. Back in school, learning. Loved it. Couldn't wait to take notes and fill up the notebook. And the gold was inspiring; it suggested something special. I remember years later when we were living in Seelisberg with Maharishi and the International movement (1974–1977), and we were sitting in on one of the semi-annual National Leaders Conferences. All the directors of the movement in different countries would come together for rest and knowledge twice a year, to report developments to Maharishi, and get feedback on their projects.

The national leader for Ireland got up and he was objecting to the movement materials, pamphlets with gold and pastel colors. Even the three-nights checking forms used when you learned TM were full of gold. He was working among poor people, he said, and they were suspicious of all that gold, maybe thinking the movement was making money on them. He preferred to use simple mimeographed forms and papers to hand out. No, no, Maharishi insisted. The gold is to give them a vision of something more, something celestial, something to evoke the splendor of Transcendental Consciousness. They were off on the adventure of their lives. There should be some flavor of all that. I don't remember his exact words, but this was the essence of it.

And it worked for me! Even now, when I see that notebook from forty-five years ago, I feel a thrill of something special. From what I know now about how Maharishi worked, I know he would have selected that color, that picture, those words, that effect, all deliberately. And that notebook is full of his knowledge and sat in his presence for a month. Some feeling of that remains. I have to say that I almost threw my notebooks away when I was in a snit with the movement many years later (to be revealed in its place), but David squirreled them away for about twenty years and brought them out when I started this project. His instincts were usually way better than mine when it came to Maharishi and the TM movement.

We had our badges, our notebooks, our schedule, our instructions on how to behave (don't pick the flowers on campus to give to Maharishi. When there was a chance to give them, flower trucks would be there, etc.). Meetings were to be held in the field house and would begin that evening. There were about 1,700 people there, mostly young college-age kids. We were thirty-one and escorted to sit up front with the senior SRM people. Keith Wallace and others had then formed the Students International Meditation Society (SIMS) and it really took off on college campuses. The field house was full of those kids, five to ten years younger than we were, wanting to see Maharishi, have the chance to round, to meditate more, maybe even become TM teachers themselves.

There was a buzz of excitement that first night in the place and then suddenly it fell quiet. Someone had spotted Maharishi coming in and we all stood up with our hands joined respectfully in the Namaste gesture. He entered the hall, climbed up the steps to the stage, came up to the front and smiled warmly at everyone and then sat down on the little couch. Jerry Jarvis, the director of the U.S. movement, welcomed us and introduced him, and Maharishi started right off, giving us a glimpse of the whole range of knowledge. It was heady; it was over my head, for sure. David saw Maharishi's aura, shining into the room as he first came through the doorway and then filling the whole room once he had entered. He told this to Maharishi years later and Maharishi nodded.

Maharishi started by talking about infinity, stretching our minds with new ideas and concepts. Individuality is localized infinity, he said. The human nervous system is concentrated Absolute and therefore more powerful than absolute, unbounded infinity. Life, he said, is balanced between Absolute and relative, between changing and non-changing. With transcending, the active mind begins to enjoy the stability of silence, even with only a faint acquaintance with unbounded absolute.

A faint acquaintance. OK, I could relate. But I didn't get the Absolute part.

We were here to learn the seven steps (of teaching TM), he said. And here came the hook! Teaching, he said, elevates the heart and mind of the teacher more than the student. Our method of teaching we owe to the tradition of masters. Teaching TM raises the teacher toward Cosmic Consciousness; it uplifts the teacher's awareness.

We had learned about Cosmic Consciousness (CC) when we learned TM. It was the state of enlightenment. Five to eight years of practicing TM and we would achieve it, and teaching would speed the way. We were excited. Our ideas of what CC was or was not were very naïve. We thought we would not age; we would never fall sick; we would totally transform the world. Five to eight years didn't sound like very long. Maharishi was giving us the encouragement we needed to persist, even if the process took longer. He later said he was shocked at the stresses in the young people due to their taking drugs, and in the collective consciousness of the world, both of which slowed down our progress.

To prepare the ground for teaching, Maharishi said, we would be gaining intellectual clarity and we would be rounding, doing extra meditations for the first few weeks of the course. You never round alone, he said, only with an experienced teacher. But rounding is essential.

Someone got on the mike and asked what the best schedule would be for a teacher, an initiator, out in the field. There were many initiators there, taking the course again, including my Robert Winquist, just to be with Maharishi, or on staff to help out, just to be there. They often asked the best questions.

Maharishi responded: best would be four months of teaching and two months of rounding, or five months of teaching and one month of rounding. Eleven months of teaching and one month of rounding would be the minimum.

He gently introduced another topic that would be expanded upon later. When you start to teach, you become known. You have become an exponent of supreme knowledge; you are an example of this knowledge and you have to dress accordingly. This, we would later understand, would mean no beards, no long hair for men, suits and ties, proper dress and behavior. We wanted to appeal to the highest level of society, Maharishi said. Nothing wrong with long hair, just that it was associated with the lethargy of hippies. We didn't want to give that impression. The meeting ended. The course had begun. It had been a very long full day. Time to get back home and relieve our babysitter.

The SCI Course Routine

The next morning began our regular course routine. We started each day by feeding the kids, getting them off to childcare, and then returning home to do our two or later, three rounds. Then off to the field house for the morning meeting. That first morning Maharishi began by saying that what motivates the mind, what principle underlies TM, is the force of life, the same force of life that motivates every activity in creation. And that force is directed from individuality to cosmic reality. Evolution, the tendency of everything to grow, to progress, to evolve, is what drives life. The force of evolution, he said, is invincible, good enough and powerful enough to fulfill its intention of the individual gaining fulfillment. TM just lets the mind flow, be in the stream of evolution. Suffering is not the way to spiritual evolution. It has been made obsolete as a spiritual path because it didn't work.

This challenged everything I had believed and practiced. I had always been motivated by gaining self-knowledge, growing, knowing more about life and myself. But my path had been experimentation on myself and observing the experiences of others (partly through reading novels). This was a slow, painful, sometimes dangerous and damaging path. No details, but I was wild and careless in my high school and college years and I had to pay the price for that. I suffered a lot. Recognizing David (on some inexplicable level) and marrying him was my salvation. I got to fulfill some of my deepest desires (a loving husband, children, and a home of my own), and now he had brought me to a path of spiritual development and growth. I resisted at each stage, God only knows why. I let him drag me along because I knew somehow down deep that this was the answer and that Maharishi was the guiding light of that path.

The course was called the Science of Creative Intelligence, Maharishi explained, because intelligence is Being, pure consciousness, the Absolute. Creative Intelligence (CI) is the basis of all creation, that ever-silent non-active pure CI—when it starts to pulsate it starts to create its expressions in the relative. It is the whole story. When meditators of wrong techniques came out to be moody and unpractical, then meditation got a bad name. Spiritual was a devalued word also. This has been a hang up—old ideas about the East, meditation, spirit. Our policy is to focus our energy on teaching TM and giving knowledge, correcting errors. For example, in the past it was said you couldn't follow two masters, God and Mammon, but wealth follows God. You need not give up the material world. You can be spiritual in the world. It is not necessary to be a recluse.

Each day Maharishi entered the hall at a back door near the stage, and it was roped off so he could get out of the car and enter the hall with the least interference. Everyone wanted to see him up close, give him a flower, get his attention, or ask him a question. It was my experience, and that of many others, that when you were finally in front of him and could ask that burning question, your mind went blank. You just stared and smiled.

Because we were in that special front section we could slip out that door from the inside and wait for him to arrive. One day I stood there with my flower and our movie camera and he came up and I aimed it at him. He stopped and posed and poured love and kindness on me for a couple of timeless moments, and then moved on. I was "in the pocket." I didn't understand much. I had a long distance to travel from my materialist perspective, but the results of TM and Maharishi's personal qualities had won me over. I was, as we say, pretty much "sold out" from then on.

As he spoke each morning I listened and took notes. After we were deep into rounding, I *tried* to listen and take notes, but sometimes I had to close my eyes. The lids were so heavy. And my head would fall forward, and his voice would play in the background while my body and nervous system tried to restructure, heal, reorient, learn and unlearn, and I could not always maintain waking consciousness. Some mornings when he was busy running his worldwide movement, he would not come to the hall and they would play a tape from a previous course. Quite a few of the kids would see he was not coming and go off elsewhere. I was not so foolish. Those morning taped lectures were equally powerful. I would become so heavy I couldn't sit up. I would flop onto the nearby folding chair and listen with my eyes closed or whatever. It was slightly less comfortable than sleeping on an airplane, but I couldn't stay erect. When his voice stopped, when the tape ended, suddenly I was awake, sitting up again, ready to go. I hadn't been asleep. I wasn't groggy. It was different. One day early on Maharishi showed up late, after all the people who didn't want to listen to a tape had left. Those of us in the hall had a special intimate meeting with him. People learned they couldn't second guess him. They had better show up.

One day Maharishi looked at the row of pregnant ladies in the front row. They had been given special comfortable seats, and many of them were knitting. I could relate. I loved to knit and my fingers moved automatically even if I was listening to music or watching a movie. Maharishi objected. It divides the mind, he said. When you are listening to him, you should give him your full attention, not have half of your awareness counting stitches or rows.

After lunch, we would all go to our small group meetings to discuss various topics, such as the qualities of creative intelligence. Because we lived in that townhome, not in the dorms with the college-age kids, our group was the SRM elders led by Curly Smith, and they had no interest in such discussions. They had heard it all before. They ignored us and wanted to chat about more esoteric aspects of spiritual knowledge that they had picked up from books (not Maharishi's), like how bars and prisons were filled with spirits unable to move along. Spirits? These people believed in ghosts? What? David and I looked at each other in amazement. What planet had we landed on? Where were we? David tried to pull them back on topic and they apologized and began again, but only for a few minutes and then they were off onto their more mystical interests.

They talked about all kinds of things about gurus and India that were new to us. Like chakras. Seems there are seven chakras, with 52 petals each and there are 52 letters in the Sanskrit alphabet and each names a petal and therefore all the sounds made by humans are there. (I am not saying this is the truth. There are other versions of this, but this is what I wrote down.) It was a relief to go back to our townhome, our place on our planet, do our two or three rounds, get the kids, have dinner, put the kids to bed and leave them with the babysitter, and go to the evening meeting in the hall. Hectic, you wouldn't believe!

David Meets Maharishi

A meeting with scientists was announced. David went and found Jerry Jarvis. Jerry knew who he was, of course, because we had been invited to the SCI course so David could present his research. Jerry introduced him and David stepped into Maharishi's presence and was overwhelmed. He couldn't think or speak. He was just stunned by Maharishi's Being, I think. The next thing he knew Jerry had guided him to a chair and he was collecting himself. Maharishi had moved on.

Later on, David hurried out the back door by the stage so he would be there when Maharishi left the hall. Maharishi got into the car and once again David approached Jerry and Jerry introduced him again. David told him he would like to talk to him about his ideas on how meditation worked. Maharishi smiled and said, "Come in the car." David told him his theory about how the inward and outward moves of the mind during meditation worked from the perspective of his background in behaviorism and operant conditioning. Maharishi listened and then raised a flower and said that with TM the whole thing blooms organically, like a flower.

David sat in the car, again rather overwhelmed by being close to Maharishi. He watched in amazement over Maharishi's shoulder as the car moved slowly through the meditators lining the road, smiling at him with love and appreciation and admiration, a continuum of beaming faces. That was how Maharishi moved through the crowds! That was his reality.

Evening Meetings

Maharishi poured out his knowledge every day. How TM works, how the mantra keeps the mind active but undirected so it can effortlessly settle inward, go from greater activity to lesser activity. He talked about how natural the process was. TM uses the natural tendency of the mind to go toward more and more. A couple of young musicians, Paul Fauerso and Rick Stanley, wrote songs about Maharishi and what he taught. They called themselves the Natural Tendency and they sometimes were invited to sing a new song to us in the evening meeting.

Following the natural tendency of the mind to transcend active thinking levels, to go inward, was easy, Maharishi insisted, simple, and not to be interfered with. You could transcend on other senses, but TM was the fastest, most efficient way. "Let Thy will be done," he said. I wrote it down. "Thy?" The highest aspiration of any religion, he said, was to be in harmony with God. It is the birthright of man. Religion? God? Man? Woman? I wrote it all down, whatever it meant, to be made sense of later, and the days rolled along. Sara took her first steps in the driveway of our town-home and David was inspired to shave his beard.

As the knowledge flowed out, somehow it became more familiar. We got used to it and kept writing it down. As I read my notes I see that I learned a huge amount, and even remember a lot of it, possibly because I heard it again and again over the next forty years. Maharishi spoke about various aspects of the Veda and Vedic literature: he talked about Vedic hymns, Vedic cognition, seers, the Yoga Sutras of Patanjali, the Bhagavad Gita, the Shiva Sutras, Niyama, and much more. But he always brought us back to TM, to personal experience and growth to higher states of consciousness. He would explain more and write commentaries later, he promised, but for now the urgency was to create teachers, and for them to create as many meditators as possible.

Maharishi emphasized the role of the mind in life. The mind is the link between two infinities, the unboundedness of the universe and the infinite value we experience deep within us, and the body is equally important. Mind and body are like good friends. Whoever moves takes the other with him. Therefore we must be careful what we eat and drink, the air we breathe, what we do. And the environment; everything influences everything else. You can't keep your influence to yourself. Each one of us is responsible for the whole universe. We can uplift our environment or pollute it with our thoughts and actions. Don't misuse the machine, he said. "A youth is not born to be the slave of circumstances; he is born to be the master of creation."

So we need a plan, and tradition helps. Nature throws off whatever is untrue over the eons. So our plan is: meditate regularly and don't do anything which we know to be wrong. A heavy responsibility, isn't it? To not even *think* negative thoughts. Don't strain, he said, be indifferent to negative thoughts. We never *try* to think anything. We associate ourselves with what is good and useful. We have no time for what is not good or not useful.

I have to confess that although I recorded as much as I could, and tried to stay alert and write it all down, it was very abstract, unfamiliar, and totally unrelated to my simple experiences. I found that I was much more interested in the questions and answers, the practical advice, and the valuable insights into living. There is much in my notes that is new and striking, about love and sex and karma and so much more. I have to share it. It's too good not to record.

Questions and Answers

Someone asked about fasting. The kids were always trying extreme diets in an effort to force better experiences. Maharishi always took a question to its highest level. Sometimes you thought he hadn't heard the question and was off on some other topic, but he always came back somehow to the question asked. With fasting, it was simple. Transcending, he said, is absolute fasting. All the senses, all the relative goes away. But as for the body, don't jolt the nervous system. Eat and sleep regularly, stay strong.

People wanted to take the natural approach and not take medicines. No, he said, take the prescription drugs. The situation will change. He always said, if you are having some problem and you think it might just be the body normalizing, give it three days. If it doesn't go away, go to the doctor. Over the years I have seen people ignore this advice until by the time they stopped trying to cure themselves naturally and sought medical advice, it was too late, way too late. But at the time we thought that once we became meditators nothing bad would ever happen, and young people think that way anyway.

We all wanted to know about Cosmic Consciousness, what it is, how it reveals itself. Do people cry in CC, someone asked him. "CC does not make a man a lump of mud," he answered. Perception becomes more refined. Everything would matter. His cry will be deeper, and all creation will cry with him. It will have a far-reaching influence.

There were questions about reincarnation. How does one's karma go from body to body? The level of consciousness stays the same from body to body, he said. The body may change, but the inner mind doesn't change. So if you raise your level of consciousness in this life, you take that raised level into the next, along with whatever karma you have accrued. The karma of the past is in the soul which enters the body of the mother, just as the whole tree is contained in the seed.

What makes individual differences at conception, he was asked: what makes genius or retardation. Is it karma or an accident? Being is the ultimate cause, he said. Accident just means you don't know the causes and antecedents. Accident only indicates ignorance of the cause. We see an accident happen to an innocent child, but the child is not that innocent. Lots of stuff could be stored inside. Everyone is responsible for themselves. Whatever a man is, he has made himself that, and that is it!

You probably are familiar with the expression: "The mills of the gods grind slowly, but they grind exceedingly fine." It first appeared in the writings of Greek Stoic Sextus Empiricus, and then was picked up by philosophers and poets over time. David quoted this to Maharishi years later and he nodded. That is right!

We have the possibility of life full of freedom yet we live a life of dependence. Knowledge makes the difference. All we have to do, he said, is *care* to live on that level and it follows. Intention, it seems, is very important. You have to let nature know what you really want and it begins to organize for you. There is research showing that if you want to die, your body begins to shut down, just from the intention. I had no idea that we were all operating on such a subtle level.

Maharishi commented on the saying "Help thy neighbor." It

became religious scripture, he said, because it is the truth. It aids evolution and supports life. The one who is helping gets his life elevated first; he enjoys greater benefits than the one for whom he acts. Interesting. I always want to help people, and sometimes I tread a fine line between helping and interfering, especially with advice. A healer once told me I should only give advice when asked. I'm trying to follow that, but this whole book is giving advice, isn't it? I can't help it. Sorry. It's my nature. Take it or leave it. But listen to this. He said that it doesn't pay to criticize someone (*mea culpa*). Just lead in the right direction. When a man knows, he'll take care of himself. It may be that a person is doing the very best that he can.

Something interesting. The student, he says, has *obligated* the teacher. The teacher has to give out knowledge. He or she *needs* to give out knowledge, he said, until it reaches everywhere. (Maharishi always said "he" but he said he meant he and she. I can't help putting in the "she." Otherwise I don't feel included.) To even *think* of the human condition raises the metabolic rate, Maharishi said. So we have to give out the knowledge, for our own sakes as well as the world's.

The kids were reading everything they could about spiritual practices and they asked about other techniques. What about the Kriya Yoga of Yogananda? It is good, he said, but there is some concentration. There is some concentration on the mantra, and this keeps the mind on the active thinking level. It is like a prop plane. Now we have TM, the jet plane, so we don't want to waste time. In TM the emphasis is laid on *transcending* (going beyond) the mantra. No concentration. No effort. And no comparison in evolution.

Some techniques suggest you remember you are an unbounded Self. You keep that in mind as you act, while you are acting. A big mistake, Maharishi said. In order to establish pure awareness in your life, you must transcend and then act, innocently and spontaneously. Fully out or fully in, alternately. Don't try to maintain the Self in activity. It will divide the mind. It will be

damaging and weakening. This mood making is maintaining the
thought of the Self, not the state of the Self.

He was asked about hypnosis. You become uncoordinated, he
said. You have given yourself over to someone else. Then you are
called back in and you are, say, twenty minutes behind your body.
It's weakening. It's criminal.

Everyone was interested in higher states of consciousness.
At that point, Maharishi was mainly talking about CC, Cosmic
Consciousness. When experiences rose to other levels he began to
talk more about states higher than that. We wanted to know: when
you get to CC, does aging stop? The body has always dropped
off, he pointed out. But in the Rig Veda, one of the major works
of Vedic literature, there is some talk about immortality. It may
sound strange, he said, but the truth is not responsible for the
present level of ignorance.

The kids thought it wasn't right to have to pay a fee to learn
TM. What about that? Maharishi observed that the initiators were
making great financial sacrifices to teach TM. They should have
salaries at least, and the payment means making a commitment.
Without regularity of practice, TM can't help much. If a high school
student convinces his parents to let him learn and to pay the fee,
he feels obligated to show results. In the West, people don't value
what they haven't paid for. In any case, he said, you are not paying
for the spiritual experience. You are paying for the chair, the hall,
etc. Transcending is without cost. You are not paying for Being.

Everyone wanted to get to CC as fast as possible. Maharishi
was a monk, so naturally questions came up about lifestyle. Is
celibacy better than being married? Spiritual growth is equally
available through married life, Maharishi said. You have a helper
and children bring love. Celibacy keeps the system stronger, but it
is the life of the recluse. For spiritual growth—meditation and action is the way. It is just a different field of activity. Married people
help each other and protect each other's meditation.

And love plays a very great role in evolution. Through TM

stresses are released and the hardness of the heart starts to soften. The warmth of purification melts the hardness and softens the heart more and more. TM removes the blocks that have prevented the heart from swelling with love. When the heart is really expanded, then it can flow in tidal waves of love which touch the feet of God. That is true devotion. The heart, he said, is a small pond which can expand into an ocean and rise in waves of love. "A small pond." I loved that. That's how I felt. My heart was a small pond with rocks in it. I needed to do better with marriage and love.

Karma was endlessly fascinating to us. Do people who have intercourse exchange karma, he was asked. This was asked to a monk! I cringed. But he would answer any sincere question. Whatever one is doing, no one is isolated in creation, he said. Every breath is exchanged by everyone. The universe reacts to individual action. So, established in Being, perform action. There is a

Maharishi Mahesh Yogi answering questions at the course on the Science of Creative Intelligence, Arcata, California, August 1971

big give and take at all times. Everyone influences everything. One pulsates into the life of the other. There's no way *not* to interfere with another's karma.

But we should know that the result of action is not in our hands. It is not in the hands of the doer. If you sow a mango tree, you will eat mangos. You can't wish for apples. You are free to sow whatever you like, but the consequences come according to cosmic will, natural law. One action can produce different results. Why? Because of the influence of past actions. If we took a loan last year, our deposits do not accumulate. They go to pay the loan. But don't brood about it. The present is more developed than the past. Our action is most powerful in the present. So we go ahead.

Religion. Not my favorite topic, but I tried to be open minded. There is a difference between the Absolute and the creator, God. I didn't get either one, but I was trying. The creator has to have some identification with the Absolute to survive relative dissolution (he explains in his commentary on the Bhagavad Gita that the whole creation dissolves and is recreated again and again—how does he know that?). The creator has two aspects, He and She, he said. The Absolute is It. The ability to create cannot be attributed to It; it has to be He or She. All this exists at the finest level of creation, and that finest level is open to experience. Our awareness opens to the finest perceptions. When we can comprehend the finest levels of the relative, then we can apprehend all that exists at that level.

Belief or non-belief is something else, he said, but the reality will be known. "I don't believe in God." "Fine, but when He comes out of the corner, what will you do?" Years later, sitting here at the computer, fingers skimming along the keys, I am thinking, Mother/Father God, OK. I am getting interested. In Jehovah not so much, but Divine Mother (Divine Father), better. I am waiting to see what unfolds. On our recent trip to France, to Brittany, in the summer of 2015 we visited many cathedrals and they all featured paintings and sculptures of St. Anne, mostly teaching her daughter Mary to read, sometimes from a book, sometimes from a scroll. Wonderful. A Jewish mother teaching her Jewish daughter to read so she could later teach her son. I bought a small statue of St. Anne teaching Mary and it fluoresces, that is, it takes in light during the day and gives it off at night. It glows and I always smile when I look at it. My small pond has grown into small lake. Not yet an ocean.

Rounding was coming to an end and the SCI Symposium was about to start. We had all been going through big changes and big mood swings. We all wanted to talk about "unstressing." As in, I am very irritable and grumpy today; I am unstressing. But better not to act on any of those negative thoughts, Maharishi said. Negative action during the day creates bad karma; it is not unstressing. If someone is depressed or irritable, it is the result of some sensation in the heart or head. Just close the eyes, locate and feel the sensation. It will cease to dominate. Don't talk about unstressing, he said, but we did anyway. It was such a handy explanation for everything that was going on.

Maharishi explained that while a person is in reality unbounded bliss consciousness, when they are negative, it is the stress talking, not the individual. This gave us an important perspective on personal relations. David and I had noticed in the early days of our marriage and during the tensions of going through graduate school that when we felt good about ourselves we felt good about the marriage and when we were feeling bad about ourselves we would doubt the marriage. It taught us even then to be patient, but with this angle we could see that it was valuable not to assume something was wrong, but to meditate, go back on the Self, and see how we felt about something after a few days.

SCI Symposium

Our schedule changed and we were now hearing from scientists and educators, famous people in their fields, mornings, afternoons, and sometimes in the evenings. Some came to meet

Maharishi; some were meditators themselves; some had children who were meditators or initiators who had brought them in. The whole event was mind expanding in a different way. Our intellects went out to far galaxies to hear about black holes, white holes, and pulsars from Dr. Mael Melvin. Dr. Robert Keith Wallace presented his doctoral research on how TM affected metabolic rate, heart rate, and so forth. We went from the body out to the galaxies and into the future.

Dr. Willis Harman was particularly interesting. He was an engineer, a social scientist, and a futurist. He was obviously a meditator and spoke about TM and consciousness. In fact, he felt it was the hope of the future. SCI, he said, meets the needs that exist. We will be going through a period of intense change, much of it violent or uncomfortable. With our increasing life span we face population problems. With more sophisticated weapons we invite the threat of mass destruction. With labor saving inventions we will create unneeded people, unemployment problems. With improved communication and transportation the whole world will become more complex and vulnerable to disruption. Our increased affluence will have a huge environmental impact. And as our basic needs are satisfied, we will need to be encouraged to seek higher needs, new goals. He said this in 1971!

We can't go back, he continued. Society needs to provide an avenue of worth for each individual; there has to be a more equitable distribution of wealth and power; we have to learn to control the impact of technology; we must find a way to inspire commitment from people; we must take care of the environment. Even motherhood will feel threatened. We must allow a paradigm shift to take place. As I read these notes now, I realize how prescient he was. Maharishi was well aware of all these problems. He lauded Dr. Harman for his creativity, openness, and vision of the goal, and we have the solution, he said. This paradigm shift must be brought about by us, he said, and the sooner the better. We will work harder for more joy. We don't look down on the present. Don't be angry at progress. Evolution has always been there. Enjoy the present and work for a better future.

Dr. Harman quoted Ralph Waldo Emerson's essay on love which talks about the evolutionary nature of marriage: "Love which is the deification of persons, must become more impersonal every day." Yes, agreed Maharishi. We want an overflow of the boundaries of love. Stress restricts marriage. TM frees the heart from the boundaries of marriage and love goes out to the universe. Personal love can lead to the boundless state of love. It is not impersonal, but personal plus.

Dr. Kantor talked about Kuhn's *Structure of Scientific Revolutions* and paradigm shifts. We social scientists have grossly underestimated human potential, he said. We ought to study healthy, creative persons, as Abraham Maslow did, and leave pathology aside. Dr. Pierce talked about alpha biofeedback and schizophrenia. Biofeedback may bring some peace of mind to some people, Maharishi said, but they report strain or fatigue after practicing it. This is true of all concentration practices. TM doesn't use any effort, so it brings results without strain. Curly Smith, one of the SRM people, often sat near me and reached over to write on my page. "Maharishi is giving an introductory lecture for all the new people here." Yes, that was obvious, but perfectly OK.

The one I really remember is Dr. Maynard Shelly. He was a professor of psychology and business at the University of Kansas and had been encouraged to come to the symposium by his student Garland Landrith. Garland is the initiator who first brought the data on the one percent effect to David's attention years later at the end of 1974. (This data showed that even one per cent of a city's population meditating can begin to decrease crime. Maharishi had predicted this and it proved to be true.) First Dr. Shelly talked generally about our transition to the post-industrial society and they will be increasingly dominated by computers, which will become cheaper, smaller, and more powerful, he predicted. Status and worth will be judged less and less by ability or desire to work and more by one's ability to be entertaining.

This was forty-five years ago, and these people were foreseeing, among other things, iPhones, YouTube, and Twitter. Very impressive. But what I remember without looking at my notes was Shelly's own study on excitement vs. enjoyment. There is a point of optimal arousal, he said, and stressed individuals need more and more excitement to get there. They turn to violence and aggression to become aroused enough to enjoy life, to act. TM or relaxation, he said, would lower the point of arousal and then a slight intensity of excitement would be pleasurable.

I was really struck by this because I had noticed that we meditators could sit around together and enjoy ourselves with very little provocation. A comment, an observation, a bit of knowledge, and we were happy and laughing. With more meditators, he said, there would be a reduced need for violence, and increased happiness; and increased happiness means finding goals to work for. There would be a lower rate of adaptation, so pleasures would last longer. We would consume less and therefore pollute less. We would not succumb to the alienation which was coming. We would appreciate the beauty of living. Curly wrote on the top of my page, He is not a meditator! I am sure of that. Well, he sure talked like one.

Geneticist Dr. Robert Sinsheimer from Caltech talked about genes and DNA. He thought it unlikely that TM could affect the gene pool. As for genetic alteration from drug use, coffee, food, there was no conclusive evidence yet. Maharishi didn't argue with him, but he suggested that "If infinity can dance in individuality, then anything is possible." I wrote in my notes that Maharishi was like St. Thomas Aquinas. TM has to fit scientific or objective truth. All truth should fit in. Interesting that just recently a geneticist has found that TM does affect genetic expression, specifically in terms of the pattern of turning genes on and off, a pattern which is associated with reduced stress and increasing the strength of the immune system (Drs. Wenuganen Supaya and John Fagan). And I believe there is now research on how life style, drugs, etc. may not change the genes, but they do affect genetic expression, at least.

We also heard from Dr. Melvin Calvin who got the Nobel Prize for his work in photosynthesis. His daughter was an initiator. Staying alive, he said, means using energy to maintain the system's organization against the thermal tendency toward chaotic dissolution. The earth, he said, is about 4.8 billion years old and it took about a billion years for life to emerge. Change is inherent in our molecular structure. We all enjoyed his talk (I took lots of notes) and Maharishi did, too. Creative intelligence is active, he said. It takes a definite direction. The mantra is a catalyst. A new structure skillfully comes from the old structure. Creative Intelligence catalyzes every structure on its evolutionary way.

I took a lot of notes on the talk of Dr. Benton Johnson (University of Oregon) on the sociology of religion. This I could relate to. He said that there is a transcendent thread that moves through many religions. Its followers become radiant, more serene yet energetic, more unselfish, less defensive and uptight, and their behavioral patterns change. Sin, which used to be so sweet, now is bitter. What causes these changes? Research shows that people who are involved in some spiritual practice, doesn't matter which one, do better in college, are more focused and effective. He observed two major trends in society. One was the decline of traditional religions, which didn't seem to be able to attract or transform their members. Another was the rise of new ideologies which tried to point to a new and better social order, though they were often anti-religious (Marx, Freud). Mainly it was often about sex; rules about sex that (without some transcendent means of living) were found to be oppressive and blocking off avenues of expression.

Maharishi was well aware that suffering as a way to God seemed to be a major component of some religions. There are two banks to the river, he said. We can choose either bank (joy or suffering) and still be along the river. Religion *can* be a means to develop the full potential of man.

Philosopher Jon Shear spoke. He would later be one of the founding faculty members when Maharishi International University (MIU) was established later in Santa Barbara, and David presented his research too.

More Questions and Answers

The symposium ended and the course was winding down. It had been quite a ride. We were now instructed to listen to tapes on the Science of Creative Intelligence and learn to prepare lectures on TM. We would read these to our small groups and practice. During the evenings Maharishi met with us and still took questions. He talked about the seven states of consciousness (waking, dreaming, sleep, Transcendental Consciousness [TC], Cosmic Consciousness [CC], God Consciousness [GC], and Unity Consciousness [UC]), advanced techniques (which would speed up our evolution), and how to talk about TM. First emphasize the benefits, then talk about how easy it is, that anyone can do it, the seven steps to learn. Don't mention advanced states of consciousness, he advised. A distant goal will put people off. Talk about improving the waking state.

We had a few more guest speakers and some interesting questions. What about thoughts of God, one girl asked. They make her feel good and happy. It is okay to mood make about God, he assured her, but don't be satisfied with that. It is no substitute for God Consciousness; it is not the way to God realization. Mood making can be a temporary relief, finding shelter from the rain. But meditate!

To someone who is doing some other technique. Good, so far, he said. But TM is the fastest. Anything *as natural as* TM will *be* TM. Put your bicycle in the rack and come in the car. See for yourself.

Why is your beard going white, someone asked, again thinking that once you learned TM you wouldn't age. The body is the last thing a monk thinks about, Maharishi said. I never thought about it until now. Maybe it's to convince people that that man has some experience.

What about the Hare Krishna people? They look down on us because they think we think God is an impersonal force and they are devoted to the individual creator. Before Cosmic Consciousness, Maharishi said, the thought of God is a mirage, just a gossip. The light of God is twenty-four hours a day, so we need the Self to be established as the essential reality twenty-four hours a day in CC. It's not possible before then. We hesitate to talk about God, he said, because talk has been degrading. Suffering has been accepted as a path to God, and so forth.

And finally, one young man implored Maharishi: Put me in CC! We all laughed and sympathized. Yes, Maharishi, just do it! Maharishi gently moved his head. We are not concerned with a magic wand, he said. We want to establish a scientific path to Unity for all generations. Evolution is computed on the basis of action (karma). Only the creator can desire that. We act in freedom and reap the consequences.

We don't desire enlightenment for all one fine morning, he said. We want the establishment of knowledge, of the true path, in accord with evolution. Freedom of action is the law. That's being realistic. Experience timelessness in the transcendent and know the value of time in the relative. Directly cognize the continuity of life and then know the continuity of time. Then time will be our friend. Otherwise it flies without our awareness. When we wile away the time in purposelessness, time is not with us.

Teacher Training

Maharishi was training us how to talk about TM, how to lecture, how to understand what he was teaching us; in short, how to become teachers of the Transcendental Meditation technique. We had had a good taste of rounding; some of our rough edges were smoothed out; we were transformed by knowledge and experience, but still our essential selves.

By the end of the course we were all talking about going to teacher training in Majorca, Spain, the next fall and winter. There would be three ten-week courses and one could take one or more of them. Private room and bath would be $9.50 a day plus $10 for medical care (half price for children). Chartered planes would leave from Los Angeles and New York, for about $260 and $175. We would need a passport and a smallpox inoculation.

David was ready. I was horrified. Living in a hotel room with no washing machine, raising two little children, one in diapers, dare I say it, "unstressing," trying to keep a marriage, a life, a family

David and Nate in the airport on the way to our TM Teacher Training Course in Italy. Look at the radiance on David's face. Huge changes were wrought by sitting in Maharishi's presence, getting his knowledge, and practicing his techniques.

together under those circumstances, and still study to become a teacher, to round, to live in a foreign country! Incomprehensible. I was very happy to go back home to my house in El Paso.

But I was also remembering Maharishi as he came to the back door of the hall and I stood outside with a flower, again and again. He was always patient, never hurried, always in the moment, smiling, warm, loving us all, someone at once very special and yet very familiar. I was comfortable with him, not overwhelmed, but only because, I imagine, I could not see who he *really* was. The one-month course had been an experience of being in an ashram, a guru's hermitage. We had been totally focused on him, on his teaching, on our meditation, and the whole program created an intense spiritual vortex unlike anything else in our lives. It was very attractive. One wanted to go back and do it again, repeat the experience, live that way again, be on the jet plane of evolution. It was irresistible.

Exponents of Supreme Knowledge

WHEN WE RETURNED TO EL PASO from the Humboldt course we felt changed. We noticed that our marriage, our lives, were happier, better somehow. We felt that we had had a life-altering experience. I returned to teaching at UTEP. We needed money for the TM Teacher Training Course (TTC)^{SM} in Spain. David put art, his sculpture, and everything else aside and looked for a job. He found an interesting position under a psychiatrist who was heading up a drug abuse program at Fort Bliss there in El Paso, and he wanted a researcher.

David brought up that he planned to go to TTC for ten weeks, maybe in the late winter or spring. His boss, Rick, insisted he promise NOT to leave the job. David considered that. Should he take the job and not go to TTC, or not take the job and figure out some other way to go to TTC? The best path seemed to be to take the job and the money and then go to TTC anyway. He is scrupulously honest, almost never lies, and this was a big one. He lied. Years later, he told Maharishi about this lie. Maharishi looked at him piercingly, but didn't say anything.

We settled into our new life. Our house continued to be the TM center and I continued to organize each teacher's visit, lectures, and courses. I was also teaching English and literature at the University of Texas at El Paso and studying for my doctoral comprehensives in my spare time (ha!). David and I also became checkers. That means we learned the checking notes and after being tested that we really did know them, we could check someone's meditation, give them the experience of the right start, and get them meditating correctly again if they had somehow warped the process and it was no longer working for them.

One day a young high school student named Rick showed up at the front door with two of his buddies. He wanted to be checked. The boys sat in the living room on the couch and I took Rick back to the meditation room. We went through the process and he was very happy. I wasn't supposed to talk about anything else, but I couldn't resist. "You did something and it spoiled your meditation?" I asked. "Yes," he nodded and mumbled something. "Like smoking dope?," I asked. "Yes," he mumbled and nodded. "Well, now you know," I said. And he did. Later he went to Maharishi International University and became a student there.

One week a teacher named David Fitch was scheduled to come give an introductory lecture in neighboring Las Cruces and then in El Paso. Then he would give the requisite second lectures and teach over the weekend. But he was delayed and asked if we meditators could give the intro in Las Cruces? There were four parts to the intro: Mental Potential, Health, Social Behavior, and World Peace. Four of us would each present one part. David and I were chosen by the group to be two of the presenters, as well as David Beaver and Tom Rosell, who had both been to Humboldt along with us. We were nervous. Who were we to get up on a stage and do that? But we did and it was fun, and afterward a small group of people came up to us.

They were a club and they were trying to see auras, all without success. But for the first time they saw them; they saw them on us. We all had auras they could see, and they signed up to learn TM. I couldn't see auras myself but that sounded pretty interesting. I had an aura that somebody could see. People could see auras. Well, okay, that was something.

Teaching TM Outside of the Movement

I remember one enthusiastic new meditator in El Paso named Austin Downey. He was a very bright guy and he took it upon himself to teach TM to all his friends and family. He wanted to save them money and he felt he knew very well how to meditate and transcend. He looked up some mantras in a book and off he went, but he was very disappointed, he told us. No one he taught "got it." No one appreciated it as he did. No one continued to do what he had taught them.

The current visiting TM teacher Gene Spiegel tried to help him to understand that teaching TM would only work with the whole package: the trained teacher taking you step by step through the procedure, the puja (the traditional ceremony that connects the teacher and the new student to the whole tradition of this knowledge stretching back to the beginning of time), the Three Nights Checking, the correct mantras correctly assigned. How could he have given the wrong mantras to his little children, his friends?

As a result of what Austin had done, his family and friends would probably never learn TM correctly. They would think they had tried it and it hadn't worked. They had lost their chance in this lifetime. At the time, I didn't realize how all the various aspects of the teaching had profound and subtle effects on the consciousness of the student. It was the package that inevitably worked, not just the separate parts. You can't teach yourself from a book. You cannot be both attempting to transcend effortlessly and trying to remember the written instructions at the same time.

The effects of certain instructions can vary, and the trained teacher knows what to do at that point, how to guide the student to experience effortless transcending. You know what they say about a self-made man? He's the product of unskilled labor! After our course on teacher training I would better understand all of this.

The *National Inquirer*

The TM teachers in Houston, Jane Hopson and Russell Hebert, had heard David's presentation on his research at Humboldt and invited him to Houston to talk to the public and to NASA. TM could be a good thing for the space program and astronaut Rusty Schweickart was an enthusiastic meditator. Jane and Russell sent a plane ticket and David went off, the first of many, many travels he would take on behalf of the movement. Rusty toured David around NASA and David spoke a couple of times and the press covered his events.

After he got home David got a call from a reporter who was a local contact for the *National Inquirer*. They had heard some garbled story about David in Houston and they sent this guy over to check it out. The reporter was looking for something strange or sensational for their readers, but David just wanted to talk about his research and the benefits of TM. The guy wanted a picture, and Maharishi always sat in front of a picture of his teacher, so David sat in front of a large picture of Maharishi from a poster we had. That was weird enough for them in 1971. They printed a small article with that picture.

Then we started to get mail. Some of it was strange hate mail from deranged minds. I could tell when the envelope was in my hands that it gave off a very sick consciousness. What was inside confirmed that feeling. After a few of these, when I recognized the feeling, I just tossed the thing out and didn't open it. This went on for pretty much the rest of our time in the movement when we were still in the public eye. On the positive side one wonderful person, unidentified, sent us a copy of Yogananda's *Autobiography of a Yogi*. We had heard about that book at Humboldt and we both read it, wide-eyed at some of the things he described. We hadn't had any experiences like that around Maharishi, yet, but we *might*. What were we getting into? Very interesting.

Off to Italy

David was determined to go to TTC, to Majorca, if possible. We were saving our money. Our friends Bill and Sue Liles wanted to go, too, in spite of having a tiny nursing baby. They were artists and didn't have much money, but nature supported. One day a guy knocked on their door and offered to buy a Volkswagon car body from their front yard. They were getting the funds together.

I gave up my reservations about another course with the children and reluctantly started to plan and to think about what to pack for a family of four and how to pay for the flights and the course. The course venue was changed to Fiuggi Fonte, Italy. The number applying were too many for the housing situation in Majorca. Prices went up slightly. We got passports. I bought an Italian dictionary and a little primer on basic Italian and started to conjugate a few verbs. I had never flown overseas and had no idea what to expect. But Europe! Italy! Wow. As a young girl, I had always taken the travel section from the *New York Times* that my father read every Sunday. I read the travel articles, looked over the ads, wrote to the tourist agencies, and pored over the brochures they sent me. I dreamed about going to Europe where all those writers I was reading had lived and written. Nature held out the lure and I went for it. Evolution was pulling me along.

All dressed up and on our way to the TM Teacher Training
Course in Fiuggi Fonte, Italy, March 1972

Learning to Whisper Infinity

WE MET OUR CHARTER in Los Angeles and flew into Rome in March 1972. One of our new young friends, Marc Freeman, took a turn holding baby Sara on his lap. She was a serene, confident little girl and preferred above all things to sit on my lap, but she would sit on others' laps if I was in view. We didn't have to buy a ticket for her because she was not yet two. I don't remember much about getting to the flight but I remember how uncomfortable it was trying to sleep and manage the kids. I do remember landing in Rome. We were supposed to be met by people and buses to take us to Fiuggi Fonte, a spa town about an hour and a half east of the airport, where our course was being held, but the hours went by and no one came to get us. The kids were hungry and the food available was strange and expensive. I asked for milk and they offered it warm, with or without sugar. We didn't have much cash. There was nowhere to sit but the floor, nowhere to nap the kids. It was painful. What was happening? Where were those people?!

I know *now* exactly what was happening. Maharishi was likely negotiating with hotel owners in Fiuggi. It was their slack season. Tourists would be coming to drink the waters from the natural springs (fonte) later in the spring and summer. Their hotels were sitting empty and they could be tempted to rent them to the movement. In order to be most cost effective for the movement, their prices had to be low, and the size of the hotel had to match the size of the group of intended occupants, leaving no empty unpaid for rooms. And there had to be dining rooms and kitchens that could be taken over by our volunteer staff, and a big place for meetings. It was complicated. Our Italian initiators were no doubt running back and forth between the hotel owners and Maharishi, offering terms, negotiating. The movement resources were slim, the course prices were kept low so many people could come, and the money had to be used carefully.

In the evening, finally, some buses came for us and we and our luggage were loaded on board and we set out on the ride. We arrived in the dark and the rain and our luggage was unloaded and left under some porch in the town square and we were led to two tiny rooms. Oh, my God. Was this going to be our home for the next ten weeks? How would we ever be reunited with our luggage and where would we put everything? Wouldn't it be stolen sitting outside in the village square? We were too exhausted to worry and fell into bed.

The next day was bright and sunny and everything improved. We were to be in the family section, a dead end street with three hotels, one of which housed our kitchen and dining room, and a nearby park. We were assigned to the Latina Hotel and we had three rooms. A small one for David, one small one for me, and a larger one for the kids across the hall from mine. All the rooms had two single beds next to each other. Miraculously our luggage was still where we left it. We identified it, put our hotel and room numbers on it, and it somehow showed up later. I don't remember breakfast or lunch, but they must have happened. I do remember dinner. The kids who were our kitchen staff were operating in a new kitchen with strange equipment, provisions probably hadn't fully arrived, and they had a hungry mob to feed. NOW. They cooked up two big pots of rice, one with vegetables and one with fruit, both burned and inedible.

There were over two thousand course participants and

probably several hundred staff. Susan Humphrey was in charge of the kitchens, and there were fifteen to set up, one of them with a wood-burning stove. Maharishi was very particular about the food. He sent Susan and her team to the markets to get the best honey, almonds, fresh fruit, and produce. Susan was responsible for menus, the well-being of the staff, and the satisfaction of the course participants (CPs). It was a big job. Soon our kitchen was fully functional and healthy, plentiful food was served.

The highlight of that first day was a rumor that Maharishi was giving advanced techniques in one of the hotels. We should all go there if we were eligible. You had to be meditating for eighteen months to get one. David had almost twenty-four. I was close. We had no idea where that hotel was and how to get there and what to do with the kids. Someone volunteered to watch them and the lovely Italian family who owned the Latina offered to drive us there. Off we went in their little car. Grazie, grazie.

We waited in a hushed, settled area outside Maharishi's room, and then my turn came and I was alone with Maharishi. The room was dark and smelled sweetly of some kind of incense. He sat on a couch and I sat nearby and we spoke very softly, just a few words to pin the thing down. I left in a daze, my mind tasting the new technique, eager to have it move in and make itself at home. My first face-to-face, personal meeting with him! He looked so kindly, and should have looked foreign, I suppose, but after Humboldt and all those video tapes I had seen for the past year and a half, he was very familiar to me, like a father or grandfather or an old, dear friend.

Maharishi met with the whole group that evening in the town movie theatre and started right out by telling us about the World Plan, expanding our minds and taking them off the mundane details of getting settled in. He later said that was his technique for drawing attention away from small issues and conflicts; he called it "drawing a bigger line." There were seven objectives of the World Plan: 1) Developing the full potential of the individual;

2) Improving governmental achievements; 3) Achieving the goals of education; 4) Solving the problems of crime and drug abuse; 5) Maximizing the intelligent use of the environment; 6) Fulfilling the economic aspirations of society; and 7) Achieving the spiritual goals of mankind in this generation. He had covered everything. The Natural Tendency wrote a song about it and sang it to us one evening. I can still hear their words and melody in my mind. Societies were already trying to solve these problems, Maharishi said. They just needed some help. The mechanics of how this would work were unclear to us at the time. Surely we wouldn't have to teach everyone to meditate, even the criminals? The world wasn't ready to hear about group effects and collective consciousness. That would wait until 1975.

Rounding

At the end of the evening Maharishi started us on a rounding schedule. We would do one round morning and evening the next day while we unpacked, got settled and organized, and rested from the long trip. He told when and when not to meditate and how to deal with insomnia if we found ourselves awake in the night and unable to go back to sleep.

Ignore any moods, he cautioned. One stress might have different layers of intensity and they would need deeper levels of rest to be released. He emphasized the importance of being on the schedule. These are not the days for planning and scheming or writing. (That was aimed at me. I was trying to find a dissertation topic and was always jotting down some idea.) Don't eat too much, he said. Gluttony causes dullness, fogginess, lots of sleep, and inertia develops. But don't skip meals. Stay on a schedule, just eat less. Go by the clock, not by moods.

Those yoga asanas were very important. Meditation changes the functioning of the body. Some stretching and turning helps to test the flexibility of the system as it increases. Due to release of stress, there are changes in our chemistry. There is a new kind of hollowness when stress dissolves. Stretching evens it out, helps in the changing value of the physical system. Asanas also help to soften the breath. They give the body exercise but do not bring any negative values such as other systems of exercise might do. And pranayama was important too. Same thing but from the inside; it stretches the body from the inside.

We were divided into areas and there were staff people in charge who would give us our daily announcements about meetings and schedules and the like. We were excited. Here was our chance to get enlightened quickly and change the world in the process. How long, someone asked. It is not wise or correct to assign a time, Maharishi answered. Could be tomorrow, or a few years. Just get on with it. Our path is the fastest!

After the meeting we walked home from the movie theatre in the dark through the quiet town toward the family area and our hotel. Suddenly we met up with our El Paso friends, David Beaver and Tom Rosell. They had found out where we were housed and had come to welcome us to the course. They had already taken one of the Majorca courses, but decided to stay on for the last one, our Fiuggi course, and continue rounding. They were already really nice people, but now, after ten weeks of rounding, they were even sweeter and softer. We could feel the difference in them. It was impressive and very inspiring. That would be happening to us.

I ventured forth by myself the next day looking for pannolini (diapers) and sale (salt). They weren't providing it in the dining room and the food was desperately bland. I found out that I couldn't get salt at the market that carried the diapers. It was sold only at Salt and Tobacco stores. Something about taxes. I don't remember the details. I tried to make the kids' room as homey and familiar as possible. They had pictures of their beloved grandparents and toys and other familiar things. David and I each had our second bed carried off so we would have room to do the yoga asanas on the floor. I also bought laundry detergent. It seemed I was going to hand wash everything for the time being. We were told not to hang laundry out our windows or on our balconies, if we had them. That was tacky and the Italians wouldn't like it. That left the radiators. Ah, well.

We also met with the childcare people. They would take the kids at 9:30 and bring them back at 5:30. We were to provide diapers, change of clothes, etc. They would see about laundry after a few days. Maybe something could be done. Later on they arranged to wash everything in one batch, but they didn't know about sorting colors. Everything white came back mauve, and everybody's clothes were all mixed up together. I decided to stick with hand washing.

The other people on the course could round from when they got up in the morning until a late dinner. One girl hung out on the square and played her guitar, and flirted with the Italian boys instead of rounding. We parents had this brief window and we had

Sara in the bidet. Happy to be back with mommy.

to make the best of it, so we skipped lunch, taking a few raisins and nuts to our rooms and going straight through until the kids came back for dinner, dirty, exhausted and hungry.

Childcare was overwhelmed and they had a policy of not changing diapers after three o'clock, so Sara came back with poop plastered over her whole bottom. My routine was to plop her into the bidet and soak her in warm water. All her clothes and Nate's went into the bathtub to soak in detergent. Then we bathed both kids, put them in their pajamas and took them to dinner or outside to play until dinner time.

The dining room was all marble or terrazzo with no curtains, nothing soft or upholstered to absorb the noise of fifty or more screaming kids running around while their parents, a little vague and quiescent from sitting in inner silence all day, sat helplessly in their chairs and tried to soothe and settle them. Hopeless. The food had improved, but if they served pizza or French fries there was a stampede to the buffet table and they disappeared within seconds.

And so went our days. Dress and breakfast the kids, put them on the bus, go round until the 5:30 bus brought them back, laundry and baths, dinner in the madhouse, put the kids to bed, go off to the evening meeting, return back to our rooms, check on the kids, thank the evening babysitter, and go to sleep. I would leave my door ajar because little Sara usually woke in the night, padded across the hall into my room, and climbed into my narrow cot. I woke up in the morning with my arms wrapped around her. Nate played hard with all the little boys and slept soundly. He was having a good time.

Rounding was, well, rounding. I found myself sitting on the asana blanket on the floor wondering what to do next. Had I just finished asanas and was ready to do something else or had I just sat down there? I had no idea. I started keeping notes. When I started meditating, when I did asanas, etc. Then I could look at the paper and see, yes, it was time to get onto the cot and move along and then meditate. The mantra alternated with thoughts, but from some level of very deep silence, of which I was unaware unless startled by some noise, only to realize that I had been very deep. And falling and falling and falling. Off cliffs, out of airplanes, off buildings. Falling and falling. Finally this stopped. When we visited the cliff dwellings in Mesa Verde National Park years later, I felt strangely at home, as if I had lived in those dark little rooms at the edge of the cliff in some past life, and that I, or maybe a child, or maybe I as a child had tumbled over the edge.

Evening Meetings

In the evenings in the movie theatre Maharishi talked about higher states of consciousness and how knowledge survives dissolution (according to the Indian time frame, the whole universe dissolves and is recreated time and again, over a vast range of time). See the relevant pages of his translation and commentary on the Bhagavad Gita. Some intelligence sustains even dissolution, he said, and gives birth to a new creation, so intelligence and existence are eternal. And when there is a time of much purity and impurity nature creates a revival of the knowledge, and we are part of such a revival. He was our teacher, our Master, and he would answer any and all questions, questions I couldn't even frame due to my limited reading and knowledge of these obscure and maybe occult areas. But this knowledge, he said, was just for us. As teachers, of course, we would avoid talking about anything controversial, such as religion, politics, or climate change (leaping forward in time here), and not confuse people with esoteric language and ideas. We would just emphasize one universal and profound truth: transcend and flourish.

One evening we heard a tape from a lecture on the status of the initiator that Maharishi had given to a course in Kashmir, India, in 1969. Transcending enlivens Being, he said, and it's infused and lived by the initiator. This vibrant Being emanates an influence of Being (to some degree or other, he said, doesn't matter how much—he didn't want us to worry about how much Being we might be emanating). The initiator is a like a big Concorde airplane; his air breezes the feet of God. The initiator is adored by the heavenly beings because he is producing a life-supporting influence in himself and in others, radiating an influence without intending to. He is the sweet child of Mother Nature. Whoever comes in his aura begins to live Being more. People are attracted to him and everything in nature has a cordial relationship with him (or her, I add).

I could relate to this because I could recognize a meditator or initiator usually by some air of softness, sweetness, and those people in New Mexico had seen our auras when we gave that introductory lecture. We had rounded at Humboldt and then meditated just before that lecture and they had seen and felt something there. David had felt that influence of Being in his friend Clint and in his initiator Casey Coleman, although I hadn't at the time. That was why we were rounding, to release stresses and be able to radiate Being more. We are passing on a vibrating influence, Maharishi said, giving life to the field of death. We are using language [in our talks] because that is all that is understood in the field of death. Language makes such a small stir. Our real influence is on the level of Being. I remember years later someone praising an initiator to Maharishi because she was very successful, attracting and initiating many, many people. No, Maharishi said, it is because the people there are very intelligent. That is, that group was very special; they had eyes to see who she was and what she was radiating.

Maharishi means great seer, we knew. Seers, he told us, are those who *see* the basic value of life, not just the surface reality, and every level of Creative Intelligence has its own special features and different expressions of intelligence. Knowledge is different in different states of consciousness, he would say. Philosophy in college is just fanciful talk. Those philosophers were not seers, just talkers. I had minored in philosophy at Vassar, and surely that was true of most of them. But some philosophers did have some experience or understanding of the deeper realities. Dr. Jonathan Shear who would be the professor of philosophy at MIU brought out the best of the Western tradition in his courses and was very popular. Later another philosopher, Dr. Ken Chandler, would do the same with the foundations of Western thought in his soon to be published books on those topics.

Maharishi kept a close watch on us all. There hadn't been much screening of who might come to the course. The door had been wide open and we had all poured through. Many of us had some physical movements during meditation as our bodies normalized and released old patterns and tensions, and Maharishi said not to mind, but just have the thought that they are not necessary.

Years later an initiator told me that he told Maharishi at Fiuggi that he was bouncing on the bed and wanting to fly around the room. No, Maharishi had told him sternly, we are not doing that yet. Yogic Flying would come later, much later, but Maharishi had the whole scheme of taking us from where we were to enlightenment laid out from the beginning. Even those early brochures on TM from the '60s said something about group practices. We thought that meant group meditations. No, it meant Superradiance, being together as yogic flyers, but I am getting ahead of my story.

The days blurred into one another. Nate came home one day with his shoe top completely separated from the sole. There would be a market at the top of the hill in Fiuggi Città in the next day or two, but he had to go to school tomorrow morning! I set off after dinner looking for a shoemaker. I found a man in a little room above some shops and showed him the shoe. Ruined, he thought, but was very friendly and wanted to know what I was doing in Fiuggi. I said, in my less than basic Italian, could he please just fix it to last one or two days, and while he smiled and hammered I gave him an introductory lecture on TM, *in Italian*.

Early Days in the Movement

On March 28, as we were two weeks into rounding, Dr. Vincent Snell, the first initiator in Great Britain, told us about the early days with Maharishi. In 1960, he told us, Maharishi travelled from India to Hong Kong to Hawaii to America and then to England. When he went to Hawaii he planned to stay only two weeks, but a man followed him in the street, and stopped him, and starting making arrangements and introductions all over the world, from place to place. When Maharishi reached England he stayed with the Snells for seven months.

During that time Maharishi sent out hand-written invitations to all top medical people to come hear him talk about the health benefits of transcending. Two people came, a psychotherapist and a doctor's secretary. Was he discouraged? Probably. When he had first spoken in the U.S. in 1958 a reporter described his lecture as presenting a cure for insomnia. He was horrified. He had talked about enlightenment and they had reduced it to insomnia. Where am I? he thought. These people know nothing about enlightenment, about inner reality. He considered going back to India. But no matter, he thought, let them come for headaches or insomnia, they would get enlightened anyway.

Dr. Snell described his experiences attending the first TM teacher training course in India in 1961. I could hardly believe what I was hearing. The course was held in the town of Rishikesh in northern India on the Ganges in the School of Sanskrit Studies. The temperature was 115 degrees in the shade. There was no sanitation; water had to be carried in and boiled for drinking. The Ganges widened daily because of the melting snows upstream in the Himalayas. The Indians left because it was too hot!

After six weeks, Dr. Snell said, the Shankaracharya of Jyotir Math visited. [There are four seats in India founded by the great Shankara, the founder of our tradition, and they are responsible for keeping the knowledge alive. The one in the north is the preeminent one. This Shankaracharya had been with Guru Dev, Maharishi's Master, who was Shankaracharya at that time.] He arrived with the traditional elephant, throne, retinue, umbrella, and bodyguard with a shotgun! He came for two nights and stayed for two weeks (he can only stay somewhere for a maximum of three weeks.). He gave the course participants exams and corrected their answers. Later he came again to inspect Maharishi's academy which was being built across the river in the forest. He crossed the Ganges in a boat to visit the digging at the site and he blessed the academy.

Dr. Snell said it was difficult to take notes because their hands were wet and sticky from the heat. Everything made a noise. The birds were incredible. Each room had a stove, a bed (with bedbugs) and a chair. There were openings at the tops of the walls

Maharishi strolling around Fiuggi Fonte. Next to him is Mr. Granville. He and his wife (you can see her head just to the right of Maharishi) were early hosts and supporters of the movement in California in the late '50s. Next to Mr. Granville is Dr. Vincent Snell, and just behind him are Lillian Rosen, the advanced technique teacher for the U.S., and Jerry Jarvis, the director of the TM movement in America. Tina Olson is on the far right.

and the Myna birds sat there and squawked. One man found his bed was in the pathway of a daily rat procession and had to move it. Everyone stayed in their rooms from ten to four. At four they went down to the Ganges and stood in it up to their necks to cool down. When David and I visited Rishikesh in May 1975, the temperature when we landed in Delhi at dawn was 105 degrees, but the Ganges in Rishikesh was ice cold and chilling and cooled our core for hours afterwards when we soaked in it for few minutes.

Maharishi lectured on the banks of the Ganges in the evenings. He had just started his commentary on the Bhagavad Gita. The course participants took notes by starlight or flashlight. As the first initiator in England Vincent had founded SRM, the Spiritual Regeneration Movement there (like those people we sat with at Humboldt). There were few guidelines, no checking notes. He was pretty much learning by experience.

There was another European course the next year in the same place and they were building a hotel next door. Noise!! In 1965 Vincent Snell went to Canada, joined Maharishi at Emerald Lake and initiated in Vancouver, Toronto, and in Montreal. In 1967 Maharishi was in England again lecturing at the Hilton Hotel. The Beatles turned up. Dr. Snell introduced them to Maharishi. They were very serious, he told us. They sat on the floor at his feet, and after that meeting George Harrison traveled around England a little with him. From that moment on the audiences doubled. There are now, he said, centers all over England, and SIMS, the Students International Meditation Society, is very big there. There are never enough people to help with initiations.

It was stunning, a look into the past of the movement, how we got from our own little unofficial center in El Paso in our living room to Humboldt and to Fiuggi in 1972. Doing laundry in the bathtub didn't seem too horrible any more. No heat, no bedbugs, real toilets and bidets, no elephants, no monkeys, very little noise really.

David and the Chart Book

One day I was deep in rounding, lost in my silence and thoughts, when there was a loud pounding on the door. Who could it be? No meditator would interrupt my meditations so loudly. A young man in a suit stood there. Where was Dr. Orme-Johnson? Someone wanted to see him. I took him next door to David's room and tapped softly on the door and cracked it open. This guy wants you, I told him and went back to my rounding. He wanted David to put on his suit and come immediately into the car and up to Fiuggi Città.

There sat Maharishi in a large room and next to him were Keith Wallace and Vincent and Peggy Snell. They made room for David next to Keith, and David was asked all about the research he had done and would present later in the course. Maharishi was making the first chart book about the scientific evidence on TM and David could assist with that. David had done a lot of

David sitting with Maharishi, Dr. Robert Keith Wallace, Dr. Vincent and Peggy Snell in Fiuggi, 1972. They were discussing the creation of the first chart book on the scientific research on TM.

research into autonomic stability, which his research had shown increasing in meditators, and he went through everything he knew. Maharishi wanted to know all the benefits connected with that phenomenon. When David finished he didn't want to leave, so he said it all again. While they were talking a photographer was moving about and snapping pictures. David thought he would love to have a picture of himself with Maharishi. He glanced over at Maharishi and saw him nod as if in agreement, but when the meeting was over, the photographer had disappeared. Ah, well.

Later on, another knock on the door showed a young woman named Judy Booth. She was on staff, often working with Maharishi or Dr. Vernon Katz on the Bhagavad Gita. Someone wanted to see David. By this time, we had realized that "someone" meant Maharishi. This time it was a meeting of scientists discussing physiology and the brain. David quickly said everything he knew about the autonomic nervous system and the hypothalamus. He was awed by Maharishi's presence and was thrilled just to be there. He saw Maharishi as glowing, extraordinarily present, his Being filling the room. Maharishi saw that David was taking in a deeper reality and he sat back, relaxed, and smiled as if to say, just enjoy.

Starting MIU

One night we got an announcement that the movement had applied to accredit Maharishi International University, a university that the movement was now starting, and that the accreditation board was coming to evaluate us. A young initiator named Nat Goldhaber had proposed the idea of a university to Maharishi at the Amherst SCI symposium in the summer of 1971, and he and Keith were pushing for a university of our own. Maharishi's idea was just to add SCI to what already existed in other universities without having to get involved with a huge physical plant. Nonetheless he let scouting parties go out and look for college campuses that the movement might purchase, and for funding that would allow such a purchase of a permanent campus. As current students of said University, we were told that we should all immediately write to our high schools or colleges and have our transcripts sent to MIU, Director of Admissions, Fiuggi Fonte, Italy. Keith was the president, Nat was the Vice-president, and Keith Wallace's mother Lillian was the librarian. We should all donate our books to her as she was setting up a library to show them. Very funny. She must have had 50 copies of *Autobiography of a Yogi* and whatever other paperbacks people had brought to the course. I hadn't brought anything but my Italian phrasebook. I knew from Humboldt there wouldn't be a minute to read.

One night David and I were invited to a meeting of the prospective MIU faculty. David had a PhD, I had an MA and I was working on my PhD. There were many others there with higher degrees, like physicist Larry Domash, who had a PhD from Princeton and who had done a postdoc at Harvard. Dr. Keith Wallace was putting together a faculty roster with our names, where we got our degrees, and all that. He was preparing for the accreditation visit. We weren't involved, thank goodness, and we gratefully went back to our daily routine.

I wrote a note to David during a lecture. I am feeling jealous about not experiencing enough silence. I'm feeling like doing more rounds. How about you? Could we somehow alternate taking care of the kids and do more? We couldn't figure out another way, and just kept going. We were doing the best that we could, releasing stress during sleep, during dreams, during meditation. TM hits much deeper than sleep, Maharishi said, like a spy going after certain thieves. It goes after the big criminals, not the petty thieves or pickpockets. TM goes after certain stresses of intense bondage which perpetuate the cycle of rebirth and which sleep cannot touch. But don't worry about karma, he said. We are set on the best karma of all, meditating, so we don't much bother about the rest.

Fourth International Symposium on SCI

Early in April 1972 Maharishi held the Fourth SCI Symposium. Larry Domash talked about the principle of least action, Jon Shear spoke about subjective experiences of pure consciousness or something like that, Demetri Kannelakos spoke and so did Keith. David presented his own research on habituation and all its implications, as well as summarizing all the research that had been done up to that time (faster reaction time, improved psychomotor activity, accelerated rate of learning, and increased intelligence). Maharishi was very happy to see this research coming out: "It is the great fortune of the scientists of this generation to be studying and analyzing the nature of infinity as expressed both in the inner life of man and the farthest reaches of his environment. The realization of the infinite value of life on both of these levels—outer objective and inner subjective—will pave the highway for a life of 200% for every man on earth."

Michael Weinless talked about set theory in mathematics, and Tina Olson, Mother Olson's daughter, danced her original choreography "And Creation Moved," describing the seven states of consciousness. Dr. John Farrow talked about chemical receptors in the nervous system. Professor Ralph Yarrow from England talked about drama and Professor Erika Lorenz from Germany gave a talk about the French poet Paul Valéry. Dr. Larry Squires, a professor of English at Humboldt State University, spoke about historical ideals of knowledge, and Dr. Bernard Glueck, who was Director of Research at the Institute for Living, a psychiatric facility in New England, was proposing introducing TM to his patients. Maharishi enjoyed these talks and commented on them all, relating them to Creative Intelligence. In between presentations he continued to take questions and talk about themes of the knowledge of consciousness. The speakers and highlights of these talks and Maharishi's responses are in the back of the original MIU catalogue.

One evening Maharishi talked about how even in Cosmic

Consciousness the mantra activates the mind. He had said in an earlier lecture that the mantra, the sound one uses in meditation, is a very vital and special aspect of the teaching, the steps of the ladder down to ground level. The mantras we use in our tradition resonate with existing impulses of the body. The Vedic seers had cognized them and for whom they would be most effective. The results are predictable. We go by the tradition; we wouldn't want to experiment with life. And even in CC, the ability to perceive the mantra is not lost, and every thought is cognized at its source. I heard once that on one of Maharishi's visits to Canada, a lady in his audience, who had been meditating a long time, said she no longer used her mantra. Maharishi quietly commented, I still use mine. At this point let me say that just as Maharishi used "he" to stand for he and she, a lifelong verbal habit, he called women ladies and preferred that term. It was politically incorrect, I know, and probably originated in the British culture in which he was raised. It indicated a higher class of female and I think he purposely used that term in that way. I preferred "women" myself, and finally, years later women became the accepted term. But in those days and times, it was lady and ladies and so it was.

But mostly the questions and talk ran to releasing old stresses, which is what we were all doing all the time. Thought is a projection of the release of stress, Maharishi said, but many stresses can be released at once, so you can't sort it all out. It's not worth bothering about. And happiness, joy, comes bubbling up from the inside also. In quiet moments, bliss zooms forth, which means CC isn't far off. The development of pure consciousness is the basis for realizing God. God Consciousness gets generated on the ground of CC. God Consciousness is the most refined value of activity of the mind; it is a forerunner to Unity Consciousness. When you get to CC, he advised, go into a year of rounding. That will propel you towards GC.

One only notices a change in states of consciousness when it first happens, he said. There is some period of amazement, of happiness. Then you get familiar with it and forget about it as it becomes an everyday reality. It is never good to talk about your state of consciousness, Maharishi said, because you can't prove it, and because others will be flabbergasted and overshadowed. Over the years to follow we saw the truth of this as we saw certain individuals claiming to be in higher states of consciousness having an undue influence over weak or ignorant minds. The doctors on the courses and around Maharishi used to joke that when someone started talking about how they were now in GC or UC, they would think, "Bring in the stretchers." I still feel this way when someone tells me they are in a particular state of consciousness. Are they full of beans, mood making, or just out of their minds?

Sometimes the SCI Symposium talks went on and on and I just couldn't take any notes. I wrote in my notebook: "I can't wait until Maharishi gets here so we can stand up and stretch. I am getting bedsores on my bum." Sigh. Irreverent me. I was changing fast and furiously and needed a little rest from all the novelty and new ideas.

We had started coming down from rounding, gradually, and I was enjoying being more active. Childcare lost their bus and we had to walk to the childcare area to pick up the kids. The Italian nuns would spot Sara with her blue eyes and golden curls and would want to swoop down on her like great black birds and pinch her cheeks. Nate would warn me when they were heading our way. They frightened her. I learned to say in Italian, don't touch her. They were offended. One day the kids all had a great time drawing with charcoal and they were covered with black soot when we went to pick them up. The Italians always dressed well and they looked at Sara and at me with incomprehension. How could I allow that beautiful child to be so dirty, and in a public place!

As rounding slowed down, and the days got longer and warmer, we got to know our neighbors a little better. After David spoke at the SCI Symposium they suddenly knew who *we* were. Keith

Wallace and his wife Barbara and their two little boys lived in the hotel next to ours. The older one, Teddy, played with Nate. Gareth was still in a stroller and Barbara wheeled him all over Fiuggi. Stuart and Moki Zimmerman lived in our family area too. After dinner, all the kids played outside and we would hear Moki calling her daughter in to go to bed, Puanani, Puanaaani. The Zimmermans would later give great financial support to the movement.

There were Stan and Yvonne Lewis and their little Lakshmi (younger than Sara). They would later gather a group of black initiators and start the black wing of the TM movement in the U.S. Many of them went to Ethiopia for a TM Teacher Training Course for 100 black Americans and 25 Ethiopians. Maharishi was very sympathetic and encouraging and he visited the course. He had suffered his own share of color prejudice. And there were Noel and Jennifer Hart and their daughter Juniper (remember Donavan's song, "Jennifer, Juniper." She said that's where that came from). Mike Love's wife Tamara was there taking the course, too, and taking care of Mike's son Christian. There were many others we would get to know better over the years. Now we would be studying together and testing each other.

Learning and Memorizing

As we came down from rounding we broke into groups and got into serious memorization. First, we were handed out papers that contained the words in Sanskrit of the ceremony of gratitude. In India this kind of ceremony is known as a *puja*. We didn't have to learn the Sanskrit language, but we did have to learn to pronounce the words properly and learn what they actually meant. We also learned what these meanings might inspire on the level of emotion. Maharishi said that the puja connects the teacher with the Holy Tradition, the line of Masters coming down through time. We learned who they all were, their special attributes and contributions. We learned how to perform the ceremony, making symbolic offerings to the picture of our Guru Dev, Brahmananda Saraswati, Shankaracharya of Jyotir Math, offerings, such as a flower, which stands for the bloom of life.

Now it is well known that being thankful or grateful has a huge, beneficial effect on one's mental health and happiness We certainly were grateful that we had found Maharishi and were in a movement to bring his knowledge to the world. In a tape we had heard earlier, Maharishi had explained that the purpose of doing the puja is to deepen the coordination between the senses, mind, intellect, and ego of the teacher. It coordinates the Self with the environment. It is a technology to transfer the knowledge to the student, a simple automantic way of teaching that would produce maximum effect for both student and teacher.

We practiced and practiced and one day, when I was doing the puja in my room, Nate saw what I was doing and brought in his own offerings, a picture of his grandparents and some little toy. My heart melted.

We were meant to overlearn the puja, as they say in psychology, to know it so well that we could just float automatically on the feel of it and not be trying to remember, first the flower, then the incense, etc. It should just be perfect in word and gesture. We got tested by each other again and again. Finally, I felt ready to go off to the hotel where they were testing everyone and present myself. A young fellow named Larry Farwell tested me. I know I performed it perfectly. He corrected some little thing which I knew I had done right and sent me off to practice some more. I was furious with him for years! Later I learned that those were their instructions. Flunk everyone. Send them back to practice some more. Test them again and again. Our instructions were that when you finally passed, then test ten other people and correct their details.

Learning to check one's meditation. These instructions had to be learned thoroughly. This procedure of checking takes a person through the correct stages of meditation and gives them the right start and experience of inner silence and effortless thinking of the mantra. Very powerful. Very precise. And almost impossible to learn because so many of the instructions were similar to each other, with just a phrase change or two, and we had to learn the timings too, 10 seconds here, one minute there. A work of genius, it was and is. David and I had been checkers in El Paso, so we were better off than those learning them for the first time. I had made a flow chart with all the instructions in their proper places. We practiced and practiced on each other. Nothing I had ever done in graduate school was this challenging.

Larry Domash was learning the checking procedure too, and was having a difficult time. We got to know him and his beautiful girlfriend Janice and we had all become friends. Larry had a quirky sense of humor and in later years he would torture David and Keith as they sat on stage with Maharishi, David ready to give his talk on the psychological benefits of meditation, like broad comprehension along with the ability to focus sharply. They were supposed to be looking like serious scientists, waiting their turns to speak. Larry would pass David a little note: "broad comprehension = comprehension of broads." David couldn't help smiling and, then, how could he say "broad comprehension" in his talk and not think about comprehension of broads. When he gave his talk those words jumped into his mind and Maharishi glanced over and gave him a stern look.

Larry was suffering along with the rest of us. A PhD in physics does not prepare one for learning the checking procedure, not at all. Well now, he said, as if he were checking someone, "You are one of those people who are unable to meditate. Go over to table number 4 and get your money back." We laughed and laughed. It really *was* difficult, and you *had* to pass the tests. Janice told me she has tear stains on her checking notes. It was that tough.

We also got sample points for the introductory lecture where you talk about the benefits of TM and the preparatory lecture, where you explain more about the tradition, and the steps to actually learn the technique. We had to stand up in our little groups and practice those lectures over and over again.

We also had to learn the notes for the three days of checking that followed initiation. These three lessons have precise instructions on how to conduct the session, what knowledge to give out, what forms the new meditator will fill out so you can tell if he or she is meditating correctly, how to answer questions that might arise, and how to deal with every possible eventuality. This training to become teachers was profound, complete, and, if you did it all correctly, foolproof. Really foolproof. All of it was essential. With the puja preparing the teacher's consciousness, with each part of the teaching being in its place, it would work. We could teach transcending to someone, and indeed, it was true. It really did work. If ever you are thinking of becoming a TM teacher, be prepared for the one of the most challenging and most rewarding educational experiences of your life! I had no idea so much went into becoming a teacher of TM and I began looking at those initiators I had come to know in a new light. They had gone through this!

So, finally, we were to learn the steps of personal instruction: the whole procedure of interviewing the person and then taking them through the series of instructions that would lead them to effortless transcending and correct meditation, and then afterwards, until they went home to practice on their own and come to first night's checking. More—being prepared to guide the student through every possible situation through questions and answers. This was the final stroke and to be allowed to learn these procedures you had to have passed all the tests and learned everything else. The course was ending. We would learn these final instructions, then Maharishi would give us the final stroke of knowledge regarding the mantras, and we would be on the bus to the airport. That was the order of things.

But first we were all together with Maharishi in the big hall and preparing to have Jerry lead us in these very last instructions which he would give out to us. Maharishi was sitting before us, radiant and loving, and very happy to have us all there about to be launched into the world to teach TM. Maharishi turned the meeting over to Jerry and he withdrew. There were almost 2,000 of us sitting in that huge movie theatre, I believe, and we were all very quiet and attentive. Jerry began with the very first part of the instruction, and suddenly the whole place transcended. We were swirled into a vortex of silence with not a whisper, not a rustle to be heard. It was a special and serious time and I felt the importance and magnitude of what we were learning. These were the instructions to take a person into their own inner silence, to guide them personally to the transcendent, as we had been guided. We were entering into a new profession, a new responsibility, and we were honored and grateful to be there, and grateful to Maharishi and to Jerry for launching us into our new lives.

Escape to Florence and Assisi

After we learned these final instructions, those who were leaving were put in one group and those of us who were staying for a one-month extension were put into another. We were going to watch as Maharishi videotaped the SCI lessons and made them into a course that could be taught at the TM centers and we would help create course materials. It looked as if we would not be missed if we disappeared for a week or so until that course began. It was a chance to see the art in Florence, to go to Assisi, where St. Francis had meditated, to Sienna, whatever. And it was a good time to have the family back together again. We had grown apart. We hadn't been with the children very much. We had been distracted by rounding and studying. We needed some family wholeness. We took a bus to a nearby town to rent a car, packed up the kids and the diapers and set off.

I had a friend from high school in Cleveland Heights, Pippy Lutz. She had been traveling in Europe with college friends in the early '60s and met a young Hungarian refugee. They fell in love but at first didn't have a common language. They wound up moving to Italy and settling in Florence. Pippy had a daughter Alessa a few years older than Nate, and Pippy found us a place to stay that we could afford and took us around Florence. It was heavenly; there was artwork wherever you looked. Even a glance up a small alley would reveal a piece of sculpture by someone's door. Pippy recommended that we visit the Parco dei Mostri (Park of the Monsters) in Bomarzo, about 120 miles south of Florence, on our way back to Fiuggi. It was designed in 1552 by Vicino Orsini. He had various artists carve huge sculptures out of the native limestone, big enough to walk into and climb on top of. Perfect for the kids to run around in and enjoy. We also drove through Sienna to see the famous cathedral made of black and white marble. The only thing I remember from there was changing Sara's diaper on top of the car.

Assisi still sticks in my mind. The town was charming and the Roman temple ruins upon which it was built were fascinating. Maharishi told us later that people would recognize a special spiritual spot and build a temple or church there. Then later another group would build their temple right on top of the old one, knowing and feeling that it was a power spot. The Basilica of St. Francis of Assisi has many frescos by Cimabue and a series of 28 by the young Giotto telling the life story of St. Francis, done between 1286 and 1304, according to Vasari. There is controversy over who actually did them, but they are wonderful and we looked and looked. I would love to go again.

We were shown a tiny cell carved into the rock of the church or friary where St. Francis had supposedly meditated. Having just spent many hours and days in our rooms meditating we could imagine him sitting there. It felt very silent and serene and holy. Best was climbing the nearby hills to where St. Francis had meditated in a cave. There we could look out on the valley below and imagine spending hours meditating and praying there. Again, it felt holy and silent and sweet.

Back to Fiuggi and SCI

Rome was noisy and tumultuous and we drove right through it and back to Fiuggi. No one knew we had been gone. Many of the kids had finished their course and left and there were just, maybe, a few hundred of us left. Childcare had shrunk quite a bit, but was still sort of functional. There was a small park near the family hotels and the little boys ran amok there. The teachers were rather helpless to control them. They didn't want to hit them and reason didn't seem to work. Being a behavioral psychologist, David suggested they "punish" them with time outs. So they appointed a bad boys' bench and sat the wild ones there for a few minutes. It really worked. The worst thing in the world was having to sit on that bench while everyone else was running around having a fine time.

The SCI course started and we were the audience as Maharishi taped lesson after lesson. We were all put to helping write materials for the course, but I don't remember any of it. The staff were also organizing the tapes and materials together to ship to the

The bad boys' bench with (front to back) Teddy Wallace, Nate, Christian Love, and another little fellow.

centers, arranging the purchase of a good tape player, and having it all ready for the following fall, an incredible feat. I do remember the night we were made teachers. On our way past Maharishi, who was seeing each of us briefly, he stopped David and leisurely chatted with him as if he were one of the top movement people, and there was all the time in the world. He sent Gavin Balhari, a tall initiator from Australia, to get a proclamation book MIU Press was producing so he could show it to David. Gavin was a speed-walker and we had seen him around Fiuggi rushing back and forth on errands for the Press. He brought the book and Maharishi showed it to David. It contained beautiful versions of proclamations endorsing TM from politicians and leaders and the press throughout the world. It would be the first of many such books endorsing TM.

Finally we were all ready to go. We collected the kids and our luggage, got on the bus in the middle of the night, and were driven to Rome for an early flight back to LA. Time to toilet train Sara who was nearly two and was ready, and to teach Transcendental Meditation in El Paso, Texas. We were initiators!

Desert Rain

WE RETURNED HOME to El Paso feeling transformed. We had a new perspective on life and we couldn't wait to share it, to teach TM. We were a part of the movement, full of hope and enthusiasm for our future, and the world's future, and it now seemed to take priority over all our other concerns. David returned to his job at Fort Bliss. His boss Rick was not very welcoming, since David had left without permission three months earlier to go to TTC, but luckily he soon moved on and the new boss was much friendlier. We quickly organized an introductory lecture and it went very well. As I looked out at the room full of unfamiliar faces, I wondered which of them would decide to learn. There were some smiling and nodding and others looking quiet and serious. When you finish the second lecture, the preparatory lecture, you just wait, smiling and serene and see who comes forth. It is a big moment of decision for them. Will they take the leap into the unknown? Does the knowledge somehow resonate with something in them? Did the picture of Maharishi on the TM poster stir something ancient in them? Sometimes you are quite surprised by who presents themselves to learn.

I remembered one such situation from the previous year. Our friend John Rechy, who had had a great success with his first novel *City of Night*, was attracted to learning TM because of what we had said about it, and maybe because of what he sensed in us, but he was very ambivalent about what effect it might have on him and his writing. Perhaps he was concerned that he would become too mellow and unable to write about the rough life he wanted to describe. He sat with the teacher at the interview after the preparatory lecture, asked a lot of questions and was struggling with himself. After a while the teacher impatiently tapped his pencil and said, Well? John said never mind and walked off. I think now that if that initiator had waited patiently and warmly until John could have settled inward and found his answer, it might have ended differently.

Soon people lined up at our stations, we gave them forms to fill out, and we started interviewing them. We each had about 20 people who wanted to learn and the next Saturday we instructed them at our house, all day long. Nate and Sara spent the day and evening with their grandparents, and we were free to give ourselves to teaching. By the end of the day we were blissfully exhausted. Our meditator helpers brought in some pizza and we sat around that evening surrounded by flowers, laughing at nothing, feeling really wonderful and fulfilled. We had taught as we were taught and it all went perfectly. Not only that, but it rained all day, a rarity in the desert. We felt blessed. We were cleansing the whole area, and being cleansed ourselves.

The first night checking, our very first, went smoothly. We could see that inner light in the new meditators, a kind of glow, and the group of strangers brought together only by having learned TM on the same day became a friendly, coherent unit. They shared their results: better sleep, more energy, less irritability, being able to do an unpleasant task without whining and resisting. They all could tell that something good was really happening to them and that their meditation was taking them to a quieter, more pleasant place. The rest of the course went well and we were thrilled.

A few of our friends in the meditator group went off to the summer Humboldt SCI course of 1972. One of them came back with a picture. He had been outside the lecture hall and some photographers had spread out their photographs of Maharishi and were selling them. He saw one of Maharishi sitting in a meeting room with David alongside. He bought it and brought it back. It was the very one David had wished for in Fiuggi during TTC. Coincidence? Had Maharishi organized it somehow? Had Maharishi seen that it would happen? Was that the reason he had nodded at David?

Our friend Jean, who had been with us when David had learned TM, had learned TM after I did. We went up the valley to visit her one afternoon. Her husband Danny, who had come up from a *barrio* in California and married one of the princesses of El Paso, remarked that David and I looked squeaky clean. Jean was a devout Catholic and later told the Monsignor at her church that she had learned TM. He went into a rage and railed against all the new age techniques that were corrupting the Catholics. Jean quit meditating and threw away all of her books on spirituality. This was typical of the ignorance about TM at the time. David has a website called TruthAboutTM and one section in it has letters from spiritual leaders of various religions describing their experiences with TM and explaining that TM is an aid to one's religion, not opposed to it, but it was too late for Jean.

David had a related experience. He was showing the new chart book of the TM research that came out that winter to a man who seemed really interested in the scientific research and all the benefits, but when David turned to the back cover where a picture of Maharishi was displayed, the man froze up. That was the end of that. Xenophobia? Fundamentalism? Very sad.

Not everyone who learned TM realized what it was doing for them. I remember one family I taught. They all did well with instruction, were meditating correctly, and the wife and daughter told the group that they had noticed changes in themselves. The husband said he had noticed nothing, no changes in them and no changes in himself. I asked the wife and daughter if they had noticed anything in him. Oh, yes, they said. He was much more re-laxed and nicer. He was astounded. He looked at them in amaze-ment. Really? he asked them. There it was, but the sad truth is that some people just don't have eyes to see it. I don't know if they continued to meditate.

Another couple stands out in my mind. The husband had good results and was very happy with his meditation. His wife was irritable and claimed nothing was happening in her meditation, insisting that it wasn't working. I could see for myself that she was softer somehow, although still her usual grumpy self, but she didn't see any results in herself or in him. After third night's check-ing I asked her husband privately if he had seen any changes in her. Oh, yes, he said, in a very heartfelt way. Why didn't you say something in the group? I asked. Oh, he said, I couldn't figure out how to say she was less bitchy. I had to laugh. It *was* a problem. I suggested a few ways he could tell her she was more lovable with-out saying she was or had been a difficult person.

One woman from a course we taught in neighboring Las Cruces offered in the group that her feet felt warm. Oh, that's nice, I said. Yes, circulation does increase in hands and feet and many people feel warmer there. You don't understand, she said, I have Reynaud's Syndrome and my feet are often painfully cold. I sometimes sit in the sun with my feet in the hot sand to warm them up. Now TM seems to be doing that naturally inside the house. Wonderful. We had seen TM improve many conditions, but you never knew what would happen. The body would heal and normalize and then you would just take it for granted.

One young Mexican girl told us when she went to visit her grandmother in Juarez, the city across the Mexican border from El Paso, that her grandmother had immediately noticed some-thing. Her grandmother always seemed to know when she had a new boyfriend or when something new was happening in her life. This time her grandmother looked at her very piercingly. You are doing something new, she said, and it is very good for you.

David taught his new boss at Fort Bliss and his wife to meditate and we also held a course for some of the senior faculty of UTEP and their wives, including the president of the college. Some of them were friends of David's parents so they knew we were from a good family. The course went very well, as usual. One amusing thing was that the wife of the art professor fell asleep during the group meditation and she snored. After the group meditation I brought up that sleep is natural. When the body has fatigue, it is quite usual to sleep for a bit during meditation, especially during the early days if one has accumulated a sleep debt. We don't fight sleep, I said, but we don't encourage it either, by starting to meditate lying down or slouching with our head back on the chair. We always sit upright when we start to meditate, and then if sleep comes, lie down or whatever. I smiled over at her. I wasn't sleeping, she said. The group laughed. Oh, yes, you were, one of her friends said. We heard you snore. She couldn't believe it. Maharishi had said that TM takes you to the junction point between states of consciousness. The transition between states of consciousness—sleeping, dreaming, and waking—is so subtle that you often aren't aware that you were dreaming or sleeping until you wake up, I explained.

One of the military officers from Fort Bliss learned TM. He was very enthusiastic and often took it upon himself to stand up in an introductory lecture to tell the group how great it was. We were having a very fulfilling time of it all, although we were occasionally frustrated that we couldn't seem to adequately communicate how profound the knowledge and experiences were, how your whole life could be changed for the better with this one simple technique. Could we have said it better somehow?

We got a call from a man who wanted to interview us for TV. We were excited and went off to the TV studio hoping that this interview would reach a wider audience and bring in more meditators. The man was rather rough and asked very negative and provocative questions. We didn't take them personally. He was obviously very stressed. At one point, I just laughed and patted him on the knee and told him he should really try TM, that it would make a huge difference to him. When the interview was over we were ushered into a nearby room to see the footage. He had interviewed a young Hispanic social worker before us and tried to upset him and get him emotional. It had worked and the young man lost his composure.

It seems that our interviewer was making a tape to submit for some job. He was trying to get hired to do confrontational interviews that were popular at that time. Our interview would not be aired on TV in El Paso. We were just being used. He thought he could get some interesting footage out of us. It was disappointing. After we finished the interview and were getting up to go into the nearby room, one of the cameramen came up to us and asked how he could learn TM. As he filmed us he could see that we had some inner Being and stability and he wanted that. Perhaps that was the reason we were there. For him.

We began offering weekend residence courses at Holy Cross Retreat in Las Cruces, New Mexico, and people came to them from all over the southwest. We recently gave an advanced lecture at a new TM center in San Francisco, and a TM teacher there told us she had attended one of those courses as a young high school girl about forty-five years ago. She was very wild in high school, she told me, and her brother had learned TM and had settled right down. Her father took her to the TM center and said you will do this or be grounded for life! She cried and cried, all through the lecture and instruction. But somehow it took. She recognized what it was and went to our residence course and others, and on to SCI and TTC.

We had ordered the thirty-three lesson SCI course and the tape machine and offered the course to the El Paso meditators. It was a brilliant exposition of Maharishi's knowledge, and the manual was very complete with transcripts of the talks, main points, questions and answers, everything you would need to teach it. We worked that into our busy schedule.

I took a brief trip to Cleveland with the kids to visit my mother and went from there to Bowling Green, Ohio, to visit one of my old high school and college friends, Susan Koppelman. Susan had introduced me to David when we were in college. She loved both of us and was sure we would love each other. We did but it took us about two years to figure it out. She was a doctoral student in popular culture at Bowling Green State University. She wanted to learn TM so I thought I would contact the local TM teacher to see what was going on. It turned out there was a course scheduled that weekend by a pretty young TM teacher named Toby Warwick. I helped teach it (we had a large response from the college kids) and folded my friend Susan, her husband John, and their little son Nathan into the course.

They all liked meditation but Susan let it slip away from her after some time. She was very busy with her teaching, getting her degree, and her role in the new women's movement. At one point, when she was living in St. Louis, her doctor told her she had high blood pressure and needed to go onto medication. She remembered that I had told her that TM reduces blood pressure in many people. At the present time TM is the only meditation technique recommended by the American Heart Association for the treatment of high blood pressure. The other meditation techniques they evaluated had either insufficient or no evidence of improving cardiovascular disease.

Susan didn't want to take the blood pressure medications with all their expense and side effects. She asked her doctor to give her a target number and to give her a little time, and then she began meditating regularly and checking her blood pressure every day at a machine in one of the college buildings. Her blood pressure dropped into the normal range; she went back to her doctor and got the okay to continue on and not take the drugs.

I was too busy teaching TM to teach at UTEP that fall, but I got one of the professors there to proctor one of my doctoral exams. The University of Maryland would allow me to take the exam if a professor would agree to put me in a room, have me take the exam, and then send it back to them. I was still searching for a dissertation topic and studying for and taking the exams as I could arrange it. There was never enough time in the day, but the kids were thriving, the TM community was growing, and David's parents were very helpful and supportive.

We taught in El Paso, in Las Cruces and White Sands, New Mexico, and I even tried giving a course in a new subdivision about an hour outside of El Paso. Only one lady and her six-year-old son learned. The little boy had had rheumatic fever and had a heart murmur as a result. He was eligible for the children's technique. Children under ten don't sit to meditate; they have a slightly active form of meditation, and they really enjoy it. The mother loved her meditation and was sure I was in CC. I had to disabuse her of that notion. When I went back for the ten-day check, the little boy told me that when he was walking around his room doing his technique that he felt sleepy and wanted to lie down. Do it, I said, lie down when you feel like it and take a nap if that's what feels right. His mother called a few weeks later to tell me that his doctor could no longer detect the murmur. It seemed to have disappeared. Could his meditation have done that? Well, I said, that is the only new thing in his life, right? He must have healed. What a great thing.

Another story or two. I initiated an older lady who had been afraid to drive or even leave her house after her husband died. Within days of learning TM she was driving again and picking up the strands of her old life. Very fulfilling. And there was a man who had severe test anxiety and was about to take a series of final exams. He was even worried about taking time off from his studies to do his twenty-minute meditations. When I asked him a few days later how his exams had gone, he looked at me blankly. He had simply taken them, breezed through them, and forgotten that he ever used to panic. He sat there in amazement trying to metabolize what had happened to him. Every TM teacher has stories like these. It is what makes the financial sacrifice so worthwhile. You are making a difference. Teaching TM is addictive, in a good way.

Then one day our perfect life changed. The phone rang. David got a call from Keith Wallace. Maharishi International University was beginning to come together in Santa Barbara, California, of all places. Maharishi wanted the prospective faculty for MIU to work on the first catalogue for our new university. First, there would be a two-week ATR (Advanced Training Resource) at the Francisco Torres Conference Center at the University of California at Santa Barbara (UCSB) over the Christmas holiday. When you taught TM you accrued credits that would pay for periodic ATR courses. Initiators from all over the country would come there to rest and round and see and hear Maharishi and get the latest knowledge. After that we were asked to stay on for a while and work on the catalogue. It would lay out the whole plan for our university, its whole theoretical basis.

Thus began our life "in the gap," as David called it. From then on we had to have our suitcases packed (figuratively if not literally) and be ready to go anywhere and do anything, to follow Maharishi around the globe. We learned to let go of our houses, our lives in various locations, and embrace the latest wave of knowledge and activity that was offered. It was exciting, but it took some time for me to get used to living like that.

David quit his job at Fort Bliss, we packed up the car and the kids, and off we went. I had no idea of it at the time, but our life in El Paso was over. We would never live in our house there again. If I had known that, I wonder if I would have gone off to Santa Barbara so cheerfully and with so few possessions. But it was only for a couple of weeks, I thought.

California Dreaming

WE MOVED INTO the Francisco Torres Convention Center on the UCSB campus, a tall, modern building with small dorm rooms and elevators, and started rounding. I could do it, I told myself. It was only for two weeks: living in two rooms and having to eat in a dining room with hundreds of other people. Dinner was too late for the kids. We had to give them a snack so they could wait until 7 or later. Sara had a healthy appetite and as soon as we walked into the dining hall and got in line, she wanted to eat *now*. She would start to scream until we could put food in her mouth. One of us would go ahead, get a tray, and the other would wait a little while, and then bring her and Nate right to the table and start their dinner. That seemed to work pretty well. We wound up eating often with a young couple, Prudence and Albert Bruns. Their little son Logan would always stick rice or some other food item up his nose, and Prudy was expecting a baby. We really liked them and we all got along well. The other course participants kept their distance from the family section. There weren't many of us with children along in those days and families can be noisy.

We learned that our new friend was the Prudence of the Beatles song "*Dear Prudence.*" She had been on TTC in India in 1968 with her sister Mia Farrow, who was recently separated from her husband Frank Sinatra. The Beatles had come with their wives, and

Donovan, too. Prudy wasn't too thrilled about hearing that they were coming. She had met many famous people in her Hollywood youth. Her mother was Maureen O'Sullivan, the Jane to Johnny Weissmuller's Tarzan, and her father John Farrow was involved in such epic movies as *Around the World in 80 Days*, for which he got an Oscar for best screenplay in 1956. Those famous people always turned out to be a big disappointment, she said. Like a well-known opera singer. She loved his music and begged to be taken to meet him when she was a child. He turned out to be an alcoholic and got drunker as the day went by, so she didn't expect much from the famous musicians from England. She wanted to stay in her room and meditate in order to get enlightened and even become a teacher of Transcendental Meditation, hence the lyrics of the song, "Dear Prudence, won't you come out and play." She describes the whole experience and what led up to it in her fascinating memoir *Dear Prudence. The Story Behind the Song* (2015).

Maharishi came to the course in Santa Barbara and met with us initiators and we got to ask questions about situations that might have arisen in our teaching experiences. It was wonderful to sit in a small room with him and have intimate discussions of our questions and experiences. When the course was over David was expected to stay on to help with the writing of the catalogue for the yet to be founded university. Some of the other faculty had already been working on it in Seelisberg, Switzerland, where Maharishi was currently established, so this was a continuation of that project. David and I and the kids were moved into a little house on Mike Love's estate on high ground overlooking the ocean. He and most of the Beach Boys were dedicated meditators and Mike offered the four little houses on the estate to the faculty. Larry Domash and Janice had one, Keith and Barbara and their kids were in another, Prudy and Albert and Logan were in the third, and we were in the fourth. In the main house were Mike and his wife Tamara and they were expecting a baby very soon.

Everyone else who was to remain and work on the catalogue,

including kitchen staff to take care of them, were put in an apartment complex in Santa Barbara called the Casa Royale. It had been one the headquarters of the students who looted and set fire to the Bank of America in 1970 after a policeman had brutalized a student carrying a wine bottle (he thought it was a Molotov cocktail). It had a nice pool in the center, a dining room, and a large room where Maharishi could meet the faculty and work on the catalogue. Alan Cobb, a very good writer and on international staff at the time, took responsibility for the draft, and everyone contributed. Except me. I was busy with family and with studying for my doctoral exams, and to tell the truth, I couldn't bear those long sessions of phrasing and rephrasing abstract sentences about consciousness, physics, and everything else. I should have been there for the literature sessions, but I didn't know about them so I missed them. Professor Sy Migdal from Humboldt State University was active in those sessions. And I remember Michael and Charlotte Cain (artists, Yale), Michael Weinless (mathematics MIT), Penny (geneticist) and John Farrow (neurobiologist, Yale), Frank Papentin (German geneticist), Paul Kapiloff (biologist), Jon Shear, and Dr. Elliot Abravanel all sitting in on those sessions.

Maharishi had TTCs going on in La Antilla, Spain, that winter of 1972–1973, and during one of his absences to visit those courses, we drove back to El Paso to get more clothes, my pots and pans (a wedding present from Aunt Bernice), and books. We left the El Paso house in the care of the other new teachers and meditators so they would have a center. The mortgage payment was only $125 a month and they thought they could handle that. It was a big mistake; we should have packed up our things and rented out the house. We could have used the income over the coming years. Instead they sold off our furniture to pay the mortgage until it was all gone. We would never live in that house again and all our possessions would eventually disappear, including David's steel sculptures and a large oil painting he had made of me during our courtship days.

We put Nate in a kindergarten just up the street. He was behind at first because he had only been in playschool in El Paso, but he quickly caught up. After school Nate and Teddy Wallace ran around together. I loved Santa Barbara, really loved it. California, with its farmers' markets and healthy foods, the fabulous weather, living on a cliff above the ocean and being able to walk down to the beach or just watch from above, was heaven. I didn't miss my house in El Paso at all. Mike had his gardeners put in a large vegetable garden on the estate and we could go and pick fresh vegetables. I remember picking some corn and running back home to put it in boiling water. It was the sweetest corn ever.

Everybody was going to a chiropractor named Dr. Meyerowitz or something like that. Everyone was interested in anything that might improve health and speed the path to CC, and that hasn't changed even today. He told us Nate was allergic to wheat and milk. He said that they produced mucus, and that was the reason for all the ear infections. With wheat-free bread and milk-free ice cream and beverages I could follow his recommendations and still keep Nate happy. These things were only available at health food stores in California in those days. After one year on this diet Nate's drippy nose dried up and he never had an ear infection again, even after we moved to Switzerland and we had to go back to milk and wheat.

In the spring Maharishi moved some Sama Veda pandits to the estate. Sama Veda is one of the four main spiritual works of the Vedic tradition and those who come from a traditional family and study and know it and can chant it are called pandits. Maharishi wanted them to audio and videotape the whole Sama Veda. They set up near Mike Love's house in a little pavilion overlooking the water. We were allowed to listen to the chanting. I was usually the only one who slipped in there and sat quietly against one wall and let those sounds pour over me. I can't say I felt anything special, but I must have, or I wouldn't have kept going back. I am a lot like those meditators who say nothing is happening, except that deep down I know something *is*. I don't know what but something is happening. We frequently saw the pandits walking about the grounds and they saw us and the children.

It had been raining heavily for days and days and people started to worry about mudslides. Albert asked the pandits if they were responsible for that rain since they are known for chanting in India to relieve drought-afflicted areas. Of course, they replied, we are chanting to Indra right now (Indra is the deva or law of nature governing rain and thunderstorms) and that is the reason for the rain. Soon they finished that section, the rain ended, and the sunshine came back. Was it true? Impressive if so. But how would that work? How would chanting affect the weather? Everything is connected on the level of consciousness? Those days I had more questions than answers, but reality was emerging as a more complex and interesting system than I had ever imagined.

A few years later, David was on a speaking tour of India,

Maharishi and the Sama Veda pandits on Mike Love's estate in Santa Barbara, California. The pandits were chanting and taping this branch of the Vedic literature. Through the windows you can see the dark and stormy rain clouds.

as Vice-Chancellor of MERU (Maharishi European Research University, more on that later), and he visited one of the major Indian temples, one of the richest in India. The head of that temple had come to Seelisberg and been Maharishi's guest. As he walked around the grounds of that famous temple, one of the pandits detached himself from his group and came over to David and introduced himself as one of the Sama Veda pandits from Santa Barbara. They were both quite surprised and delighted to see each other.

Maharishi came from time to time to join in the faculty discussions and hear what they had written for the catalogue in their academic areas. He had many projects going on, so he didn't stay with us for very long. When he visited Mike's place, everyone would give him flowers and he was especially warm towards Teddy and all the children and he gave them flowers in return. Sara was blissed out by being close to him and we have home movies of her standing around smiling and waving a flower he had given her. One time he gave her a choice of several flowers and invited her

Sara giving Maharishi a flower, Santa Barbara, California, 1973

to pick the one she wanted. She looked them over carefully and selected a deep, rich red rose. Ah, Maharishi said, she wants something substantial. Once when he was meeting us in the largest room of Keith's house and we were sitting at the back, I asked her if she wanted to give him a flower. Maharishi was sitting in a white chair that had been appropriated from our house and was slightly raised so we could see him and he could see us. All by herself, Sara, only three years old, walked to the front and reached up and offered him a flower. He beamed down on her and gave her a flower and she walked back through the row of chairs to me, smiling and wide-eyed.

In a small private meeting with Maharishi at Keith's house Maharishi told David that he was now Director of Research for the International Center for Scientific Research. Paul Levine had been doing that and was a bit miffed that David would now have the title and be responsible for collecting all the research being done on TM all over the world, and for conducting new research. There would be laboratories on the west coast and the east coast, Maharishi said. Paul Levine was an MIT and Caltech physicist, a top guy, who had founded his own company and could build computers. Paul was tied to his company, to some extent, although he could get away to be with Maharishi and help with the research, but David could be sent anywhere, do anything. He was "in the pocket" and could be depended on to do whatever Maharishi asked.

There was beginning to be a flood of research to be collected and disseminated. Jean-Paul Banquet from France was beginning to publish his research on brain wave synchrony during TM. Keith's research on lower heart and respiration rates during TM was being replicated. Others found faster reaction time, increased perceptual ability, superior perceptual-motor performance, increased intelligence growth rate and learning ability, improved academic performance and even results in business settings: increased productivity, job performance, satisfaction, and improved relations with coworkers and superiors.

And there was more. Larry Farwell, my old nemesis from TTC in Italy, found decreased anxiety, and various psychologists found increased normality, improved mental health, increased psychological health and so forth. David was charged with collecting and examining these studies and creating charts on them that could go into the latest version of the chart book. David has a genius for looking at data and seeing trends and effects and translating findings into charts that would illustrate them. He was also responsible for sending relevant papers out to new researchers who asked for them. Many of the charts he created on the new papers made it into the catalogue. Everything went in there.

David was stunned. All that responsibility. Honor, yes, but all that responsibility was overwhelming. It stretched his mind way beyond his small daily concerns. It was both exciting and alarming to see that Maharishi envisioned a huge expansive future for you. David had already been doing the work, but imagining himself as director of laboratories on both coasts was a stretch. Not only that, but with all the research coming in, Maharishi was thinking about collecting these papers into a volume and printing it. It was very difficult to get papers on meditation published in those days so the idea was to get permission to reprint all the ones already published and to also publish the best of those that were not yet published. David would be the editor of the first volume along with John Farrow.

I have to confess that after Maharishi left town and everyone had returned to their work, but the room was not yet put back to the way it had been, I slipped in there and sat in that white chair he had sat in and meditated. Nothing. Ah, well, I tried.

The faculty had been put to taping one-week core courses connecting their discipline to SCI. Each week-long course would have ten lessons, the first one giving an overview of the whole discipline, then eight important topics in the field and the last one exploring the latest developments and knowledge in the field. All of this would be connected to consciousness, to the Science of Creative Intelligence. Maharishi was training the faculty to make these connections as they wrote their sections of the catalogue. Maharishi International University (MIU) would begin with 20 of these core courses, taken one at a time and thus the students would have an overview of all the possible majors offered and could thus make an intelligent decision. The second year would have one-month courses in selected disciplines, and then the students would go into their major field, each one offering only one-month courses. That way a student could focus on one area and not be divided by taking four or five different courses at the same time. It was a radical proposal, but it proved to be very successful. MIU began by offering a Master of Arts (MA) in Interdisciplinary Studies and initiators came to take the course, get their degree and then offer those core courses in the TM centers, as well as at MIU once it got started. Maharishi wanted to get the knowledge out as soon as possible, not wait until we had students coming.

We had a wonderful summer with lots of birthday parties: Sara's third birthday, Logan's, Gareth Wallace's, Teddy's too, I think, and in the autumn Nate's. There must have been some for the adults too, but I remember the kids' parties with tables of cake and ice cream and all the adults running around playing ball games on the large lawn overlooking the Pacific Ocean, while the children raced around with icing all over their faces. Prudy gave birth to Paulie and Tamara gave birth to her daughter Summer Love. My mother and my sister Linda and her boyfriend Mark visited. Mom and Linda learned to meditate soon after we did, and they had great results. Mom helped out the movement by attending center events, telling her friends about TM, and providing a place for the local teachers to live, like Guy Hatchard from England. They all remember Fay fondly.

It was an ideal life in many respects. We were all devoted to Maharishi's vision, to actualizing it. And thus he was "present" to us in many ways. It was not exactly a hermitage or ashram, but in the sense that we were all his students and tuned to his ideas and goals, and under his direction, it actually was.

In the fall I signed up for an evening pottery course offered to the community through adult education. I loved working with the clay and found I could center a lump on the wheel and raise a bowl. David tried but it just wouldn't work for him. I was a natural. My fingers and thumbs just knew what to do. I still have two little bowls with my initials and October '73 dates scratched on their bottoms. I must have been a potter in a past life. It felt so good, natural, and blissful to be back with the clay again.

That autumn on one of Maharishi's visits we all went up into high hills near Santa Barbara to look at a piece of land that the movement was considering buying in order to build a permanent academy there. Jerry was there, all the faculty, and lots of initiators. We roamed around the beautiful land and the small house already on the property. David climbed up on the roof and took Super8 movies of us all following Maharishi around and listening to his questions and comments. It seemed there was a water problem. Not enough water available up there to sustain a facility but nevertheless a beautiful piece of land high in the hills.

David's parents visited around Halloween for a few days. They had been very sad when we left El Paso and the kids loved seeing them. They missed us, but they could see we were having a wonderful life and were enthusiastic and passionate about what we were doing, and as parents who wished for our happiness, they could only approve and support us. In addition, I had managed to get some professors at the UCSB to proctor some of my doctoral exams. I had only one to go and I was studying for that one, on the modern American novel. It was a great life. I could have gone on there forever. I still fondly remember that time and wish that we had founded MIU there and we could have lived there for the rest of our lives. Not to be.

Part Two:
Ashram in the Alps

Maharishi Mahesh Yogi, about 1974

Lakes, Mountains,
and Alpine Meadows

IN NOVEMBER OF 1973 David was called to Switzerland, where Maharishi was then based, to join a Scandinavian tour with Maharishi and other scientists, and after the tour they ended up in Seelisberg. David was in the car with Maharishi who was being driven to the airport, uncertain whether he was going to go back to Santa Barbara or, ideally, staying with Maharishi in Switzerland. Maharishi wasn't committing himself, but he smiled at David and said, "We will bring Rhoda." Me! I took the kids to stay with my mother in Cleveland and left on a six-week excursion ticket. I was excited about being with Maharishi and in Switzerland, but I fully expected that we would return to Santa Barbara after this project or whatever it was.

When I arrived everyone was settled in a tiny village at the western edge of Lake Lucerne in Hotel Hertenstein. The overflow, and there was always an overflow, was in neighboring hotels, such as the Seeblick and the Alexander, and nearby guesthouses and chalets. It was the off season and Maharishi was quartered there with the principal international staff and faculty. Those weeks in Hertenstein were my first experience of really being in the ashram. Our time in Santa Barbara had been a preparation for this. I had seen how Maharishi's visits were prepared for and how he was cared for and treated. Traditionally, an ashram means a spiritual hermitage or monastery. Now it means anywhere that is a center of spiritual activity, like yoga or meditation.

The Hotel Hertenstein was an ashram in the sense that Maharishi lived there and managed the whole movement from there. All of us were focused on him, on his projects, and on his knowledge. Our group was comprised of the people who did the videotaping, transcribed the tapes and produced them, and the scientists and faculty, the people who helped him create the tapes and pamphlets and displays. And the 108s. This was a group of mostly young people wealthy enough to just *be* there, with or without portfolio, we might say if we were English. This 108 situation was designed to give these initiators an evolutionary program. The idea is that one third of the group would be living and traveling with Maharishi, learning from him and benefiting from his attention and presence. One third would be on a rounding program, deepening their experiences and developing their consciousness directly. This could be on a course, or living in Maharishi's hotel. And the other third would be sent on projects around the world. These projects would help the growth of the movement, it would be hoped, but mainly they would give those 108s an evolutionary opportunity to mature, grow in consciousness, and learn how to operate in the world with Maharishi's knowledge and direction. The idea was that they would rotate through these different programs. If they were on a rounding course or living with Maharishi, they paid a generous monthly room and board charge which helped to pay for the rest of us on staff, I am sure. They saw Maharishi often and had a nice meditation routine, and sometimes he held special meetings for them. They rather resented me and David and some of the rest of us who didn't pay to be there.

The name? There are 108 beads in a mala, or necklace, representing the 108 devatas or laws of nature, a flattering name for a group of people who didn't seem to contribute much to what was going on, as far as I could see. Over the years I saw that some of them did do valuable projects and that Maharishi took responsibility for their evolution in any case. They came and went. There was one young man who spent considerable time with the international group around Maharishi. At one point, Maharishi asked him to go to some difficult country, perhaps Afganistan, I am not sure. The fellow retorted, "I am paying to be here. I don't have to go there!" Are you shocked? I am. Did he not understand that Maharishi was directing his evolution and that he was being sent off *for his own sake*, not Maharishi's? He disappeared immediately and that was the end of his participation in the 108 group. I understand he was very bitter about this, possibly because he still didn't understand what had happened. We did.

I have recently learned about the 36 righteous individuals described in the Talmud (36 is one third of 108!). With each generation 36 righteous ones greet the Divine Presence. They might or might not know they are part of that group or know of any fellow members, but their presence on earth allows civilization to continue without being totally destroyed. They are humble, spiritual, ethical, and their mere presence supports and allows the divine on earth. Think Sodom and Gomorrah. God destroyed them because Lot could not find even one righteous person in those towns. Isn't that an interesting coincidence or similarity? There was trading and cultural interaction between India and the Middle East at the time of Abraham, about 4,000 years ago. Who knows what might have percolated from one civilization to the other.

I was a novice. I didn't know the rules. I didn't know proper behavior. You never point your feet at anyone, especially Maharishi. Very rude. Always tuck your feet under you. You always stand up when Maharishi arrives or leaves the room. Sleep with the head to the east (most auspicious) or south (okay for householders). I learned why much later, but from then on when David and I traveled, we would always use a compass to see which way our beds were oriented and sometimes sleeping with our heads toward the foot. This could be important. Why take chances? Just reserve judgment and move the bedding. Whatever did the maids think when they saw the bed rearranged at the various hotels we visited?!

Birthday Blessing

David and I had a room on the second floor and Maharishi met the whole group downstairs in a medium-sized meeting room every evening. He sat on the west wall and the place was crammed full of everyone whom he had called to be there as well as various guests, drop-ins, and visitors. David was an important scientist so we sat to Maharishi's right, not too far from the front. Once Maharishi got going, talking about the knowledge or his plans to enlighten the world, he was having too much fun to stop. Mother Olson and a young woman named Rindi Schwartz, who had just arrived after visiting her family for the holidays, and a few other old timers, thought he should get more rest. (Me, too. I could barely stay awake some evenings.) Maharishi agreed that Mother Olson and Rindi would stand up at ten o'clock to signal that it was time to wrap it up and go and rest. They would stand, Maharishi would smile and nod and keep on going. Mother Olson would start to leave the room. No, no, he would motion her to sit back down, and on he went.

It was at that time that David and Rindi began writing the Fundamentals of Progress. In a meeting one morning with Maharishi, David remarked that he noticed that there were several themes coming out in the research papers that he was collecting. For example, certain studies were showing physiological adaptability and others were showing psychological adaptability, and also stability and integration as a result of TM practice. Some of the studies were showing integration in various different aspects of mind and body. These were scientific concepts, but Maharishi began to expand on the idea immediately. Could the research be interpreted in terms of purification and growth? David had to think about that one. It was not immediately obvious. Maharishi got very excited about the idea of fundamental aspects of a concept and started scribbling notes. He went up to his rooms after the meeting, still thinking and talking about this. Rindi had gone up with him and a few others, and came back downstairs to David very impressed. Maharishi had said, talking about David, "What a beautiful mind!" She was now to work with him on creating the Fundamentals of Progress. She was a good choice. Rindi had an MA in philosophy and is a brilliant person. From that time on, she and David were constantly working together, often in our small room.

Maharishi identified the Fundamentals of Progress as being adaptability, stability, integration, purification, and growth. Each could be illustrated with the research across the physiology, the psychology, sociology (behavior), and ecology (effects on society as a whole). David and Rindi set to work thinking about the research and putting charts to each one of these areas in the Fundamentals of Progress. There would later be the Fundamentals of Health, of Rehabilitation, of Balance, and so forth. The earliest versions of the Fundamentals made it into first catalogue of Maharishi International University, 1974–1975. Look for them in the back pages. The Fundamentals project went on for years, expanding in all directions, and they often figured prominently in displays and pamphlets.

Maharishi was now talking about establishing Maharishi European Research University (MERU). Larry Domash would be Chancellor, David would be Vice-Chancellor, and Jacques Verlinde would be the chief administrator, or something like that. Again, a title and responsibilities way beyond anything you could imagine. MERU was only right there in our little hotel, but it sounded as if it would take on a much larger presence. MERU would conduct three areas of research: 1) Experiential research on higher states of consciousness (what people were experiencing on the various courses Maharishi was offering, like TTC and ATRs); 2) Empirical research (EEG, biochemical, psychological, sociological, etc.) which would be conducted on the initiators coming for ATR courses; and 3) Theoretical research, integrating the deepest principles of modern science (and also art, literature, business, etc.) with the knowledge of consciousness. This would also include research into the Vedic texts, Maharishi explained. It was a different angle from Maharishi International University, which was getting started in Santa Barbara, California, and it all sounded very huge and exciting.

David's birthday is January 17 and Maharishi always made a big fuss about birthdays. Mother Olson had organized a cake and a little celebration in the now traditional movement way. First you light the light, then cut the cake, and so forth. Mother Olson cut David the first slice and he was to offer it to Maharishi. Maharishi closed his fingers on the edge of the plate but didn't let go, as he was supposed to, and as David and he both held it, Maharishi closed his eyes and went inward and then whispered some phrases we couldn't hear. Finally he released the plate and smiled at David. Mother Olson was very impressed. What a blessing you were given, she said afterwards.

Maharishi liked to take boat rides around Lake Lucerne, which amused the Swiss people. Why would we want to boat around in circles on the lake and not go anywhere? they wondered. We would get a call, or someone would notice that a boat with a big bubble top had pulled up to the dock. We would all descend into the boat, the lucky ones up front close to Maharishi. There was a lot of jostling and hoping and disappointment if you were left to find a seat in the back. It was kind of a test of your importance and status, and you were lucky to be on the boat at all; it wasn't that big. I had no expectations and no sense of any status or worth so I was never disappointed and was just happy to be there. If Maharishi wanted to include everyone, then two boats would come, but you wanted to be on *his* boat. Maharishi continued to work on whatever he had been doing, writing a pamphlet or presentation, or to hear the text of the latest chart. Those who were working on the

Boat ride from Hotel Hertenstein with Maharishi. Mrs. Gill on the left. Theresa Olson, Mother Olson's youngest daughter, and Marco Steifel, national leader of Switzerland, are standing behind Maharishi.

project sat close by.

Maharishi heard every word of anything that would be printed. He would study the layout, the colors, the design, and the text. It all had to be perfect; it had to create the right effect on its audience, and it went back to the writers or designers or press people again and again until he was satisfied with it. Nothing went out without his scrutiny and approval, but he made it all somehow into a joyful game with lots of laughter. At a recent graduation ceremony at Maharishi University of Management (2016), commencement speaker was filmmaker David Lynch. He opted for a question and answer session rather than a formal talk. He was asked what the most important lesson he had learned in filmmaking and had carried with him into his future successes. "Always get the final cut," he said. Just like Maharishi. You can check out the interview on YouTube.

Sometimes we would go on a boat ride just to air out after working all day on a project, or as a treat for an invited guest, people I didn't know, but who had been helpful or important in the early days. One such guest I remember was a lovely older lady with white hair named Mrs. Gill. She had been one of the leaders of the movement in England in the early days. When Maharishi first traveled to England in the '50s he set off by plane but had no contact in London who might meet the plane or pick him up. His method was to go someplace, sit in the airport, and wait. Someone would approach him and offer to host him and his activities. He said he had, you could say, cosmic dates with long-time seekers who were waiting for him to arrive. As he sat on that plane to London he chatted with an older, very upper class English lady in the seat next to his, a Mrs. Marjorie Gill. She was a life-long spiritual seeker and was impressed by Maharishi's presence and knowledge. She invited him to her home and it became the base for TM activities in London for years. One of my friends remembers being a meditator in London and learning the checking insructions from Mrs. Gill.

Dr. Vincent Snell was another such seeker. He was a surgeon, and for most of his life had been looking for spiritual evolution. For twenty years he had been practicing some techniques that had been taught by Gurdjieff and his disciple Ouspensky. Gurdjieff was a Russian mystic, philosopher, spiritual teacher, and composer of Greek and Armenian descent. His teachings were influential during the first part of the twentieth century. Russian mathematician Ouspensky studied under Gurdjieff and taught his practices in England and America. Dr. Snell was coming out of the London tube one day and saw a poster advertising TM with Maharishi's picture on it. This was what he had been waiting and preparing for. He immediately embraced TM and became the first British TM teacher. Maharishi never forgot these people. They would be invited to Switzerland, to India, wherever Maharishi would be for a while. He provided them with living quarters, cooks, and made them as comfortable as he could. If Dr. Vernon Katz visited, it was always an occasion. He and Maharishi were working on translating and commenting on the various Vedic texts, such as the Brahma Sutras.

I didn't have much to do but meditate and enjoy and study. I had brought my notes and books along for my next doctoral exam. I would walk around the beautiful grounds along Lake Lucerne with David or with Janice Ahlborn, Larry's girlfriend.

We had become friends in Fiuggi and deepened our friendship in Santa Barbara on Mike Love's estate. It was lovely to have a friend there. The others were working on special projects for Maharishi and had no time to cultivate friendships or wander around the lake through the melting snows. Janice and I sat together on the boat rides while David and Larry sat up front with Maharishi discussing the latest chart or scientific theory.

Or I would go to the dining room where Mother Olson would often take a cup of tea in the afternoon. I knew her personally from our small group at Humboldt and I had read her book about when Maharishi first came to the U.S. and stayed with her family. I especially loved one story she told about how she was complaining to him about how much work her theatre group required of her and how difficult it often was. Maharishi commented, "See the job, do the job, stay out of the misery." What a life lesson. I have evoked it ever since. I learned a lot from her on how one behaved around the Master and she answered my naïve questions.

I got permission to call my mother from time to time. Long distance to the U.S. was a big deal in those days. No Skype, no internet. I was worried about her and the kids. Nate was pretty active and my mother wasn't used to having two little ones around. My sister Linda was 17 and was living with her so that was some help. On one call, Nate said, "Mom, I almost put my eye out!" I heard my mother say in the background, "I told you not to tell her that!" Nate had run into the corner of the dining room table and broken the skin on his forehead right near the eyebrow. My mother, an alarmist and worrier, had no doubt exclaimed, "You could have put your eye out!!" Good grief. I was ready to go back home to Santa Barbara, put Nate back in school, and resume a normal life. Normal, hah. Not what Maharishi had in mind for us.

My six-week ticket was running out. I brought this up personally to Maharishi. It was time to go back, I told him hopefully. The children could come here, he suggested very sweetly. Jerry could bring them. Oh, my God! Jerry Jarvis, the national leader of the

TM movement for North America, with no children of his own, picking up my wild man and my little daughter in Cleveland, a total stranger to them, and taking them on a transatlantic flight and to the bathroom every hour or two!? Maybe it would have been evolutionary for Jerry, but it was incomprehensible to me. I am sure my face showed the great horror that I felt. All right, he agreed. You can go get them. I was so relieved and eager to be gone that I didn't process the inevitable conclusion that we would remain in Switzerland and not go back to Santa Barbara. Not go back to my perfect life in California. Not ever.

Setting up MERU

Soon after I got back with the kids we were all moved into the Hotel Seeblick in Weggis, just east of Hertenstein. It was a small family hotel owned by a man we all called Herr Hasler (Mr. Hasler). He and one of his sons also owned the Hotel Alexander next door. He was a kindly old man and he and Maharishi had a very sweet relationship. In later years Maharishi invited him on a tour to see some of the grand hotels in India. It was a shock to him to see those enormous luxurious Indian hotels, like the Ashoka in Delhi, and compare them to the small family hotels he was used to with their simple amenities.

There was a farm out back, and another of his sons, a middle-aged man, worked there. The kids liked visiting him and the animals and wandering around by the lake and hills. The oldest son was not terribly interested in the family hotel business and over the next few years, Herr Hasler gave the Seeblick completely over to the movement. He also stood up to the other hotel owners, who were unsettled about this Indian guru renting all their hotels in the winter season. What would people think? The Swiss are very conservative. Hotels cannot be sold to foreigners; they must remain in the family, or at least in Swiss hands. But they are also very practical and must have liked the extra income. We often made interesting demands of them in the course of renting their hotels. Larry, who was a great mimic, would joke, in their accent and speech rhythms, "Yes, you can *do* it, but you have to pie [pay]."

Paul Levine and his wife Lee came frequently to Weggis, and Paul and David set up a laboratory in the Seeblick at the end of our corridor with equipment Paul had built and programmed. He had adapted concepts from physics to study the phenomena of EEG signals. Paul came out with a display he called COSPARS, which showed that brain wave coherence increases during TM and is even more evident in long-term meditators. They measured Theresa Olson, who had spent the most time meditating around Maharishi, and her coherence was really striking, quite visually apparent. David began doing research on how that kind of EEG coherence was related to creativity and to a host of other aspects of psychology and physiology. It would not be known for years what the full value of coherence might be. It was a brand new concept in EEG research.

Around this time, Maharishi took his immediate entourage, including David, to Ostend in Belgium to finish up a TTC. Or it could have been the one in Knocke, Belgium, or Vittel, France. We heard that some fellow who got up on the mike to ask a question; he was wearing mismatched clothing, and Maharishi pointed this out to the poor guy and the group. He signaled to David and to Tom Factor, one of his immediate staff, to stand up, and there they stood in their blue suits and red ties, looking very professional. Dress like that, Maharishi told them. It was the regulation attire for the men around him at the time. We want to look like professionals, he said. We *are* professionals. That was my handsome husband!

I found a day to slip away to Zurich, only about an hour away, and find a professor at the University of Zurich who would agree to proctor my last doctoral exam. It was on the modern American novel. He notified me when the exam arrived and I went up there to sit for it. He took me into a small room and looked at me very sympathetically. This is a very difficult exam, he said. Who cares? My life has been a series of overcoming one obstacle after another. I sat down and wrote and wrote until the two hours were up. I passed. I still had one foreign language exam to take and then on to the dissertation. Maharishi had emphasized the need for me to get this PhD. He was even more set on it than I was. I couldn't fathom how it would help the movement. I think the reason was that it would help me, that it was important and evolutionary for me to do it.

After a little while, it became obvious even to me that we were not going back to Santa Barbara. David had brought it up to Maharishi, and he wanted David to stay. I was really upset. I wanted to go back. David wanted to stay. This was his life. He was Director of Scientific Research; he was Vice-Chancellor of MERU, whatever that was or would be. He was collecting and doing research; he was writing charts illustrating the findings of all the new research, and Fundamentals of every kind; he was on every speaking tour; he was putting together the first volume of what would become the *Collected Papers*. All he ever wanted to do was to help Maharishi. I knew that. I knew that it was important and worthwhile. I wept and wept. The children were baffled. Why was Mom crying? I really don't know what the past life mix was. I just knew I was unhappy about it and was grieving about letting something go and taking on life in the ashram. Had I done it before and it hadn't turned out well? Unfathomable is the course of karma, it is said.

There was really no argument. We would stay. But, I asked, where would we live with the children? How would it be anything like a normal life? There were no other children around. There were no English schools that Nate could go to. David asked Maharishi where we would live. "Wherever Rhoda would be least miserable," he offered. How embarrassing. I was known, thoroughly known, but still accepted. That is kind of freeing, isn't it? Maharishi quietly took me on, tried to find ways I could evolve and serve the movement, and subtly engineered improvements in my family life and my consciousness.

Someone from senior staff came over one day and said we were to have a nanny for the kids. Whom would I like to have? There was a young American girl named Nadine working in the kitchen. I would go into the kitchen with the kids looking for a snack in the afternoons. Nadine had offered to make cookies with them, and they stirred and chopped nuts and cooked together. I asked if she would like to play with our kids and teach Nate to read and all that. She was thrilled. That would be fun and much better than chopping vegetables and washing dishes. She cheerfully hung up her apron and joined our family. Her Australian boyfriend Gareth was also on staff and both of them were working for credit to go on TTC.

Soon it was time for the Seeblick to host its paying guests for the Easter holidays. We knew we would be moving soon but had no idea when or where. One day Nate, who was aware of everything going on around us, came to tell me that the buses had arrived and were out front. I ran to a window. Sure enough, there they were, rumbling and smoking. Find Nadine, I screamed, and started hurriedly to pack. I later heard that Maharishi had said that if you had three days to pack and get ready, it would take three days. If you only had an hour, you would do it in an hour. (Never mind if you had a suit at the dry cleaners.) Nadine helped me pack up and we all moved to the Victoria-Jungfrau, a grand hotel in Interlaken, right on a huge central park. This hotel had mainly summer guests booked, so we could stay there for a few weeks until the summer season started. Then, as the snow melted, the ski hotels in the Alps would come available. We would return to Interlaken again and again over the years.

Marco Steifel was responsible for negotiating with the Swiss hotel owners, for finding appropriate hotels the right size for each group and trying to negotiate good rates for however many weeks we would use them. He was constantly around our hotel, working

very hard, especially in the times between our long winter rentals
and the long summer rentals coming up. We needed hotels for a
few weeks or even one week at a time, as the ones on Lake Lucerne
were putting us out and opening up for spring and summer guests
and as the ski hotels were closing down and were amenable to our
summer rentals. Later his younger sister Carmen would join him.
They were always really well dressed and seemed to be running
around day and night.

We settled into our rooms in the Victoria-Jungfrau and into
a routine with meals and childcare. I especially remember one
morning there. Maharishi had come down early into one of the
smaller meeting rooms and was sitting there, pretty much alone.
The video team was setting up. Very few people had finished meditation or breakfast, but I was a mother. I was up and I happened to
pop into the hall with the kids. Maharishi saw me and mentioned
for me to come over and sit next to him. I was startled. Me? That
was where Keith sat, or Larry, or Jerry. Me? Oh, no, no, I backed
away. He wanted to encourage me to think big, to take my role
in the movement, something he may have seen but I sure didn't.
I wanted to keep a low profile and not get some job I didn't even
understand, let alone be able to do.

However, it seems I did participate in some jobs and did write
some things, not that I remember any of it. One day in the main
hall when Nadine was on her day off, she was enjoying being able
to see Maharishi interact with the scientists. I had tried to introduce her to him once when she and the kids were all dressed to go
out and play in the snow, she remembers, but she was embarrassed
at being seen in her snow clothes and hid behind the blackboard.
Someone in the hall was going to read something that I had written, and Maharishi said, "Rhoda should read her words." Nadine
was watching him and then saw he was looking directly at her
and she realized she was supposed to get me. She giggled and ran
off to find me. Where was I? Who knows? On one of her days off
I took the kids on a local bus to a neighboring village that had

the ruins of a castle, so we could walk among the stones and then have lunch somewhere. I habitually embarrassed the children at lunch by asking the management to turn down the loud music and by trying to find something edible and vegetarian, and the castle terrified Sara. She must have heard something about ghosts in castles or something, or maybe she just didn't like the feeling of it. It did feel creepy.

Nadine and Gareth were soon ready to go on to TTC. I brought it up to Maharishi. Should I find another nanny? No, he advised. Nadine should stay. She and Gareth should go separately. It would be better for them. (How did he know them?) I passed this along to them, but they wanted to go together. As it turns out, perhaps he was right. So it was coming time to leave Interlaken, and I would be without a nanny and wouldn't be able to study. I was constantly reading and looking for a dissertation topic and I guess I was also helping to write things.

An English initiator named Peter Russell told David about an English girl who was applying to be on staff and who seemed to be perfect. She had mistakenly been sent to the TTC in Belgium and then to Seelisberg and she was taking care of some small children there, probably Alisha Isen, the daughter of Eric Isen who was a filmmaker and also Josh Geller, whose father was a brilliant cartoonist.

We went to check her out in Seelisberg. She was a trained and experienced teacher and she had created a real schoolroom with artwork and projects in just one week. I wanted her. Nate was going on seven and needed someone to teach him reading and writing and Sara would soon be old enough to start to learn to read. David asked Maharishi if we could have her teach our kids. Oh, no, he laughed. The 108s can do it, David reported back to me. The 108s!! Are you kidding? A couple of those rich girls getting up early and spending all day with my kids actually teaching them something? No, I insisted, Rachel! It went back and forth, but I was adamant. Nadine called her Mary Poppins. When we landed in Arosa later that spring, she was there!

Looking back I guess I could speculate that Maharishi thought it would be evolutionary for some of the 108 girls to have the responsibility of teaching my kids and the resources to get materials for them. The kids would have been all right, I imagine, and it might have worked, but at the time I couldn't conceive of my kids being a stage in someone else's evolutionary path. I heard a story years later about one young woman, who was going back to the U.S. after years of rounding, and Maharishi had told her that she needed to get married, to have a relationship with commitment and responsibilities. No, no, no, she would never get married, she insisted. Then get a dog, Maharishi said. Had she done it? Not yet, she laughed, but she was making friends with her neighbor's dog. Maharishi seemed to land right on the area you are least able to manage, and would tell you that's what you need to do, and you would find it almost impossible to do just that. Perhaps that's what he had in mind for one or more of the 108 girls but I wasn't having any of it.

Florence

In May we were all moved to the Palace Hotel in Mürren, a holiday resort in the mountains. It was just for a few weeks until we could move up to our permanent summer quarters in the Prätschli Hotel in Arosa. The Mürren hotel was available because the skiing season was over and it was too early for the summer crowd who would hike in the mountains. Soon Maharishi took the scientists, including David, and went off on a tour of England from May 6–12, celebrating World Plan Week, which was summarized afterward into a fancy pamphlet. It began with a symposium at the Royal Albert Hall at which everyone spoke, including Dr. Snell. David, Keith, and Elliot brought out the scientific research on TM through the framework of the Fundamentals of Progress. Nobel Laureate Brian Josephson, who was a meditator and Professor of Physics at Cambridge University, spoke at the

Cambridge session. Dr. Banquet presented his EEG research, and David and the others presented all of MERU's new research in the EEG and related areas.

I was grumpy to be abandoned just when we were about to pack up and move somewhere else, without his help. I don't think I told Maharishi what I was going to do, but the kids and I got on the train and off we went to visit my friend Pippy in Florence. We stayed with her and had fun doing children's things around the city with Alessa, her daughter. Pippy was pregnant and we just mostly hung out together and talked while the children played. Her husband and her Italian friends called her Elizabeth. You must go way back, they observed, if you are calling her Pippy. That was way back, sixteen years before, in Cleveland Heights. Almost a past life, it seemed, so remote from what I was currently doing.

When it was time to leave, Pippy took us to the train station and it was a typical Italian madhouse. She ran along the side of the train we were supposed to be on, looking very pregnant, and calling up to the passengers who were hanging out of the compartment windows, asking if there were a couple of empty seats. One man offered the compartment he was in so she passed our luggage up to him through the window and led us to the nearest door. We went down the aisle passing compartments loaded with people (think Harry Potter on the train to Hogwarts!) and finally came to our guy. He was surprised not to see Pippy but welcomed us in. We had seats for the return journey and didn't have to stand in the aisle outside of the compartments like many other people. What a system!

Soon after we got back, David and Maharishi returned from England. I was very happy to see them, and I think now that Maharishi was giving me a new view of David, helping me appreciate him more. If there were rocks in my small pond of a heart, there were definitely rocks in my marriage, and Maharishi often did things to improve our situation, and everything he did created effects on many different levels. One time the phone in our room rang. David picked it up and it was Maharishi himself calling. We were both shocked; he had never called our room before. "How is Rhoda?" he asked David. Rhoda? David looked over at me. I was standing there blankly When the call ended he came up to me. How are you, he asked, looking at me closely and lovingly. Maharishi had drawn his attention to one of his responsibilities that had maybe slipped from his awareness during his intense focus on his projects. Me. I must have needed his attention and Maharishi felt that need.

Swiss Cows and Alpine Bouquets

From Wengen, or Mürren, or wherever we had been, we were taken to Arosa and we landed in Swiss heaven. Arosa is a small village in the Alps, and Maharishi's hotel was high above the town. It was called the Prätschli. We had a gorgeous, large corner room on the second floor with a huge balcony and windows looking out onto the mountains. It was late May or early June 1974 and although the skiing had ended, there was still snow on our balcony and definitely on the hills and mountains. The kids' room was right next door, but not connecting. Maharishi's room was in the same location, two floors up. Everyone was envious. We would be getting Maharishi's *darshan*. Darshan means the auspicious (and evolutionary) glimpse or view or sight of a deity or a holy person. In India people would spend time with a saint, a holy person, in the belief that merely being in his or her presence would have a good spiritual influence on them. Here everyone wanted to see Maharishi, be with him, to sit in his presence, to attract his attention. This even meant trying to crowd into the elevator with him when he headed upstairs from the meeting hall. He would get into the elevator and motion more and more people to come in with him, smiling and enjoying, until it seemed the elevator was surely too full to go up.

We were almost the only family there and everyone was kind to us, even all the staff. A word about staff. It was like traveling with a small army as the whole operation moved from place to place. Besides our hotel, there were courses everywhere: TTC for Americans or Europeans with kitchen staff and translators and course leaders. They also had to be moved seasonally as hotels opened and closed, and as the courses started and ended. In our hotel around Maharishi there would be his Indian cook Hari and his personal staff and secretaries (we called them the boys on the door). They were there, taking shifts around the clock, letting people in and out, bringing people and things to him, carrying out his instructions, and so forth. When did Maharishi ever sleep? When he finished with one group and told them to go and rest, the next group would come in to work with him on their project. There were cars and drivers; there were the video and electronics staff doing all the taping; there were various boys and girls (some of them were men and women, but not many) helping to transcribe tapes, write materials, help create everything. Lillian Rosen, the only American advanced techniques teacher, would come and go between her tours.

There was also a constant stream of guests to be housed and taken care of. There were always a couple of doctors around, mostly Elliot Abravanel and Eberhart Arnold from Germany, a very sweet and saintly man, who came and went from the courses, checking on the people there. And there were the workers, the kitchen staff, the boys who got the boxes of food and unloaded them, the people who cleaned, and so forth. They were all working for course credit. They didn't have enough money to go to TTC so they worked until they had enough credit to get on the bus to a course and go become teachers. Our hotel was a little village in itself and I got to know almost everyone. Nate was found in every corner and did know everyone. I was friends with Susan Humphrey who seemed to be the one responsible for setting up kitchens, engaging staff, helping with housing, doing everything, just as she had in Fiuggi. She was very fond of Nate and Sara and always tried to help us out.

We located and claimed Rachel Parry. She was the daughter of a Cambridge don, an educated teacher of small children, and there were now several of them of various ages. There were Alisha Isen and Josh Geller, and I think Adam Phillip, whose mother was on the Vedic Science course. Rachel needed a school room, a place where the children could work and draw and write. It seemed to be impossible to find one. Every room in Maharishi's hotel was precious. Everyone wanted to live there. She found a room in the basement, and I must have had some clout as David's wife, and probably Susan helped, because they reluctantly gave us the room and found a place for Rachel, too, so she wouldn't have to try to get a ride up the mountain every day to teach the kids. She turned that dark basement room into a real schoolroom. The walls became covered with charts and their drawings, and there she taught the kids to read and write and do math and science. When spring started to come and it warmed up, she took them into the hills for hikes and picnics and biology lessons and wildlife viewing.

There were cows pastured very near our hotel. One day one of the 108s, Freddie Cadmus, climbed on the back of one. She was a tiny thing and the cow didn't seem to mind. Freddie had digestive problems and was very thin and constantly hungry. She was always down in the kitchen making some pasta. I found out all these things from Nate. He knew everything. Rachel took the kids higher and higher to small lakes and great views. We began to walk outside after dinner and Sara picked flowers. Sara had a little Swiss dress that we had bought in a tourist shop, with a sewn on pinafore, very cute. It was red, white and dark blue. We had to get her a few more because she didn't want to wear anything else. If they were all dirty, I had to wash one at night, dry it while she slept, and put it back on her in the mornings. Nate would wear anything and usually destroyed his new pants within a few weeks by jumping over some wire fence. I was constantly shopping for new clothes for him or ironing knee patches on the ones he had.

On June 30 it was Sara's fourth birthday and she wanted to give a flower to Maharishi. She picked a little bouquet and I took her up to Maharishi's area on the fourth floor. John Cowhig was on the door. He asked Maharishi if we might come in. Maharishi was sitting with Jemima Pittman, one of the leaders of the movement in England. Sara went right over to him and offered her bouquet. She was shy around other grownups, but not around him. Maharishi took a little globe pencil sharpener that was sitting in front of him and held it out to her. What we are doing, he said, we are making homes for ourselves all over the world, and he touched the globe again and again with his finger and then gave it to her. She was, as we say, blissed out. Many was the evening she wouldn't go to bed until she had given Maharishi a flower. I would take her upstairs and John would peek into the room, get Maharishi's permission, and Sara would pop in, give him a flower, get one in return, and happily go to bed. What a life we had.

I had one more exam to go, and that was in the German language. I needed two languages for the PhD in Comparative Literature and I had already taken graduate seminars in French, so I didn't need to do an exam in that language. I had had one year of German at Vassar and I was trying to learn more. In those Cantons where Weggis and Arosa are located they spoke Schwyzerdütsch, Swiss German. They could understand my German but their language took some getting used to. Even the numbers were different. There were many German staff around Maharishi (and Italians and French and Dutch, etc.) but everyone spoke English. I tried to speak German whenever I could and my accent wasn't too bad, but our hotel was way up in the hills and not anywhere near the shops and restaurants of the town, where I could have practiced.

I found out that the Princeton language exams would be given in various locations in Europe. There was one scheduled in Germany, but I didn't know anyone there and didn't particularly want to go there. There was one scheduled in Paris. Ah, Paris. Yes. A Vassar College friend lived there, Marie-France Siegler-Lathrop. She was a filmmaker working as an assistant to the great Jacques Tati who had made *Mr. Hulot's Holiday*. She had an apartment in the Latin Quarter. Siegler was her father's last name. Her parents had divorced and her mother had married an American, Bill Lathrop, and moved her and her brother and sister to Alabama when she was about ten or eleven. She spoke fluent English, of course, but with a southern accent. She helped Tati get American tourists to be bit players in his films, among other tasks, and she hoped to make her own films.

I took the train to Paris with a young woman named Coral who would later marry Bill Scranton and try to help him get into politics, like his famous father. A word about Coral. She was a beautiful young woman with a real glow about her. We first met her in Interlaken at the Victoria-Jungfrau and Nate was smitten. When she came into the dining room he would dive under the table and peek out at her. Bill would pretend to be jealous. I don't remember why she was going to Paris, but we got sleepers on the train and had a fun, although noisy and uncomfortable ride.

Marie-France welcomed me. I taught her TM and we talked through the three nights checking as we drove all around Paris and went to the big castles in the south, like Versailles. Tati took us out to dinner one night and was very charming. Marie-France held a big party for all her friends and I wandered around Paris on my own while she worked. I even took a tour of the Bastille one day, a French tour! My French was coming to life and I was getting to a whole new level of fluency. I could almost speak and understand it without translating in my mind, something I had always wanted to be able to do. I wasn't ready to go back to Arosa. I felt totally at home there, as if I had lived there in a past life, a very happy one. It was also exhilarating to be a person again, however briefly, not just a mother, a wife, a disciple, just an individual. I called David and asked him if he could manage a little longer with the kids. No. He couldn't. I should come back at once. I did. Incidentally, I took the German exam and passed it.

When I got back I learned that David had told Maharishi I had gone to Paris to take my German exam. No, she didn't, he said, she went to Germany. Maybe he had heard something about the

German exam and misunderstood. Or maybe he knew very well what I had done. Whoops! What did that mean? I should have asked him? Those 108s asked him everything: should they color their hair, what colors should they wear, should they invite their mother, should they go for a visit home, God knows. I am an independent person. I can make my own decisions. But that wasn't the way in the ashram. I had the laws of nature there in person, the Delphic Oracle right in my hotel, and I was a fool not to ask him anything important. I tried to do better, but I never got very good at being the perfect disciple. Add this to my list of mistakes and lost opportunities.

On Rachel's weekly day off I would borrow a car or somehow get us a ride down into the town and Nate and Sara and I would wander the streets, visit the toy stores, get a hot chocolate at a café, and just have a fun time. Often we had lunch at a little bistro. Money was tight but we managed. We could always buy some little toy or something for our rooms to make them more homelike. David and I had sold a piece of land we had bought on the Eastern Shore, Maryland, in our graduate school days and the buyer was sending us a check for about $85 each month. It was enough to meet our very modest needs. At some point we began to get a very small salary from MIU even though we were no longer living there.

Maharishi met with the scientists every day. Larry Domash was brilliant. He could explain and summarize complicated ideas from physics so that they became easy to understand. He also was bold to connect the vacuum state with Being, which was quite a stretch for a conventional physicist. Brian Josephson, a theoretical physicist from the University of Cambridge, came around that summer and he was a restless fellow with very few social skills. He had gotten the Nobel Prize for his work on superconductivity and quantum tunneling, which is the phenomenon of a particle apparently tunneling through a barrier and appearing on the other side. It is called the Josephson Effect.

An interesting aside. Josephson had predicted this effect as a twenty-two year old student and was trying to publish it when he heard that some other physicists were working on the same problem. It can take months, even a year or two, to publish a paper in the scientific journals. He arranged something with the editor of the *London Times* and published his results, preventing his competitors from shutting him out. He was the youngest man to get a Nobel Prize for his work, which he had just received in 1973, the year before he came to Arosa. He was not as bold as Larry, and rarely spoke to the group or explained his ideas. I think he knew that Maharishi hoped he would be able to connect these advanced topics in physics to consciousness, but I never heard him go beyond the idea of transcending lowering entropy, which Larry first discussed. Still, his name and position were useful to the movement as we wrote pamphlets and hosted symposia.

I remember one special day in the large meeting hall when Maharishi had been discussing neurophysiology. I had meditated early as usual so as to be ready to take over the kids from Rachel so she could meditate and get to dinner on time. Maharishi had just ended the afternoon meeting and had told everyone to go and rest. He was still sitting there on the little couch; a few people were wandering around, and the video guys were shutting down. There was a biology book open on the table before Maharishi. He had been meeting with the scientists and talking about TM and the physiology. Fearlessly Nate walked right up to him and looked down at a big illustration of the brain. He looked at Maharishi. He knew he was a very important person to us. How big is *your* brain? Nate asked.

Maharishi cupped his hands together to form a little ball. It's small, he said, but like a light bulb, it fills the whole room. Nate accepted that. He nodded and moved on. Why are there lions carved on Guru Dev's chair? he asked, pointing to the big painting behind Maharishi. Oh, Maharishi said, it reminds him of the forest. Nate was satisfied. Here was an example of what Maharishi had always told us. Answer a child's question simply and briefly; don't go into a big abstract explanation. I listened and learned.

One day in the hall one of the main initiators in the U.S., the regional director for the western region, Stan Crowe, was showing Maharishi a large two-page (maybe four) colorful newspaper he had produced with lots of little articles on various aspects of TM, with scientific charts, and it was all very readable and very impressive. It was a great tool for advertising TM. Who did it? Maharishi asked. Stan said he had produced it in California. But who did it, Maharishi probed. Who wrote it? Who put it all together? "Bob Roth" was the answer. Send for him, Maharishi said with a glance at one of his secretaries, and Bob turned up a few days later. He stayed on and wrote and made himself very useful.

Reluctant Disciple

Maharishi had tried to get me involved in little projects, often writing projects, but I was not ready. I lacked confidence or was afraid to jump into something too big for me to handle. It was an old stress but still prevailing in my consciousness. He kept trying to draw me in, to give me a chance to evolve through serving him, but I couldn't do it. One day he asked me to look into the finances of the Vedic Studies PhD program going on down in the town at the Hotel Eden. It seems a number of the students were months behind in their room, board, and tuition. Could they afford to be here? I knew Maharishi felt, and had often heard him say, that if a course fee would be a financial pinch, then the person should save their money and go later. He didn't want people draining their resources or their parents' resources. If they were on that program they should be able to afford to stay and be guided by Maharishi as he saw fit, to educate and direct their activities for their evolution. Someone, probably Helga, who was in charge of paying bills and kept a tight watch on the money, brought me a list of course participants (CPs) and their arrears. I jumped right on it. This was a job I could certainly do. Limited and unambiguous, and I am good with money and people.

The Vedic Studies course had begun with discussions of the structure and nature of Vedic literature in Interlaken. A group of those interested in pursuing a PhD in Vedic studies had been organized and had been moved first to the Seeblick and then up to Arosa ahead of us and put into the Hotel Eden, which had become available early. Maharishi loved to go there. It gave him an opportunity to talk about the Vedic literature, to explore themes and avenues of Vedic expression and structure to an interested audience. Most of his time was taken up with administration of the entire worldwide movement, the national leaders of each country for the movement, the management of the various courses around Switzerland, and the logistics of constantly staffing and moving from hotel to hotel.

The Vedic Studies program was like a vacation for him, a chance to pursue his real interests and his lifelong goal to reestablish Vedic knowledge in India, and from there to the whole world. He frequently had various pandits brought from India and they would chant from the Vedas and he would comment on what they chanted. We could tell that he really enjoyed these sessions and was enlivened by going deeply into the meaning of each word and phrase and commenting on the effect of even the sound alone on our consciousness, which was good, because we understood nothing of the chanting and very little of the commentary (speaking for myself).

It was with that group that Maharishi developed some of his own contributions to his Vedic Science[SM], to understanding its structure and organization. Later he would lay out the theoretical framework for the TM-Sidhi® program and make the tapes that would be shown on the six-month courses that would begin in late '75 and '76. One of the CPs recalls that he was with Maharishi from Interlaken on and met with him personally in the Prätschli before he went to join the group in the Hotel Eden. Maharishi gave him a 50% scholarship for the course. The fellow had a BA in Sanskrit, was very intelligent, and became one of the coordinators for the group. Maharishi wanted him to be there. I imagine that the other 50% covered his room and board at least. It was a very precious course, but it could not continue if it couldn't at least meet the costs of running that hotel.

I got a ride down the mountain, informed the course that I would be having interviews with some of them, and started right off. They were not happy about it and there was some reluctance to cooperate. I don't remember if I told Maharishi that or if he just knew it, but soon there was an announcement that he would come see them as soon as I was finished. It took a number of days. I tried to be very compassionate and delicate with everyone, but it was obvious that some people were just running up a debt they might never be able to pay, and the movement has a long memory. Others just needed to shake the money tree and get current with their account.

One day I was riding back up the mountain in a taxi. It was very difficult to telephone the Prätschli to get someone to come get me because the few lines they had were always busy with people doing important things, and if I did connect, it was hard for the person on reception to get someone to the phone who had the authority to send one of the drivers down to get me. I had to get back, meditate, relieve Rachel, give the kids dinner, entertain them until bedtime, put them to bed, and sneak doing some laundry into that. I wasn't about to sit around the Hotel Eden for an hour trying to call the Prätschli. I called a cab. I would pay for it myself.

As I was heading up the mountain I saw that I was about to pass a limousine, probably Maharishi going to see one of the groups down in the town or in a neighboring town. I moved close to the window and pressed my hands together in the Namaste gesture and smiled to see him as he drove by. It was always a joy. He definitely saw me and understood where I had been and what I had been doing. I didn't think much about it, but a few days later a brand new Fiat turned up outside and the keys and papers were given to us! Really to me! I had a car. It was clearly meant for me to do my job since David never went anywhere unless he was going somewhere with Maharishi. It was a help and a reward for both of us for doing our jobs, and we did them well.

Charts, Fundamentals, *Collected Papers*, the kids, my projects, laundry, and so the summer was going by. David and I led very busy but pretty much separate lives, but we tried to spend meals together as a family and some time together after dinner or at a special event in the meeting hall. One such event every year was Swiss National Day on August 1, and it's a big deal. Our balcony at the Prätschli faced the neighboring mountains and after dark huge bonfires were lit all over the mountain, some in the shape of the Swiss cross, Rachel reminded me, and fireballs rolled down the mountain, and men carrying torches ran down the mountain also. We watched until late. Luckily it was a clear night and we could see it all. I had connected with Rachel on Facebook after forty-two years, and we were both trying to remember what had happened in those precious days in Maharishi's hotel.

Some time that summer Maharishi began talking about how even a small number of meditators, something like one percent, could affect the larger group. This was way before the research that validated this prediction. It seemed far-fetched, but one of the initiators took it seriously and began to order data from the FBI Uniform Crime Report.

MIU Moves to Fairfield

Near the end of August we heard that MIU was moving from Santa Barbara to Fairfield, Iowa, onto the old Parsons College campus. When the college became a party school and lost its accreditation, it had gone bankrupt and had been on the market for over a year with fourteen million dollars in debt. They had sold off the library collection and some other assets, but no one seemed to want a college campus with 40 or more small buildings outside a little farm town in southeast Iowa. The movement had bought it, or contracted to buy it, for about two and half million dollars.

The place had been empty during the bankruptcy proceedings and in all the time since then. When the Parson College staff heard about the bankruptcy decision, they had stood up, grabbed their purses or jackets, and walked out the door, leaving paper in the typewriters, flour in the barrels, food in meat lockers, and lunch in the cooking pots. By now it was incredibly dusty and the grass had grown very high all over the big campus.

MIU had been holding classes in Santa Barbara and suddenly everyone was scheduled to fly to Fairfield. New students for the autumn term were told to go to Fairfield, not to Santa Barbara, and everyone would be arriving soon. It was very exciting. Our own university with everyone a meditator: students, faculty, staff, and even the grounds people and all the workers, all volunteer meditators. No smoking, no drinking, healthy food, silence, an ideal life. Everyone wanted to be part of it, but first the place had to be cleaned up, and about 20 volunteers, including great souls Margie and Jerry Leahy, Roger and Nancy Leahy, Charlie Borden, and others, arrived to steam clean the whole kitchen, clean out the first buildings, and get the place ready for the September 3 arrival of the Santa Barbara contingent. The Fairfield community pitched in to help. Gas lines had to be repaired; grass had to be mowed. It was formidable. The liquor store hired another employee, thrilled that college boys would be coming back to town! They had no idea who we were.

On September 3, the whole group flew on chartered planes to Des Moines and were driven by bus to Fairfield. There is a picture of them on the front page of that day's *Fairfield Ledger*, getting off the buses wearing suits and ties, dressed really nicely, initiators many of them, looking very happy. That day Maharishi sent a telegram which was read out to them that evening. It said: *It is my delight to receive you in the new campus where you will be developing your full potential. Let every day structure a new step of progress. Infinite is the range of knowledge and so is your consciousness. Rise to wholeness and prepare to lead the world. Jai*

Guru Dev, Maharishi. Charlie Borden, who was in charge of getting the campus opened up, recalls that it was a very beautiful day.

How do I know all this that happened over forty years ago? I had heard stories over the years, but when I was writing this chapter I asked my Facebook friends for dates and memories and they flooded in, everyone joyfully remembering the excitement of those days. Charlie remembers meeting Jerry Leahy in his office, as president of the Bank of Pella, Iowa, earlier that summer. Charlie posted articles from the *Fairfield Ledger* and that telegram on Facebook. It had been Jerry Leahy who had told the movement about Parsons College and had been instrumental in the negotiations. Paul Stokstad remembers Jerry himself cleaning a bathroom in what would later be the literature and art building, Foster Hall. Diane Frank came as a volunteer and then stayed to be a faculty member teaching writing. You were heroes, I posted. "It was a very heroic time," Mark Keister posted back. It was all very inspiring, and still is, to think about those times and our enthusiasm. Those who posted are still enjoying their memories and what they gained from the whole experience.

One of the Santa Barbara faculty drove our car and camper across the country. He didn't secure the camper properly; it got loose and disconnected. When we next saw it, it was dented and useless. All our clothes, my pots and pans, and all our personal things were packed up, sent to Fairfield, and stored in one of the buildings. When I finally found them several years later, they had been rifled through and my clothes were sadly out of date. Pretty much all was lost. Ah, well.

Summer was coming to an end. It was starting to get chilly in Arosa. In September Maharishi was going off on a big tour and taking David along. I was rather grumpy about it. As he was leaving the hotel, I told Maharishi I might go off somewhere. I don't remember his response. When they all left and the hotel seemed very deserted and empty, Rachel and I packed up the kids and along with Paul Glossop headed for England to visit her parents. We stopped briefly in Paris to visit Marie-France, Paul remembers. We crossed the Channel on a ferry and the waters were very rough. I get motion sickness easily, but this was the worst I had ever experienced. If I had asked Maharishi rather than told him, I might have avoided this. I was throwing up and vibrating all over and if there had been a button I could have pushed to end it all, I might have pushed it. Rachel took the kids out on deck and they came to visit me from time to time, but it never let up. Even when we were back on land, it took me several days to stop buzzing and feel normal again.

When we arrived we went to Roydon Hall, a movement facility, for a few days and I recovered. Then we visited Rachel's parents in Cambridge. I learned to drive on the wrong side of the road, which forever broke my automatic confidence that I was driving on the right side of the road, and we had an okay time. I remember almost nothing of the trip and Rachel admits to a total blackout about it. Maybe not such a good idea, all in all. When we arrived back in the Alps it was snowing. Nate got a toboggan, Peter and Kristen Sandel had joined the school (their parents were part of the video team), and the kids had fun playing in the snow. David returned from his tour and we left Arosa and moved into a big hotel in Mürren for a midseason stay until we could get into our winter home somewhere on Lake Lucerne.

Mürren

The resort town of Mürren was in between summer season and ski season and snow was starting to fall heavily, especially on the mountains. Maharishi took us up in trams to the top of one of them above the clouds and we all stood there in the snow and sunshine and we threw snowballs and took pictures, like a bunch of children. So much fun for everyone, Rachel remembers. We were what we were, and we were what he had, so he made the best of us, both for the movement's sake and for ours.

Nate had learned the meditation technique for young children back in El Paso and it had really settled him down, but he couldn't be trusted to go off and do it himself. He was too easily distracted by all that was going on around us. Could one of us walk around with him, I asked. Yes, that would be all right, I was told, so either Rachel or I would walk around with him wandering through all the empty meeting or dining rooms in that huge hotel. Sara was nearly four and a half and eager to be initiated too, but we were supposed to wait until she was about five. All the other kids in the school had their technique and she wanted hers.

One day I went down the hall to Maharishi's suite to ask him some questions and Nate was with me. Maharishi was not feeling well and he was resting in his room and just meeting small groups privately. After we left and we were walking back along the corridor, Nate asked me loudly, "If he's so holy, how come he's sick?" Dr. Elliot Abravanel had asked Maharishi virtually the same question on his TTC in Rishikesh some years before. "If you are enlightened, Maharishi, why do you have bronchitis?" Maharishi explained that the body has its own karma. One could witness it and not be overthrown by it, but it had to be lived. It was what we all had wondered right from the beginning, gauging from those questions in Humboldt. I told this to Nate.

Maharishi then took David off to Nepal where he planned to initiate thousands. Leaving again. I was sad, Rachel remembers. I would have to do the whole move, including boxes and boxes of David's papers, by myself. Marco and Maharishi were still negotiating with the hotel owners. We were waiting to hear where that would be.

When David finally came back from Nepal and India he brought me two beautiful sarees. His Indian host had taken him shopping and urged him to buy them for me on the movement's tab. One was green and had golden-beige embroidery and a red and green embroidered border. It was very elegant. When I first wore it, Maharishi noticed it and praised it. David also brought me a purple and gold wedding saree that was extremely heavy. I still have them both and I wore the wedding saree to a big wedding in Delhi in 1980.

Daily Life in Maharishi's Hotel

WE WOUND UP THAT WINTER in the very fancy, five-star Park Viznau right on Lake Lucerne, east of Weggis. At first I got a corner room, not very big, with a double bed, a chair, and little table, and there was a small room next to it for the kids. I was not very happy with it. David and Maharishi were not back yet from Nepal so I was on my own trying to make a home there. There was no place to sit and read the kids a story; it could not be made very comfortable for the family. Susan Humphrey saved us. There was a room on the other side of the kids' room, a large and spacious room with a living area and a sofa and chairs, and there was a huge balcony off of it. It was elegant and beautiful. It was being reserved for some special guest, but they hadn't come, and Susan got it for us and we had it that whole winter long. The kids' room was tiny but it had two beds and a bathroom, so it was very valuable, and it connected to ours. Was Maharishi consulted about this? I expect so. In later years I would hear people complaining about something, saying Maharishi would never have done that or said that. Well, I knew that he micromanaged the whole movement, every aspect of life around him, and it is entirely likely that he *was* behind whatever directive or activity being questioned. One has to assume so.

There was no room in the Park Vitznau for Rachel or the school room. She was sent to live in a little guest house with other staff, but she was given a large, light-filled, airy room for the school in a hotel very close by. The kids built a little town with roads and zoomed their toy cars around it. She had a science area with a microscope and a solar system hanging from the ceiling, and she got some men to build her a pyramid and play houses the kids could crawl around in. She filled the room with their artwork and the place looked like a real schoolroom.

Housing was always tricky, and not just for us. The hotel was always full but some rooms had to be set aside for the important visitors, the visiting dignitaries and the staff Maharishi often called to come. Some of them were never satisfied with their rooms. Lillian Rosen was one of them. She was a great heroine. She traveled all over the U.S. giving advanced techniques by herself. She was all sweetness and devotion in front of Maharishi, but let her turn around and she might snap at you. She wanted everything done just her way and didn't stand for any insubordination. She was famous for bossing her helpers around and was not always delicate with their feelings, although she was completely soft and sweet to her initiates. A young Canadian, Rig Gelfand, was one of the boys on the door then and he was in charge of housing in Maharishi's hotel. He told me that he had a method of dealing with Lillian on her visits. First he would have her taken with her luggage to some small, perfectly acceptable private room with bath, but definitely below her status, real and perceived. She would immediately roar back up to him, complaining loudly. He would act surprised, ask her to take him to the room, and then tell her it was all a big mistake; that was not at all the room she was to have. Then he would take her to the room he had originally planned to give her. She was mollified and pleased and content. It was over for that time.

I have to tell a Lillian story, although it is not my story; it is Charlie Donahue's story. Charlie was our regional coordinator for the Eastern U.S. First, you have to understand that sometimes people would take Maharishi's knowledge and gather a following about them. They would pretend to have some consciousness and standing that they may or may not have had, and instead of referring all gratitude and deserving to Maharishi and Guru Dev, from where the knowledge had come, they would accept flowers from their little group, and have an undue influence over them. Maharishi called them cuckoo gurus.

OK, the Lillian story: One day Charlie asked Maharishi, why Lillian? She was such a terror out in the field (the field was wherever Maharishi wasn't, like the U.S. was "the field." If your time around Maharishi was over, you were sent out to "bless the field.") Why choose Lillian of all people to be the one advanced technique teacher in the U.S.? Charlie asked. Maharishi replied, I wanted someone no one would follow [someone who couldn't develop a following of their own]. Charlie smiled broadly and said that if that was your intention, Maharishi, you chose very well. Charlie says that Maharishi almost fell off his couch laughing.

Next door to us on the second floor lived Barbara Klein. She was in charge of the cash box. That meant that she was the one you went to if you needed gas money to drive to Lucerne to pick up some part for video. She was the one who organized Maharishi's travel if he was flying somewhere with a group. Her big bed was covered with piles of papers and she never seemed to sleep. There was a constant stream of people going past our room to consult her. She was careful with the money but seemed to know exactly how and when to give it out. I am assuming she was given guidelines by Maharishi, was handpicked by him, and that she turned directly to him or to Helga when something fell outside her guidelines. Helga was the main finance person and the buck (or Swiss franc, as the case was there) stopped with her. Any major purchase had to be approved by Helga and she was taught to be very careful with the money.

We had a lovely Christmas in Vitznau. We had a tree in our room and decorated it and the kids got lots of presents. We got Nate a bike and David taught him to ride right outside in front of the hotel in the big circular driveway. Some people were resting and rounding in the rooms above the driveway and they grumbled at us. Sara insisted on learning TM and so I taught her that winter of '74-'75. It was about that time that David received some data from a young researcher and initiator named Garland Landrith. It was he who had brought his professor Maynard Shelly to our Humboldt course. Garland had compared the crime rate in four Midwestern towns that had at least one percent meditators with four matched towns that didn't. One couldn't know if those people were actively meditating, but at least they had been taught. The door to infinity had been opened. Garland found that the crime rate began to decrease when the one percent threshold was reached, just as Maharishi had predicted earlier that year. It was a wonderful discovery, showing that we didn't have to teach everybody; one percent would start the trends in a positive direction.

Maharishi was thrilled. It was a huge shortcut in his plan to enlighten the world. Maharishi wanted charts made right away so the initiators on their ATR courses in nearby hotels along the lake could take them back with them. He took the news with him and went into silence. For us silence meant the period Maharishi took every year, the first seven days of the new year. He would withdraw from activity and go inward. Meals were brought to his room; he saw no one. If you could, you took silence, too, and surfed on the waves of his deep consciousness. Never me. What could I do, not talk to my children? When Maharishi came out of silence he was refreshed and ready to launch into new activities. Everyone was eager to hear about his new directions, ready to leap into action for his January 12 birthday celebration.

While we waited for Maharishi to come out of silence, David had asked Garland to get more data, to look at cities large and small all over the U.S. to see if crime rate was affected as the meditating numbers grew. Crime statistics are hard to come by and don't get published until at least nine months after the year end, but surely the trend could be found in some of the larger cities. TM was taught everywhere and the effect must have been evident. However would the world be convinced of the finding, which was soon named the Maharishi Effect since Maharishi was the originator of it, on the basis of a couple of small towns in the Midwest? David and the other scientists worked very hard to enlarge Garland's original findings. Garland's data was analyzed by Candice Borland who was with us that year. She was a statistician and helped to construct the publishable study, now to be known as authored by the team of Borland and Landrith.

Dawn of the Age of Enlightenment

MAHARISHI CAME OUT OF SILENCE ON FIRE. "Through the window of science," he said, "we see the Dawn of the Age of Enlightenment," and we would now announce and inaugurate the Dawn on every continent. We would start with a big celebration on January 12. Get prepared!

Ceremony on the Flagship Gotthard

For the occasion the movement got the largest ship available on Lake Lucerne, the Flagship Gotthard. The interior of the ship, especially the large dining room, which became our meeting room, was filled with flowers, and the inside and outside of the ship were decorated with lights, scientific displays and huge banners saying Inauguration of the Age of Enlightenment. You can see pictures in the large gold occasional book printed at our press in Germany, *Inauguration of the Dawn of the Age of Enlightenment* (MIU Press: W. Germany, 1975).

Many small boats were also rented so everyone from the courses around the lake and all the guests could come along and be part of it and we sailed around the lake in a big flotilla for hours. The visiting national leaders of our TM organization, scientists, and senior staff were all crammed into that meeting room, video cameras had been set up, new scientific charts were on the walls, and we started out with the traditional candle lighting and cake cutting ceremony (performed by Lillian).

Jerry began as Master of Ceremonies and introduced Keith, the president of Maharishi International University. Keith began by honoring our hosts in Switzerland, men from the families of Hertenstein, Seeblick, Gersau, Brunnen and Lucerne. I didn't remember this, but was interested to read in the *Dawn* book that their communities had donated all the flowers. It was very sweet, and Maharishi really appreciated those few men who stood up for us, like Herr Hasler, and facilitated our being able to host the movement and all our courses in politically neutral Switzerland, the most ideal country for us since its history was peaceful and not full of violence and suffering.

Keith then named all the scientists who had come to speak from MIU and from around the world. What were we inaugurating? The Age of Enlightenment. What did that mean? Keith said: the state of enlightenment represents the ultimate development of what we ordinarily consider to be the most valuable qualities of human life. Enlightenment results from the full development of consciousness. And what makes it unique today, he went on to say, was that Maharishi had re-established this knowledge, made it accessible to scientific investigation, brought it to each and every human being. As Maharishi had said, "There's no reason in our scientific age for anyone to remain unenlightened."

Keith rolled through the achievements of the movement from its inauguration in Madras, India, in 1957, to Maharishi's world tours, TTCs, international symposia on SCI, scientific papers, right up to the discovery that one percent of a city's population practicing the Transcendental Meditation technique improves the quality of city life. Then he introduced Maharishi, who had been sitting with his eyes closed.

Maharishi began by chanting softly in Sanskrit, bowing down to the tradition of Masters, from Lord Narayana to the current Shankaracharya. He prayed to Mother Divine: "Mother Divine!

Now on Thine own, think of bringing the dawn of enlightenment to the whole world and destroying the fear of all that is not good. . . . Thine immeasurable influence and strength is beyond the reach of prayers even from the Lord Almighty, the Lord of Creation, and the Lord of Dissolution. May all the good belong to all the people in the world; may the rulers go by the path of justice . . . ; May this world be free from suffering and the noble ones free from fears." He ended by paying homage to his own Master, Guru Dev, Brahamananda Saraswati, the supreme teacher, full of brilliance.

Maharishi exuded happiness. This was a fine and joyful moment for him. He spoke at length referring to the most recent news of the one percent effect and all the possibilities now open to us to really enlighten the world. It was still dark, yes, but the dawn is there, and it should not take long for the first rays of light to be seen, and that would be good enough to dispel the darkness while we awaited the full sunshine. My joy today is the joy of the gardener, he said, to see the tree growing, blossoming, and producing fruit, and that fruit becoming ripe and sweet, "and this will be the fruit of knowledge eaten by the whole population on earth." Then he called up the traditional "blowers of harmony and peace in this land of peace," asking for the alpine horn to be blown. These are huge horns that extend about six or seven feet from the men who will blow them. The performers have to be big men and they really blow forcefully, and then a low, full tone vibrates the whole room. Men in traditional Swiss dress waved the cantonment flags and it was all very colorful and exciting.

Keith then welcomed the press and news services who were there and then we launched into the scientists' presentations. David was the very first one to speak. Keith asked him to present the now more than three hundred research projects going on all over the world (how it had all expanded since David was named Director of the International Center for Scientific Research!), but David opened with his latest findings, his work of the past few weeks. A series of charts had quickly been produced and hung on the walls and they showed nine major cities in the U.S. with their crime rates before and after reaching one percent and the same for control cities matched for size and resident and student populations. And not just crime, David added. A recent study of the fifty U.S. cities ranked on quality of life (crime, health statistics, income, air pollution, etc.) showed that the best cities had the highest number of meditators. Statistically significant! $p < .01$. That means, he explained, that the chances of this being an error were one in one thousand. Good odds!

Yes, Maharishi said. Just a few meditating houses in the city will take care of all the negative tendencies in that city. This will take away all the headaches of the mayors. They just have to encourage a few households of meditators, erect a few meditating houses here and there.

David then went into a review of scientific interest in consciousness, from Abraham Maslow through a summary of the now hundreds of research papers on TM. It was all very impressive, and Maharishi said he hoped the press was taking note.

Six physicists, one chemist, one neurobiologist, one geneticist, one neurophysiologist, one mathematician, one educator, a couple of psychiatrists, one psychologist, one legal theorist, and a two restless children coming and going. Maharishi commented on all the speakers, and Michael Dimick introduced the various administrative bodies for the movement, presidents, Board of Advisors, Board of Directors (including Jemima Pittman, Sally Peden, and Rindi) and the Directors of the Seven Divisions (which seemed to include me and David and Susan Humphrey and Theresa Olson and everyone else we worked with).

Larry gave the concluding speech. He not only made physics interesting and understandable, he was a great and inspiring speaker. Truly, he said, "Maharishi has created a sort of miracle. In only seventeen years . . . he has come to the point where he is satisfied that this knowledge is well-established and here to stay . . . ," he said.

"The true meaning of today," he went on to say, "will be evident far in the future when people see these videotapes and read these words and understand the full value of what Maharishi has brought about."

Inaugurating the Dawn in Amsterdam

Weeks earlier a symposium had been set up by the Dutch movement in Amsterdam for the end of the month. Maharishi and the scientists would give talks at the RAI, the largest conference center in Amsterdam, on January 31 and hold a big symposium at Vrije Universiteit on February 1. A group of scientists and other top staff would fly there with Maharishi, and David and I were on the list. It was my first time traveling with the entourage. David was going to present the Fundamentals of Progress and Candice was going to present the research she and Garland had just done on the Maharishi Effect. The conference had a theme or purpose, which I do not recall, but Maharishi hijacked the event to declare the Dawn of the Age of Enlightenment, stretching everyone's minds, especially the minds of the Dutch leaders who had envisioned a rather conservative display of Maharishi's knowledge and the scientific research.

It was very exciting, and Amsterdam is one of the major capitals of Europe. I was overwhelmed by being there and wanted to look around (I had already heard all the talks, several times!). David didn't want to go out and about; he wanted to perfect his upcoming talk on the Fundamentals of Progress. It all went off beautifully. David was pleased with his talk and so was Maharishi. We grabbed a quick lunch at our hotel (the Dutch cheese! the Dutch butter! the watery vegetarian soup [ugh]. Did no one understand how to give vegetarians a balanced protein?). The first day we grabbed a taxi and sped to the Rijksmuseum and sprinted to the Vermeers, which were way in the back of the huge building. Small they were, but brilliant with light and consciousness. The second day we went to the Van Gogh museum and tasted and saw what we could in so little time. It made an indelible impression on me and the desire to return was born, which didn't happen for nearly forty years, but it did happen.

At some tourist shop I picked out a pair of little earrings of tiny blue and white Delft china, which I still wear, and we found some traditional wooden clogs for the kids, which they loved. They clattered around the Park hotel in them, up and down the uncarpeted marble stairways and corridors until we were persuaded to ban them from the hotel and consign them to outdoor wearing only. Imagine! People were meditating and were disturbed by the noise. We were the only family living in the hotel.

Spring on Lake Lucerne

Scientific discussions went on every day and evening in the big hall and various guests came and went. Alaric Arenander, who was working on his PhD in neuroscience at UCLA, talked often about the wonders of glial cells and the other scientists tried to figure out with Maharishi the physiological basis for enlightenment. Some of the staff were working on tapes and lessons for teaching TM in schools and there was a big video group to support all these projects. Lots of activity: writing, speaking, taping, printing, and administering. There was a TTC in Vittel, France, to be seen to, as well. Maharishi had formalized the TTC. It was no longer the open-ended experience of Majorca, La Antilla, and Fiuggi. It was a systematic presentation of lessons, video tapes (including many made by Larry Domash and David), and studying. Maharishi was consulted on who would be accepted to these courses. David remembers one of the first times that he was in the car with Maharishi discussing not science, but administrative matters: the course office was considering a young man who had been a bit "off the program" on his previous courses. Was he unsuitable? No, no, Maharishi said, young boys can be a little mischievous; it will be all right.

David, Keith, Jacques Verlinde, and Dr. Byron Rigby were sent off to an inaugural dinner for Canada's World Plan Week that February at the Chateau Laurier Hotel in Ottawa. Or national leader Jeff Dreben had set it up. A short, exhausting, jet-lagged trip. Susan Humphrey regularly went to check on the kitchens and housing at the various courses. There were ATRs going on around the lake for Maharishi to visit as well. At some point Maharishi was told that the young initiators were quite distracted by each other, falling in love and even getting married, only to find out when they got home from rounding that they had made a big mistake. We had always been told not to make any major decisions when rounding, but who listens? After this the groups of men and women were sent to hotels in different towns so they could focus on their consciousness and their rest before going back to the field.

One day Maharishi announced that a small group of us in his hotel would have a chance to rest and round also. David had been working really hard and travelling a lot, which was very hard on him, so he did deserve a rest. I was part of that group, too, and we gratefully settled into a routine of extra meditations and tapes while the kids played in their schoolroom and in the hills around the lake with Rachel. We were put into a small meeting room near the main hall. We didn't go into the main hall, which would have been too exciting; we might have gotten drawn into discussions and tasks. Instead our little group sat together and watched Maharishi on tapes on the little TV at the front of the group. One of those tapes was called Guru Dev: Blossoming of Life from the Depth of Silence. It had been made on Guru Purnima July 8, 1971.

In this talk Maharishi describes how his beloved Guru Dev set out as a young boy toward the Himalayas in search of a master to guide him. One of his requirements was that the saint be kind and not given to anger. It seems he had heard of a famous saint in the area who belonged to an order that doesn't use fire. He went to the man and innocently but purposefully asked him for some fire. The man exploded with anger. Didn't this ignorant boy know that he didn't use fire!? The young boy answered him, something like, if you don't use fire, where is all this heat coming from? Maharishi laughed and said that maybe the man was in some kind of "grumpy CC." I was horrified. I wanted to be free of my grumpiness. I was hoping that evolving into CC would purge me of that irritability and grumpiness that I so often fell into. Grumpy CC? What an awful idea. David says Maharishi probably meant that the man wasn't really what he claimed to be. I hope so. I am less and less grumpy, so maybe there is still hope. I wish I had asked Maharishi that question.

One day in the middle of rounding during one of our small group meetings, Maharishi himself entered the room and sat down there in front of us. We were, what can I say, stunned. It was as if he had stepped out of the television and into the room. How would you react if suddenly Cinderella or some TV personality had jumped into the room and began to talk to you? He had a huge presence in that little room and we were awestruck. Questions? No way. Just gape and listen.

The World Tour

Around us we heard rumors that Maharishi was preparing to go on a world tour to inaugurate the Dawn on five continents. One of the boys came by our room. Would David like to go on the world tour? No, he wouldn't, he said, he would rather stay and keep rounding. We heard that Maharishi laughed when he heard this, and said, "David is deep in his two and two" (which I take to mean that he was so tired he was sleeping a lot and barely able to do the rounding schedule). Our friend Bob Oates was invited to go along to the Indian, European, Canadian, and American parts of the tour and he later put his experiences into a book with beautiful pictures of Maharishi, *Celebrating the Dawn* (Putnam, 1975). Maharishi went first to Delhi and then he took a short side-trip to Rishikesh to visit the Academy and rest a bit. Maharishi addressed a big gathering in Delhi on March 11 (and was very pleased that the current Shankaracharya of Jyotir Math attended), and then one at Benares University and one in Bombay.

Then the group flew on to London, while Maharishi took a side trip to Vittel to see the TTC which was winding up. In London they had interviews with the press and spoke at the Royal Albert Hall on March 19. In Canada they spoke in Ottawa at the Chateau Laurier on March 21 and then Quebec, then moved on to New York, Atlanta, Chicago, Fairfield and Los Angeles. At each of these places well-known politicians and public figures spoke about their personal experiences with TM and the press responded pretty well. Bob quotes a number of them in his book.

In Los Angeles, we heard, Maharishi was to be a guest on the Merv Griffin show. Merv Griffin was a very popular TV personality, and his audience numbered about thirty million. He had just learned TM, he announced to the cameras, ten days before, and was very impressed. He had invited Clint Eastwood, also a meditator, and several others to join him and Maharishi. We got to watch the taped version when they returned, and I remember the moment when Clint Eastwood reached into his coat, as if he were going to draw out a pistol, and whipped out a flower to give to Maharishi. We all gasped collectively. The show was a huge success and thousands of people, thousands, wanted to learn TM. Initiations ran to about forty thousand a month following the show. For once the initiators had enough money to buy a new suit or even a car.

Maharishi announced that we should build a Capital for the Age of Enlightenment on each of the five major continents. We didn't realize it but he was planning to start this project with a groundbreaking ceremony in the Himalayas in May and we would be there.

Maharishi went on to inaugurate the Dawn in South America and Africa and got back to Switzerland in early April. By then the Park Hotel had opened to tourists and we had moved into the Hotel Seeblick in nearby Weggis. Rachel had lost her schoolroom in March, when that hotel opened to tourists, and the organization

Rachel Parry and her students: Sara, Alisha Isen, Nate, and Adam Phillip

had rented a chalet way up in the hills as a substitute. It was a twenty-minute walk straight up the mountain. The kids ate snow from the window sills and had to light the old wood stove to stay warm, but it was a great adventure. Spring was coming, snow was melting and flowers were peeking through the ground and the snow. We were coming down from rounding and we followed the kids up the mountain one day to see where they had been playing. Heidiland, David called it.

The Establishment of MERU

MERU was coming together in the Hotel Seeblick: labs, displays and all. David was very busy with it and I had my role. Maharishi said, "David will be in charge and Rhoda will organize everything," or something like that. Maharishi called me the mother of MERU. Rachel wrote to her mother that I was enjoying the work and responsibility but was looking rather exhausted. David's parents came for a visit. One afternoon they were sitting out on their balcony while we were meditating, I guess, and Pop was having a smoke. He couldn't smoke indoors, he knew, but thought the balcony would be all right. Then a little piece of paper on a string came floating downward. Bill and Lois Avery lived up above and the smoke was disturbing them. Bill was the engineer who had designed the electronics for the Nepal initiations, which was a brilliant solution to the challenges of speaking to large crowds without loud speakers and a proper sound system. Lois was handling the cash box. Maharishi had asked me to do it, and I had respectfully declined. It would be awful, I told him, thinking of Barbara Klein. People would be coming up to me at all hours, especially when I was trying to have a peaceful lunch with my family. All right, he conceded, Lois could do it and I would supervise. Now I look back and wonder if anyone else refused Maharishi and negotiated with him as I did. How difficult I must have seemed! How patient and forgiving he was with me.

At one meeting in the hall, someone asked Maharishi about children, and he said that children choose their parents and become part of their families based on timing and karma, of course. I stood up and asked about adopted children, since we had adopted Nate and Sara. Had they chosen us? Same thing, Maharishi said. Adopted children just come by another route. I felt that was true, I told Lois afterwards. Nate and Sara seemed to be our very own, no matter how they had come to us.

I found myself in charge of trying to house everyone who showed up and I was busy with many administrative details. I was often abrupt and maybe severe at times. I can be very short with people. Unfortunately I am often not very cordial and courteous, especially when I am stretched. On one occasion I got a message from Maharishi not to be so "mean." I was ashamed and shocked. I do have a mean streak. By sending me this message Maharishi was doing at least two things, I believe. He was showing me to myself, and that was not pleasant but necessary. Secondly, I think he was pointing his finger at one of my stresses, one of the rocks in my heart, and incinerating it. Our friend and fellow scientist Dr. Byron Rigby, a brilliant psychiatrist, used to say that being around Maharishi was like having open-ego surgery. Today we might call it tough love. It *was* love and it was sometimes painful.

Maharishi was often with the PhD students in their hotel, bringing out his vision of Vedic structure and techniques, and he also often met with our intimate little staff group in the Seeblick. One day Eileen Gallagher, who was in charge of the mailroom, had a birthday. She was a shy English lady who quietly and modestly did her very important job of directing the mail that came in and making sure nothing went out that hadn't been authorized. I was in charge of asking the kitchen for a cake and finding a moment to present it. David and I had some trick candles that automatically relight after you blow them out. We put them on Eileen's cake. She dutifully tried to put them out after we sang and all that, and then, after about ten to fifteen seconds, the candles suddenly they sprang back to life! We all laughed and were enjoying ourselves, but she was very embarrassed. Maharishi was very sweet to her and made some comments about immortal candles and we finally snuffed them out. (Sorry, Eileen. It was thoughtless of us.)

The boat rides continued on lovely days whenever Maharishi was in town. Once he was sitting up front as usual with the special guests and David and I and the kids were about two-thirds of the way back. We never got seats for the kids so they always sat on our laps. Nate got restless and climbed off of David and was moving about nearby in the aisle. Maharishi caught his eye and beckoned him up front. Nate zipped up to him and leaned over while Maharishi whispered something in his ear. Then he zipped back to us and said seriously, "Dad, Maharishi wants you." David got up and went up the front. Everyone was smiling. There really wasn't any need for David to go up there. Maharishi was giving Nate something to do for him and seeing if he would do it.

Late one morning there was a group meeting in one of the smaller meeting rooms on the fourth floor, Maharishi's private meeting room near his suite. Sally and Rindi were there and Lawrence Sheaff and Stephen Benson. Lawrence was one of the chief designers for the Press and Stephen got things printed, first in Germany and then later in Seelisberg when our presses were set up there. They were hard workers; they checked everything with Maharishi and hurried off to do whatever he wanted done. Lillian must have been there, Jacques, and a couple of others. I was not usually included in such meetings. It was the first time I was in that room, and I had been specifically invited. Hari, Maharishi's cook, came in to ask Maharishi something about lunch. Maharishi asked us all if we would enjoy an Indian lunch. We, of course, were very enthusiastic. Then for the only time that I ever heard, Hari began bringing us all an Indian lunch, plate by plate.

When Maharishi's plate was delivered, he waved his hand over it and whispered something we couldn't hear. We were used to the usual bland course food which meant very few spices and herbs. This was delicious, full of black mustard seeds, cumin, coriander, ginger and other spices from Indian cookery. I learned this later when I learned how to cook this cuisine once we were back in the U.S. David was happily wolfing it down until he noticed Maharishi watching him. Maharishi then slowly and deliberately lifted the food to his mouth. David slowed down.

Maharishi announced that we were all going to India to inaugurate Capitals of the Age of Enlightenment. All? Me? I asked out loud in amazement. Yes, he nodded. Oh, my goodness. When? In a few weeks. Visas and plane tickets were being organized. It would be my first trip to India, exotic India. Wow. I would need stuff, sarees, oh my God. Maharishi was drawing me closer into his inner circle.

Rachel had a birthday, too, that May, and since she was loved by all the staff, they made her a huge birthday cake decorated with marzipan swans. The children had chipped in to buy her a real Swiss cuckoo clock with a little bird that comes out and chirps and they were bubbling with excitement about the purchase and giving it to her. She wrote all this to her mom and told her that the kids were reading *James and The Giant Peach* at the time. Nate was enjoying the slapstick humor, Josh liked the adventure, Alisha liked the magical bits, and Rachel loved the natural history. She wrote to her mom that she was living in a tiny room in an old chalet on the banks of the lake. A huge gilt mirror on one wall gives the feeling of space, she wrote to her mother. She felt surrounded by real and reflected leaves and soft green light. Her staff time was coming to an end and she was going to go to TTC. We had no replacement for her, and our trip to India was coming up.

Off to India

PASSPORTS IN HAND we landed in Delhi at dawn and it was already 105 degrees, the pilot had told us. The sun was blinding and the heat was dry and intense. We got off the plane and walked across the tarmac to the building to claim our luggage. It was a madhouse of people running around shouting, luggage being loaded onto some buses, taxis being loaded, and horns beeping. Finally we were off to our hotel. I clearly remember thinking and feeling, I am back home, and I don't think I like it. It was utterly familiar on some level, although I had never been to the Far East before in this lifetime, and it was also with a sense of it not being a place of happy times. Our destination, the Ashoka Hotel, was a five-star with all the amenities, and the girls wanted to go off shopping immediately for sarees and sandals for the trip. Ma (Jemima Pittman) said she needed some new sarees, and the rest of us didn't have any, or very few, and we would be wearing them every day. I did have a pair of yellow sandals with narrow straps that I had bought somewhere in the U.S. that I could wear with sarees so I didn't need to buy sandals. They all did.

First we went to a tailor shop and the girls picked out fabrics for the short blouses that go with the sarees. We got measured, but when we went back to pick them up, mine were too small. They had made them too tight in the arms, too high in the midriff and too tight across the bosom, and they hadn't even been washed yet and would shrink farther. We saw that some of the Indian ladies wore theirs with seams popping and stretched in all directions and their bellies exposed over the waistline of the sarees. Not an attractive look. Our funds were limited so I bought a couple of sarees off the rack at some shops and I got a cotton saree slip and went to a shop that had ready-made blouses and insisted on large ones, which I tried on, much to the shopkeeper's disgust, until I found some that were comfortable, large enough, and had room to shrink when washed. We visited many shops in the major shopping areas and were guided around, but it was still overwhelming, as well as noisy, polluted, crowded, and a bit frightening.

Rishikesh

After a couple of days of shopping and resting from the long flight (and waiting for a few other people to arrive from various parts of the world), we all piled into Ambassador taxi cabs for the drive up to Rishikesh, where Maharishi had his Academy of Meditation built in the state forest. The cabs were modeled after the British Morris Oxford. The Indian version, the Ambassador, was the first and only car made in India for many years, starting in 1958, and it was pretty much the same year after year. This was 1975, so some of the cabs we were riding in may have been nearly twenty years old. Most couldn't manage to go uphill and run the air conditioner at the same time, and the whole trip was uphill with the driver and at least four passengers. Some of those cabs died *en route* or broke down and we had to reshuffle. Our cab broke down in the middle of the plains north of Delhi, hot and dry and dusty. We sat by the side of the road, all alone, wondering what to do. An oxcart moved slowly by, drawn by the biggest ox I had ever seen with a small driver perched high above the cart. There were no other cars coming or going. It was silent and deserted. Maharishi had always sent us in caravans in Switzerland. Now I could see why.

Nat Goldhaber, the first Vice-president of MIU, was in our taxi.

Nat had been teaching TM in Korea and Afghanistan, and was on his way back to the U.S. when he heard about the tour from Jerry and he had joined us in Delhi. Nat told us that the Afghan people had a custom of killing saints and holy people and burying them there so they couldn't leave and so that their good influence would bless the countryside. "What rude behavior," Maharishi had laughed, Nat told us. Nat and the driver looked under the hood of the car. They deduced that the car needed a gasket and Nat took out his Swiss Army knife and proceeded to carve one out of some cardboard we found near the road (plenty to choose from). That worked and we were on our way again. But for a time there, we had stepped back thousands of years into the age of ox-carts and deserted plains, far away from civilization as we knew it.

On our way to Rishikesh we stopped at Haridwar, one of the holiest places in India. It means "Gateway to God." There are many pilgrims there who come to bathe in the holy Ganges. Huge gatherings (*melas*) are held there every six years, and the major ones every twelve years, as well as other festivals, drawing hundreds of thousands of pilgrims. We were passing through at a quiet time and the taxis took us right down to the *ghats* where people bathe. These were stone steps leading into the water of the river and women were washing and bathing with very little privacy. Beggars approached us, and the personal space in Asia is very different from what we are used to. A very dark-skinned nearly naked man with long, unkempt hair came right up to me, inches away, with his hand held out. I was shocked by how close he was, and I didn't know what to do. David pulled me to his side.

We ate lunch and then headed further up the Ganges to Rishikesh. TM teacher training courses had been held at Maharishi's academy for years. This was the place where our friend Prudence and the Beatles had sat with Maharishi in 1968. This was only seven years later. It was historic! We were given rooms and sent to rest. We would leave very early in the morning, we were told.

Our group had expanded. Jerry had come and Dr. George

Sudarshan, a theoretical physicist who was a professor of physics at the University of Texas in Austin, and would go on to win many honors and awards. He was a devoted meditator at the time and he popped into Seelisberg or wherever Maharishi was whenever he could get away. There was Frances Knight, who later painted the Holy Tradition, the tall narrow painting of all the sages from Narayana through to Guru Dev and Maharishi, the one that you see in every TM center in the world. She had been studying art in India and she turned up. Had Maharishi called her? Probably. There were others too, a few initiators who had been working in southeast Asia, like Richard Eidson and Leon Weiner, and we also had Maharishi's secretary, a Canadian named Martin Karklins, as well as Lawrence and Stephen and Sally and Rindi and Lillian and Ma.

We got up early, mainly thanks to the huge monkeys who were in the trees near our room and making a big noise. We were wrapped in our sarees and waiting to leave, but the leaving got postponed. A group came to see Maharishi and he gave them a lecture in Hindi. Sally, Rindi, and I sat on a low wall and listened and watched. More old Ambassador cabs began to turn up to replace those that had died on the way to Rishikesh and to handle the extra people. There was a bus loaded with various Indian men, including the numerous pandits Maharishi had called. Peter Warburton, we later learned, was organizing for all the Indians. The important ones, like the elderly Brahmarishi Devarat and his son, and others, like Satyanand who had been with Maharishi and Guru Dev in the old days, and Brahmachari Nandkishore, who was always with Maharishi and was kind of a secretary and special disciple, were assigned to taxi cabs also. Some taxis set out, but we westerners were waiting for more taxis to arrive.

Finally we left for Jyotir Math, high in the Himalayas. Sally and Rindi and David were in the back of our taxi and I sat up front with the driver because I get less carsick in the front seat. It was a long, hot journey up a narrow, dusty, very winding road.

We climbed and climbed. Sally and Rindi and David were getting carsick so Sally and Rindi started singing show tunes. They knew them all and sang away. I could sing along with a few, but their knowledge was very impressive, and it passed the time and took our minds off our queasy stomachs. We stopped once to eat a sack of oranges we had bought. We found a place by the side of the road under some trees and ate our snack. There was a slight breeze and I unwrapped the saree from my shoulders and just sat with my damp little cotton blouse exposed to the air so the sweat could dry. David had a Super8 movie camera and took footage of us all, laughing and having a grand time.

We stopped once at a spring pouring out of the mountain from a pipe set into a concrete watering place. I ducked my head under it and got my hair wet in order to cool off. We gratefully drank the water, but later we learned that although the spring water may have been pure, it was full of mica and would irritate our intestinal tracts. We had to pee, but there was nowhere to go. We walked down the road, Lillian, Ma, Rindi, Sally, and I, under our umbrellas (to keep out the heat and the sun) and found a rocky place by the side of the road that was insufficiently private, but would have to do. We stopped later in a small village and bought watermelons and cokes. Dr. Sudarshan cut up his watermelon and was trying to eat it, but the buffalos in the street tried to take the pieces from him. The villagers stared at us. We were the first Westerners to visit up there in thirty years, and many of them had never seen one before: white ladies wearing sarees, pale-faced blond men in blue suits and red ties.

By late afternoon we reached the village where we would spend the night. It was what is called a hill station, either built by the British or the military. A crowd had gathered and it seems Maharishi was expected. He gave them a talk in Hindi and our men sat arranged on either side of him on some sort of stage, and, as he talked in Hindi, the men, and we women sitting in the front rows of the audience, took this opportunity to meditate. Soon our heads nodded and dropped onto our chests. We may have gotten as far as a mantra or two before we fell asleep from the heat and exhaustion. Someone in the audience asked why, if meditation was so great and gave you so much energy and all that, why were we, his people, all slumped around him, Nandkishore later told us. Maharishi explained that we were worn out from the drive. Embarrassing. We were led to a small room and dinner was placed before us. We were hungry but were almost too tired to eat.

David, Lillian, and I were sent to a room nearby to sleep. David was extraordinarily kind to Lillian. She was doing her best to keep up and stay cheerful and be helpful. Our room had three cots, but no linens, no pillows, no towels. Lillian and I unwrapped our sarees and laid them on the cots like sheets and pulled them back over us. It was too hot to need blankets. We had a room with the kind of floor toilet that you squat over, and a room to wash in. It was a small bare room with a pipe and faucet coming out of the wall and a bucket. That was it. I couldn't believe it, but there was no alternative. Just march on. It was an adventure. Up for breakfast and another day!

Jyotir Math

When we finally arrived near Guru Dev's ashram in Jyotir Math, we stood by while Maharishi entered ceremonially. He had last been there many, many years before with Guru Dev and now he was returning, his mission to spread the knowledge around the world underway, if unfinished. The pandits he had brought with him lined the stone stairway up to the ashram and chanted as he climbed up. He was greeted by the current Shankaracharya, Swami Shantanand Saraswati, and taken to his rooms. We had stepped back into the past in a very foreign country.

Our rooms were in a little guest house in the surrounding town of Jyoshi Math. We called it the Jyoshi Hilton. Our rooms had cots with only a few thongs to support the mattresses. The bus had brought our own (hopefully) bed-bug-free sleeping bags and that would have to do. I don't remember them being uncomfortable but that may have been because I was totally overshadowed by the bathroom. It was a small room with a floor toilet. I was now used to that, but the pipes leading down from above were full of spider webs and large, very large, spiders. You had to keep an eye on those guys and make sure they didn't move while you were in some delicate and vulnerable position. There was a small sink with a cold water faucet, which was dripping, and a sort of shower head on the ceiling right in front of the sink, which was also dripping right on your head when you tried to wash your hands. There was a drain in the floor. Holy smoke!

We assembled for some meal, I guess our first up there, and we waited and waited. Finally, one plate came out. We waited some more. David went to explore. There was a small kitchen (?) with a small man hunched over a small open wood fire, cooking our food, one plate at a time. That day we walked around the ashram following Maharishi as Swami Shantanand showed him around. We visited a famous tree, very ancient, with a cavernous space under the roots, and several other small shrines. There were various saints living around the ashram and they came out in their ochre robes to see Maharishi. They had white hair and beards and looked ancient and timeless. The villagers below spotted David taking movies and were suspicious. Who was that foreigner? What was he doing? He explained to the Indian entourage that he was looking for the ancient shrines and caves he had heard about.

Were our meditations up there fabulous? Don't ask *me*. I don't remember, but I don't think so. We spent our days in the meeting hall of the ashram, sitting without back support on wiry grass mats, the men on one side and the women on the other, traditional ashram style, along with other Indian visitors, men and women. Guru Dev had had that two-story thirty-room building constructed in his time, and we were later shown Maharishi's room when he was there, a simple chamber opening onto the meeting room. When the long days were over, Maharishi would say, go and rest.

We asked Maharishi, what about go and meditate? Oh, you will do that here in the hall. Being in the presence of the Shankaracharya is your meditation, he said. What? There was a loud speaker, constantly blasting the chanting and lecturing from the hall (in Hindi) out to the grounds and the village. There was no silence. None. Inner or outer, as far as I could tell.

Swami Shantanand (it means the bliss of peace or the peace of bliss, I think) sat before us on a large carved raised chair with a canopy over it. He had been named by Guru Dev in his will to be his successor, and although there had been some dissention at the time, Maharishi had made sure the will had been carried out. Maharishi sat to his left on a small raised platform, not as high as Swami Shantanand's. He was a very peaceful, kindly seeming man and he looked out on us with interest. It was painful to sit there hour after hour with my lower back aching. There were some places against the walls, but they were few and always occupied. One day, someone tapped me on my shoulder and pointed me toward David. He had seen an empty spot along the wall and quickly slipped into it and he was motioning me to go there. I gathered up my voluminous, awkward saree skirts and tried to creep surreptitiously past and around and over lots of people in the path. I finally got there, David popped out, I popped in, and I got my saree arranged and looked up. Swami Shantanand had been watching the whole thing and he was smiling and nodding warmly at me.

Once, when the crowds had gone for the day, Swami Shantanand addressed our group, in Hindi, of course, and Maharishi translated. The Shankaracharya said that we were very, very fortunate to be there in that blessed place, the result of many lifetimes of good karma. He lauded our desire to help the world out of its misery, but, he told us, we had to start with ourselves. We had to get enlightened ourselves, first and most importantly, and then we would be in a position to help others. Maharishi didn't tell us everything he said, but Nandkishore filled in some of the details. It seems

Swami Shantanand had told us that we were especially fortunate to have Maharishi as our Guru and had praised him very strongly.

When we were alone with Maharishi on one occasion, David asked him, "How do you feel, Maharishi, coming back here where you were with Guru Dev?" Maharishi answered, "I think of all the things I haven't done yet." "That's exactly how we feel when we come to see you, Maharishi," David said.

The Yagya

Then the day arrived for which we had come. It was an auspicious time to start a new activity and the heavens would supposedly bless that activity with success. We were going to lay the cornerstone (symbolically) for a Capital of the Age of Enlightenment, for a university that would teach Vedic Science there in the Himalayas, and this would be the seed capital for all the rest in the world. Sometime everyone would be able to come up here, Maharishi

Shankaracharya Swami Shantanand Saraswati walking with Maharishi from the ashram to the yagya setting

told us. I think now that he meant to the Himalayas, to the places he would later design and build for meditation.

We walked into the hills behind the ashram, all of us, to the designated location. Shankaracharya Shantanand first stood, then sat in a chair under the trees and Maharishi stood next to him while various saints stood around them. We stood nearby under our umbrellas and watched as the ceremony (*yagya*) unfolded. There was chanting from all four Vedas, and the digging of a hole. Then into the hole went milk, various powders, and a rose, all with appropriate chanting. Unlike the carefully orchestrated puja we had been taught, this performance was considerably looser. Everything would pause as the pandits searched for a particular powder or item and then would resume when it was found.

We were totally absorbed and fascinated by the yagya and it went on and on. David and Martin scrambled around quietly taking Super8 movies and Stephen and the others took pictures. The sun was strong and the day was hot, but we didn't seem to notice. When the ceremony ended we all came back into the present and I noticed that army helicopters had been flying overhead. It seems we were really close to a disputed part of the Himalayas and they were keeping an eye on us. I hadn't heard them at all until that moment. The inner silence had completely dominated my awareness. I later told that to Maharishi and he nodded.

Since we were in a military zone, some high ranking military officials came to see what we were up to. Nat was designated to give them an introductory lecture and explain our presence. They were apparently satisfied and we were allowed to continue up into the region close to Tibet and its Chinese invaders, all the time being closely watched by the Indian government.

Badrinath

Our next stop was farther up into the Himalayas along the Ganges River to the Vishnu temple at Badrinath, one of the holiest pilgrimage sites in India. Somewhat like the Christian Trinity, in India the Godhead has three aspects, as I, a Jewish girl with little interest in traditional religions, understand it: Brahma, the Creator; Vishnu, the Maintainer; and Shiva, the Destroyer. Similarly, the female aspect is also a trinity, Saraswati, Lakshmi, and Durga, all faces of Mother Divine, Devi, the most profound level of divinity. The road was narrow and very winding and had been completely closed to tourists and most other traffic for about thirty years, since the Chinese had invaded Tibet. We saw military vehicles and Tibetan herding families along the road, dressed in black with very colorful trim and accessories, right out of the pages of *National Geographic*. The road had opened up only very recently to pilgrims and travelers and then the army closed it again after we left. We had slipped in through a very short window in time. We had been very fortunate indeed.

We were told that the road was too narrow for two cars or buses so there was a gate system. People would leave from below at a certain time and traffic would be halted from above until the last car came through and then it would be reversed. Ha! So much for the theory. As we headed up, driving on the left-hand side of the road, as in England, and looking down thousands of feet to the river below, we would come face to face with another car or bus. Then we would have to back up until a wide spot in the road could be found, pull onto the slight shoulder on the hillside, and let the other vehicle pass. This happened a number of times and was pretty scary. Better not to look down into the valley way below.

Our destination, the Vishnu temple at Badrinath, was at an altitude of over 10,000 feet, and from there you look up at the snow-covered peaks of the Himalayas, far, far above you. We heard that an early version of the temple had been destroyed by a religious sect, and that the black stone statue of Vishnu had been thrown into the river to save it from destruction. Adi Shankara, the first Shankara, visited there in ancient times, according to the Gita. He took a boat onto the river and pointed down. Divers located the stone where he indicated and brought it up, and Shankara had a new temple built to house that stone and those of other deities. You can look up the temple on Google and see images of it.

We entered by a grand stairway and through a pillared hall to come to the main shrine area, everything carved and beautiful. Just below the temple area were a couple of pools filled with steaming sulfurous water from the hot springs. Pilgrims were supposed to bathe there and purify themselves before entering the temple area. These waters were said to wash away all your sins. We women held back but the guys shed their outer clothes and enthusiastically jumped right in. It's so much simpler to be a man when you are rough traveling. David came out feeling totally pure and transparent and without stress. He went to stand right next to Maharishi, feeling he could stand there and not be overwhelmed by his stresses. A thought popped into his head, as if right from Maharishi, "Take care of Rhoda." Rhoda? He looked around and there I was, freaked out by the crowds closing around me, the strangeness, the foreignness, the whole experience. He came to save me. I always felt comfortable and protected in his presence. I could be at ease if he was close by.

We went from shrine to shrine around the enclosure and the pandits chanted at each one and we sat and listened and asked Nandkishore where we were and what was going on. One shrine was for Adi Shankara, the founder of the four seats of Vedic wisdom (Jyotir Math and three others), Kubera, the god of wealth, the sage Narada, Lakshmi (Mother Divine, consort of Vishnu), and finally the main enclosed Vishnu shrine. Temple guards were there to move people along. You were supposed to go in, see the Vishnu stone, get the darshan for a moment or two, and then move on. Maharishi motioned us to all crowd in there, our whole group and our pandits, and indicated that we were to sit down. The pandits began to chant the *Thousand Names of Vishnu*, a chant that lists all the divine attributes of Vishnu. There was a young woman who happened to come in with us and she also knew the chant and she joined in. The whole things lasts about half an hour. The temple guards gave up trying to move us along, accepted the situation, closed their eyes, and sat down also. It was very profound and intense, like the yagya in Jyotir Math, ringing with human voices and yet full of inner silence. One of the guards told our group that it was the most spiritual thing that had ever happened there.

We were offered the *prasad* from the ceremonies. That means that some of the food that is offered in the ceremony is then given to the celebrants and they eat it and get some of the darshan from the ceremony. Sometimes you get a flower or some other part of the offerings. And lunch. We had lunch somewhere and walked past the vendors selling sweaters and other artifacts, including conchs. Jerry is a trumpet player, and he picked one up and got a good sound out of it. David chose a small war conch with a loud piercing sound (we still have it). The vendors were amazed to see us Westerners there at all, and being able to blow their conchs. We started down the mountain, leaving at the required gate time and having exactly the same experience as we had coming up, only this time we waited while those coming up had to back into a wide space in the road.

Traveling Back to Delhi

As we began our descent back to Delhi, it began to rain and storm. Maharishi commented that nature hadn't wanted us to leave. A landslide covered the road ahead of us and someone had sent for the military. We climbed over the pile of rubble blocking the road and walked to a nearby guest house and sat for hours in the near dark with only candles to light the room and talked with Satyanand, who had been with Guru Dev along with Maharishi, until we got word the road had been cleared and our taxis could continue. We drove down in the early dawn and arrived at the place on the Ganges where we could ferry across to the Academy, but the ferry wasn't running. We walked to the hanging bridge nearby and walked over the river, swinging and bouncing high above the turbulent waters.

When we reached the other side we sat there on the ground with Maharishi and the rest of the group and waited for cars to come for us and the day began to dawn. Finally, tired of waiting, we got up and started to walk toward the Academy. Maharishi rustled some man out of his dreams and asked him to carry our hand luggage. We piled it up on him and he took a few paces, decided never mind, put it down and went back to sleep. We laughed, picked it back up and began walking again. Finally a few cars came along. Maharishi jumped into one and motioned for us to get in also. When we came to his house, he got out and motioned us on to our place. What a night that had been.

Once back at the Academy we rested and recovered from the trip. Sally and I were dehydrated and they brought us water that was supposed to be pure. We filtered it though our handkerchiefs and laughed to see that it was full of the hair from the donkeys that had brought it. Maybe it had been pure, but now it was full of hair and sand. We drank it anyway and liberally salted our food. Then back we went to Delhi to connect with our flight to Switzerland. People at the hotel asked us where we had been and were astounded to hear that we had been to Badrinath. Most people save up for a lifetime to make a pilgrimage to that holy spot. And for many it is still impossible. How fortunate we were. And how ignorant.

When we got back to Switzerland, Dr. Elliot Abravanel told us we most likely had parasites. There are two kinds of people in India, he said, those who know they have parasites and those who don't know they have parasites. He gave us a horrible drug called Flagyl but we survived it. I had brought back Tibetan knitted sweaters for the kids and a shawl for Rachel. Sometime later in Courchevel, our destination that summer, we got to play the videos David and Martin had made for Maharishi, and he had me comment along with the movies. He had told David to make sure everyone got in the picture and David did his best. Unfortunately, since he was the camera man, he was mostly left out.

On the road to Badrinath

Summer in Courchevel, France

WHEN WE ARRIVED back from India Rachel was leaving for TTC in Arosa and everyone else had moved to the Hotel Annapurna in Courchevel in the French Alps. Courchevel is a ski resort in Saint-Bon-Tarentaise, France, the largest linked ski area in the world. Of course, the skiing season was over and the hotels could be rented for our summer courses. There were several villages called Courchevel at different altitudes as you went up the mountain. We were in Maharishi's hotel high up along the hills. I am sure that Maharishi chose that hotel for the summer because of the name. Annapurna is the name of a collection of mountains in the Himalayas in India and Nepal. The Sanskrit name means "full of food." The dining hall at Maharishi International University was named Annapurna when the group moved there from Santa Barbara. *Annapurna devi* is the kitchen goddess, the giver of food; without her there could be starvation. There is a lovely inconspicuous temple to her in Varanasi (Benares or Kashi, as it used to be called) on the Ganges, where all her priests wear richly colored, deep-red vestments. We visited there in 2014 and loved the feeling. We entered into it as an afterthought, and stepping into its quiet rooms from the crowded, busy, and intense walkways around the main Shiva temple was like being sweetly at home.

The Annapurna Hotel would be Maharishi's summer base.

There was a helicopter pad up the hill so he could easily visit all the TTCs and ATRs being held in France and Switzerland that summer of 1975. Everyone in those days kept an ear open for the flutter of helicopter paddles; that meant Maharishi was coming home, or coming to visit your course. The Annapurna was full when we arrived, but Susan managed to get us one room with a king-sized bed and a desk. She had mattresses for the kids placed along the wall on the far side of the room, and so we lived there pretty comfortably for about four or five months. I never complained; we were lucky to be there. Eventually David got an office just down the hall so he could work in peace, and since my MERU responsibilities (housing, cash box, personnel, etc.) were back in Weggis I didn't have much to do except read and search for a dissertation topic and help out as tasks presented themselves. I told Maharishi I was having a difficult time finding something in literature to relate to consciousness. Just take a little from here and there, he said, and put it all together. I thought, he knows nothing about how you write a three-hundred page dissertation, going deeply into one topic, but it turned out that he was right; I did both.

I got to sit in on many meetings in a small meeting hall near the top of the building surrounded with windows looking out on the Alps. It was there that the video guys played our Super8 movies of the trip to Jyotir Math. Maharishi had me comment the movies as they rolled along, and my voice may still be on those tapes. I remember another session where Keith told Maharishi that we finally bought the MIU campus. We bought it? he asked quietly with surprise in his voice. Or so I remember. Could this be right? MIU had moved to Fairfield the summer before. Could it be that papers hadn't actually been signed until then? And it hadn't been checked with him before the final inking of the documents? David says I am misremembering.

There was a school for staff kids (and maybe course kids) about half way down the hill in Pomme de Pin Hotel and a young

Australian initiator named Bevan Morris, who had just arrived, was delegated to drive Nate and Sara down there every morning and bring them back in the late afternoon. Later he became one of the secretaries, one of the boys on the door, filling in gaps as John Cowhig and Ron Decter came and went on various missions.

The lessons and manuals for teaching SCI in schools were a big focus that summer. Maharishi frequently met with that group and gave input on their lessons. Several lessons were to be on great men and women who embodied the qualities of creative intelligence. David should be one of the great men, Maharishi insisted, with the qualities of insight and foresight. David's research and work on the Fundamentals exemplified those qualities. When the earliest versions of that material came out, it was under David's rubric as Vice-Chancellor of MERU and with his signature. David was always embarrassed about his messy signature, but Maharishi thought it looked all right.

Our dear friend Emily Levin, who was one of the 108s, had written the first song of many to come that summer; it was on the Dawn of the Age of Enlightenment. The day after she wrote it, she was eager to play it for Maharishi, who was preparing to leave for the day. He was getting into the elevator and he waved her in and asked her to play the song then and there. He kept beckoning more people into the elevator and as it filled, the guitar neck gradually moved higher and higher until it was completely vertical. She played it like that and sang her song. Maharishi listened, and as the elevator opened, he said "Very good. Teach it to Nate." Nate! Emily dutifully tried to find Nate and get his attention, but he was always running somewhere and didn't want to stop and listen while this lady played her guitar for him. Finally she cornered him and he sat and politely listened. Emily had done her duty. Nate ran off. I don't think he had been inspired to learn the song, Maharishi had his eye on Nate.

Later Emily would write and record many wonderful songs, including a beautiful birthday song that became the movement version of Happy Birthday ("To be born at this time of mankind, when the path to enlightenment lies before you . . . to be blessed with a Master divine . . ."). I fondly remember one she wrote particularly for one of Lillian Rosen's birthdays ("Happy birthday, Lillian, You're one in a million. . .").

Maharishi and the secretaries were very busy that summer of 1975, coming and going. There were several ATR courses there in Courchevel to visit, as well as those in La Plagne, Flaine, and Avoriaz. There was even a European TTC in Isola up in the French Alps north of Nice, and there would be another TTC in Vittel, France, that autumn. Susan Humphrey visited these courses to check on the kitchens and make sure the CPs were happy with the food. She and Marco flew to Biarritz, France, to scout out hotels for the next winter.

Maharishi was going to offer the first AEGTC^SM for a men's group there. That would mean Age of Enlightenment Governor Training Course^SM, six-month courses on the theme of the Yogic Sidhis as described by Patanjali in the Yoga Sutras. The idea was that even though one meditated without any intention, sitting in the transcendent, what Maharishi called the home of all the laws of nature, one had an effect on the larger society. As the source of that effect, we were, despite our imperfections, Governors of the trends of time, and so we would be known after that. As the courses read and reread Patanjali, they began to have experiences of the Sidhis or perfections that Patanjali describes. Maharishi was very interested in hearing these experiences and monitoring how the CPs were coming along.

We in Maharishi's hotel were very busy with another one of his new projects. He wanted to see if any of the alternative medical or non-medical techniques for improving health or expanding consciousness would help us evolve. We were to be the guinea pigs. He invited healers from all over. Daniel Maurin, the national leader of our French movement, brought some kind of alchemists to us, part of a long tradition dating from the Middle Ages. Alchemy was a forerunner to modern chemistry, but it was historically focused on refining gold from baser metals. David was amazed that these ancient "sciences" continued to flourish along with the modern scientific revolution. Who knew? Modern alchemists seemed to be interested in refining consciousness or health by drinking gold. Lesley Goldman and I tried everything.

One initiator brought her father, Dr. Bloodworth, a chiropractor who believed his adjustments would show results in the brain waves. Maharishi insisted that David accommodate him, but the EEG didn't show any noticeable results from a session or two. I had several sessions with him; they always seemed to help my lower back. Massage therapists came (yummy!) and numerous others. Lesley remembers one of the Greek initiators, Taman, leading a group up into the hills, insisting they walk barefoot on the grass, put their faces in the grass and breathe it all in. Grounding? Chlorophyll?

And various kinds of fasting. We did an extensive grape juice fast. That was delicious, but when we were deep into it, Krishna's birthday came along. That year it fell on August 29. The Indians around Maharishi would always celebrate the day by making trays and trays of Indian sweets, and we were all told to enjoy, in spite of the fast!

That summer Maharishi opened the door to healers, energy workers, body workers, and supplements, and I ran right through that door and am still running to this day. Faithful to my program, to be sure, but interested in anything that might enhance my progress, health, and comfort. More recently, during the founding of the movement's new medical school program, Maharishi told Keith and the others to explore any modality that was proven to be successful, to be open to any techniques that would help with the evolution of consciousness and mind-body coordination.

MIU and Niagara Falls

David and I even had a brief stint as secretaries in late September. Maharishi wanted to take a group of us to visit MIU and South

Fallsburg, where the movement was buying a new facility. I found myself in charge of plane tickets, the travel roster, and other details. Once David and I popped into Maharishi's rooms to ask some questions about the trip and check some details and there he was sitting on the asana mat on the floor. That was a lesson to me. Asanas often got forgotten in my busy family life. Maharishi was busier than any of us and yet he found time to do the asanas!

There would be a big group of us going on this tour to the U.S.: Maharishi and his secretaries and other staff like Vesey Crichton from England (who had been around for some time and on the Jyotir Math trip as well), Rindi, Sally, Michael Dimick (whose family had been instrumental in purchasing MIU), and some others. Maharishi meant for Dmitri Kanellakos to go, but somehow he didn't make it onto the list. I got gently chided later for

Maharishi meeting with MIU faculty and staff. Behind him are Michael Dimick (left), Vesey Crichton (center) and John Gorup on the right. My mother is sitting along the wall with a big purse on her lap. Jerry Jarvis is standing and facing Maharishi. I think I am the person two back from Jerry.

forgetting that (sorry, Dmitri). I hadn't seen my mother in a while and I asked Maharishi if she could come to MIU and join us there for the visit. Yes, he said. Some initiator should bring her from Cleveland. He didn't want her to travel alone. I called the TM center in Cleveland and one of the guys, John Gorup, I believe, was thrilled to be able to escort my mom and be part of Maharishi's inner circle for a few days. Maharishi met with the faculty a couple of times and my mother got to sit in on those meetings and spend a little time with us before we moved along.

We felt very comfortable and at home on the MIU campus. Sally, David, and I walked around smelling the rich vegetation of the Midwest and enjoying the late Indian summer sunshine. One of my Facebook friends remembers that while we were there with Maharishi the weather was unusually gorgeous. He accompanied the entourage to the airport, and, he says, the very second Maharishi's plane left the ground, a cold wind and blizzard blew in.

Sally and I were Midwesterners and it all seemed very familiar to us; it was our laws of nature. Little did we suspect that we would be living there a mere two years later. When you are with Maharishi you think you will never do anything else, be anywhere else. The "now" is all consuming and you just don't or can't think of leaving. Ever. But once we climbed aboard the movement jet, so to speak, we were living in the gap, ready to go in any direction at any time. Life could change utterly with a knock on the door or a phone call.

From MIU our little group went to New York and we drove some campers along the Hudson Valley to South Fallsburg, a small hamlet in the Catskills. We visited a hotel complex there that was for sale. That area used to be very popular with New York Jews. They would take their families up for the whole summer and the husbands would work in the city and come up on the weekends. These hotels and others like them were called the Borscht Circuit. This era was over and the whole area was up for sale. Other spiritual movements were buying hotels there as well.

An older couple owned the hotel we were visiting. They had hosted the summer crowds for years and proudly showed us around the place. They were particularly eager for us to see their dining room, which was lavishly decorated with plastic flower arrangements, plastic grape vines going up the walls. We were all rather disgusted (they would be the first things to go!), but Maharishi praised them and the whole place. He was uplifting them and being kind, as he always was. They were clearly unhappy to have to sell their home and business and Maharishi was soothing their feelings. The movement did buy it in the end, and allowed them to live in their family home on the grounds until they were ready to give it up. We visited some other hotels, too, and one of them had guests, some older people playing shuffleboard. Maharishi studied them. "They are playing like children," he said. He couldn't believe that people in the wisest time of life would be satisfied playing childish games when they could be pursuing knowledge and their personal evolution and working to improve society. What kind of culture was this?

From there we drove north to Niagara Falls, which Maharishi really liked and had visited before. I think the Falls are holy somehow, and there is a delicious celestial quality in the rushing and spraying water. We stopped at a gift shop and there was a tank with oysters in it. You could select one; if there was a pearl in it, you got to keep the pearl. Maharishi asked Michael to select some for the ladies in our party. He pointed, they opened, and there was a pearl. The woman helping us was amazed. Pearl after pearl. It had never happened like that before. We got enough for all of us. Maharishi handled them all, blessing them, I think, gave them back to Michael, and Michael kept them until they were handed out to us later that autumn back on Lake Lucerne.

I got the last or second to last choice, after all the 108s who had been with us. There were two pearls left, a little one, and a large rose one with a black spot but lovely nacre. I chose that one and David and I drove to Lucerne that winter and found a jeweler to mount it on a post. The post went through the black spot and it disappeared. I showed it to Maharishi and he handled it and liked it, but, he said, the pearl should touch my finger, not stand above the ring. That was for jyotish purposes (Indian astrology), but we didn't know anything about jyotish at the time. Well, the pearl often slipped to one side and touched my other finger so I didn't seriously think about having it reset. I still treasure that ring, although I have worn it a lot and chipped the nacre in my busy, rushing, careless way.

The kids missed us while we were at MIU. Rachel was on her TTC and although there was someone on staff to take care of them when they came back to the hotel after their day at the little school, they were sad. Lillian was very kind to them, and she sent a message to me to call them and reassure them we would be back soon.

Winter on Lake Lucerne

We returned to the lake for the winter of 1975–76, or so we thought, and were housed in Seelisberg. When David and I drove into Lucerne to get my pearl set in a ring, wonder of wonders, I found a small portable washing machine in one of the department stores. You may laugh, but *you* didn't have to do laundry and I did. The little tub sat in the bathtub, you plugged it in, and it swirled the clothes and soapy water around and around. When you were ready to rinse, you put it under the faucet, turned it on, and ran the clear water into it. Eventually all the soapy water overflowed and the clothes were rinsed clean. They just had to be wrung out and hung up to dry. I was very happy and proud of my machine. Nandkishore heard about it and came to see it. He was responsible for washing and ironing Maharishi's silk dhoties. He looked at it dubiously. Not for him. He would continue to hand wash.

Maharishi had begun offering the AEGTC courses then to develop the Sidhis, the perfections, in the Governors. These replaced the usual ATR courses. From the Yoga Sutras of Patanjali, Maharishi developed the idea that by working within consciousness, one could effect changes in the self and in the outer world. One might ask the body and mind to do something it might not be able to do, but in the attempt to do it, the physiology and psychology would be challenged, and in the process, more fully integrated and evolved. Stresses would be thrown off, perception would be refined, and enlightenment would be developed.

A Family Holiday

That autumn Maharishi was going off to visit a men's AEGTC in Biarritz, France, and a group of us were going to go along, including the kids! We got on a small plane and flew to Biarritz. We got there late at night and we were taken to Maharishi's meeting rooms to wait for him until he came in. I sat in a big chair and Sara climbed onto my lap and promptly fell asleep. Maharishi came in and everyone stood up except me. I was pinned down by a heavy, five-year-old sleeping child and I didn't want to disturb her. I felt bad about not standing up to greet him properly, but what could I do? I was hoping he wasn't thinking I was disrespectful.

We had a few lovely, sunny days in Biarritz together. Maharishi met with the course and David got to sit in on some of the experience meetings. A young man named Andy Rhymer was known for having very good experiences and he stood up and told Maharishi that he experienced being with Jesus around the time of the crucifixion, that he was one of those people there then. Oh, yes, Maharishi said dismissively, we all were, and went on to other things. Maharishi was developing what would later be formalized into the TM-Sidhi program.

We borrowed a car one afternoon and took the kids to the beach. It was very late autumn or early winter but the weather was unusually sunny and warm. We played on the sand with John and Sarah Konhaus and David remembers going into the water and turning his back on the surf. He then noticed we were all watching him with horror. A big wave hit and he was tumbled into the surf. We had lunch at a café and even took a drive into Spain, since the border was very close by. It was the time of the Basque rebellion and the streets were full of soldiers armed with machine guns. We quickly turned around and went back into France. It was just a little treat for us to go there and play together as a family instead of leading our separate busy lives, and David got a peek inside one of these new courses.

Maharishi left us in Seelisberg for a while and went back to MIU, this time for the First International Conference on Science and Consciousness. He had the faculty there give talks in their area and then he connected them to SCI. It was a grand training session for them. Sy Migdal gave the talk on literature and Maharishi's response is included in the book *The Flow of Consciousness: Maharishi Mahesh Yogi on Literature and Language* (MUM Press, 2010 that Susan Andersen and I wrote later). This would be volume I of the series Consciousness, Knowledge, and Enlightenment: Selected Lectures of Maharishi Mahesh Yogi. Michael Cain spoke on art and Maharishi's response is in the second book of the series, *The Unmanifest Canvas: Maharishi Mahesh Yogi on the Arts, Creativity and Perception 1970–2006* (Lee Fergusson and Anna Bonshek, MUM Press, 2014). These are insightful and brilliant talks and I hope more books follow in the series: music, law, government, sustainable living.

Nobel Laureates in Weggis

One of MERU's physicists, Alex Hankey (who had trained under Nobel Laureate Steven Weinberg at MIT) had the idea for a similar symposium at MERU in Switzerland just before Christmas, which he thought might be called Evolutionary Models of Nature. He suggested inviting his friend Nobel Laureate Brian Josephson, professor of physics at Cambridge University, and Larry could call Dr. George Sudarshan, who was director of the Center for Particle Theory at the University of Texas at Austin and professor of physics at the Indian Institute of Science in Bangalore, India, the Indian equivalent of Cambridge, as well as visiting physics professor at MERU. We also had our own space scientist, John Lewis, who came with his family, and who held a double professorship at MIT and was later put in charge of NASA's missions to the outer planets. These three would then attract other top scientists, Alex believed.

René Thom and Ilya Prigogine accepted our invitation. René Thom was widely considered to be the leading mathematician of our time, known for developing the basis for singularity theory and catastrophe theory (don't ask!) and Ilya Prigogine was head of the Department of Physical Chemistry at the University Libre de Bruxelles in Belgium and also Director of the Solvay Institute. He was famous for his work on dissipative structures and complex systems, and was awarded the Nobel Prize in 1977 for discoveries in non-linear thermodynamics. (You can look this up, but briefly he figured out how order is surprisingly created in physical systems under certain conditions. Heated oil creates channels in the liquid for heat dissipation, just as heated water in the Gulf of Mexico creates channels in the air to dissipate heat, phenomena we call hurricanes. Or how termites, aware of little bits of wood, would add their piece, and somehow without an architect, a huge termite nest would be built). Alex thought they would be able to appreciate our manner of talking about TM as creating a low entropy experience (less entropy, more order) in the transcendent. Larry would present that and Maharishi would preside.

The symposium was a great success. Maharishi used the occasion to honor Professor K.P. Sinha from the Indian Institute of Science in Bangalore, by giving him the Maharishi Award for Physics, 1975. Larry gave a talk at the symposium and so did our new physicist Dr. Geoffrey Clements. The talks were brilliant and all the scientists, including Drs. Thom and Prigogine, were eager to hear Maharishi's response to their theories. As Vice-Chancellor of MERU, David (and I) helped welcome and entertain them and found them to be very natural, friendly and comfortable around us all. René Thom was a big bear of a man, but very sweet and humble. They all seemed to really be enjoying the symposium. David clearly remembers them vying for Maharishi's attention and being very appreciative of his understanding of their fields and his intuitive comments on their work. Maharishi was impressed that Prigogine and Thom had come to our little conference. When it was over, he asked David how this conference had come about. It was Alex's idea, David told him. David reported that Alex thought that with Josephson and Sudarshan on the program, perhaps other really top scientists would come to join them and at least have the occasion to talk to them if nothing else. Maharishi laughed.

There were frequent small meetings in the Seeblick or Alexander Hotels with Maharishi in those days, and that was when I showed him the pearl ring. Immediately after January silence, once again everything changed. Much to our surprise, David and I, other couples, and the ladies group, including many 108 ladies, were all put on a bus and moved away from Maharishi to Interlaken to begin our own AEGTC course there. We were going to be Governors of the Age of Enlightenment! Hopefully.

Governor Training

IT WAS EARLY WINTER 1976 and here we were in Interlaken once again. We had three small rooms in a row in our hotel. Child-care was set up and we started to do the new program, rounding, of course, with some new techniques and angles. Maharishi frequently came to meet with our group, and with the men's group in another town, and the various TTCs, of course. When you are deep in meditation, he told us, desire to be in the far corner of the room and see if you are found there. I never was. We frequently met with Maharishi and the ladies in our hotel and we talked about Yogic Flying® and invisibility and various other special powers. He wanted to hear all of our experiences. One of the older 108s, Joan Meechum, had joined the course and she was very vocal. She had been on TTC in India in 1970. (Maharishi sent her to Roydon Hall in England later when she needed assistance and they took care of her for years. One of my Facebook friends remembers her there in 1990, and she was well taken care of by the staff.) The whole point, however, was to challenge the physiology to do something beyond its current ability and therefore urge it to new levels of integration, purification, and growth.

One of our friends, Vernon Barnes, told me that he was teaching TM in Calgary and wanted to go to one of these courses. He took a loan on his house for $25,000 and used it to put TM ads in the media, hoping to cash in on the excitement that had followed the Merv Griffin show. In exchange for this, all of the initiators who would enjoy the rise in initiations, and therefore the resultant income, agreed to give him their ATR credits to be used toward his course fee. It was a gamble, but it worked. Vernon paid off his loan, Calgary became a one percent city, and Vernon had the credits to go to his AEGTC. Vernon later got his PhD and has written and published a number of excellent studies on the effects of TM on cardiovascular disease (especially in adolescents at risk for cardiovascular disease, which is important for prevention). He showed that TM changed how they responded to stress: less rise in blood pressure and heart rate, and ideally, less disease in adulthood. He also published a paper on the effects of TM on war veterans with PTSD. It reduced their need for psychotropic drugs (among other benefits).

On January 12, 1976, Maharishi was going to celebrate the Year of World Government, not on Lake Lucerne in a big ship like last year, but in a huge hall in Lucerne. Everyone wanted to go, so a bus was made available from our course in Interlaken to go to the celebration in Lucerne and come back later that night. The bus trip would take over an hour each way. I was rather reluctant to go on a long bus ride, come back late, and be exhausted the next day and sleep through my rounds. I stayed home, but David went. Maharishi was training and had promoted a new crop of people who were sitting on the stage along with some of the old ones; there was no special seat or welcome for David. He was a spectator, meant to focus on his evolution, I would guess, and not be involved in the movement's affairs at this time. Also, in retrospect, I believe Maharishi was doing what he could for our personal evolution before he sent us off to MIU.

Sara began to have stomach pains and Dr. Eberhard came to check on her. He feared it could be appendicitis but he wanted to be sure before he subjected her to doctors and hospitals. She had a little fever, wasn't eating, and was losing weight. I went in to check on her in the middle of one night and there he was by her bedside, quietly checking her stomach while she slept, listening with his stethoscope for gurgling that would indicate that there was no blockage and that things were moving along all right. David went down into the kitchen and cooked her a bowl of oatmeal the next morning and she started to mend quickly. When Sara was better, but still in her bathrobe, I took her to the big meeting in the hall and put her up on the stage so she could walk over to Maharishi and give him a flower. He was very pleased to see her looking well. He had been monitoring her progress. All of our progress, to be sure. He wanted to hear what was going on with all of us.

On February 23, 1976, on Lesley Goldman's birthday, she remembers, Maharishi gave one of his fabulous talks. This one was on the fullness of fullness and the fullness of emptiness (please don't ask!). He was pleased and a little surprised that this deep knowledge emerged at this place and time. Ah, he said, it is because we were in Interlaken (between the lakes), between Lake Thun, the Thunersee, and Lake Brienz, the Brienzersee, between two fullnesses. And he was before a group of people doing deep and long meditations and open to such knowledge, drawing it out of him.

When it came time to leave Interlaken, our car was off somewhere, put to some other uses since we were rounding. The four of us were put on a bus with Emily Levin, Meredith Williams, and the other 108 ladies on our course and told to drive toward Zurich and call back in hour. We did, and then we were told to keep driving and call back in another hour. This went on for most of the day. We were getting weary. Apparently negotiations for midseason hotels were not yet settled. One just the size of our group had not yet been contracted. Finally, we were sent to a hotel in Zurich where we had a memorable vegetarian dinner (a little pile of peas, a little pile of carrots, and a little mound of potatoes) and spent the night. At breakfast Meredith announced that she had discovered the perfect diet: eat whatever you want and move every day. Dr. Elliot Abravanel was working on a diet book and

Meredith thought he should include her discovery. After breakfast we were finally directed to the Goldey Hotel (back in Interlaken!) on the banks of the Aare River, which actually was contained in a little canal on its way through the city and past our hotel.

The hotel was small and charming and the food was pretty good. We had a balcony overlooking the canal, bare trees, and the wintery landscape. Still, it was beautiful and often sunny, and we had a lovely time there. The ladies were kind to the kids and we had no nanny so the kids played around the hotel and we walked all over town. I remember one trip to the laundromat. All of Sara's Swiss dresses were in the wash and she wouldn't put on anything else that was clean. I think she was upset by the constant moving and wanted something loved and familiar to wear. She sat in her underwear on one of the machines and cried until her dresses went through the washing and drying cycles. The Swiss ladies looked at me with horror and obvious disapproval.

On one of our walks along the river we passed a little old lady on the street, bent over and barely able to shuffle along. Sara pointed to her. She had never seen anyone like her. All she knew were the young women around Maharishi and the spry older guests like Lillian. What is the matter with her, Mom, she asked. Oh, I said, she hasn't been doing her asanas and she has gotten all stiff.

On Easter Sunday, we staged a little Easter egg hunt for the kids and that afternoon Nate was invited on a walk with Meredith and Joan Meechum. He was comfortable walking around town with them and took a picture of them with Meredith's camera. He was very interested in cameras and knew all about them. Watches too. He would look at everyone's watch and pry into the details of what they paid, how good it was, and so forth. He had an encyclopedic memory.

Exploring Perfection

In March we were moved out of the Goldey and were separated from the ladies. We got our car back briefly and we moved up into the Alps to Davos, another ski resort town. Paul and Josie Fauerso had arrived in Interlaken and drove with us and the Sandels up to Davos. June and Lincoln Norton joined our couples course, too. Maharishi visited us in the Seehof Hotel in Davos on May 22, and gave us a very inspiring talk. I scribbled fast to keep up with his speech. He was explaining the value of the TM-Sidhi program (why anything is possible with the Sidhis, the perfections we were attempting to develop). He began with concepts with which we were already familiar. Physics tells us, he reminded us, that the observer changes the object observed. Larry Domash had often described the phenomenon in quantum mechanics that when the observer observes the object, it becomes selected or fixed. Until then it is in the field of possibility. The non-localized wave function of all possibilities becomes a discreet, localized particle. Looking at it pins it down.

Vedic Science fills in the story, Maharishi told us. As perception becomes more and more refined through transcending (keep to the course routine; rounding is the key, he insisted), then subjectivity imposes itself on objectivity. The object comes to mirror the consciousness of the subject, the knower. The world is as you are, he insisted. If the knower is fully living himself, then the object is fully enlivened in his consciousness. Whenever you look at anything, you see Being, your own Self. If pure consciousness is permeating everywhere, everything, then liveliness follows. One area lively, another area lively, like the twinkling of a star. Then twinkle, twinkle everywhere, the twinkling of the entire universe at the same time: twinkle, twinkle total star. This is Unity Consciousness: "The total universe breathes with every breath of the knower."

Unity Consciousness can be developed through the mechanics of observation. The process of observation, of knowing, is what structures the mechanics of living Unity Consciousness, the enlivenment of silence in the field of activity. If the subject (knower) is crystal clear Being, then the object seen changes into the value of Being, and this change can be observed by the knower. The object is seen in terms of the Self: this makes Unity Consciousness.

So whatever you want to do to the object, he said, you must do it to yourself. If you want to do something somewhere, in the relative field, you must do it in the Self. No effort needed. Do everything where you are. Refinement of perception is the important thing. When the object is seen in terms of the Self, then the Self has doubled itself. In ignorance, the subject is annihilated by the object. When perception is crude, it is a means of bondage; the object can localize and trap unbounded awareness. Only the object is perceived and not the Self. In liberation (Unity Consciousness) the subject is doubled in the object. The object mirrors the subject. It all hinges on how sharp perception is, how refined it is. The world is the same. The mechanics are the same. What changes is the knower. When the knower changes, life changes. Stress blurs perception; what takes away stress is rounding. Just follow instructions. Simple. Go by the routine. The field of all possibilities awaits us.

By refining perception we develop microscopic vision, Maharishi said, which can locate the parts within the wholeness of our own Being. If perception can be refined to the level of perception *in the field of the transcendent*, then the whole play of life can be seen in the transcendent. In the state of least excitation of consciousness, consciousness flows without flowing, without friction, without loss of energy, the same from start to goal, and then the object is found in the sameness of the Self, subject and object are infinitely correlated, and this is Unity Consciousness. I do not believe our experiences at that point justified this wave of knowledge, although perhaps some of us were ready for this knowledge. Maharishi was speaking to the future, not just to us, recording himself for generations to come.

Gaining knowledge is the great art of living, Maharishi explained. Physics has evolved to the level that it provides a scientific understanding of the basis of refined consciousness, that everything is compactified in Being. Physics finds that the reality of the totality of natural law is present in unmanifest form as the virtual fluctuations in the vacuum state (we weren't yet talking about the unified field; that would come later). These fluctuations contain all possibilities of natural law, all possibilities existing together in an unmanifest form. In the Vedic literature, in the Puranas, the same ancient story is told. *Puran* means ancient. *Being* is the ancient one, Maharishi explained. Everything else is a fluctuation of that. The Puranas talk about behavior in the field of Being. They sing the glory of the unmanifest.

At the time, we understood very little of the Puranas, that branch of Vedic literature. That would come later. And as for myself, the refinement of perception in or out of the transcendent, was very abstract and outside my sphere of experience. In fact, this whole vision of the advanced stage of the evolution of consciousness, and the experiences that were beginning to be reported by the evolving meditators, would be the focus of the Invincible America Assembly which would begin in 2006. For now, it was inspiring, while, for many of us, the experiences he described were out of our range, out in the twinkling stars. We rounded. We did our asanas. Hotels were changing. I packed and the couple/family course moved to Mürren.

Research Personal and Experimental

We settled into the grand Palace Hotel in Mürren. There was a cute group of children there, including the Jump kids, little Michael Dreben, whose parents were national leaders of the TM organization in Canada at the time, and others. There didn't seem to be a beginning or end to the course, just an evolving continuum. Spring was coming to the Alps and we could walk the trails with the kids after lunch and dinner. If you held out your hand with birdseed in it, little birds would fearlessly perch on your fingers and eat the seeds. I have to say I remember very little of the whole course. We were rounding and the days slipped one into the other. The only excitement was when Maharishi came to see us.

One day we heard that hot air balloons would be taking off near the hotel very early in the morning. We waited with the kids in one of passageways overlooking the fields filled with these beautiful, colorful, huge balloons. David and the kids went down for a closer look. One of the balloonists offered to take David along; they would land somewhere in Italy. David was tempted but baffled by what he would have to do in Italy to get back to the course. We waited patiently and finally the big creatures lifted soundlessly into the skies and floated off. It was the silence and the beauty of it all that we remember best. Back to our rooms and the program!

Even though he was rounding, David was still directing the research going on in MERU. This seems to be his lifelong rounding program. I could just give myself to the course and to the children (and to the laundry, of course), but David's responsibilities never seem to cease. Russell Hebert and Chris Haynes were carrying on with the EEG research in Weggis. They were measuring synchrony and coherence, but nobody knew what they were good for in those days. Most scientists of the time thought that the more complex the brain waves were the more intelligent or active the person might be. But if meditators were increasing in coherence, as Paul Levine had shown, then it must be a good thing. Meditators were certainly more creative, so why not look at that?

As part of MERU's mission to do research on higher states of consciousness, David and his team had been routinely testing the initiators who came on ATR, and now on the AEGTCs, giving them standardized tests of creativity, intelligence, and whatever they had available, as well as measuring their EEG coherence. The boys had also measured some Swiss non-meditators and found they were also high in coherence. Of course, our Swiss lab tech Urs Stroebel said, they are *Swiss*. David had the insight that Russell and Chris should look at the correlation between coherence above a 95% threshold and creativity. Would there be a strong relationship between coherence and other positive measures? He ran the idea through his rounding brain, and like cherries rolling up and down in a slot machine, the number slid up and down and landed on .71. He told Russell that the correlation would be about .71 (1.0 would be perfect correlation, so anything that high would be significant.). The next day Russell called. It was exactly .71!! Very highly correlated, and more correlations would be found with high coherence over the years, both psychological and physiological; it was even related to moral reasoning.

What about higher states of consciousness? David set them to make a questionnaire asking the initiators about experiences of Cosmic Consciousness. Were they unbounded witnesses to waking, dreaming, or sleeping? Data was gathered, the experiences were rated, and yes, there was a correlation between high coherence and the best reports of higher states of consciousness. It was the first look into this area. A recent book confirms that high coherence and its associated qualities are found in the top people of every field, from music to athletics, and that TM increases coherence. Take a look! *Excellence through Mind-Brain Development. The Secrets of World-Class Performers* by Harald Harung and Frederick Travis (Gower, 2015).

Neurobiologist John Farrow had the idea of looking closely to what happens with the EEG and breath when a person transcends. Well, you can't know that until after they come out of the transcendent, so John had our old friend Theresa Olson, Mother Olson's youngest daughter, push a button when she realized she had just transcended to unbounded consciousness. There, just before the button press was high coherence and a long pause in her breathing, not stopping exactly but becoming a mere flutter for maybe forty to sixty seconds, and no gasps afterward, just a subtle transition back to normal quiet breathing. This had never been seen before. They were beginning to understand coherence and what it might mean. Fast forward to today, researchers are just now realizing that brain wave coherence is responsible for organizing the whole brain, like a conductor managing the whole orchestra, and is responsible for better motor and perceptual performance, learning and a host of other important activities. TM increases it. They are finally catching up to us. David was a visionary.

In one small group meeting David told Maharishi he was having some good experiences but also an awful lot of unstressing. Maharishi nodded. When the Ganges floods, he said, it stirs up a lot of mud. The supply seemed to be endless!

A couple of professional writers arrived to see Maharishi in Seelisberg. They had written a number of popular books and they wanted to cash in on all the interest in TM. They had gotten their publisher interested in a so-called TM Diet book and they came to research it. Maharishi didn't want to spend time with them. They wouldn't be a help to the World Plan; they would just waste his time. So he sent them to Mürren to talk to Dr. Orme-Johnson, Director of Research, etc., etc. David showed them around and took them to the dining rooms, explaining that there was no particular TM diet. There were no special requirements. We all ate healthy vegetarian food like yogurt and seasonal vegetables and honey and nuts. Oh, well, they said, at least we came to a beautiful place. If this were to happen now, we would emphasize organic and non-GMO food as being essential to health and evolution.

This wasn't the first time someone had come around hoping to make money or fame from some association with the movement. I heard Maharishi dismiss these attempts with a smile: When a tree grows big and tall, every little dog wants to lift his leg against it, he said. Every little dog wants to mark it as his own territory.

An Intimate Year with Maharishi

IT WAS MID-JUNE 1976 and time to come down from rounding. Our six months were up and we had things to do, like get the *Collected Papers* off to the Press. Before we were fully back into activity we got word that we should come back for the semi-annual National Leaders' Conference. We really weren't needed, of course, but it was an excuse to get us moving. The conference was to be held in the grand hall in the Sonnenberg in Seelisberg, which had been completely rebuilt and redecorated, and we found that Maharishi had created a new movement with new staff and a new order of things. This would happen again and again over the years. He said he could create a new movement every day if he chose to do so. Vesey Crichton passed me a note telling me it had all changed radically. Maharishi was living in the Kulm Hotel and no women were allowed in there, just members of the men's section of the World Government (which meant the upper administration of the global movement). The Ladies World Government (they had their role also) was in Arosa, as were the couples AE-GTC and the "clear" men's AEGTC. There were TTCs in Avoriaz and Austria, and probably other places as well. Greg Conaway, an initiator and helicopter pilot, and his wife Vicki had arrived and Greg would be taking Maharishi around to all the courses. We had no idea what our role would be in all of this.

Maharishi was preparing to offer a version of the AEGTC to meditators in various formats. What would we call those meditators? Not Governors. That would only apply to initiators who had taken the course. At one small meeting in the Seeblick before we moved up to Seelisberg I suggested Citizens, Citizens of the Age of Enlightenment. He loved it. It stuck.

The Chalet Antique

The Seeblick had also been renovated and restructured and was full of MERU labs, personnel, displays, and staff, so we were put in a guest house a little to the east and right across the street from Lake Lucerne called the Chalet Antique, and antique it was. It had eleven tiny rooms, which even included a second unused kitchen upstairs. The ceilings were low, maybe under seven feet, and doorway lintels were even lower, under six feet. David had to duck his head passing through them. There was no real living room, just a room with straight-backed chairs lining the walls, but we had a kitchen and we had quiet and privacy and could cook, or bring food over from the Seeblick. We could be a family again, just us. There were no screens on the windows and the mosquitos would come buzzing around our ears and wake us up. I went to Lucerne and bought nylon curtains and we pinned them up on all the bedroom windows. A Dutch boy named Paul was sent over to take care of the kids and they had a grand time swimming in the lake. Our house had a lot and dock across the street right on the lake and figs were ripening on the trees there. For the first time we were here on Lake Lucerne in the season, in the summertime, and it was warm and beautiful and full of tourists. I began to think seriously about really living in Switzerland from now on. I envied those beautiful houses along the lake. Might we live in one of those someday? How, I couldn't imagine.

David and I were finishing up the last writing and proofing of the *Collected Papers* and it was nearly ready to go to the Press. There was also a researcher from India finalizing his research on

TM and athletics and David was asked to help him turn his study into a viable research paper. His wife was with him and the weeks went by until it was finally finished. They were eager to return home to their children, but somehow it took forever.

We made frequent trips over to Seelisberg, but I somehow missed the best event. My birthday falls on July 6 and we should have dressed up, driven over to Seelisberg to see Maharishi, to give him flowers and all that. But the kids didn't want to drive there and wait around all day. They wanted to celebrate with just the family on the lake. As it turned out Professor Peter Malekin, a Lecturer at the University of Durham and long-time initiator from England, was visiting and Maharishi sat with him in the big hall and they talked for hours about literature. If I had gone over for my birthday I would have been part of that discussion. Add this to my list of mistakes and lost opportunities. The transcribed talk, however, is included in my book *The Flow of Consciousness*. How it got into the book is a whole other story, which I will tell in its proper place.

Maharishi told us later that month that David was appointed by the trustees to be the new president of MIU and that we would be going there in a few weeks to live in the big president's mansion on Burlington Avenue just off the square in Fairfield. David was actually the second president of MIU. Little known fact. A few years later, riding around in a taxi in India with Keith and David, Larry would joke, "Everyone in this taxi has been president of MIU, except the driver." The kids were excited: America, Superman, kids who spoke English. But first, David's parents were coming to visit us. They were on a trip to Africa and would arrive August 3. We moved them into the Chalet with us and Pop bumped his head dozens of times on the low lintels. He was losing his sharp mind, but we weren't aware of it at the time. We boated around on the lake and went swimming and took short trips to other sights and walking trails. Nate was in his own little heaven. He loved walking around with his grandpa. Pop always jingled the coins and keys in his pockets as he walked, and to Nate that music meant ice cream, candy, treats, love.

The end of the summer came and David and I strolled around on the lake soaking in the warmth and beauty of it and seeing it as if for the last time, nostalgically and sad to think of leaving Maharishi and Switzerland. Somehow the weeks went by and we didn't leave. Lenny and Lesley Goldman were supposed to go with us yet we stayed and they left for MIU; Lenny would be Executive Vice-president. Susan Humphrey was asked to go there too and be part of the administration. We were in a meeting with Maharishi in the Sonnenberg one day, and there was talk of us going soon. Inside I cried out, not yet, Maharishi. I am not ready to go. I am not ready to be on my own. He knew my heart, I am sure. We were to stay for another year, a very important and evolutionary year. There had been a silent and subtle but very definite movement of Americans out of Seelisberg and out of Maharishi's immediate entourage and back to America. We observed it. We speculated why. We were to be some of the very last Americans to leave.

Moving Up to Seelisberg

At the end of the summer we were moved into the smallest of the three hotels the movement possessed in Seelisberg, but didn't actually own, as I understood it. Maharishi was in the Kulm with the men, staff and administrators; the top ladies (I called them the Rindis because they were always in a group around her, all dressed in sarees) had been moved from their summer quarters in Arosa to the Sonnenberg, and we and other couples and staff were in the Pilgerheim. There was a glassed-in passageway from the Kulm to the Sonnenberg over the little road that bisected the village. Maharishi met with scientists, couples, and everyone in the grand Sonnenberg auditorium or in the smaller Gold Room or the Pink Room. Outside there was a park with benches looking down on Lake Lucerne, and a candy shop, and other small hotels and guesthouses ranged along the small road leading down from our hotels. Way down below, directly on Lake Lucerne, was a mead-ow called the Rutli, which legend describes as the place where the Swiss Federation took birth. The kids climbed down there with some of the European staff. There was also a boat station there for catching a ferry to Brunnen across the lake, a connection to trains to Zurich and the north, or other towns farther on.

We lived there about a year, and I can see our rooms clearly in my mind. David's and mine was on the second floor northeast corner. There was a defunct shower in the corner of the room full of boxes of research papers, Fundamentals, and other papers. My twin bed was on the right; David's was on the left, and there was a big desk for David in front of the windows looking onto the lake. We were in a little area of several rooms and a door to the hallway. We had Lawrence Sheaff's mother (Baba) next to us, Nick and Nan White across the hall, and a full bathroom we all shared.

We were also given two additional rooms out the door and down the hallway, one for the kids and presumably one for me. Not even connecting rooms, but rooms through that door and down a hallway. I was spoiled by having our own little home on the lake, and although Sara was six and Nate would be nine that October, that was too far away for the kids to be. I offered those two rooms to Nick and Nan in exchange for their double room across from us and we switched so the kids could be close to our room. That wasn't how it was done! I hadn't consulted the hous-ing office. I was used to being the housing director for MERU in the Seeblick and I just went ahead. Wrong! We got to keep the kids' room but Nick and Nan lost those two rooms and were moved into a double somewhere else.

Baba was a very sweet person and the English ladies would often come over to take afternoon tea with her. She was very tiny and Lawrence was very tall; it boggled the imagination to think about tiny Baba producing such a large son, the youngest and tall-est of eight, I think. We enjoyed having her there, but sometime the next summer she went back to England, and we got her room, so we had the whole little closed off area to ourselves just before we left. We got a Dutch boy named Marcel to be the kids' teacher and he had Nate reading the *Odyssey* and modern novels, whatever he could find in English, appropriate or not. His girlfriend was taking care of a little boy whose mother worked for the Press, so they all played and worked together in the kids' room.

Nate was once again the master of our environment. In those days Maharishi often wanted to slip away quietly and secretly for some destination. There was some concern for his safety. Nate would see his car pull up and call up to our room from the street, "Mom, Maharishi's leaving!" This was important news, of course, because you could run outside and try to get him to answer a question or give you direction on your project. We never got told to stop Nate from doing this, so I guess it was all right.

Dr. Eberhard Arnold was driving Maharishi everywhere that year and Maharishi was keeping him close. We didn't know it, of course, but he wouldn't live too much longer. He died unexpectedly a few years later of a rare and unusual pneumonia-like disease, and everyone was really saddened. He and Elliot Abravanel had been the doctors for thousands of people attending TTCs in Spain and Italy and all over Europe. Everyone knew and loved him. Did Maharishi see his time on earth coming to an end and wanted to give him as much attention as he could? I like to think so.

Maharishi took us along on his visit to an AEGTC in the Bellavista Hotel in Arosa on October 13, 1976. I think he wanted to give us a break from our work and let us just enjoy him and the knowledge. He emphasized to that course that experiences of the Sidhis are on the way to Unity Consciousness. The sutras or threads are structuring unity, and therefore much would be accomplished along the way. A total transformation will come about, he insisted. The potential of human life is infinite; much more profound than some isolated perfection. He had teased us with the Sidhis or perfections, divine hearing, Yogic Flying, knowledge of past and future, but the real goal of the program was growth of consciousness, mind-body integration to the highest degree. Each sutra or thread would have an effect on consciousness. The basis for success would be what he called clear transcending and soon he would divide all the winter courses into clear and not so clear transcending. He was hoping for scientific research on the Sidhis. It should be possible to objectively demonstrate what is happening in consciousness, he thought. He was impatient to have more research done.

When Nate heard the helicopter paddles he would run to the pad behind our hotel and wait there, sometimes with Ronnie Bach, whose mother Leona was living with the ladies in the Sonnenberg. Once Maharishi offered to take both boys up the helicopter, but Nate was unsure about the whole thing and declined. His birthday is October 23 and we had a big party for him in the Pilgerheim dining room, mostly adults, of course. Right in the middle of cutting

Nate and Sara with Maharishi's little helicopter

the cake I got tapped on the shoulder. Maharishi wanted to see me in the Kulm. I handed off the knife and left, but I felt really torn. I didn't want to have to choose between my family and Maharishi, but I did it all the time when we lived there. I tried to balance it as best I could. David, I think, got short shrift in the deal.

It was an amazing time. The Press was always printing something; David was always writing something; and I was asked to write, edit, and proof some of that. Stephen Benson was sure it was perfect when he gave it to me. Maharishi wanted perfection, no typos. The first volume of *Collected Papers* had been sent out to the courses to proof as well. I remember David taking the ferry from the foot of Seelisberg over to Brunnen across the lake and taking and bringing back the proofed sheets. I always found some mistakes, which was good, because they should be fixed, but bad because that part of the text had to be redone. In those days and during many late nights, the text was printed on transparent paper or film, then cut and pasted on a page, photographed, and the pages put in the correct order, mixed up and some upside down, so that when the huge sheet was folded and refolded the pages came out in the right order. Mike Davis was the genius behind the folding. Maharishi expected you to see your own work, your own writing, to its conclusion. You personally had to proof and check it and make sure it was right. No delegating responsibility, no passing it off to someone else. It was a good lesson for the rest of our careers. Just like David Lynch, we know we have to have the final cut. I'm working on that right now with this book.

Once the kids were in bed I was often roaming the Kulm, going from the Press to Maharishi's meeting room to ask him the questions that Lenny was sending over from MIU. Issues arose, and they wanted Maharishi's suggestions and guidance. David had no taste for administration; he was deep into research, making new charts, and writing Fundamentals. We both met frequently with Maharishi to ask these questions and bring up these issues. The students wanted a new dance floor. Money was tight. Should they build it? David felt that the questions were really trivial and his work would be influencing the whole world. He tolerated it but didn't really take part. It fell to me to corner Maharishi, try to get his attention, read him the questions, explain the issues, and pass along the responses.

Along with his research on high coherence (being achieved on the AEGTC) and creativity, David had also been directing Barbara Granieri to test participants on the AEGTC courses at the beginning and end of their stay on measures of intelligence and creativity, both of which were found to be initially high, no surprise since these people were long-time meditators. They increased even more on fluency and originality (more original ideas, more quickly) during the courses. Most of the CPs finished the field independence test in half the usual time and even so showed significant increases by the end of their course. Geoffrey Clements was working with a visitor from the National Institute of Scientific Research in Quebec, a man named Stephen Milstein. They tested eight women who had been rounding with the AEGTC for eight months and found that their hearing was unusually acute, and when they were tested right after doing the sutra to enhance hearing, their sensitivity increased even more. These three studies on creativity, hearing, and field independence (along with flexibility of cognitive and motor behavior, i.e. thinking and acting quickly) were being completed and written up, but it wasn't happening fast enough for Maharishi. They would be finished and make it into the first volume of *Collected Papers* later in the year.

Since that time numerous studies have found the TM-Sidhi program increases neurological efficiency, the stability and efficiency of the endocrine system, and long-term increases in alpha coherence and total broadband coherence in various parts of the brain. Geoffrey also led a group of guys in Mentmore, England (Michael Beresford, Andrew Jedresak, and others) and they found reduced biological aging, and increased coherence, intelligence, and creativity.

The most interesting thing to me was Maharishi's explanation of mind-body coordination. He had always said that mind and body were like friends; one went along with the other; they were in tune with each other. We used to talk in TM introductory lectures about how if the mind is excited, say by watching some thrilling ballgame, then the body gets excited too, shows faster heart rate and so forth. So when we meditate and quiet the mind, the body quiets down, too: slower heart rate, lower metabolic rate, and so forth. However, considering the TM-Sidhi practice, Maharishi took a deeper view of it. When the mind is in the transcendent, in the field of Being, or nearly so, then it is extremely free from the body, yet still has some contact with it, he said. Through impulses, the mind-body coordination is maintained. When the mind is in a non-impulsive mood there in the transcendent, then it is completely free and can command the body much more than when it is merely in tune with it.

In this state, he explained, the mind becomes superior to the body; it develops mastery over the body. The body then follows like a servant, not a friend. The body even tries to do things that are completely unfamiliar to it; it dare not disobey because the mind is so powerful. The mind in this state becomes the master of its own projections; it can override the body; it is freed from the limitations of the body. It becomes the master, the governor, and the body would attempt to obey, and in the attempt mind-body integration would be greatly enhanced. The mind stays independent, witnessing the body and its fluctuations (mind, ego, sleep, dreaming).

The Vedas, the Vedic literature, he said, are the expressions of these basic relationships, the relationships between different kinds of impulses, which give rise to different kinds of creations. The stress in the atmosphere has been holding us back, he told us. It was lifting now, and subtler values were coming to be experienced. We need a few thousand Sidhas in the world practicing those sutras. Every sutra has that wholeness. Every sutra structures wholeness, he said. Today we might say that every sutra pings the system and it responds by structuring greater wholeness.

That autumn Maharishi had us reading the Upanishads in Seelisberg. One evening in late October he talked about how the great sage Yagyavalkya was enlightening his king. Whereas the Vedas bring out the gap between the Absolute and the relative spheres of life, the Upanishads bring out the knowledge of the Absolute, the unmanifest absolute value of life. When we hear the Upanishads, he said, part of our minds can comprehend the

Absolute. Yagyalkya gives the king confidence that he can comprehend the Absolute. You have to study the Vedas on the level of pure consciousness, the Absolute, Maharishi said. That is where the cognitions of the Seers are recorded. To know the Absolute, one has to *be* the Absolute. So Yagyavalkya elevates the king toward enlightenment. Every word, every phrase, tells the story of the Absolute. It is not a knowledge that can be gained on the basis of language; it's the story of consciousness being told to consciousness. We were reading or hearing it on the basis of our consciousness, which was not that of Yagyavalkya or surely not even that of his king, I can tell you, but we were meant to be getting elevated in some way, just from the reading experience. One hopes so. Vernon Katz has brought out a new edition of the Upanishads with Tom Egenes that is worth looking at (Tarcher Cornerstone Editions, 2015).

Maharishi was always meeting with a small group consulting on projects or just hearing the news of the day, and I could slip in, sit in the front row near him, and be part of it. That autumn there was a very contentious presidential election going on in the U.S. Nixon had resigned over the Watergate scandal. The Europeans were surprised we were making such a fuss about it. Everyone milks the cow, they said. Politics was always corrupt. Gerald Ford was running against Jimmy Carter and it was a very lively race. One night in the meeting, Vesey was telling Maharishi all about it. Imagine, he said with disdain, months and months of haggling over this election. In England we choose our Prime Minister in a very civilized two-week period. I was incensed. Humph, I said, two weeks! Well, that's all it's worth. Maharishi laughed and laughed. Vesey was not amused.

Swami Muktananda's Visit

Sometime that fall we had a visit from Swami Muktananda, who had founded the Siddha Yoga group and written a number of books. He was well-known and traveled with a large entourage of young people. He didn't actually teach his people a technique, we had heard, but gave them taps on the head that created spiritual experiences in them. Several years later one of our people in Australia was asked to visit him on his visit there and pay Maharishi's respects to him. Our friend sat in front of him and silently wondered what those taps might feel like. Swami Muktananda caught his eye, left his platform, wended his way through the audience, and popped our friend on the head. It was something, he said, but compared to his experiences in long rounding over the years, not much.

We didn't know he was coming until we were invited into the hall and saw that huge banners had been posted around the walls welcoming him. Maharishi had a platform built for him at a level higher than his couch. It was a sign of respect. He was showing us how one guru would respect and entertain another. Swami Muktananda had a young western man, his "Jerry Jarvis," we whispered to one another, whom he was calling Arjuna. Arjuna is the warrior whom Krishna educates and enlightens in the Bhagavad Gita, the classic epic of India that Maharishi had translated and written a commentary on years before. The name seemed a bit grandiose, but we were listening and watching. Arjuna introduced Swami Muktananda who gave a brief talk with one of his people translating. I don't remember what he said, but after years of listening to Maharishi speak, we did not think his talk was especially profound, or that he seemed to be a very spiritual person.

Swami Muktananda then directed his entourage to chant the *Guru Gita* or Song of the Guru, which is one of the Vedic scriptures, said to be authored by the great sage Veda Vyasa. It describes the qualities and powers of the guru. They did it very well and we closed our eyes and listened and enjoyed. The young people chanting seemed to be in some sort of altered state with their eyes closed or rolled back in their heads, as if carried away by their chanting. When Swami Muktananda and his entourage were ready to leave, he jumped off his platform and onto Maharishi's couch and hugged him. Maharishi did not look pleased. We were shocked.

Later that day, perhaps at our usual evening meeting, Maharishi told us that since we had listened to the *Guru Gita* from our refined levels of consciousness that we were no doubt getting as much or more out of the chanting than his group was getting. He told us that Swami Muktananda belonged to a Sanyasi order. The Sanyasis were said to be enlightened saints who had completed their third period of life (twenty-five years of meditating in the forest) and were sent to spend their next twenty-five years blessing the field, that is, spreading their coherence around as they traveled through the people. In order to tie them to their roots in the tradition, to remind them of their place in the long lineage of enlightened Masters, they carry a staff and do a little ceremony to it every day. Maharishi always sat in front of and below a portrait of his Master, Guru Dev, and all gratitude and recognition of the source of the knowledge were directed toward him. I would add love to that. Maharishi clearly loved his Guru Dev.

Writing and Editing and Enjoying

Much else happened in those precious days. Vernon Katz often came to work on translations and commentaries with Maharishi. I was invited to one of those sessions with Susie Levin, but I was bored and useless. I couldn't relate to endless variations of words and phrases of experiences that were way beyond me. I was a practical woman, a woman of action. Susie thrived on these sessions, but not I. I was not invited a second time.

I remember being in the small meeting room when one of the 108s, Ava Kennedy, came in to read Maharishi a transcript of one of his lectures. She had been put to transcribe and edit the lecture and she began to read it to him. He stopped her. He didn't like it. It was over-edited and his unique voice had been lost. He sent her back to try again. I was there in another meeting when she returned with her next version. This one included all the umms, and aahs, the endless repetitions, and the impossible grammar of a person speaking and thinking in front of a group, starting one sentence right in the middle of one in progress. He didn't like that one either. His talk had to be paragraphed and edited, of course, but it should show him as the intelligent, educated person he was, not subjecting the reader to every cough and pause. I didn't realize it at the time, but when I went to transcribe and edit his talks on literature and language for the book *The Flow of Consciousness*, I knew just how to do it. I had been trained without realizing it.

Life in Seelisberg was not all work. Maharishi liked to enjoy life and he wanted us to have fun. There were boat rides on the lake and meetings where some visiting musicians would sing or play. If someone like Emily had written a new song we were invited to hear it, and there was always some Indian festival to be enjoyed, like Krishna's birthday at the end of August with lots of sweets, or the Nine Days of Mother Divine with much heavenly chanting going on for hours. Evening meetings offered the news from television clips, and various friends from around the world were always passing through with their news and their projects. I remember one particular visit from Bruno Romano, the national leader of the TM movement for Italy. He came with his new wife. When he was younger, years before, Maharishi told him to tell the Italian government to tear down the Colosseum in Rome and build a Capital of the Age of Enlightenment there. The ruins were filled with the suffering and pain of thousands who died there and were polluting the city. They should be replaced.

Bruno had broken into a sweat. How could he ever tell the authorities such a thing? They would be horrified. Destroy their national monument, their heritage, one of their major tourist attractions?! Build some building in which to teach meditation? It was incomprehensible. It was beyond belief. What was he to do? When he told us the story we all laughed sympathetically. It was a terrible conundrum. I don't know what he actually did do, but consider for a moment what might have happened if he had done what Maharishi suggested he do. Perhaps there would have been a great outcry, press coverage, ridicule, discussion, lots of discussion, maybe some TV interviews. Maybe this would have spread the knowledge, brought people in to learn TM, made him a national figure. Who knows? He had grown up, gotten married, and had a child. The new national leaders of Italy were soon to be a pair of enthusiastic, bright-eyed, and charming young fellows named Carlo Canteri and Iseo Squaranti. I remember them well and hope I spelled their names correctly.

Reading the Planets and Stars

That winter Maharishi had begun to talk about the science of jyotish, the Indian astrology, an ancient predictive science. This opened the door for all our ex-hippies and beatniks, and everyone who was interested in Western astrology, but hadn't been able to connect it to meditation, to what we were doing. They jumped right in, enthusiastically studying whatever books they could find, writing some, traveling to India and studying with jyotishis, and having numerous readings. Not I. I thought those columns in the newspaper telling you to stay in bed today based on your birthday, that is, your sun sign, which constellation your sun was in at the moment of your birth, were ridiculous. How could everyone born between June 21 and July 21 have the same fate? There was a boy from my high school class born the same night as I was who was completely different, but Maharishi thought there was something there, so I tried to be open-minded.

There had been some mention of jyotish on our trip to India, but nothing much had been elaborated on it at the time, so our first real encounter was with Richard Eidson who had been along on the trip to Jyotir Math and was living then with the 108 group in Seelisberg. He was studying jyotish very seriously and had reached the point where he wanted to test and confirm his knowledge. He asked me to give him ten major dates in my life and he would try to say what may have happened on those dates. He took them away and studied and came back with his answers.

The first date he addressed was in May 1966. I think he chose this one first because he felt most confident in his reading. Richard looked at me with sympathy and understanding, his eyes round with shared pain, and he offered, "The death of your father?" God, yes! It was sudden and unexpected. My dear, dear father had had surgery for a benign chest tumor that he thought might be interfering with his breathing, which was labored and difficult. He was a smoker and drove from appointment to appointment with the car windows open breathing in exhaust fumes, now known to be a deadly combination. They failed to restrain him and he unconsciously pulled out his oxygen tube and his heart stopped. I kind of remember hearing that they had put a DNR (do not resuscitate) on him because his heart was enlarged, and he had emphysema, and chronic bronchitis.

I came home from some errand and David looked at me with compassion and took me into his arms and told me what had just happened. That death tore me apart. I grieved and grieved, and it still comes upon me unexpectedly with a sharp sense of loss. He was 55 and I was 25 and we were living in Washington, D.C. We drove to Cleveland for the funeral and I cried painfully and wrenchingly the whole way, and came out of it only when we arrived and I had to deal with everything and everyone and help out.

How had Richard known? Was this "written," as we used to say about things after seeing the film *Lawrence of Arabia*? My father's death was booked and meant to be? I was shocked and yet somehow reassured. I could stop resisting and accept it. Later a jyotishi would tell me that my family had been royalty in the Middle Ages and my father worked the serfs hard, and that was why his life was full of hard work and an early death. When I told this to my sisters, Linda, that lover of jewels and fine living, said, "I *knew* we were royalty!!" And Adele instantly retorted, "*I* never abused the serfs," and probably she was right, looking at her easy life, full of travel and lots of money.

The next date he addressed was October 23, 1967. Richard looked uncertain about the exact meaning, but was pretty sure about the general significance, and asked, "You learned to meditate?"

No, I answered.

"You got an advanced technique?"

No.

"You went on course with Maharishi? Teacher Training, something like that?"

No.

It was the birth of our son Nate, I told him. He was surprised. He said there was nothing in the chart on that day about children, birth of children, sons, anything. It was rather an event of great spiritual significance, something major to do with my evolution, according to my chart.

And it was. It was just that. I had yearned for that baby. I was devastated to learn I could not have children. I ached to have a baby in my arms. I made baby clothes for my friends. I knitted sweaters for them. Finally, we applied to an adoption agency. Over the summer, Mrs. Klein came out to our house to look us over. She was a working mother with three children of various ages, but that wouldn't do for me. I was taking graduate seminars, going for a PhD in Comparative Literature, not sitting around the house baking cookies. Our marriage was too young, she said (it still is, but we are growing into it after 50+ years). We were denied. It felt like the end of the world for me. It was my deepest desire at the time, the very deepest.

Then one Monday evening in October, my cousin Shelly called. He was a lawyer in Philadelphia, and he was in a restaurant with his wife Jill and her mother, Janet Fleisher. Janet had been telling them how interesting it was that that day one of the clients of her art gallery came in, a lawyer named Marvin Lundy. He had arranged for the adoption of a baby and the adoptive parents had just learned that their older child needed open-heart surgery and they couldn't take on a new baby. So that baby was born, was in the hospital, and had nowhere to go. Shelly jumped up and asked for the restaurant phone and called. Were we still looking for a baby? The father was a doctor, he thought, and the mother a nurse.

Yes, yes, yes, we said. OK, he said, I'll look into the Maryland laws and see if you can do a private adoption and find a lawyer and call you back tomorrow. That was it! I was too excited to eat or sleep. David was studying for his eight doctoral preliminary exams which would begin the following Monday and he had no time to drive to Philadelphia and whatever else this entailed. And we had no money to pay the lawyer, the hospital expenses. But no matter. No matter. I couldn't sleep from the excitement of it all. David studied for his exams and I read Dr. Spock's *Baby and Child Care* from cover to cover, twice.

The birth father, it turned out, was not a doctor, but he had an MA in Journalism. The mother was a student. The father was Jewish with dark hair and eyes. The mother was blond, blue-eyed, and Swedish. What a match! This could be our own son. We met with Marvin Lundy in Philadelphia three days later. He approved us. Both getting PhDs. Perfect. He was Jewish too. What better recommendation. The blue bundle would arrive at Shelly's house the next day. We clumsily cooked up our first batch of formula and waited. We fielded names: Nate for my father, dead these three years, or Leif, because the mother was Swedish. We took the bundle in our arms and pulled back the blanket, and there, looking out at us with bright eyes, dark hair and a cute Jewish nose, looking like an international banker, was Nate, clearly Nate. Jill's mother, Janet, arrived to share the bliss. We fed him, burped him, and he performed exactly as Dr. Spock predicted. We unwrapped him to change his diaper, and there on his little penis was a tiny bandage with a drop of dried blood on it from his circumcision. I panicked. What if he was ruined?! Oh my God. No, the pediatrician assured us the next week, he was fine and we were doing a great job.

We put him in the VW camper between us on the front seat

(these were the days before seat belts and baby seats) and drove back to Maryland, laughing and inventing nicknames: ornate, neonate, cognate, etc. etc. He slept his first night in the bottom drawer of our dresser, and then in a borrowed carriage which a friend brought over the next day, and finally, when he outgrew the carriage, a real, also borrowed, crib. I hung over those beds: the drawer, the carriage, the crib, and watched him sleep and poured love on him and, what can I say, it was a huge, huge step in my evolution. It took me to a new place in my life where I could grow and be happy. Richard was right. My chart was right. Jyotish was amazing.

Next Richard picked June 30, 1970. Again, he was certain it was a major spiritual moment in my life, a significant advance in my evolution. Yes and no, I smiled. That was the day Sara was born, our precious beautiful little girl, with her crown of golden curls. We were living in El Paso at the time, Nate was approaching three years old, and it was time, we felt, to adopt another baby. Again, we applied to adoption agencies, but we didn't get very far. They would just not handle a mixed marriage. Good grief. All marriages are mixed. What could be more different than a man and a woman? An indifferent Jew and a lapsed Episcopalian were almost identical. But we were experienced now. It seems doctors did a lot of setting up adoptions, so I went to two gynecologists and told them we wanted a baby. I offered that the baby could be part Mexican since my coloring was dark, brown eyes, dark brown hair, perpetually tanned Middle Eastern skin.

Some weeks later the second doctor called. He had a patient, a young unmarried high school girl who was about to give birth and he hadn't found any prospective adoptive parents yet. He would consider us. The baby was due June 12. We had rented out our house and were about to leave for Maryland to sell our house there, empty it out, and move back to El Paso permanently. We quickly met with the girl's young lawyer and he approved us. The birth mother was beautiful, he told us, and she was huge. Maybe twins, he said. I gasped. Twin boys? OMG. Nate was a wild man, a real challenge. Two more? Please God, let them be girls. The mother was Irish Catholic (David's grandfather was Irish), and the birth father was an art student at the University of Texas, and his father was an architect. Perfect. David was an artist and his grandfather was an architect and had built many of the public buildings in El Paso including Hotel Dieu, the hospital where the baby would be born. The renters we had found moved into our house and we moved into David's parents' house and waited, and waited. I asked the hospital to notify Dr. Huchton, our pediatrician, when the baby was born. We just didn't have the resources to take a special-needs child, and we wanted him to check out the new baby, or babies, God help us.

On the morning of July 1, over two weeks past the due date, David was meditating, Nate was running around, and the phone rang. Hello, I said. "She is the most beautiful baby I have ever seen," Dr. Huchton said. A girl, I cried out. David had heard the

phone ring and my cry and came rushing out. A little girl. She would be Sara after my father's mother, who died young and left him a five-year-old orphan, and after Sara Monday in Joyce Cary's *The Horse's Mouth* and *Herself Surprised*, and it was an Orme-Johnson family name too. I had prepared a woven baby basket that we had gotten in Juarez, lined it with foam and flannel (in yellow and green because I couldn't choose blue or pink), and we were ready to put her in the camper and head out. My mother freaked. You can't take a new baby across the country. Yes, it'll be all right, Dr. Huchton said.

Beautiful baby Sara

Wait two weeks and then it'll be fine since you will be camping and not taking her into hotels and restaurants where she might be exposed to something. So we drove across the country with Sara in the basket, and often on my lap, and Nate in the back seat, stopping first in Cleveland so David could rebuild my mother's back porch. Nate helped by smashing the old floor tiles with a hammer.

Evolutionary? Yes. I was (am) a selfish, insecure kind of person with a sharp tongue, critical like my mother, and Sara was delicate, easily hurt. I had to tread carefully. I had to become a nicer, more generous, better kind of person. I had to change and grow in a new direction. She was a gift from God. Still is.

One more date. June 15, 1963. This was 1976. The date was about fourteen years earlier and we looked and acted pretty young, so Richard was uncertain. It looks a lot like marriage, he said, but it doesn't have to be. He didn't think we could have been married that long ago, so he kept searching for alternative interpretations for the date. I let him flip flop for a minute or two and then told him, yes, it was our wedding date. Well, he exclaimed, you couldn't have picked a more auspicious time if you had a jyotishi find one. A *muhurta*, or auspicious date, is given by the jyotishi for the commencement of any important activity: buying a house, moving into it, getting married, starting a new business or a new project (like building a Capital of the Age of Enlightenment in Jyotir Math).

David's mom was our jyotishi on that one. David was graduating from Columbia in early June 1963 and we were thinking of getting married at the end of the summer. We would live together and work at summer jobs in Boston, and then move to Maryland where David would start his PhD program in experimental psychology and I would start working as a new computer programmer in D.C. for Bellcomm, Inc. Bellcomm was part of AT&T with a contract to explore abort trajectories for the upcoming moon shots. No, said David's mom, I am only coming east once, either for the graduation in New York City or the wedding at the end of the summer (which would be in Cleveland, of course). So we moved up the wedding date, David's parents moved in with his mom's sister on Long Island for a week or ten days after the graduation, and David and I traveled to Cleveland to get ready to be married. Our guardian angels were organizing for us even then, before we ever heard of Maharishi or TM.

I don't remember any other dates. Richard told Maharishi he was getting about 80% of his predictions right. No, no, Maharishi insisted. Maharishi Jyotish^{SM} is 100% accurate. Now the trip to Jyotir Math made sense. There may have been a muhurta that May for founding Capitals of the Age of Enlightenment and/or a Maharishi Vedic University^{SM}. Or possibly it was what is called *aksheya tritiya*, the day of lasting achievements. On this day each year, the sun and moon are both exalted and supremely bright. This is an extremely auspicious day in the Hindu and Jain calendars. It is thought that any activity begun on this day would be extremely fruitful. Aksheya means never diminishing or never ending. The day is ruled by Vishnu, and everyone looks to the north, to the major Vishnu temple in Badrinath. After the yagya we had travelled up to Badrinath. This day fell on May 13 in 1975. I don't remember when we were there, but it was definitely around that time.

In any case, we did that yagya and Capitals started springing up everywhere. The movement began to expand like lightening, striking in all directions. I came to have more respect and admiration for jyotish as the years went by. Some people didn't understand their jyotish predictions, but I was always able to get something out of them. Years later I showed Sara's chart to a jyotishi and told him I was thinking of trying to locate the parents of her birth father, who had been an only child and had been killed in Vietnam. I thought his parents would be happy to know they had a really wonderful granddaughter and great granddaughter, who had been born by then. The jyotishi took one look at the chart and said definitively, "Don't do it!" I don't know what he saw, but I dropped the idea.

MERU Degrees

Sometime that autumn of 1976 Maharishi asked me if MERU could give degrees to our Governors, to those who were attending our courses. Our precious initiators had dropped out of college in order to teach TM, to travel all over the world for Maharishi, work for the movement and to put their personal lives on hold. They should have degrees for all their work, professional recognition for what they had done so they would have some standing when they met important people or spoke before an audience. At least they should have transferrable college credit if they wanted to get a degree elsewhere in something specific. This was my area. I was an academic person, familiar with credits and transcripts and the new trends in giving credit for practical experience. I went right to work on this. First I designed transcript forms, admission forms, folders to hold each person's paperwork, and all the items needed to evaluate their courses and practical experience. Lawrence Sheaff and Adam Craig of the Press began to design gorgeous versions of these forms and the folders to put them in, all gold and rose sunrise colors, and real gold lines and flourishes. Maharishi liked them, boxes of them got printed, and I immediately put them to use.

That autumn and winter there were six-month AEGTC courses going on all over Switzerland and France. I took the car, and sometimes the kids, and visited the courses, explained what we were going to do and gave the CPs application forms to fill out and instructions to have their college transcripts sent to me as Registrar of MERU (it was Fiuggi and the start of MIU all over again, a familiar path to tread and no accreditation board to account to). I began to construct files on everyone. I had visited all the courses that had started that autumn, and by late December I had reached the ladies in the Seeblick. Maharishi loved to be down on the lake and he was going to take silence there with the Rindis and special guests. Vincent and Peggy Snell were there, too. I drove over there at the end of December and met with the different groups in the Seeblick, giving them applications and instructions. During one small group meeting with the Snells and others I suddenly couldn't sit up any more. I lay down on the floor. I felt all right, but I couldn't sit up or stand. Dr. Snell looked me over and asked me some questions and told them to get a room for me and somehow I got to the room and into bed. I was exhausted, I think, and had some kind of flu. Dr. Barry Charles was around in those days and he came and listened to my chest. Nothing major, no drugs, just rest, bed rest. I sent a message to David and lay there for several days while Maharishi went into his yearly silence. I was in Maharishi's hotel while he was in silence and I was asleep with exhaustion and the flu. What kind of karma was that!

The National Leaders' Conference, January 1977

After silence Maharishi hosted the usual semi-annual National Leaders' Conference and then inaugurated the Third Year of the Age of Enlightenment, The Year of Ideal Society, again on the Flagship Gotthard on a snowy, sleety day. No matter the weather, Maharishi was welcoming the sunshine of the Age of Enlightenment, which he was basing on the experiences of the Governors on the AEGTC courses. We can accomplish our goals by just relaxing into the simplest form of one's Self, he said, a purer state of consciousness, which allows us to skillfully make all of our activity in accordance with all the laws of nature and bring in an ideal society. And this is based on practicing the TM-Sidhis, he said, the strength of our movement. The whole talk is printed in the publication *The World Government for the Age of Enlightenment, Achievements, First Quarter, 1977*. We still have our copy. There are also a number of pages dedicated to the national leaders who attended the conference and summarized their achievements: Argentina, Australia, Austria, Belgium, etc., right on to Yugoslavia. The movement was now alive and breathing in nearly every country in the world.

As I studied my copy of that publication while preparing to

write this section, I especially liked seeing the picture of Michael Marchese, because we stayed with him and his family in California during our MIU days when Nate was getting married. Michael was there representing the national leaders of Thailand and Burma. He had taken the MA in SCI that we had offered in Santa Barbara and was on his way to teach TM in South America when he got a call from Michael Dimick. Someone in Thailand had a school and wanted to put TM in the curriculum. Michael changed his ticket and arrived in Thailand only to find that the school was a four-room building in a rice paddy. No matter. He found a translator and set about teaching TM and setting up the movement in Thailand. The Buddhist monks were very appreciative of the knowledge. Maharishi came to visit the early start of the movement in Thailand along with Vesey Crighton and Lawrence Sheaff.

While Michael was single-handedly building the movement in Thailand and offering the first TTC there (with the help of John and Jane Clapp), he got a call from Jerry. Someone from Burma had written to the movement (then operating out of our beautiful facility in Pacific Palisades) and asked for someone to come teach them in Burma, and there was a phone number in the letter. Michael's small stipend from the movement would cover a plane trip to Burma to these Indians living in an English-speaking colony. Why not? He called the number and the man who answered was very happy and enthusiastic. "Oh, Guruji (honored guru), please come to our colony." "No, no," said Michael. "It's just me." He got a tourist visa and flew there. He got off the small plane in a small airport and looked around and, as Maharishi always did, he sat and waited. Finally, an Indian man approached, recognizing him as the only Westerner around, and took him to a hotel. Michael taught out of that hotel room, putting people to meditate for the first time in the large closet, the only other available room. He had made eight trips to Burma by the time of the National Leaders' Conference and had come to give the news as a representative of the national leaders from both those countries. A hero of the Age of Enlightenment! Just like Nat Goldhaber who had set up the movement in Korea and Afghanistan. No doubt Maharishi had invited Michael to come to Switzerland to rest and revive himself and had provided the airplane ticket.

A young half-American, half-English girl named Wendy Unglass appeared in our lives that month. Maharishi sent her to me to be my personal assistant. I didn't ask for help, but clearly I needed it with the MERU degree project, as well as all my other work. David and I were also printing a pamphlet that spring on all of MIU's programs. She pitched in and typed papers for David and did whatever else needed doing. Wendy was a bright light and fun member of the family. She remembers Nate as having an adventurous and inquisitive spirit (I'll say!) and Sara as a playful and sweet soul (yes, very sweet).

The Vice-Chancellor of MERU Tours India

Right after the Conference and Inauguration, David left on a long, solo trip to India. Dr. Sudarshan had been invited to speak at a conference on "Mind—Approaches to Its Understanding" in Jammu, the capital of the northern Indian states of Jammu and Kashmir. Dr. Karan Singh, who was Minister of Health and Family Planning in India and a direct descendent of the Maharaja of Jammu, was the chairman of the conference. Dr. Sudarshan thought someone should come representing and speaking on Maharishi's contribution to an understanding of the mind. Dr. Singh was persuaded and David was to go and a whole tour around India was organized for him.

Maharishi called David in his hotel room in Jammu, India, the night before his talk and instructed him to place his tape recorder on the table right in front of him and tape his entire talk. David thought that Maharishi wanted to hear what he said and having the tape player there would keep him focused. He was going to present MERU's neurophysiological and psychological research on higher states of consciousness and he was supposed to invite the government of India and its responsible organizations and institutions to create an ideal society by making TM and SCI widely available.

As the conference convened and people began to speak David observed that Dr. Singh was constantly interrupting and overriding all the speakers, no matter their importance, giving his views and opinions very authoritatively. David had been placed at the head table next to Dr. Sudarshan and right in front of Dr. Singh, who was sitting in the front row. When David's turn to speak came around, he placed his tape recorder on the table in front of him and deliberately pushed the record button. Dr. Singh sat back in his chair and stayed silent during the talk. He didn't want to be recorded. David got to present his whole talk uninterrupted. Was that why Maharishi asked him to place the tape recorder there? The whole talk (dutifully recorded and uninterrupted) is printed in the *Achievements*.

David was sent from there to speak at the All India Institute of Medical Sciences and the Department of Psychology at Delhi University. He then traveled to Allahabad where the Kumbha Mela (which occurs every twelve years) was being held, in order to talk to the press and carry out a few missions from Maharishi. Traveling in India in those days was a red-eye nightmare. When he arrived in Allahabad no one was there to meet him at the plane. How was he to get to and into the enormous gathering by the Ganges; he had no idea where to go or how to find our people. As luck (!) would have it, his German seatmate on the plane took him in his car to see a judge he knew. The judge knew Maharishi, gave David dinner, and the whole dinner party escorted David over the grounds of the Kumbh and found Maharishi's encampment. When David introduced himself to security at the gate a great uproar ensued. The guard ran around the camp yelling, Dr. Orme-Johnson is here! Dr. Orme-Johnson is here! Everyone went running about shouting. The judge was impressed. David was taken to his tent to rest. He had a big press conference the next day.

After the incredibly spicy dinner at the judge's home, David had a bad night (no details necessary) but he spoke anyway.

David was also supposed to deliver a big book of proclamations honoring Maharishi and his teaching to Prime Minister Indira Gandhi. She was known to be visiting the Kumbha Mela, but she slipped in and out secretly and David missed her. She would be assassinated just seven years later by her own bodyguards. He was also supposed to give greeting and flowers from Maharishi to Anandamayi Ma, a great saint who also had an enclave there, but she wasn't receiving people when he went. David felt really bad that he had failed to do those two things, but he did get to do the ritual bath in the Ganges on a beautiful, sunny day, escorted by the camp entourage.

After stops to speak in Bangalore, Chandigarh, Hyderabad and Bombay, David finally returned. The kids and I went to the airport to pick him up that evening. He had been away on his birthday and we had missed him. He didn't want to go directly home to Seelisberg; he wanted to see Maharishi in the Seeblick and deliver gifts to him and report on his trip. Maharishi was expecting him. I can see that night clearly and vividly in my mind. David had just returned from an exhausting tour and a long flight, but he seemed youthful and glowing. India is sometimes called *karma bhoomi bharat*: India – the land of karma. Well, forget the small suitcase of karma we take into this life. David had burned a whole mountain of karma on that trip.

We sat in Maharishi's little meeting room in his suite and David told him about his adventures and gave Maharishi all the gifts people had sent along. Praveen Shrivastava had sent a little bottle of Ganges water which Maharishi promptly drank down. Someone had sent a Shahtoosh shawl made from the neck hair of the Himalayan Ibex, incredibly soft. Maharishi and David sweetly talked together like old friends and companions. It was really the first time I had ever observed their very personal, intimate, and loving interaction. The kids sat with us for a while and then ran around the Seeblick, their old home, when they got restless. I was feeling we should go home (an hour's drive up winding roads) and put them to bed, but they were okay and David was enjoying a very special personal time with Maharishi.

The First MERU Graduation Ceremony

Wendy and I had been traveling to the AEGTC courses and getting everyone to fill out applications and have their transcripts sent in. Now they were arriving and we were filing them in folders along with applications and other paperwork. It seemed very reasonable to give credit for the SCI course, the TTC course, ATRs, number of people instructed in TM, all those activities in the field (think Michael and Nat), and most recently, the six-month (AE-GTC) course. Quite a few of our Governors were truly eligible for a BA or MA in SCI. They had earned it with hours spent on their courses and activities in the field. Many large courses were ending that April and we needed to structure a big graduation ceremony. We had gorgeous diplomas printed and hand lettered with their names. Maharishi, Larry, and I pored over the wording in that diploma. It wouldn't just give a degree and name and date. It would spell out the knowledge they had gained and what it represented. It was an education in itself with gold lettering and flourishes galore! Each graduate's name had to be hand lettered by anyone in the Press who had some calligraphy training or talent (Tony Miles comes to mind).

At a small meeting that fall Larry Domash reported to Maharishi that I was doing a great job creating the academic side of MERU and preparing to give out degrees. Yes, Maharishi nodded, you can put a competent person anywhere and they will do well. David just remembered and told me about this conversation. He may have told me at the time, but I have no memory of it. I was busy trying to create the event, the graduation ceremony where the diplomas would be handed out. It must have erased everything else in my mind.

Just a few problems. No caps and gowns and no way to tell who was on what bus coming from what course as the day would unfold, so no way to put the diplomas in order and organize the ceremony. The German ladies solved the first problem by quickly sewing a fabulous robe for the Chancellor of MERU, Larry Domash, with a very European gold velvet crushed cap with little gold tassels hanging down. They also made four or five cap and gown outfits for the other faculty who would be witnessing the event. Vernon was there, and Larry coveted Vernon's crushed gold velvet cap, which he thought was more professional and academic looking than his with the gold tassels. They also made about five cap and gown outfits for the graduates, all golden but not so elaborate as Larry and Vernon's but we had maybe a hundred or more graduates!

I figured out how to do it. Larry would stand at a podium on one side, call out the graduate's name, Rindi would be seated on Maharishi's couch (per his instructions) and and then would give each one a flower after they got their diploma. The faculty sat on the other side of Rindi. I sat behind Larry in the area just below the stage with my pile of alphabetized diplomas. Behind the Sonnenberg stage was a small backstage area which couldn't be seen from the audience.

As each bus arrived, the CPs were directed into the hall. Those in the front row would approach the backstage area in a stately manner. The second row would quietly fill in the front row and wait their turn, etc. Our Governors are very clever people and they caught right on. The first graduates entered the backstage area, quickly put on their cap and gown, walked behind the stage over to me, and whispered their name. I found their diploma in the alphabetized pile on my lap and handed it up to Larry's back-stretched arm. He pulled it up with a flourish, and read out the graduate's name and degree. Then he or she climbed up onto the stage, past me and right in front of Larry, received their diploma with a handshake from Larry, a flower from Rindi, crossed the stage, came down the other side, went behind the stage and quickly removed their cap and gown and handed it to the next person and returned to the audience!

It all went flawlessly. Maharishi watched the spectacle on video in his rooms. From the front and from the video it looked smooth and orderly. It wasn't alphabetical, but no one noticed. The cap and gown clad graduates flowed smoothly across the stage. The wild and hurried exchange of costumes behind the stage was invisible. The CPs were in bliss. They got to see the big hall, to get their beautiful diplomas and degrees, to shake Larry's hand, get a flower from Rindi, and leave on their bus to go back to their course. They remember Maharishi being there, giving him a flower. They obviously felt his presence and believed he was somehow there. Or they remembered giving him a flower on their course another time and conflated the two. I had been in the background, the unrecognized genius (!) behind it all, but I was happy and relieved that it was accomplished. I was worried that I hadn't done exactly what Maharishi wanted, but it seemed to be okay. I think I was supposed to check the list of names with him so he could eliminate any unworthy ones, but I am not sure. I was never corrected, and life went on.

New groups came that spring to begin their six-month AEGTC or extension courses (you could stay on after the course for several more months), and we had to start all over again. We continued to visit the new courses starting up, taking applications, filing away transcripts and preparing for another graduation to be held in the fall. When I learned that we were finally leaving for MIU, I trained Barbara Holdrege, who was working on the programs and materials for teaching SCI in schools, and Wendy, and turned all my paperwork over to them. There would be another big graduation in October with Larry and my replacement presiding. I would get questions about MERU degrees for maybe the next ten years, but I was no longer involved. But what I started did live on, and MERU degrees continued to be issued ceremonially for a number of years.

Maharishi later had MERU issue PhD degrees to various leaders of the movement and to those who were responsible for giving out the highest levels of knowledge and techniques.

Our TM-Sidhi Course

One day in May or June I was told that I had been given a room in the Sonnenberg with an intercom in it. In those days, Maharishi talked by intercom to various groups. It saved his time and strength. The important ladies had them. I was suddenly one of them. The room was tiny; no bed, no closet, nothing but a mattress on the floor and that intercom. When Maharishi wanted to talk to you the red light went on and you knew he was there. What was I supposed to do? Hang out there all day and night?

About that time Maharishi began a TM-Sidhi course just for those of us on international staff. We had been watching with envy as each new group got launched on the Sidhi program and we felt left behind. Finally our time arrived and we were all organized into groups and given the first instructions of the program. David and I were in a small group with Geoffrey and Di Clements and Adam and Bobbie Craig, who were designers and illustrators for the Press. We were supposed to discuss experiences with each other. It was subtle, but something important seemed to be happening. Each technique was like an arrow launched from the transcendent, speeding toward its target, and on the way it changed things. Each zinger created an effect.

The experience meetings were fun. We all seemed to be noticing effects, enjoying the process, and excited about the results. One night I went to my room up there in the Sonnenberg and the intercom light came on. Maharishi was with someone in his rooms, Walter Koch, I think, one of the movement founders from the old days, and I told him I was enjoying the techniques, feeling changed by them. "Yes," he said, "you are more, more . . . better." I think he didn't want to name any particular quality because then I might think I had been deficient in that before now. So I was more better. It was good!

I took my work with me and hung out there as I could. But if I spent any significant time in the room hoping Maharishi would connect, the kids would come looking for me. Where was Mom? And they clattered up there noisily, disturbing the meditating ladies. I couldn't abandon my husband and family and hang out with the ladies. It didn't feel right. Was Maharishi trying it out on me? Was I supposed to feel a pull in that direction? Should I think of myself as one of Rindis? I decided to test that notion out.

Now, there was a thing called "resting." Some of the ladies had difficult times with their monthly cycles. They were then all told to take three days off, not work, take meals in their rooms, rest and rejuvenate. You could tell someone was "resting" by the food trays outside their door. OK, I would try that. On the next occasion, I put myself to bed with a novel, and prepared to "rest." Well, that morning an unusually large parade of men came into our room to talk to David, to consult him on something or other. I sat in my bed watching and listening and feeling awkward and not very restful. The kids needed me. Who was going to bring me a tray? Not David or Wendy. They had too much to do already. It was ridiculous. It was hopeless. I got up and went about my business. Resting was not for me. I would never be a Rindi, just a mom and whatever else I was.

As for the intercom, I talked to the electronics guys and asked them to take it from the Sonnenberg and put it in my room in the Pilgerheim, to string a long wire between the two hotels to make it reach. They must have checked with Maharishi because soon it was done and I could lead my normal life and still be available to Maharishi.

My mother came to visit and I took her on my trips to the courses along with the kids and got the new groups to send in their transcripts and prepare to get degrees. The weather was beautiful, Switzerland was beautiful, my little Fiat was perfect. We had a grand time. The courses were delighted to have someone, anyone, come and talk to them, and I was entertaining. I don't remember anything I said, but I had them laughing, being grateful they were there, that we all were there doing what we were doing.

When I got back from one long trip the intercom had disappeared, but I got it back. TM-Sidhi instruction continued, meetings continued, and I asked if my mother could sit in. Maharishi looked dubious. What would my mother make of these small meetings discussing administrative issues? She expects nothing, I assured him. She is just simple and innocent and will enjoy being there with us. All right, he said. At one of those meetings, I asked him, Maharishi, when are we *really* going to have the Age of Enlightenment? A few more big stirrings of the pot, he said. The TM-Sidhis were one, jyotish was another, and there were obviously a few more to come but he didn't go into details and I foolishly didn't ask.

That summer Maharishi was preparing to offer the TM-Sidhi course to the meditators and we were grappling with how we would promote these courses. He let the designers and Press go wild with ideas: Superman flying, supernormal powers, the works. The Press printed sample posters and other materials. David, Larry, and I went along with the whole thing for a while because Maharishi seemed to be encouraging it, but we started to worry about the implications. We felt we had to say something. Someone had to say something. We told Maharishi we felt that the movement could be accused of false advertising. We could be sued for telling people that they would learn to fly and then having them learn the techniques, even the Yogic Flying technique, and find that they could not reasonably expect to either fly or immediately have the other powers being advertised by the preliminary posters.

Yogic Flying comes in several stages, according to the Vedic texts. Hopping like a frog indicates the first stage, and later one could move through the air. Many of us were definitely at the first stage, which was rather funny, ungraceful, and very undignified. It was often very blissful, the CPs reported, certainly integrating, and stirred up lovely experiences of inner unboundedness, but it wasn't flying in any sense of the word. Maharishi was waiting for someone to bring some reality into the situation, and the posters and other materials quickly came back down to earth. We would stop talking about levitation. That would be misleading. We would talk about Yogic Flying, our specific term for what was really being taught and learned and practiced.

David had been sent off to give a lecture tour of Iowa and he went to MIU, organized a tour, and had a pamphlet printed advertising A New Breakthrough in Human Potential. Scientific Symposium on Levitation and the Transcendental Meditation Program, presented by the faculty of Maharishi International University. David (as Professor of Psychology and Director of Research, MERU), Keith (as Professor of Physiology, MIU), Jon Shear (Chairman, Department of Philosophy, MIU) and Leonard Goldman (Professor of Law and Government, Executive Vice-president, MIU) were the scheduled speakers. The pamphlet contained experiences of course participants "while practicing the technique for levitation." The abstracts of each speaker's talk related the Sidhis to the scientific research on TM. They spoke in Des Moines, Omaha, and various Iowa cities: Sioux City, Ames, Iowa City, Cedar Rapids, and Davenport.

Maharishi heard about the wording of the pamphlet and called David on the phone. He wasn't happy about the word levitation when he saw the pamphlet. Why did you put that there? he questioned. It might have gotten us into trouble. You dictated that title, David replied. Oh, he said. We aren't going to use that term any more. Somehow that had slipped by.

Our Last Summer

It was our custom on Guru Purnima to give wishes for the next year. Guru Purnima falls on the first full moon in July and it is a time to remember and celebrate the guru. This year it fell on July 1. These times were precious to Maharishi. He would speak lovingly of his time with Guru Dev, his guru, and sometimes tell stories of their years together. We were often asked to jot down our hopes and plans for the next year, successes we could lay at the feet of the guru when next we celebrated. We usually wished for fulfillment of our many projects, for our personal enlighten-ment, world peace, etc. This year Maharishi asked people to read or speak their wishes out loud before the group. David was sitting on the stage and when his turn came, he spoke not from his role as Vice-Chancellor on the research or publications, or as president of MIU, but right from his heart. He wished immortality for our dear guru, Maharishi. The hall exploded in cheers and applause. It was what we all desired.

After Guru Purnima my birthday (July 6) rolled around. There weren't many of us in Seelisberg, David was away again, and it seemed it would be a non-event. I didn't mind, but that afternoon people seemed to have found out, and when I went to the Gold Room Tina Olson had hurriedly gathered together an armful of roses that were meant for the podium and surrounding area and handed them to me. I was supposed to offer them to Maharishi, lay them on the table before him. Nate appeared at the back of the room. He had come to see that I was properly recognized. The roses were beautiful, but they had not yet been prepared for Maharishi; they were full of long, sharp thorns. I knew he would immediately rummage among them, choose a rose for me, and give it to me. Should I let him do that and probably get pricked? They were pricking my arms as I held them. I decided not to put them down in front of him. I still wonder if I did the right thing.

Late one night I was walking in one of the corridors of the Kulm or Sonnenberg or the bridge over the road connecting them, and there was Maharishi walking along by himself. How had he slipped past the secretaries? Wendy had a similar experience of running into him all alone, but early in the morning. I would guess Maharishi had been checking on something somewhere, perhaps the Press, or going to a small meeting in the Gold Room. In any case, we were unexpectedly face to face. I couldn't think of anything to say or ask. He extended a flower toward me. I took it, but he didn't let go. We stood there for several timeless minutes, he tugging gently on the flower and smiling at me, and me tugging gently and wondering if I should let go of the flower, or what to do. Eventually he released the flower, and dazed, I went on my way. I remembered when David had offered Maharishi a plate of cake on his birthday several years before, and Maharishi had held on to it for a few moments before releasing it. Mother Olson said afterward that David had received a great blessing from Maharishi. I suspect he was rearranging my molecules that night before letting me go back to work.

During the summer of 1977, what would be our last summer in Switzerland, Maharishi had the idea of sending the graduates of the current AEGTC extension courses to MIU to reinvent it, to make it more successful on all levels of academic and administrative activities. They would revitalize MIU by bringing their refined level of consciousness to bear on every aspect of the university. Everyone wanted to join the new initiative. It was very appealing to join in Maharishi's latest project. You would have his attention on you; there would be frequent phone calls and lots of feedback. You would be living in the vortex of his energy. It was irresistible. Everyone who could would try to drop what they were doing and jump on board.

Larry, Susie Levin (who had an advanced degree in Education), and I were interviewing and organizing the group, which would be called the Council of Executive Governors, the CEG. One young man who had just gotten an MA in Physics from Harvard was eager to drop out of his PhD program and join Maharishi's new wave. Susie, Larry, and I didn't think that was a great idea. He would be more valuable to the movement with a PhD in physics, we thought. Anybody could wash dishes or be a teaching assistant or whatever, but he was serious about going. We were up in Arosa where the courses were being held and were concluding. We found a public phone booth and called Maharishi at the Kulm in Seelisberg. Larry asked, what did Maharishi think about this young fellow John Hagelin going to MIU with the CEG or should he go back to Harvard to finish his PhD? Back to Harvard was the unequivocal answer. Maharishi had spoken. John went back to Harvard, and the CEG went on to MIU without him.

David was then sent off to be part of a big tour of India: "Consciousness—The Field of all Possibilities. All-India Conference on Veda and Science, 5–22 August 1977," starting in Rishikesh. Dr. Sudarshan was one of the chairmen, and they spoke in over ten venues around India: Tirupati, Hyderabad, Bangalore, Bombay, Ahmedabad, Benares, Delhi, Jabalpur, and Kaladi. Brian Josephson spoke as did Larry Domash. David and Keith weren't pictured or listed as featured speakers, but they did speak and David's research showing maximum coherence during flying, and especially at the moment of lift off, was prominently featured in English and Hindi. The text read: . . . "Now the time has come to proclaim that the advances of modern science are reaching the frontiers of Vedic wisdom. The age-old whisper of the Veda has given a new direction to the scientific age—raising it to the Age of Enlightenment."

Under three pictures of various American course participants joyfully hopping and airborne was this quote from Maharishi: "They are all up in the air, inviting everyone who still has their feet on the ground to join in bringing in the rising sunshine of the Age of Enlightenment." Maharishi joined the tour and when it ended Maharishi led the group to Kanyakumari, the southernmost tip of the Indian subcontinent, the site of a Mother Divine temple, and one of the places where Maharishi first had the idea to bring Guru Dev's wisdom out to the world. David remembers this visit especially well. His experiences there and in other places with Maharishi will be featured in his own book, which will ideally quickly follow mine. He had more private time with Maharishi than I did and has a much better memory.

I remember once returning from a trip around Switzerland that year and Vesey telling me that someone had reported something to Maharishi that I had allegedly said, probably something I shouldn't have said. Maharishi retorted that I hadn't said that! He stood up for me. I recently was back in touch with Vesey and we were reminiscing about those days. I asked him if he remembered what it was I might had said. He didn't and neither do I. But he did say that in all those years he never heard Maharishi say anything bad about me. It gave me confidence that he thought well of me and supported me again and again.

Leaving for Iowa

The summer was ending and the time had come to leave. We all loved our life around Maharishi and in Switzerland. We hated to leave, at least I did, but it was happening anyway, and since Maharishi was directing us, it would be the best thing for us all. David and I were to move to MIU where there would be a school, other children, and where David could carry on his research and still continue to travel for the movement. Larry was now the new president of MIU, I would help with administration, and David would be the chair of the department of psychology and still Director of Research. Susie would join the education faculty. Unfortunately for me, David was still away, so it fell to me to pack up the kids and go. It was a difficult time. I went through all the things we had accumulated during our four years there, like bed-spreads for the kids' beds (to make them feel at home in every new location), toys large and small, papers, and clothes for all three of us. I gave away everything I could. I believe I left David's clothes and papers for him to deal with when he returned to Switzerland. I was warned that we were limited to two suitcases each and they didn't want to pay overweight. I found some large cardboard box-es and filled them up. When they were lifted, little Lego pieces rattled and skittered around inside.

I asked the two ladies in the Communications Office, the Eileens, to please alert MIU that we would be arriving the next evening in Cedar Rapids, Iowa. The next morning as we were getting ready to be driven to our flight from Zurich, Nate noticed that the light on the intercom was red. Maharishi was on the line! Jai Guru Dev, I said. Was I all right? he asked, sensing that I was uncomfortable. Not exactly, I said. I am feeling rushed and like I am being pushed out of here. No, no, he said. You can stay. It's all right, I said, the kids and I are ready to go. After a bit more conversation there was a knock on the door. Susie was leaving, too, though not directly for MIU, but when she went to see Maharishi and have her final interview with him, she was told he would be on the intercom in my room. The kids and I stepped out in the hall to let her have a few minutes privately with him. Then off we went. It was exciting and sad at the same time. For months I had been singing the lyrics of a John Denver song to them, "I'm leaving on a jet plane, don't know when I'll be back again. . . .." They were eager to go.

After a long flight to the U.S., a plane change in Chicago and another flight to Cedar Rapids, we arrived in the late afternoon exhausted, only to find there was no one to meet us. We waited for several hours, it seemed to me, and then, finally I called MIU and got connected to Susan Humphrey. She hadn't heard anything about our arrival and felt terrible that we were there, had been sent by Maharishi, and had been neglected. She immediately sent a car for our luggage and a small plane to bring us quickly to Fairfield. The apartment we were to have was in an old fraternity building that had been made into faculty apartments. It was not yet available, so we would stay in some rooms nearby until it was. We got into the small plane and took off over the fields of Iowa in the sunset and arrived at the tiny airport in Fairfield, just north of the campus.

We went to bed in our spare, unfamiliar rooms and woke up the next morning in another universe. We had left the intense but silent whirlwind that was life around Maharishi and had landed softly in the quiet middle of nowhere. Our new life would begin here in Fairfield, Iowa, a life that would last nineteen years before everything changed yet again.

Part Three:

Ashram in Iowa,
the MIU/MUM Years

Maharishi Mahesh Yogi, late 1970s

In the Cornfields

DAVID WAS STILL TRAVELING around the world, so the kids and I settled into our temporary rooms in one of the old fraternity buildings on campus and explored MIU, which would be our home for the next nineteen years. We also toured the town of Fairfield, Iowa, and the surrounding farmlands and lakes. Nate and I went over to Lincoln Elementary School, which was very close to campus, and met the principal, a very kind and welcoming Mr. Brown. He kept an eye on Nate as he entered fifth grade, his first real school in over five years. He knew Nate was adjusting, not only to a new school, but to new routines. When music lessons were offered, Nate had the embouchure for a trombone and he took right to it. Sara entered our little MIU School and played happily with all the kids. I was supposed to be part of the administrative team with Lenny and Lesley Goldman (Executive Vice presidents) and Susan Humphrey. They all welcomed me with a cake and candle-lighting ceremony and I started to attend administrative board meetings, but it just didn't take.

I was drawn to the Department of Literature, headed by a beautiful, very warm and intelligent woman named Margaret Butler. She had a PhD in French literature and she and her faculty were very ably teaching the first-year literature core course, the second-year one-month course on the quest theme of Joseph

Campbell's *Hero with a Thousand Faces*, and third and fourth-year courses in the literature major, which was one of the most popular majors on campus. I had in mind that Maharishi had insisted repeatedly that I get my PhD, so I felt that was my most important task. I quickly took my place in the department, took on a teaching load, and slid away from administration. Someone brought up to Maharishi that I had moved in that direction, and he approved, so that was that!

Let me say here that although we were now in Iowa, thousands of miles away from Maharishi and from our old life in Switzerland, surrounded by farms and acres of cornfields, I felt (and continue to feel) connected to Maharishi. I sensed that he was (and is) guiding my evolution and that I should just work with what came along. The whole mission of the University was Maharishi's project to bring Vedic knowledge, the knowledge of consciousness, into the academic world. Everyone at MIU felt the same way: faculty, staff, and our first students, who were largely our own initiators or Governors, if they had already taken the TM-Sidhi course, and their children. We all wanted MIU to succeed. We all wanted Maharishi's attention and approval. Over the years David frequently toured and visited Maharishi wherever he was, we both went to big courses he was holding, and sometimes we went over to Switzerland or elsewhere for special projects, so we felt very close to him and his projects. We felt that we were still "in the ashram," a part of his movement and under his eye and direction. We gave ourselves wholeheartedly to making MIU a success in whatever way we could.

Finishing up the TM-Sidhi Program

We moved into our apartment in Frat 113 and made a nice home for ourselves. Parsons College had taken a couple of the fraternity houses and divided them into apartments for married students or staff or faculty, and we got one of those when it became available a few weeks after we arrived. We had a large living room, a full kitchen with a horrible grey rug on the floor, and four bedrooms, one of them full of the previous occupants' belongings and unavailable for several months. The bathroom had two toilet stalls, a gang shower, and a row of urinals. I immediately had them removed and a bathtub and small sink installed. David and I would each have our own bedrooms and so would the kids. We got accustomed to separate bedrooms on our six-month AEGTC. We slept better, had room for our own desks, and had a little privacy. Nate had difficulty explaining to his friends why his parents slept in separate bedrooms. But, as Virginia Woolf insisted in her books, a woman needs "a room of her own" if she is to write or have any kind of creative life.

Outside of our apartment door and downstairs was a laundry room with a washer and dryer (yay!!) and an area covered with thick slabs of foam where the faculty who were living in the building could do their TM-Sidhi program. Upstairs was the main lobby where all the children played together while their parents were downstairs on the foam. And they played on the foam when we weren't using it. Maharishi hadn't forgotten that David and I hadn't finished the TM-Sidhi course that we had started in Switzerland with the other international staff. He sent Bevan Morris to MIU that autumn to give us the final part of the program, the Yogic Flying instruction, and once we had it, we joined the group downstairs. Nate had turned ten that October and insisted that David teach him TM, the adult technique, so we were all moving along.

The Yogic Flying instruction kicked loose a big stress as well as starting some profound healing. I was enjoying the new, deeper program, but I soon went into a depression. My mother was bipolar, one of her brothers was seriously depressive, and so was her father, and my brother Jay and sister Adele were afflicted to some degree. I had always had periods of depression, though not very lengthy ones. As this depression hung on, I found that, thanks to the new program, I had sufficient physical and emotional energy to get the kids fed, dressed, and off to school and to see my teaching and administrative responsibilities through the day. When the depression ended, it ended forever. I have never had another like that one, or even like the shorter ones I used to have. Yogic Flying did not give me wings, but it did create a healing and integration that have stayed with me. In general, I have found, and I am surely not unique in this, that while one might take months and months to work through certain deep stresses, like gnawing on an old bone, the TM-Sidhi program pushes the stress release to move along, like those hot house plants that are forced, or brought into full bloom for the spring season. "Bloom where you are planted" (1 Corinthians 7:20-24). I bloomed and continued to bloom where Maharishi had planted me.

Teaching at MIU

I discovered I was a natural educator (or performer, it often seemed to me), but the teaching experience at MIU went beyond anything I had ever known before. I had taught English and World Literature at the University of Maryland and the University of Texas at El Paso, but MIU students were a new experience for me. They were alert, interested in literature and in consciousness, not reading the newspaper in the back row, eager to learn, and very comfortable speaking in class and participating in any assignment. They were, in short, a teacher's dream class. Under their bright, lively attention, I found I could develop new ideas, new methods of teaching, and I thoroughly enjoyed the whole thing. Other faculty members discovered the same thing; Larry called the classroom a particle accelerator of consciousness. Standing before those students I had new insights and epiphanies about the literature I was teaching. Sometimes I stopped to jot them down so I wouldn't forget them.

The most successful course we taught was our second-year one-month course that all the students took at that time; it was based on the quest theme as described in Joseph Campbell's *Hero with a Thousand Faces*. Former students still come up to me, to this day, exclaiming about that course, telling me how it taught them to see their evolutionary path, their growth of consciousness, in everything they read. More about that below.

One of the joys of teaching in the Literature Department was that I could develop new courses and explore new areas of literature. I had taken Classics at Vassar and I thought that a course in the Greek and Roman epics, drama, comedy, and poetry would be a great basis for the study of English and American literature. I started rereading all the old beloved and familiar works, like Homer's *Iliad* and *Odyssey*, and reading works I had never read before, like the Latin novel *The Golden Ass* by Apuleius. Novels were my favorite literary form and this was the beginning of putting together a little bit from here and there, as Maharishi had said, and beginning a dissertation project, although it took me a while to pull all the pieces together.

Creating a course at MIU meant much more than putting together a reading list, figuring out where papers and exams would fall, and starting class. You had to create lesson plans for each day with learning aids to help the students: Main Points (two or three of them) with the accompanying SCI points (how each point related to the knowledge of consciousness, to the experiences of meditation the students were enjoying), and other materials like that. We would later add a Unity chart at the bottom, that is, four points going from the most superficial level of the lesson to its deepest connections in Unity Consciousness. This meant really thinking through the *Odyssey* in a new way. What points did I want to make about it? How were they related to Maharishi's insights into consciousness? How could I take it to the deepest levels?

There was also a challenge on another level. At Vassar we had read only primary sources. We thought things through for ourselves. We were not fed an angle or a viewpoint. We learned how to learn. I wasn't content creating these charts (and mounting them on the wall each day). I wanted to stimulate the students to think. First, I thought they should actually read the work I had assigned. Ha ha. As you probably know from your own academic experience, students often show up in class without having even opened the book, so I gave daily quizzes on the reading material. Sometimes these were just on details (meaningful, but not something you would pick up in Cliff Notes, for example) and sometimes they were open-ended essay questions. As we went over the answers together after the quiz, I found they provided the springboard for discussions and eventually we reached the salient points. Or I would leave the SCI part of the chart, or some section of it, blank, and ask the students to fill in that part. Make the connection yourself, write the sentence, read it out, share it with everyone, discuss it. I wanted them to make it theirs! They were terrible at this at first, but they improved over time; they learned how to relate their ideas to consciousness, and after a while they could do it themselves. In fact, once a group taking a course in playwriting grumped to me, do we have "put in SCI?" No, of course not, I said, but when I saw what they had written, there it was! It was an inseparable part of them.

If the quiz I gave was an essay question, I broke them into small groups, had them read their answers to one another, pick the best one, and have the author read it out in class. It was very good for them to see what their peers could come up with. Discussions were lively and classes were really fun for all of us. I gave the exam on the day before the last day (and graded furiously that evening and night) so we could discuss it in the last class. When the students read out their "A" answers to each essay question, there was no grumbling from the others about "why didn't I get an A?" I would also include a survey page: was the reading too much, too little, just right? The kids were shocked at the answers. Half the class thought there could be more reading! What? Who were those traitors? Their own friends sitting right next to them!

I designed a seminar on the novel and whenever I gave it, I would separate the class into groups and give each group the responsibility for teaching their particular novel, for preparing the teaching materials, main points, quizzes, discussion questions, everything. I met with each group and guided them along. Now this is called Active Learning or Project Learning. I was ahead of my time. I was known as a tough but popular teacher and in June 1979 the students voted me best teacher of the year; they gave me the Most Enlightened Educator Award. Of course, it helped that the literature major was one of the largest so I got more votes than the most brilliant mathematics professor. Other literature faculty got awards too. They were all excellent teachers and much appreciated by the students: Susan Setzer, Silvine Marbury, Bryan Aubrey, Tim Truby, Tim Ambrose, Carol Inman, and some fabulous visiting faculty governors from all over the U.S.

I didn't shy away from real life in literature either. That means death and sex (we didn't get into taxes). Think about Aristophanes *Lysistrata*. In case you have forgotten, Lysistrata organizes her women friends to deny their husbands any sexual favors until they end their endless wars. It was lovely to have a female heroine in a Greek comedy, and the issue is always timely. Spike Lee has just made a film version of the play set in modern Chicago. The main scene in the comedy shows a warrior on leave trying to get his wife to make love with him. Faithful to Lysistrata's instructions, and against her own inclinations, she puts him off again and again, sending him on a series of errands. She can't make love without perfume, etc., etc. She mischievously asks her husband, what is that tent pole under your tunic? The students looked nervously at each other. Was that what they thought it was? Were we really talking about this in class? David says I have a rebellious streak and love to shock people. I guess that's true. I felt that they couldn't really fire me because I was part of the David package, but I did get questioned from time to time. Someone would tell Maharishi that I was teaching such and such. She shouldn't teach anything depressing, he said.

Ah, depressing. That is a different story. The Vedic view of art is that it has certain *rasas* or flavors, the best of which is the bliss toward which art can lead consciousness. It is important not to take someone's precious consciousness, or your own for that matter, on a journey through words, images, and events that might pollute or stress their minds. Death is natural; it cannot be avoided, but reading about torture or seeing it in a film could be unnecessary. There is considerable discussion today in academia about such issues. Does the teacher have the right to ask students to read about slavery if that might trigger overpowering emotional reactions in them? Students who are meditating have a way to flush things out twice daily; students who are not meditating may be left with indelible impressions. Maharishi often commented that in ignorance, experience makes a line in a rock, which is difficult to erase. As consciousness expands and becomes more flexible, experience may make only a line in sand, or water, or finally, air, easily erased. I read with new eyes and as time went by found I had little taste for reading about gratuitous suffering and evil. I found growth, emotional or spiritual, to be of the greatest interest and gravitated toward works that helped my own consciousness to expand and would therefore be suitable for the students.

I used to read whatever I began right to the bitter end. No more. If something isn't giving me joy, understanding, empathy, whatever, I drop it. It helps to have the view that everything is evolving, growing, moving toward greater and greater fulfillment. Even if a character goes through some difficult times, one can see it as karmic and necessary in its way. In one of his talks on literature Maharishi said, "No matter what one sees, one sees evolution there, and because evolution is one's own nature, one sees one's own nature in everything, and this reference to the Self makes everything enjoyable. So the study of literature would even go so far as to develop Unity Consciousness" (July 6, 1976, Seelisberg, Switzerland). See *The Flow of Consciousness, Maharishi Mahesh Yogi on Literature and Language* [MUM Press, 2010] for the whole talk. A work would only be depressing if the central characters failed to learn, to grow, to get to a deeper level of understanding, or if the reader didn't.

Another point. People have different physiologies and respond differently to works of art. When Maharishi brought out the principles of Maharishi AyurVeda after 1980, we could see that a person who was predominantly *kapha* (solid, slow thinking, to name a few attributes) might find excitement, even violence, stimulating, while a predominantly *vata* person (light, quick thinking, a tendency to nervousness) might find the same thing irritating and disturbing. One has to know oneself and choose accordingly. I can't read or watch anything on the Holocaust. It gives me nightmares.

The Square Root of One Percent

In 1978, the year after we arrived at MIU, Maharishi conceived of a program to create an ideal society. One province or state would be selected in each country and groups of our Governors would be sent there to introduce local governments to the value and effect of having one percent meditating in each city or state. These teams of four women or men would live and meditate together and work together to spread the knowledge of consciousness and its benefits to a local government for creating one percent of the population meditating in the city or state: less crime, fewer accidents, fewer suicides, and on it went. The Maharishi Effect research had become a substantial body of studies by that time.

Larger countries like the U.S. and Canada required two ideal provinces. The U.S. had Rhode Island and Washington State. David, Jon Shear, and others were sent to talk to the press and support the activities of the teams. I missed the Rhode Island tour, but joined David and Jon for the Washington tour that summer. One of the Governors in Rhode Island had the idea of collecting some data to support their claims, a young fellow named Walter Zimmerman. International sent him there along with one other scientist to gather data and write up what he found. They found that the approximately 300 TM-Sidhi graduates in Rhode Island were already affecting the quality of life. Data from government sources showed improvements in crime, deaths, motor vehicle fatalities, auto accidents, unemployment, pollution, and alcohol and cigarette consumption, trends that were not found in the surrounding states. A young woman named Fran Hodges worked with Walter on this study. It was one of the first clear indications of collective consciousness affecting society (see paper 321 in *Collected Papers*, Volume 4).

When Maharishi heard about these results he was very stirred. If a number smaller than one percent meditating together and practicing the more powerful TM-Sidhi program could influence these trends in society, that brought social change much closer. Sitting with Larry Domash and Geoffrey Clements and other scientists, Maharishi worked on this idea and elicited ideas from the group. It is known that when elements in a system are coherent they are much more powerful than a greater number of incoherent elements. Here I go again with the physics (I was a math major, you remember). Take the phenomenon of laser light. Since in a laser the photons are coherent, the light reaches much farther than beams of incoherent light where the waves neutralize each other. Here's another example: if ten men are pulling on a rope together, they are more successful than 100 men pulling more or less together but also in various directions. In short, the square root of 100 is ten. If our Sidhas could be considered more coherent than meditators, and one percent of a population meditating could produce results, then possibly only the square root of one percent would have the same or greater effect, doing the program together in one location, not scattered about. The summer programs ended and everyone returned home. Over but not forgotten.

In November a letter that had been written to the editor of a newspaper was read out to Maharishi. A man living in Nicaragua had written about the Sandinista revolution against the dictator Somoza. Thousands of people were being killed and he pleaded for help from anywhere. Maharishi decided to help that man out and, as usual, took his thinking and planning global. He proposed sending teams of Governors to five major trouble spots in the world: Central America (Nicaragua, Costa Rica, Guatemala and El Salvador), the Middle East (Iran, Israel, and Lebanon), Africa (Rhodesia), and Southeast Asia (Thailand and Kampuchea). Groups of our Governors, approaching the square root of one percent of each country's population, were sent to these places, housed in hotels, and told to quietly do their meditation program and not go out or mix with the people. These were very dangerous locations. In Iran, we heard, some of the Governors went up on the roof of their hotel to see what was going on in the streets. They were spotted and some of them were led into a courtyard to be executed. Somehow it didn't happen and they were allowed to go back inside. Maharishi immediately pulled them out of there.

Larry, David, Keith, and Steve Drucker traveled to the Central American countries and talked to their governments. There were meditators in high places and they arranged audiences with Somoza (word was that his wife was a meditator), the president of Costa Rica, who was a meditator, and others. In Nicaragua, they met Somoza in his bunker, which was riddled with bullet holes. The Nicaraguan Governors were lecturing on TM and teaching it to many people. The revolution was losing its steam and violence was quieting down. Somoza dismissed the whole thing, but the Sandinistas knew that our Governors were somehow supporting peace, and that meant upholding Somoza, and they ordered our group to leave. They sent a message threatening the group with machine guns. Maharishi pulled them right out. When the Sandinistas later overthrew Somoza and he fled, they held celebratory parades. Our Nicaraguan Governors recognized the men leading the parades. They had been sitting in the first row of their lectures, learning what we were doing. They believed us and Somoza didn't.

Maharishi commented that the revolutionaries were more in tune with the collective consciousness than Somoza. He will regret it wherever he goes, he said, and so it was. The Sandinistas followed Somoza into exile and bombed his car. Apparently they forgot what they learned from us because they were later attacked by the Contras, and Nicaragua became a Cold War battleground. They lost to the Contras and lost in the subsequent elections. They were ousted. If they had really learned their lesson and set up a group of meditators or Sidhas there might have been a different outcome. I should add one point. Although peace or the reduction of violence may have been seen as supporting the status quo, in effect, the coherence created by the Governors would have gradually led to a resolution of the conflict *and* an improvement in the society, but without violence and loss of life. We would have the same issues come up later in our projects in Venezuela, the Philippines, and even in Armenia in 1990.

David came home just in time for us to go to El Paso for Christmas at the end of 1978. When we got back from El Paso, a huge blizzard hit Iowa. We were snowed in. It was weeks before they plowed our little road to the frats. We had to take out the kids' sled and pull it down to the main dining room to get our groceries from the commissary. We felt just like pioneers. I had been teaching Willa Cather's great Midwestern novels, *My Antonia* and *O Pioneers!* Now I could relate to those early American experiences of winter on the prairie.

The Youth Invincibility Course

That summer of 1979 Nate was eleven, going on twelve, and Maharishi began a new TM-Sidhi course for teenagers. They would begin their TM-Sidhi program, advance a little with it each summer, and be eligible for the two-week flying block when they reached sixteen. Gregg and Georgina Wilson were put in charge of the course. They had no children of their own and they had no idea what they were getting into, taking charge of a dozen or more wild and creative meditating children and trying to keep them in their dorms, on a schedule, and on their program. Nate was excited. Since the kids had to be thirteen to attend, Nate got special permission to be on the course (this had to be from Maharishi, who micromanaged every detail of all the courses, whatever you may think). Nate packed up and moved into one of the pods (smaller residence buildings on campus) with the other kids, many of them his friends from MIU: Eden Wallace, Chris Danaher, and a few others, some from far away. We visited Nate in his room and our hearts melted. There was his asana blanket on the floor and incense burning on his dresser. Would he take to the knowledge as we had? No, not so much, but he had a fun time, and there was a big graduation and he wore a suit jacket and tie, gave a speech to the whole dome celebration, and enjoyed it all thoroughly.

Jumping ahead a bit, Sara joined the Youth Invincibility Course the summer of 1981, again with special permission. She had just turned eleven, but she was very mature. I think Maharishi thought she would be just fine. During the previous year she and three other little girls wrote essays on what they thought about this idea of Yogic Flying. The Wilsons paraded them around to the TM-Sidhi courses that others were taking. The courses loved them and Sara loved doing it. She learned to pause when she knew that certain things she said would elicit laughter and she became quite a performer. Nate, on the other hand, was thirteen going on fourteen and very interested in girls. Gregg and Georgina had a hard time keeping the boys and girls in their rooms in the evenings. One evening they found the boys' rooms empty, and when they inspected the girls' rooms they found Nate hiding in the cabinet under the sink. Gregg sent Nate back home to us for a few days. He winked at us and told us he would let Nate back on the course, but he had to discipline him a little bit. I am sure that Maharishi was told all of this. Embarrassing! The courses went on every summer and the kids moved along with the Sidhis.

'They Are Crying for You at MIU'

I was teaching the *Odyssey* one year, probably September 1979, and I was having a difficult time. Not with the *Odyssey* or with teaching, but with my moods and life in general. I was feeling alone and in need of David's love and presence and support. He had been off in India with Keith on a speaking tour and they had stopped in Switzerland and were spending time there with Maharishi. As I read about Penelope crying for her husband, who had been away at war for twenty years while she had to raise her son alone, run the household and estate, take care of his elderly parents, and defend herself against her enemies, I found myself crying as well. I called Rindi. You know, I told her, I have been very strong through many, many long separations over the years, but I am not doing well this time. I am embarrassed to bring this up, but I need help.

That night Maharishi called David and Keith into his meeting room and told them, "They are crying for you at MIU." David and Keith were both on the plane the next morning and home to us that afternoon. I felt validated and supported by Maharishi. If he had thought my need was unimportant or passing, he would have said, tell her he will be home in a few days. I had seen that happen many times in the years around him. A few days, a few days more, and weeks and months could go by. Around Maharishi you were in the gap, and cosmic matters (not necessarily apparent) overruled daily ones. I knew a woman who was heading back to the U.S. and Maharishi asked her not to leave yet. She insisted and when she returned she had a terrible automobile accident and injuries and it took her years to recover to some functional level. I believe he saw the possibility of that or that it might be a bad time for her without specific details and knew that if she stayed until that time passed, she might avoid them or soften the karmic blow. Who knows? I was not embarrassed or ashamed of myself. I felt loved and valued and grateful.

Accreditation

MIU was preparing for a visit from the accreditation team of the North Central Association of Colleges and Secondary Schools in the autumn of 1979. An accreditation team had come in 1976 to evaluate our application and found that the nineteen senior and twenty assistant faculty were "creative in their vision for higher education and eminently qualified" and granted us "candidate for accreditation status." We were then granted accreditation for our undergraduate programs and even our Masters programs, but we wanted our new doctoral programs included as well. We wanted to be accredited to the doctoral level and to become a full member of the North Central Association.

Larry came back from Switzerland and spearheaded the effort. There were forms and descriptions (self-studies) to write for each department. This was extremely important because accreditation to this level would help MIU in many ways. Students would be eligible for grants and financial aid and so would the University in many ways. Each department had to prepare documents about what they taught, the professors, and so forth. Margaret and I were responsible for our section of the report. Lenny and Lesley were busy on the administrative side. They had to talk about the physical plant, our future plans. The report must be thorough, comprehensive, academic, yet true to our mission, which had to be explained in terms the team (a panel of academics from other universities) would understand.

In preparation for the visit, the whole place had to be improved in appearance as well. We wanted to make a good impression on the team. It wouldn't be easy because there was little money for repairs and improvements. Tuition and donations barely covered operating expenses. David remembers that Susie and Emily's mother, Helen Levin, was visiting at the time. She was a very impressive woman, a professional educator, and a member of the North Central Association (she recused herself from voting on MIU). Mrs. Levin noticed that the large glass doors leading into the library needed cleaning. She didn't tell anyone about it. She just got a bucket and cleaning materials and set to work herself to clean them up. David and Larry noticed and appreciated her pitching in. She must have thought they were *schmutzig* (Yiddish for dirty), Larry commented.

There was a community spirit and excitement about the whole thing. The team came, looked, asked questions, interviewed students, faculty, administrators, staff (most of whom were volunteer, getting small stipends and course credit for their efforts), child-care, the whole place. Maharishi had sent Geoffrey Clements to be there when the team visited. After they toured one of the science laboratories and the faculty had left, they asked Geoffrey what he himself thought about our faculty. When they came out after talking to him they looked at our guys with a newly evident respect and admiration, David remembers. They finally left to consider and evaluate all they had read and seen. After the visit we waited anxiously through the autumn and winter to hear the results.

The Golden Dome

The TM-Sidhi program had spread throughout the faculty, staff and students and morning and evening program spaces were set up with small groups all over campus. It would be best to combine the small groups into one or two large ones. Eventually we were all moved into the University fieldhouse, depriving the students of a gymnasium. At first there was a sheet partition hung across the huge space, men on one side, ladies on the other. We meditated and did our program in comfortable clothing, often fell asleep during or after the program, so it was like a big pajama party and we were more comfortable with the sexes separated. David and I especially remember Friday evenings when there was a lively current of interest between the boys and girls on either side of the big curtain as the weekend approached, expressed in terms of whoops and hollers and other sounds. There was plenty of room on campus to build some big buildings for the men's and women's programs, and after much deliberation, the dome structure was decided on. Builders and products had to be researched, money raised, and volunteers with expertise gathered together.

People in Iowa were somewhat concerned. Would we be flying

around and creating air-traffic problems? There was a lot of interest and confusion. It was all very exciting. Would the place be under roof before the blizzards hit? The project was getting enormous support of nature. It didn't seem possible that it could be done in time, but the cold weather miraculously held off while concrete slabs and foundations were being poured. The structure began to rise up out of the field and take shape against the sunsets. It would be a beautiful wooden building, natural and elegant. The roof would somehow be golden. This was the late autumn of 1979 and winter was coming on. So was Christmas. We liked to fly to El Paso to spend Christmas with David's parents, Nate and Sara's beloved Nana and Papa. David's mother suggested that we all meet in Florida in Key West instead.

Our little camper had been destroyed on the trip to Fairfield, so we had bought another used tent camper and taken various trips with it. The University had given us an old Dodge to drive around campus and we had put a hitch on it. We were ready to go. Nana and Papa would rent a camper van when they got to Florida. David's sister Jeanie would stay with them. David's brother Bill and his wife Nan would rent a place in Key West with a pool and we would all hang out together in the warm weather and swim and play. We packed up the car and camper and headed south with our tofu sandwiches, planning to camp and picnic along the way in order to keep it affordable (we had a very small faculty stipend). I think we may have been getting about $250 or $300 per month from the University at the time (and an apartment, and food, and gas, and medical care), so we would have very little cash to operate on until we joined up with the family.

The first evening on the road we had a disaster. We pulled into some little Iowa town just as the car leaked out all of its transmission fluid. We got it refilled and we checked into a motel, trying to decide what to do next. I think the sensible thing to do would have been to return to MIU and forget the long trip south in an old iffy car. Was this a sign? We didn't consider that aspect of it.

In the morning, the ground under the car was dry. The fresh transmission fluid seemed to have soaked into the gaskets and expanded them and maybe we were okay. I really don't know what I am talking about here, so I may be getting it wrong. In any case, we were advised that we could proceed and keep checking the fluids. We couldn't turn back. Christmas lay ahead of us, and Nana and Papa, and the warmth of Florida.

We met up with the family, picked up sister Jeanie, brother Bill and his wife Nan, in Miami and headed south to Key West. Somewhere along the route we saw a cloud of white, something like smoke, in front of us as we drove along. David immediately stopped to investigate. Bill pulled the camper in behind us. David saw a truck upside down in the black, wide ditch running along the highway. It was slowly sinking into the watery muck. It must have come around the curve on the far side of the ditch, probably slid on the gravel, and flipped over. David jumped out of the car and dashed for the disappearing truck and jumped into the water. He kept diving down but the water was a murky green and he couldn't see anything anywhere. At one point, he found the truck door with his hands and tried to open it up. A few other cars and trucks pulled over to watch.

David tried one last time, felt his way along the truck body, pulled himself lower and lower until he found a window, reached in, felt a head of hair, pulled, and the young man easily slid out. David pushed him to the surface and followed him toward the shore. Bill saw the black head and at first thought it was David covered with slime. They pulled him out and Bill started doing CPR with his hands and mouth, but it was too late. The boy had probably hit his head on the steering wheel and become unconscious. In his pocket was his Christmas pay check. When the other men saw who it was, they disappeared. Police showed up and a 911 unit as well. They treated David's eyes in case he got something in them in the poisonous soup, told him to quickly get a tetanus booster, and we all moved along, stunned and sad for the boy and his family and feeling helpless against what had happened. David felt a need to isolate himself, purify, meditate, and reground himself. Everyone was silent. Pop was proud of his boys. Nate and Sara thought Dad was a hero. We found our campground in Key West, dropped Bill and Nan at their hotel, and life moved on.

We had a wonderful vacation and family trip and drove back home to find out that in our absence Maharishi had unexpectedly turned up to see the progress in the first dome. There had been meetings there in the open air with snow on some of the beams, and the whole thing was magical. We had missed it. Susan Humphrey had tried to locate us, calling every campground she could find in the phone book. We felt out of tune with nature, terrible, awful. Had we made the wrong choice? Was it a mistake?

A Very Busy Year

IN EARLY 1980 David went off to Thailand with Maharishi and Nandkishore and the entourage and was gone for some time. After that came a meeting of the American Association of Physicians Practicing the TM program in New Orleans. This group of doctors had formed to introduce TM to the medical community. In the spring David went on a rehabilitation tour of European capitals with Art Anderson, Jon Shear, Frank Papentin, and George Ellis, and they stopped by Roydon Hall, in England, where our Wendy was settled with a ladies' group there.

The Golden Dome was finally finished and the men would begin doing their TM-Sidhi program there. But before they started, we ladies were invited in to do the first program there, to inaugurate the Dome and get a taste of the Dome atmosphere. It was difficult to close the eyes. The curved beams crossing each other high above us, the little opening at the top letting the evening light come in, the vast expanse of silence, the presence of all that beautiful natural wood and the subtle effect of all those hours of dedication—overwhelming. A deeper purpose for this first program in the Dome may have been to inspire our minds and put our consciousness to work on the desire for our own Dome, which was next on the agenda and only awaiting funds.

Our beloved Margaret Butler, the chair of the Literature

Department, had to leave MIU. Her husband Ed developed a brain tumor and needed surgery and then radiation. They moved to Iowa City, closer to his doctors, and she got a job at the University of Iowa, way below her abilities and education, but the best she could find in that university town filled with academics looking for positions. It was very difficult for her to leave her life, career, and friends, and painful for us as well. I became the chair of the department that March and my administrative load increased.

One day Larry called a special meeting in the Dome. He got up before the whole community and announced that MIU had been awarded accreditation to the doctoral level. We were now a full member of the Association of Schools and Colleges in our region. We had tears in our eyes; we hugged each other and whooped and hollered. We had worked very hard to make it happen, but the wonder of it all was that the team had seen beyond the old campus buildings, the insufficient groundskeeping, and the low remuneration of staff and faculty, had understood our vision and dedication and judged it to be important and worthy. We couldn't help but think that the coherence created by our groups of Sidhas had influenced the collective consciousness.

The PhD

My goal in this life, even before I started TM, had been to get a PhD, and Maharishi had repeatedly emphasized this as well. Why? I am not sure. Something on my karmic check list? Something that would affect my evolution? There was a subtle urgency propelling the project, something that I now recognize as a push from nature to hurry me along on this evolutionary path, usually a bit faster than is comfortable. As I look back I see that the bits and pieces did indeed come together for me. I had been teaching our second year one-month literature course which was based on Joseph Campbell's book *Hero With a Thousand Faces*. Working with the ideas of Carl Jung and others, Campbell took the idea of archetypes (patterns of consciousness) and applied it to story patterns found in all cultures. He called it the monomyth or hero's journey or quest.

The hero of the quest faces all sorts of obstacles, but if he perseveres he finds union with God in the end. This is the universal truth of all religions, Campbell believed, underlying their various cultural details. We read epics, dramas, and other works of literature and saw the various stages of the quest everywhere, and we could see that the end point, or goal, was the gaining of enlightenment, God Consciousness and Unity Consciousness. It wasn't a big step from Campbell's thesis and it enabled to students to enjoy movies, stories, and plays in a very personal way and to see their own growth of consciousness displayed large.

This book was a big influence on George Lucas when he was working on his *Star Wars* films. Moongadget.com spells out the stages of the quest in *Star Wars* in a table. Lucas had learned TM over forty years ago and there is speculation that "the Force" was inspired by concepts from SCI and Yoda by Maharishi. Whatever the case, Lucas has come out in recent years in support of the TM initiatives of the David Lynch Foundation, especially the Quiet Time programs in the San Francisco schools.

As I widened my knowledge of classical literature, I had discovered *The Golden Ass*, by Apuleius (c. 124 – c. 170 CE), the only remaining novel written in Latin. It describes the adventures of a boy named Lucius who experiments with occult magic and get turned into a donkey as a result of his foolishness. He goes through many adventures, finally encounters the Mother Goddess Isis, eventually gets on the right spiritual path, and moves in the direction of enlightenment. At the center and heart of the novel, as Lucius passes a long winter in his donkey body waiting for the spring roses that would transform him back, he hears the tale of Cupid and Psyche. Psyche, the soul, goes through her own difficult quest in order to be reunited with Love and be made divine and immortal. Although Campbell builds his theory around male "heroes" and his temptations are all described in Judeo-Christian misogynist terms (woman as temptress, Eve as the villain seducing poor Adam, etc.), I could see the monomyth operating in that tale. I would have to strike out from Campbell and the Christian mindset, however, and find my own way.

Especially telling was the central event in Psyche's journey where she is sent to the underworld (think inner world), to bring back a box of Beauty (Plato's version of the Absolute). Her journey underground is described as a descent involving less and less activity until she reaches the silent depths below and converses with the goddess Proserpina, queen of the underworld. It is the story of transcending. Did Apuleius mean that? Was it an accident?

I had begun to do research on Cupid and Psyche, on the Lucius frame folk tale, on Apuleius's neo-Platonic education and writings, and I found that it was all coming together. I spent days in the University of Iowa library in Iowa City and brought home piles of books and photocopies of articles. Sometimes I stayed overnight at my friend Tracey's. She had been on faculty at MIU and was getting an MA degree from the University of Iowa. I found a number of modern novels based on the Cupid and Psyche theme. Would they depict Psyche's descent in the same kind of inner or transcending manner? Would they respond to what I believed was the ultimate archetype in this way? I read and read, but I had to fit my research into the off months between courses during the school year, between all my domestic and administrative and academic responsibilities, while the kids were in playschool and in between trips, and travels. I found a sympathetic advisor at the University of Maryland, a former teacher of mine named Lewis Lawson, and I was on my way.

In the summer of 1980 I set about actually writing my dissertation. As soon as the kids ran off to camp, I sat down to write and only stopped when I had to eat lunch. When the kids came back in the afternoon, I dropped my pencil until the next day. One day Nate popped in and asked what was for lunch. I said, well, I could stop writing and make something, or you could make something and I could keep working on my PhD. He considered that. He was very interested in me being an important person. What should I make? Anything, I said. How about an omelet, he asked. Fine. Nate likes to cook and he set to work. We had a lovely lunch together, just the two of us, and then he disappeared and I went back to work.

Summer Fun

In June there was a big inauguration of the College of Natural Law which the movement had opened in Washington, D.C. We all went and the event was held at the Omni Shoreham Hotel. Sara had turned ten in June and pestered me until I found time to teach her the adult TM technique. She was radiant with her practice. Nate took another Youth Invincibility Course block with all his friends and drove the Wilsons crazy, I am sure.

That summer we also went camping in Rocky Mountain National Park with Nana and Papa. Nate checked out every rig in the campground and declared ours to be the poorest one there. Well, it was, and cost and status have been important to him since his birth. The mountains and wildflowers were gorgeous and we swam and hiked all over, and then we stopped in Denver so David could appear on a TV show talking about TM. There was a TV personality named Denver Pyle there. He played Uncle Jesse on the Dukes of Hazard, a show that the kids watched. He was also being there taped for an interview. The kids were impressed. Dad was a TV personality! That summer David was on tour again with Keith and Alex Hankey and Geoffrey Clements and they got to visit Maharishi in Seelisberg and make some tapes there. We have photos of David on stage in the Sonnenberg. When he came back we all went tubing on the Des Moines River with Tracey. We had a lovely family summer. David had another trip to Europe, this time to speak at an International Symposium of Consciousness in Barcelona. He hated to travel and was constantly on the move. I loved to travel and envied every trip.

Halloween stands out in my memory bank, aided by a photograph. Teachers at the Maharishi School suggested that the students dress up as familiar characters for Halloween. Sara chose Harpo Marx, probably because of her halo of golden curls. We have a picture of her sweet, happy face shining out from under a top hat.

Autumn Session of the World Government of the Age of Enlightenment

Suddenly Maharishi called together a big one-month course to be held in Delhi, India starting on November 5, 1980. My mother came to Fairfield and moved into our apartment to live with Nate and Sara (he was thirteen, she was ten). I packed up my sarees and off we went. It took a few days to organize the MIU group so we left MIU on November 7 and arrived on the 9. Maharishi told us to rest for a day or two, so the first meeting we attended was on November 11, a few days into the course. One of Maharishi's supporters had lent the movement his commercial building, which would soon house the presses for his paper the *Indian Express*. It was a huge building with many floors and a terrifying opening down the center looking into the basement of the structure. We were housed in hotels and guest houses but we were to eat lunch and dinner in the Indian Express building. We were bussed there from our hotels for the day, through slow and noisy traffic and past horrifying city dumps and landfills (think *Slum Dog Millionaire*, if you have seen that film). I wore an allergy mask on every ride and by the end of the course, the pink felt had turned dark grey with soot and pollution.

The men were given the option of being housed in large tents in the fields outside of Delhi. David thought that would be adventurous. Indian tents are like Arabian ones, large and decorated and like little homes. The sunlight would pour through the beautifully printed fabrics creating patterns of color everywhere. They could also hear the chanting of thousands of pandits from a nearby encampment. The sanitation facilities were not ideal, however, and soon everyone was having Delhi belly. David lasted a week or two, pulled rank, and moved into the Lodi hotel with George Todt, who was really sick. I had been living with faculty members Shelley Levin and Carol Bandy in a little guesthouse. We were soon moved into the Ambassador Hotel for ten days and then to the Rama Inn.

Enough of that! I insisted we live together in the Lodi Hotel. Frances Knight was in charge of housing. Why was that necessary? she asked. Was I helping him with his work? Really! I was finally allowed to move in with him November 24 once his roommate was moved somewhere else. She probably checked it with Maharishi. When we were together the course became more comfortable for me emotionally. And I have to say that one of the highlights of the whole adventure was the traditional South Indian breakfast which we shared every morning at the Lodi Hotel. At least we had one really delicious meal a day.

The ostensible reason for this course was to introduce us to Maharishi Vedic Science^{SM}, to all the works of the Veda and their organization. Maharishi published a full page description of the course and his intentions in the *Sunday Standard,* which gave the whole overview of the course and why we were there. I can't do better than to put it in his exact words. The newspaper showed a huge photo of Maharishi with the caption, "His Holiness Maharishi Mahesh Yogi, founder of Vedic Science and the World Government of the Age of Enlightenment, who brought to light the 'Apaurasheya Commentary' of Rig Veda and inaugurated the Dawn of the Age of Enlightenment." These words appeared to the left of the photo: "This World Assembly is to unfold the full potential of Vedic Wisdom to create a powerful evolutionary influence in world consciousness and give its benefit to the world to eliminate the age-old problems of mankind in this generation.

"Thousands of traditional Vedic pandits performing their cherished yagyas and thousands of Governors of the Age of Enlightenment during the morning and evening yoga practice (the Transcendental Meditation and TM-Sidhi programme) are contributing an intense influence of *sattva* [purity] for the entire world's population to enjoy.

"The Vedic programme of yoga and yagya is purifying world consciousness and creating an evolutionary influence by enlivening natural law so that life everywhere on earth is evolutionary for everyone and health, happiness, peace, and prosperity reign in society."

The article continues with more of Maharishi's words: "It is most fortunate at this hour of human evolution that there is a global awakening to the oldest theme of knowledge about life, the Veda. Having repeatedly verified this knowledge over the last 21 years on the level of direct personal experience, and having found that it enriches all aspects of life of the individual and society, we feel tempted to dive deep into this beautiful wisdom and to come out with a complete understanding about it. That was the reason I invited you here."

He went on to say that Vedic Science would be correcting the problems created by modern science: "Playing around with the fine particles of nature, science has discovered the destructive potential of natural law and has delivered total annihilation at the doorstep of human existence. World events daily impress upon us the urgency of developing a new sense of wisdom in the human race if our existence is not to become ever more precarious." He told us in one meeting that he didn't think the world had ever been more ignorant. The Governors, he said, will create a greater power than the stupidity of the great power blocs.

We later learned that U.S. and Russian submarines were positioning themselves near each other in the Indian Ocean and there was a serious danger that some incident could trigger a world war. So the practical significance of the Assembly was that enough pandits and Governors of the Age of Enlightenment were gathered together in order "to enliven the collective consciousness of India and the entire world."

Maharishi lectured on Vedic Science every day and we lettered posters illustrating what he talked about and hung them on the pillars of the hall. I am no expert so I am going to quote what Maharishi said about the Vedas, what he published in the Delhi *Standard*. He went over every word, I am quite sure, so his words are the best entry into the subject matter of our course. It is significant that he published his whole program for all of India to read, regardless of their readiness to hear it.

"On November 5 the World Assembly started by reviewing the range of knowledge offered by Vedic Science. Maharishi described how Vedic Science covers the entirety of knowledge by including everything that ever could be known about the 'known' (the object of perception), the 'knower' (the subject or self) and the process by which the knower and the known come together to produce any aspect of 'knowledge'. Of the six Upangas, systems of gaining knowledge in Vedic Science, Nyaya and Vedanta are dedicated to pure knowledge, Sankhya and Yoga are dedicated to the knower, and Vaisheshika and Karma Mimamsa are dedicated to the field of the known.

"Under Maharishi's guidance the World Assembly reviewed every aspect of Vedic literature and saw how all this literature, taken together, presents the full range of Vedic Science, how the Upangas, Upavedas, and Smritis present the path of discovering the Veda; how the Veda is discovered in the simplest form of one's own awareness and has two aspects: Mantra, reflecting pure knowledge, and Brahmana, reflecting the infinite organizing power inherent in pure knowledge; and how the Vedangas, Ithihasas and Puranas present the complete study of the Vedas; their structure, modes of expression, universal applicability, verifiability, and eternal validity.

"The Assembly then moved on to analyse the compatibility of Vedic Science and modern science." One section of the newspaper page is a chart illustrating "The Six Upangas and Modern Physics," the result of discussions between Maharishi and the

Vice-Chancellor of MERU, our old friend Geoffrey Clements. Prominently displayed is a photo of the stage in front of us in the main hall. The caption reads: "Maharishi with Vedic scholars and scientists discussing the relationship between Vedic Science and modern science. At the front of the stage are all the major works of Vedic literature. Maharishi is seated beneath the picture of his Master, His Divinity Swami Brahmananda Saraswati Jagadguru Bhagwan Shankaracharya of Jyotir Math, Himalayas." Geoffrey is sitting to the far right. Bringing out the Vedic knowledge in the name of Guru Dev was one of Maharishi's main ambitions. Reestablishing the vitality of the pandit culture and its activities was another, and it would take years to accomplish.

There is also a big section on the newspaper page delineating all of Maharishi's impressive achievements around the world, from the World Plan, to creating 16,000 TM teachers, the discovery of the Maharishi Effect, inaugurating the Dawn of the Age of Enlightenment, founding MERU in Switzerland [he leaves out MIU, possibly to avoid being seen as being on the American side of the Cold War], establishing the World Government of the Age of Enlightenment, developing the TM-Sidhi program in 1977, training Governors of the Age of Enlightenment to administer the trends of time, the Ideal Society campaign in 108 countries simultaneously in 1978, the Ideal Village program in 1979, and starting the Global Super Radiance Program to coordinate groups of Governors around the world, thus intensifying their effects on collective consciousness. And all this while developing his unique commentary on the Rig Veda, and now bringing this knowledge to India and through the Governors to the whole world.

We sat in front of Maharishi on very thin mattresses on the stone floor, crowded together uncomfortably. Very uncomfortably. I don't even want to talk about the food. Our flying hall was carpeted with the same thin mattresses and nearly as crowded, hot, and miserable. There were two toilets on that floor, hardly sufficient for a large group of women. We waited and waited in line. Somehow the pull of the knowledge of the Vedas and the TM-Sidhi program took over and we settled into silence and had deep meditations. I joked to one of my friends as we sat around discussing the challenges of life on the course, "No wonder the knowledge has been lost, if this is what it takes to revive it." Every now and then someone reminds me of these words.

Sometimes at our evening meetings Emily Levin would get up to sing her birthday song. She was given a list of those people who were having birthdays that day, but the CPs had come from all over the world and many of their names were mostly consonants with no discernable vowels, and when she got to the line, "Happy birthday to . . ." she had to stumble along, hoping they would recognize themselves.

Maharishi told us that he was bringing out a new name for the knowledge he was giving us, Vedic Science, my course notes say. It is a new science because its rules are not included or recognized by any other science. The name couldn't be used until now, he said, because the knowledge of the Veda was too dim to be heard, even in India. Natural law had been sleepy because of the vastness of ignorance, but our presence here is entering into the nerves of nature's functioning, he said. This is a very historic gathering, and by the time we finish this assembly we will have unobstructed knowledge of the structure of pure knowledge, he insisted.

The Veda shouldn't be associated with various times or religions, he said. It is not a faith; it describes the mechanics of nature. It is eternal. How do we enter into this eternal field? How do we get to the Cosmic Self when we are immersed in the senses and the mind? Through the gap, he explained, the junction point, the meeting point of opposite values, the field of all possibilities, the home of all the laws of nature, the structure of pure knowledge, the infinite spring of organizing power. That is our own unbounded awareness.

It's like the meeting of the Jamuna and Ganga Rivers at Allahabad (where, it is said, the underground Saraswati River joins the confluence). There the Saraswati River blossoms. Sar means lake, swa means self; the wisdom of the Self blossoms at the meeting point of the two, the pond of the Self, the pool of pure knowledge. With the TM-Sidhi program we are creating an effect from the gap; the fog is lessening, pure awareness is increasing, and the relationships between the fine fabrics of creation are being experienced clearly, he assured us.

How does the Cosmic Self get individualized in the Governor? Through the instrumentality of feelings, through refining feelings, and culturing life through the TM-Sidhi program. Don't allow harmful things to enter the system, he cautioned. Don't muddle awareness with thorny perceptions. We were given some behavioral guidelines to follow, which I faithfully wrote down: truthfulness, non-anger and no intoxicating drugs, pleasant speech (feelings should be saved from irritation and anger), patience, friendliness, good hygiene on all levels, generosity, life in balance, and balance of rest and activity.

Every cognition of the Veda is in terms of a deva, he explained, an intelligence [or law of nature] that directs the flow. Through the Sidhis, awareness opens to the finer values of the devata level. When you observe something, he said, you enliven its devata aspect. The approach is important; gentle, loving approach is best. Modern science is dangerous because it approaches the subtle layers of creation violently. Each Sidhi sutra is a channel for the simplest form of awareness to make an entry into the senses in a gradual, effortless, natural way.

Each Vedic hymn has two values: word and gap. Both are the same Self, he said, but it is difficult for the Self to find itself broken into two pieces. It takes quite a long time to settle down, even for a perfect Sidha. The neurons get upset when they are faced with two opposite experiences of infinite magnitude. So the Vedas have the branch called the Upavedas, to help the physiology adjust and balance itself. One of the Upavedas is Ayurveda, the science of life. The time had come to bring it out.

Sitting prominently on the stage with Maharishi was a large elderly vaidya, or Ayurvedic medical man, named Brihaspati Dev Triguna, who was president of the All India Ayurvedic Congress and was the personal physician of the president of India. He sat there along with several other vaidyas, and pandits of the various branches of the Veda. Maharishi wanted to hear from them about how Ayurveda balances the physiology through its mechanics: pulse diagnosis, the five elements, herbs, behavior, the three doshas or types [vata, pitta and kapha], and various treatments to balance those types.

Maharishi was very interested in the notion of immortality at the time. It should be possible, he said, to see the element of non-change in the structure of the physiology. Change will always be there, but it should be restorative, not corrosive, from one day to the other, from one hour to the other, from one moment to the other. He asked the pandits to chant some verses from Sama Veda on immortality. One pandit said that Ayurveda is for immortality. Certain herbs, called rasayanas, give vitality, radiance and bliss; they prevent suffering and old age. Long life has a purpose, the promotion of *dharma* (one's duty, right action, or best evolutionary path), not just longevity for its own sake.

During the mornings, people were going off to see Dr. Trigunaji at his clinic, to have their pulse taken, their doshas assessed, and then getting herbs to address their imbalances. Each dose was wrapped in a tiny scrap of newspaper; each elixir was bottled with alcohol. Not to be left out of anything, no matter how unusual, David and I took a taxi to the area of Delhi where he practiced and picked our way carefully along a scary, narrow, trash-filled street. Suddenly an enormous elephant came down the street towards us. We plastered ourselves up against the walls and waited while he lumbered powerfully and slowly by, indifferent to us but taking up most of the street. Colorful! We waited for Trigunaji and when he saw us, he took my pulse first. Vata, vata, vata, he proclaimed. Bloodless body! (What did that mean? I do have low blood pressure.) He took David's pulse and told him he was strong and healthy. Why are you here? he asked. David explained that he wasn't enlightened and wanted to be. David was pleased to be told that I was delicate and he was strong. Me Tarzan, you Jane. He liked that. I am such a noisy, control-freak, bossy person that the reality of the situation is often lost on him.

We were there at one meeting when Trigunaji told Maharishi that his people had been coming to see him in great numbers. Are they sick? Maharishi asked. No, Trigunaji answered, they want to get enlightened. Maharishi took that in. The time had come for another big stirring of the pot. The time had come to bring Maharishi AyurVeda out into the world. Vaidyas then appeared regularly at the Indian Express building and dispensed strange looking little irregular pills or powders. After we returned to MIU, Maharishi gathered famous vaidyas about him in India or Switzerland and began to develop the purest, most efficacious version of Ayurveda (the science of life) that he could. Courses were developed on Ayurveda and were then offered at MIU to faculty and staff. I took them all and learned how diet, the seasons, body types, pulse diagnosis, cooking with certain herbs and spices, and many other elements of this ancient and traditional medicine, could influence health and balance.

Soon a traditional herbal remedy, a rasayana suitable for all types, was developed by Maharishi and the vaidyas. His formula was called Amrit Kalash™ (a container of the nectar of immortality) and we all began to take it. At first it came in metal cans and contained, among other things, the occasional large wooden twig. Later it was refined and bottled in glass jars with beautiful labels. They also developed a program of treatments designed to balance the physiology at each change of season: massage, steam baths, and so forth. Soon we had a campus clinic and the faculty could get a five-day treatment several times a year for minimal cost. It was heavenly. We found Maharishi AyurVeda to be very valuable knowledge. It was a great gift.

I took copious notes on the course since it was all so new and not always easy to follow. I won't repeat or explain or try to teach Vedic Science here. You can take courses and degrees in Maharishi Vedic Science at Maharishi University of Management, but I do want to share a few things that strike me now as I read through these notes. Follow along as you can. Maharishi emphasized the role of the pandit in Vedic Science. Remember that he said in that newspaper page that he had organized large groups of pandits during the course whose chanting would also create world peace. That's what the men were hearing from their tents.

Maharishi explained that the flow of consciousness within itself is the pattern of the engineering of the universe, and the Vedic hymn, as it falls from the pandit's mouth, is a copy of the quiet murmur of nature within *para* (the Absolute). Even when the knowledge of refining consciousness is lost over time, the sounds of the Veda are kept, memorized, and passed on.

The pandits traditionally assemble year after year to chant together in order to keep their pronunciation pure and the sequence of sounds pure and exact; it's a very foolproof method for maintaining the correctness of the Veda, Maharishi said. The daily routine of the pandits ensures the benefits for everyone. They begin before dawn, settle into themselves and begin chanting. By the time the children wake up they can hear the sounds and start to learn them. The whole population wakes up under this influence of *sattva* (purity). The pandits repeat their chanting at noon and again in the evening. So everyone reveres them for the gift they give to the whole society; they enliven the basic functional aspects of nature; they create coherence and mistake-free life. Today, Maharishi has established groups of pandits in each Maharishi School in India, and in a room apart from the classrooms they do their traditional practices and thereby enliven the intellects of all the students.

The pandits also perform yagyas or ceremonies, and these performances are a technology to think in the outward direction and produce an effect. I was remembering when the Sama Veda pandits in Santa Barbara created copious amounts of rain in the area while they were recording those particular verses meant to bring rain. They told us they were hired in India to go to areas of drought and bring the rain. The *sankalpa*, the intention, the resolution of the yagya, gives the intended target in time and space. In specific yagyas, Maharishi said, mantras combine on a transcendental level to produce a specific effect. Groups of pandits have now been set up in India and the U.S. in order to influence the trends of time, to dissolve negativity and create world peace.

Back in Delhi, one of our friends was planning to get married and decided to have a traditional Indian wedding, with Maharishi's blessing. I had the purple and gold wedding saree David had brought me from India years before, and as I stood dressed in it in front of our hotel waiting for a taxi, I noticed the Indian women giving me strange looks. I tried to explain that I was dressed for a wedding and they nodded politely. I didn't know it then, but the wedding season is during January during the cool weather, not on a hot November afternoon. Google Indian weddings and you will see processions with the groom on a white horse, people marching and making music, and huge noisy celebrations lasting late into the night. Ours was a quiet simple one, with a central fire and the bride and groom walking around it with the ends of their clothes tied together. There was a lot of chanting, and we didn't understand the many traditional and symbolic offerings and gestures, but it was all very interesting. Maharishi dampened down the enthusiasm of some on the course to rush out and get married also in order to have the ceremony by reminding us not to rush into marriage, which is essentially a great sacrifice of time and energy, along with the love and companionship possible.

Towards the end of the course Maharishi put another full page message to the Indian population in one of the papers. We had taken a group photo under the banner "Autumn Session of the World Government of the Age of Enlightenment" and it was put to the right of Maharishi's picture, right at the top of the page. Under Maharishi's picture it said: "The Veda, from the clear vision of a modern physicist, has the characteristics of a superparticle— the ultimate basis of all creation in the theory of supergravity— and should be studied in the light of quantum electrodynamics, quantum chromodynamics, geometric dynamics, and the gauge theories that are currently being developed towards a unified field theory." Got that? Below a little text about science and the Veda was a huge chart showing the seven divisions of the Veda on the left and parallel entries in columns for Physics, Chemistry, and Mathematics. Wow. Who would understand that in the whole population of New Delhi? Inscrutable but impressive.

By the time the course ended, Maharishi was pleased with the effects of the Governors. Secretly, beautifully, they have robbed the power blocs of their leadership in the family of nations, he said. Yes, there were some conflicts here and there, but a lot had been accomplished. On the Vedic Science course the fine feelings of the Governors were enlivening *para* [the Absolute]; they were having an enriching influence on the whole world. He wanted us to do program together at home. *Sattva* is coherence in English, he said. Just as little straws make a great rope that can pull a big ship, and little impressions [stresses] can make a *jiva* [a soul] continue through eternity, so our group coherence would affect the whole world. It is enough to be born as a human being, he said, with a birthright for full enlightenment. We will soon cognize those laws of nature which are guiding life at this time.

We were inspired but not feeling very healthy. Many of our friends were staying on for the course extension, but we had a Christmas date with the kids and grandparents in El Paso. When we got there we went to see a German enterologist right away. He took samples. Was it Giardia, I asked, remembering our earlier trip. David had been on many trips, so who knows what he had. It's a zoo in there, he said (his professional diagnosis), and gave us the hated drug Flagyl. I learned that if I took half the amount twice as often I could survive the nausea. I remember lying on the bathroom floor in the middle of the night waiting to see if I would have to throw up. When we had finished the drugs we felt good, full of energy, back to normal. We took the kids to White Sands National Monument near El Paso and played in the white sand, rolling down the dunes with Nate and Sara and laughing and laughing. They hated to leave the place. Mom and Dad were rarely such fun. We thought we might go back to India and even arranged for a couple to move into our apartment to take care of them, but we were told to stay at MIU. Our time with him was over for now. Back to work.

Around this time our brilliant friend Larry Domash left MIU to pursue marriage, a family, and a career in physics. He had been an ideal president: academic, intellectual (and I mean this in a good way—deeply interested in knowledge), inspiring, and with a great sense of humor. We would miss his presence and leadership.

The Ladies' Dome
and Another Busy Year

I CONTINUED TO DO research and some writing on my dissertation and sent chapters off to my advisor in Maryland. Construction was proceeding on the ladies' Dome, and David continued to travel for the movement. In February 1981 I gave a paper on the transcendental aspects of Doris Lessing's *The Marriages Between Zones Three, Four, and Five*. I related it to what I called an archetype for the evolution of consciousness. I presented it at the Ninth Annual Conference on Twentieth-Century Literature at the University of Louisville in Kentucky. I got the idea from my dissertation research on the archetype of transcending and I later worked these ideas on Lessing's novel into my dissertation. It was very exciting; it was my first conference presentation. I got to stand up in front of my academic peers and present my research connecting literature to Maharishi's knowledge of consciousness.

That spring MIU got a grant to host a series of colloquia in the different departments, to bring in experts in each field and interact with them in order to develop our own vision of education in the light of Vedic Science and SCI and to learn from their more traditional perspectives. Each department published a brochure containing an abstract of the proceedings with long excerpts from the talks and photos of all the participants. I have mine for the Literature Department colloquium, a beautiful exposition of talks by our guys: Dr. Ralph Yarrow of the University of East Anglia in Norwich, England; Peter Malekin of the University of Durham in Durham, England; Dr. William Peden of the University of Missouri in Columbia (Sally Peden's father); Peter Nelson, a great poet and teacher who was visiting faculty that semester; and Dr. Carmen Sarracino of Elizabethtown College in Pennsylvania. Our invited guest was Dr. Robert Scholes of Brown University. We had been reading his books on literary criticism and were eager to hear his response to our talks during the panel discussion. I gave an overview of my interpretation of the Cupid and Psyche archetype and Silvine asked him questions about his critical position. Professors Doug White and Jon Shear spoke too. The whole thing was videotaped, and Scholes leaned over to whisper to me, "This is hard!" He was unused to performing unscripted in front of video cameras.

The whole thing was brilliant and inspiring to us all. It took quite a lot of our time to set it up, invite people, manage the finances for the grant, organize the event, and create the brochure, but we felt strong and competent with the knowledge. I felt bolder and more confident about putting it out there to my peers.

Staying Young

Later that spring (1981) Keith dragged us into his laboratory. He wanted to see the effects of TM on aging. He had tables correlating near-point vision, blood pressure, and vital capacity (lung power, you could say) with chronological age. He wanted subjects over forty. David had turned forty in January, and I had turned forty the summer before. We dutifully showed up and were tested. I came out to have a biological age of twenty-eight, twelve years younger than my chronological age. Great! David had a biological age of twenty eight and a half. Even better. He always wanted to be older than me, and now he was. A joke. We laughed about it, but aging is the ultimate stress test, isn't it? It was good to know we weren't aging as fast as we might, thanks to our TM and TM-Sidhi program.

This wasn't the end of it. Geoffrey made a chart a few years later (that Maharishi loved) illustrating all the changes TM made in the direction of decreased ageing and increased longevity: increased cerebral blood flow, faster reflex recovery, better temperature homeostasis (not by me: my hot flashes had started and my internal temperature regulator was seriously demented—cold flashes followed by intense hot flashes all day and night), better serum cholesterol and glucose tolerance, improved memory, less depression, and less insomnia (except for me with my hot flashes). Of course, these findings are statistically significant, meaning that most people experience them, but not everyone.

A few years later David would do a study based on Blue Cross of Iowa statistics on a group of 2,000 meditators compared to non-meditators at similar locations, with similar professions, and all that, and not only did the TMers have half the rate of hospitalizations and doctor visits of the non-meditators, the effects became even more striking with age. The TM over-forty group did much better than the other over-forty groups. Medical care utilization went up steeply for the non-meditators with age, as expected, but much more slowly for the meditators. David told Blue Cross about these results *using their statistics*, but they weren't interested, except possibly for their own employees. He later learned that insurance companies aren't concerned with wellness; their profits are regulated, so they are only interested in cash flow, which they then invest for their shareholders. Less sickness, lower premiums, less cash flow, less profit for the shareholders. Greed triumphs over social wellbeing.

Family Fun and Travels

Once again in the summer of 1981 Nate went on the Youth Invincibility Course, and Sara, only eleven, was given permission to join the course as well, by Maharishi, no doubt. Who else? She did her hair in a crown of braids to tame her unruly curls and to look older. She was the youngest one on the course, but many of the others were her friends from Switzerland and MIU. Another big challenge for Gregg and Georgina Wilson, but they did a great job and the kids had a lot of fun.

I spent every morning that summer writing my dissertation, and I sent in a conference proposal for a paper on Psyche's archetypal journey within. It was accepted by the Fifth American Imagery Conference in Chicago that autumn. I didn't actually go. Silvine presented the paper for me and I stayed home and taught. By the end of the summer I was finished with a draft of the whole dissertation and was ready to edit, rewrite, and send off polished chapters to my advisor. I still needed to do some research to fill in a hole here and there, but it was all going very well. David went off to give a paper at the American Psychological Conference in L.A. and had a great time surfing with Tom Factor and Peter Wallace and all his California friends. In November I dragged

Emily Levin and I inside Wally DeVasier's plane on our way around the East Coast on our fundraising tour. Young and beautiful!

the literature faculty, Susan Setzer and Silvine Marbury and Tim Truby, to the Midwest Modern Language Association meeting in St. Louis. None of us had a paper accepted but we got to hear quite a few, and I was hoping some of them would be inspired to submit and present one.

The ladies' Dome was being completed and I flew off with Emily Levin on a small plane to raise funds to finish it. Emily sang and I spoke to groups of meditators in Washington, Philadelphia and a few other cities and I got to visit family and friends at these places.

Inaugurating the Ladies' Dome

In early December 1981 the Bagambhrini Golden Dome would be finished, and Canadian magician Doug Henning had chosen it to be the venue for his wedding to his fiancée Debby Douillard. Doug had been on numerous TV specials and he was a famous figure in those days. He and Debby were dedicated meditators. In the past few years he had worked closely with Maharishi and they were planning a theme park filled with magic and the knowledge of meditation. It would be called Vedaland. Some of the rides would attempt to give the experience of what higher states of consciousness might be like. The University decided to make the wedding the inaugural event, but forty-eight hours before the day of the wedding, the windows had not yet been installed, nor had the stage, lighting, or heat! Hundreds of students, staff and volunteers worked all hours of the day and the night to get it done. We all felt Maharishi's attention on us. Very blissful.

The Dome was named for Rishi Bagambhrini whose cognition is in the Tenth Mandala of the Rig Veda. Her consciousness is so expanded that she says at the end of her cognition, "I breathe forth like the wind, giving form to all created worlds; beyond the heaven, beyond the earth so vast am I in greatness."

The day before the event, Doug and Debbie rehearsed the ceremony while the walls were being painted, final windows were being installed, the orchestra was rehearsing, and the chairs, eighteen hundred of them, were being set up. By the afternoon of December 6 the finally finished dome was filled with flowers and decorated with candles and flags of every country for the occasion. There was a huge arch of flowers that the couple would walk through. Over forty cameramen and reporters were swarming over the place; there was even some TV coverage. Doug and Debbie had moved to MIU and Doug was generous with his interviews and his praise of the community and the TM program. He was planning to build a huge, magical house, and to use Fairfield as his home base, going out to do projects like Vedaland, and spreading the knowledge of enlightenment.

We began the inauguration with a call from Maharishi, who

Susan Humphrey on the left, then Susan Shatkin, Naomi Kleinman, then Catherine Castle behind the cake, Maureen Wynne behind her, and I am on the far right.

emphasized the need for sixteen hundred to meditate together at MIU. Dr. Sudarshan spoke, describing the significant role MIU was playing at that time in history. We ladies were hosting the inauguration and I was one of the last to speak, right before the wedding would take place. I remember saying something like a very special event would be occurring there in the dome today, but the really significant event would begin when they cleared out the chairs, brought in the foam mattresses, and the ladies on campus, resident and visiting, would all assemble for their first TM-Sidhi program that evening. The coherence they would radiate into the community, the state, and the whole world would have an effect on the trends of time, long after this particular wedding was over, and this has been proven true.

The Bagambhrini Golden Dome is still the site of conscious-ness-changing activity and silence morning and evening. From that time on, I structured my days around morning and evening meditations in that Dome, tromping there from our nearby apart-ment in rain, snow, ice, and subzero wind chills. Inside that dome, my meditations were clearer and crisper. At home I was easily distracted from doing my full meditation program. In the dome, once we started it was effortless to move from part to part. And the sleep I sometimes drifted into, when we lay down to rest at the end, was profound, delicious, and other-worldly.

Doctoral Orals
and *The Cosmic Psyche*

WE SPENT THE CHRISTMAS HOLIDAYS with my family in Cleveland and then David and I were invited to Seelisberg for the January 12 celebration in 1982 and it was wonderful to see Maharishi again. We had to stay in a little guesthouse in a neighboring village, however, and commute back and forth to the hall for the meetings. We didn't get much sleep or have very long to meditate but it was good to be back in Switzerland and for me, to feel like part of the international movement again. I always enjoyed the National Leaders' Conference with all the news of the movement's growth around the world, and we knew nearly everyone there even though five years had passed since we had left.

That summer there were numerous events at the College of Natural Law in Washington, D.C. The movement had fitted up a big hotel downtown on 11 Street, even installing new double-glazed windows to keep out the sounds of the city, and courses were being held there. Nate didn't want to go. He was nearly fifteen, and there was a girl he really liked in Fairfield. He resented being away from her, and with good cause. While we were away one of his friends moved in on her, and eventually married her. We took them to the fabulous art museums in the city and the museums on the Mall, Nate grumbling away, but both kids enjoying them pretty much.

Defending My Dissertation

My faculty advisor at the University of Maryland, whom I knew from my days of studying there, Lewis Lawson, was not only a southern gentleman, but he was honorable and just, without ego or personal agenda. He sincerely tried to help me get through. He helped me greatly with the structure of the manuscript. Chapters of my dissertation had gone back and forth by mail over the past few years, and I had even visited once or twice to do research at the Library of Congress or meet with other faculty there in order to build a committee and be guided by them. The man in the Classics department thought I should learn Latin since that was the language of the *Golden Ass*. That was unnecessary, and a ridiculous thing to impose on me since my thesis was based on plot elements, not the style or language, and it would take me years of studying Latin to get to the level where I could make even an amateurish translation of the work. When I needed to discuss the translation of a particularly meaningful phrase I could consult someone. We didn't invite him to be on the committee.

MIU had acquired a big computer a year or two earlier, the DEC 11, and it had a very sophisticated word processing program called Word 11. I took classes in it and became proficient, in fact, the local expert. It did footnotes and all kinds of fancy things that would have been agony to type or retype page by page (I had laboriously typed David's doctoral dissertation in 1968 and 1969). The MIU typing pool had entered all my hand-written pages and I could just edit and move things around. This was over thirty-five years ago. We take cut and paste for granted now. Many of you never even had to type on a typewriter and grew up with word processing. To me it was a miracle. David did his time-series analysis for the Israel project on that computer the next year. I had been working for several years on small computers and did word processing on them: Wordperfect, Wordstar, MacWord, etc., but this was in a whole new class.

By September we had a full committee and they were ready

to read the final draft of my dissertation. It was called *Psyche's Descent into the Underworld: The Transcending Pattern in Myth and Literature*. David was in Switzerland at the time, and he told Maharishi that I was finished and was ready to submit the final draft to my committee. She should submit it to Harvard, he said. David didn't know what to say. Maharishi had told Skip Alexander, too, that he should have his PhD from Harvard. Skip was well into his doctoral program at UCLA but he dropped it and started all over again at Harvard. Did Maharishi mean I should start all over again at Harvard? Or did he mean that I was Harvard caliber? David's mind was spinning. She is at the University of Maryland, he said. Oh, that's all right, he replied. The PhD will give her more confidence. She lacks confidence. David was surprised. He hadn't thought of me as lacking confidence because I was so bold in my speech and actions, but that was just a cover-up for my basic insecurities. I think Maharishi thought that getting the PhD would help, and it did, but there would be considerably more growth of consciousness, more to do, more to learn, much more to accomplish before I would sit comfortably in myself and know that I could do anything. David had a new view of me. Maharishi was always tinkering with our relationship, thank God!

Tell her to put this in, Maharishi said, and he dictated the paragraph below. I have italicized what I had to add to work it into the subject matter of the dissertation. I couldn't just plop it in there without any reference to the hundreds of pages that had come before. Here is what Maharishi said:

The purpose of literature is to enhance life, to allow it to flow in bliss, *in inexplicibilis voluptas* [inexpressible bliss, a reference to how Apuleius had described Psyche's bliss when she is made immortal]. Every expression of speech and writing is the flow of *the* consciousness *and coherence of its author*. Speech should be such as to awaken the inner life of the individual, to bring the listener *or reader* into harmony with the laws of his *or her* own nature and thus to gain the support of these laws of nature, *which are, in fact, identical to the very laws that describe the workings of nature herself.* It is the role of literature *(and of literary criticism)* to create models and examples of the kind of writing that will produce this effect. *The wide range of effects produced by transcending, as reported by the scientific literature on the Transcendental Meditation technique* [which I had included in footnotes earlier when I talked about transcending, even Yogi flying, which he had told me to put in!!], *suggest that the whole quality of life could thereby be greatly enhanced.* Literature records the flow of consciousness, not only on the level of superficial reality, but on the level of infinite correlation of consciousness *described by the various individuals who have experienced its existence.* The purpose of speech, of writing, is to inspire thought, feeling, and action. The purpose of action is to end action in its goal—fulfillment.

I can hear Maharishi saying these words. Those are his expressions and the thoughts he often expressed in the many tapes he made. We played these tapes to our literature majors, and I would take the phrase "the flow of consciousness" to be the title of my next big project, the collecting, transcribing, editing, and printing of these tapes. David had telexed me this paragraph.

Maharishi always embraced the latest technology, which at the time was the telex, a system of network and phone-based printers. You could put something, pictures or text, in the telex machine at your end, make the phone call, and it would print out on the destination telex. This technology made the telegram old-fashioned.

It was easy for me to insert the paragraph Maharishi had dictated to David at the very end of this dissertation. I didn't have to reprint the whole thing, or even change the page numbers on the long bibliography that came next. I sent the requisite copies for the committee to Lewis Lawson and he scheduled my oral exam.

David was still in Switzerland, working with Maharishi and the other psychologists on the Cosmic Psyche project. I flew to D.C., stayed at the College of Natural Law, and someone drove me out to the University of Maryland to defend my dissertation on the appointed day. Lewis Lawson was there, along with a woman who was an expert on folk tales, two other people whom I do not remember, and a sour-faced man from the English department. He thought I didn't know what Neoplatonism was. I thought I did. Plotinus, whom Apuleius studied and wrote about, and whom I read and studied, was generally thought to be the founder of that school of thought. I thought I did a good job of defending my knowledge and use of the term. I was a bit nervous, but confident about my work. Many questions later, someone commented on the last paragraph, the one dictated by Maharishi. "You seem to be putting forth a new theory of literature here." Yes, I said, I am. It would have been too much for them to understand where it really came from. Maybe I should have tried. If I had had my volume, *The Flow of Consciousness,* in hand, I might have had a case, but it was too early for that.

They had finished with me and Lewis asked me to wait outside while they deliberated. I wandered around in the hallway looking at posters and notes posted on faculty doors. Then I heard voices and footsteps clattering up the stairway. I overheard a faculty member telling her student that she had to go now. It was time for her to do her Transcendental Meditation in her office. I met her at the top of the stairs and cheerfully told her I was a teacher of Transcendental Meditation. She wasn't interested. She was on a schedule. She went into her office and closed the door and presumably started meditating. Well, if that isn't support of nature, I smiled, what is. She may have been a highly evolved person; her powerful vibes may have influenced my fate.

Lewis soon beckoned me to come back to the conference room. He whispered to me before I went in that they had accepted my dissertation without changes! Almost unheard of. They do like to make you suffer; they like to put their stamp on your work, to show they have done their job. I would have had to make whatever changes they required, reprinted the relevant pages or perhaps the whole thing, and then resubmitted it for their approval, and since I was headed off to Seelisberg the next day to join David there, it would have had to wait for several months at least. I thanked the committee, and Lewis and I took two copies of the dissertation and walked down to the Administration building to turn them in. I was finished. It was over. I was Dr. Rhoda Orme-Johnson. It was a bit difficult to really believe it.

I took a public bus back to the College of Natural Law and headed up to my room to get out of my fancy suit and silk blouse and do asanas. As I rolled around on the floor I felt some hard lumps in the carpet. I pulled back the asana sheet and felt around. No lumps there. They were in my back, knots of tension. It was over, but I was still adjusting. I called David and told him what happened and when I would arrive. He told Maharishi the story, especially the part where the committee noticed the paragraph he had dictated. I suspect most of them read the introduction, skimmed the body, and read the conclusion, and there it stood out. Maharishi was happy to hear that I now had the PhD and he laughed and especially enjoyed that last bit of the story.

The Cosmic Psyche

I flew into Zurich and joined David in Seelisberg, where he and Susie and Michael Dillbeck and Skip and Vicki Alexander were working on what would be called *The Cosmic Psyche*, a volume of chapters on all aspects of modern psychology related to higher states of consciousness, to Vedic Science. Every day David and the others wrote and wrote. I tried to help by typing, editing, listening. It wasn't my area and I was feeling like resting my brain. I had passed a huge evolutionary milestone in my life and I was elated. I was then in what psychologists call a post-reinforcement pause. (After an experimental animal gets its reward for pushing a button, it stops for a while, and then resumes.) Nearly every day we met with Maharishi and discussed the ideas and read out what had been written by Skip and Michael and David. Maharishi appointed Michael and Susie to be the editors, and they honed the writing down to what had already been said and written somewhere else. None of David's new ideas and connections to modern psychology made it into that draft.

We all ate and walked about together and enjoyed the celestial air of Seelisberg and the weeks went by. David's parents had promised us a trip to Greece with the kids, my chosen destination, as a reward for finishing my PhD. I wanted to visit the places I had read about in my study of Classical literature: Delphi, the temples, the islands. The kids were home with Brad and Joy Garso, staff at the Fairfield Maharishi School, and were eagerly awaiting our return and their Christmas vacation. Nate would be appearing in a Shakespeare play just before Christmas. Would we be back in time? He was being a bit wild and Lenny and Lesley took it upon themselves to spend time with him and settle him down.

At one point Maharishi had business elsewhere and wanted to slip away unseen, so he sent the six of us off to Lake Como in a limousine with a driver for a little holiday. I thought this was wonderful, a chance to be alone with David out from the pressure of the project, seeing a beautiful part of Italy, and eating some real food. It was my idea of heaven on earth. It was still warm and sunny there and lovely. We took a boat trip around the lake and our guide pointed out the houses belonging to famous, wealthy people. Our hotel was simple but nice. Susie got nervous. Susie is a yogi of vehement intensity, as the saying goes. She didn't want to be away from Maharishi. She wasn't comfortable just enjoying a respite from intense evolution as I was. She fired up the others and we rushed back. When we got there, we found that Maharishi had disappeared. We had hurried back for nothing. Back to work. I think he knew we (or at least some of us) needed a few days to air out, to relax and ground ourselves in the world. I, for one, found it a relief to have an occasional break from the intense and rarified air around Maharishi.

Weeks became months and Christmas was approaching. I was

in denial, but soon it was apparent that the Greece trip would not happen, that we would just be eventually returning to the U.S., hopefully in time for the Christmas holidays. The parents decided that we should meet in Boston and have Christmas there with David's brother Bill. Nate was keen to get a black leather jacket for Christmas and was eager to pick it out. We were happy to all be together again. We had a good visit, a nice holiday with the family, but it wasn't Greece. David admits that he owes me that trip, but with the current state of affairs in that region and our advancing years, I may never get to collect.

Israel and the Taste of Utopia

WE WERE INVITED for the January 12 celebration again, and this time it was being held in Chianciano, Italy. It is a spa town with mineral waters, and I have no idea why the celebration was being held there. Maybe a big course was being carried on there. I don't remember. Many MIU people were invited: Bevan, Dennis and Linda Raimondi, Susan Humphrey, Keith and Samantha and Lila Wallace, Michael Dimick, and lots of others. David, Skip, and Michael got to read out parts of their *Cosmic Psyche* chapters to the big group, but the group had heard it all before and wanted to hear Maharishi instead. David's birthday rolled around, but Maharishi was busy with other matters that day and didn't come out. He did send Nandkishore twice to tell David that he was thinking about him all day. We got invited to a semi-private meeting that evening, or the next one. Chris Wege was there. David invited Keith to come along. We chatted with Maharishi about this and that, nothing significant, and when we got up to go, I thought deep in my heart, that it would be the last time I would be in a small room with him like the old days, yet I couldn't think of anything cosmic to ask or say. Was I now off on my own? It was a lowering thought, but just as when we were first told we would go to MIU and an important year passed before it happened, this was a glimpse of the future, even if it did take about thirteen years to play out.

Maharishi then sent the whole group to Rome to do a little sightseeing, "to see the Pope's museum," as he called the Vatican. We were taken out to dinner by one of the wealthy University donors and we walked around Rome as tourists. We somehow happened into the Gucci store. David asked them if they had any non-leather belts. He wanted a belt he could wear inside an Indian temple (no cow leather allowed), and the salesman was horrified. You would ask for something like that in a Gucci store!! We decided to look around anyway. Everything was terribly expensive. I wanted to bring something home to the kids. What if I could find something with a Gucci label? Nate was overshadowed by famous labels at the time. At the back of the store there was a display of tennis shoes, low tops, with the Gucci colors. For some reason they were on sale; maybe they were no longer a featured item. They were only $12 a pair and there was one pair left in Nate's size. I was delirious. I was imagining and foreseeing his great joy and excitement. I couldn't wait to get home. We decided not to tell him how inexpensive they were.

Nate was thrilled with the shoes, so much so that he hesitated to wear them. They sat on his dresser just being admired for weeks and weeks. We didn't tell him how little they cost. He was sure we got a bargain, knowing how we thought and how little extra money we had, but he wanted to think they were worth a lot. He wore them to shreds eventually.

The Israel Project

In late July 1983 David and Skip and Vicki and Howard Chandler went off to Israel to begin a big Maharishi Effect study. Skip had gotten a grant to support the project and he was the main organizer. Israel was going through a difficult time and war was raging in next-door Lebanon. Lebanon had become a battleground for various forces inside and outside the country trying to get power in the region. They gathered a group of Sidhas together in a hotel in Jerusalem and notified as many experts as they could about the project and its likely results. The Israeli meditators, particularly their national leader Gad Tick and a man named Ami Rochaek, worked very hard to get the group together, gather data, and even help with the early stages of analysis. The group ranged from 60 to 240, depending upon whether the Israelis had to work or could get away. The square root of one percent for Israel at that time was about 200. The scientists were collecting data on war intensity in Lebanon, war deaths in Lebanon, the Israeli national mood (based on newspaper content analysis), the Israeli national stock index, auto accident rates, number of fires, and crime rates for both Jerusalem and Israel as a whole. It was a very ambitious project and difficult to analyze because the group size fluctuated widely.

The scientists gathered data and talked to people and watched the situation anxiously. They were able to watch the events of the war and read the number of deaths posted daily in the newspapers and it soon became obvious that the numbers of Yogic Flyers and the people dying were very closely related. David would wait at the door of the flying hall to see what the number was that day and if it was low, then he knew people would be dying. It was very real and serious.

In order to analyze all this data they made indices that combined all the variables and the results were clear: when they topped the super radiance number (200), the composite index of quality of life (few deaths, fewer fires, better national mood, less crime) followed along. There was even some evidence that the effect was felt first in Jerusalem, where the hotel was located, and then, as the group grew in size, in the whole of Israel, and then even in Lebanon. One visible effect of the group practice was that Israel got out of the fighting in Lebanon and dropped back just to defend its borders. David, Skip, Howard, and Wally Larimore (an expert statistician they brought on board) worked on the paper for nearly five years. The wrestling match they had with their journal (*The Journal of Conflict Resolution*), which is published out of Yale University, would give rise to a whole book in itself. In fact, it became the subject of a dissertation exploring bias and subjectivity in reviewers and journals (Dr. Carla Linton Brown, Harvard, 1996). How could they think of publishing something called "International peace project in the Middle East: The effects of the Maharishi Technology of the Unified Field" even if the statistical analysis was impeccable, even though it might be a very important contribution to the field. Maharishi Technology of the Unified Field! No wonder they choked on that. But to their credit, publish it they did in 1988 along with numerous disclaimers and explanations and other sorts of material to keep them from being embarrassed. It stirred up quite a riot in the academic world. The fact that it even got published at all attests to the rise in collective consciousness that the group at MIU was creating.

College of Natural Law

Early in October an organization in Norway had the idea of gathering a big group together and having it practice meditation for a few minutes, thereby creating an influence on world peace. Maharishi sent David, Neil Paterson (our Governor General of North America for the TM organization), and many of the scientists and other movement leaders to attend the event and to attempt to present our ideas on the theme. There was a big countdown, lots of noise and fanfare, and everyone meditated in their own particular way for a few minutes, and then it was over. The organizers thought they had done something for world peace, but it was a ridiculous concept and execution. In order to have some lasting influence on the world, a group had to convene for more than a few minutes, and they had to have some significant form of meditation to practice. No other type of meditation had ever been proven to have any effect on collective consciousness, only the TM and TM-Sidhi practice.

At the end of October Maharishi suddenly called all the faculty who weren't teaching at the time to Washington to the College of

Natural Law. We were going to celebrate the rising sunshine of the Age of Enlightenment for North America. David was still in Norway, but I could go, so I asked a couple on Maharishi School faculty, Lawrence and Laurie Eyre, to move into our frat and keep an eye on the kids for a few weeks and I flew to D.C. with the group. They were the kids' favorite teachers and saw nearly as much of them in the school day as we did at home.

It seems that Maharishi was seeing that events in America and around the world "have shown that the continental consciousness of America has made high jumps in the progress toward purity and is now sharing its happiness with other parts of the world." He had taken out full-page ads in newspapers in many countries offering any government the chance to establish life in accord with natural law. He was feeling very fulfilled with the news that we had the ability to change the world in a more peaceful direction much faster than we ever had. It had been eight years since the Dawn was declared and we were seeing the day rising. Soon, he said, not too many more years, and we would see the noon sunshine.

What was the basic cause of all the problems in the world? Violation of natural law. We have annoyed nature, Maharishi said. Life according to natural law (promoted spontaneously through the group practice of the TM and TM-Sidhi program) will be the one solution to all problems. We weren't talking about the vacuum state any longer. Physicists were now recognizing the unified field of all the laws of nature to be the basic level of creation, and to us it meant that state of mind where consciousness or intelligence is open to itself in the transcendent, what he was describing as self-referral consciousness, through the technology of the Unified Field. Modern Science and Vedic Science had founded one beautiful secured platform so any nation can flower, he said.

Life according to natural law doesn't mean going camping, or going to live in the forest, Maharishi laughed. To err is *inhuman*, he insisted; it is due only to ignorance, not knowing how to perform right action. We can train our awareness, our intelligence, to always be evolutionary. Evolution is no longer a mystical word; it is a practical solution. What we need are a few people who by profession can purify national consciousness. We need the technology of the unified field in the educational system so everyone grows up not to make mistakes, not to violate natural law. Why were we in Washington, D.C.? Problems come here from all over the world, he said. A group of Sidhas here could influence the whole world. And, again, he gave credit to the Vedic pandits in India for preserving this knowledge (and performing their yagyas) and to all the meditators. The world is definitely a better place than it was when he came out of India twenty-five years earlier. He said he felt great joy. "I feel so fulfilled to be celebrating with this knowledge and authority."

Bevan took over the meeting and I slipped away to meet David's flight from Norway at Dulles airport. The next two weeks were intense. Maharishi made tapes on rehabilitation for a prison program, and on defense. He organized the decoration and expansion of the meeting hall so it would look like the grand hall in Seelisberg, worthy of being a capital, and he commented on the various Unified Field Charts created by the faculty in their disciplines. He also gave a profound lecture on Sankhya, one of the six systems of Indian philosophy, and began to talk about Utopia, Heaven on Earth. All in just a couple of weeks.

George Ellis, a Governor who had taught TM inside several maximum security prisons, asked Maharishi to make a tape for a prison program he was spearheading. The best system of rehabilitation, Maharishi said, would give a man the spontaneous ability to think rightly. There has to be an infinite, unshakable state of balance created in the consciousness of the prisoner, so he would be incapable of wrong action, either for himself or for the environment. That's rehabilitation: disallow the sprouting of negativity. The technology of the unified field is the technique of rehabilitation: enliven the unified field in a person, and let that be the reality through the thick and thin of life. The most ideal behavior is self-referral behavior. Then it is natural, the behavior of nature. Correctional programs are necessary because the state has not taught people to behave with each other with such perfect friendliness that the pain of the friend is the pain of the self. Awaken the self-referral performance within the consciousness of the prisoner and *then* let him out in society, he said.

That afternoon the celebration continued. Bevan introduced all the movement luminaries sitting to the right and left of Maharishi; Neil, Benny Feldman (our Governor General of South America), Keith, David, Kurleigh King, Nandkishore, and others. In the evening the discussion revolved around supporting a big group in D.C.: jobs, housing, and all the details of setting up such a group. He liked the renovated hall. It is a very royal set up, he said. Very comfortable feeling; it gives a spacious feeling. It just needs some workspaces, microphones so people can contribute to the discussions. He wanted to launch into minister training programs and leadership training programs under Lenny Goldman.

All the faculty had been directed earlier to create Unified Field Charts for their area. This meant summarizing all the aspects of one's discipline on one chart, ranging from the subtlest values of the field to its most expressed areas at the top, parallel to a vision of consciousness going from the subtlest to the grossest levels displayed along the side. These charts would be displayed in the classroom, so students could see where the current course, even the current lesson, fell on the whole structure of the knowledge of the discipline, and how it related to their own consciousness. All the departments had been working on this project, discussing and organizing their discipline, even our Literature Department. Maharishi was most interested in the ones for physics and mathematics and spent time going over them and commenting on them. We all learned from the discussions how to improve our own charts. This was not only a brilliant educational tool, it made each department think deeply about their field and the courses they taught. I had taught and attended several universities and there was nothing like this anywhere else.

John Hagelin, our own brilliant physicist, now a Harvard PhD, spoke on the qualities of the unified field and the mechanics and dynamics through which it liberates energy rather than consumes energy. Maharishi loved that point. If it's a continuum, it has to be self-generating. With less consumption of energy there could be more longevity. He also took some time, for his own joy, I suspect, to explore the Vedic literature with us. He went deeply into Sankhya, how it unfolds the structure of the Veda just by counting numbers. The first *richa* or verse of the Veda shows how infinity is contained in a point and how the laws of nature sequentially emerge from that point. The sequence of progression, the whole structure of the Veda, can all be understood by counting, counting number of words, phrases, suktas, mandalas, and so forth. In this system of counting, the relevance of the significance for different parts of the Veda, the relevance of each part of the laws of nature becomes clear, as well as their relationships to each other. The flow of the whole Veda, he said, goes from point to infinity, from the seed to the whole tree.

If you hold on to that point in your consciousness, Maharishi said, and one can hardly breathe at that point, then the nervous system, which is responsible for any state of awareness, cautiously, carefully functions with such profound balance that total awareness at the point becomes real, lively, fully awakened. And together in that state of balance is that state of authority to hold on to the main switchboard of creation. That state embodies the chief commandership of the whole creation. It was Sankhya that had enabled Maharishi to cognize his Apaurusheya Commentary on the Rig Veda. We could see how fascinating this was to Maharishi. We followed along as best we could. The seed was being planted for the programs in Vedic Science that would unfold over the next twenty years at MIU leading to MA and PhD degrees in Maharishi Vedic Science.

Maharishi went on for the next few days talking about his

theories of government and defense. If you educate the civilian population to act in accord with natural law, then the nation will not need military defense. The first duty of the military is the prevention of war, to smell out the ugliness and correct it. Every country is the concern of the whole world. Everyone is connected to the whole universe. As world consciousness rises all systems of government will end up on a plateau of fulfillment in their own vocabulary. This will be Utopia. In the Brahma Sutras, the seer Vyasa says that Brahman is the devourer of all. When awareness is fully awake within itself (Brahman Consciousness), it realizes that it is all that there is to anything. Devour all diversity and sit fulfilled in the Self.

Maharishi was particularly pleased that president Reagan had said that nuclear war cannot be won; therefore it should not be fought. Reagan said he was looking forward to a day when all nuclear weapons could be banished from the earth. Maharishi thought that was a very historic, timely statement showing the changing value of time. That was the voice of America speaking, Maharishi said. Reagan was reflecting the rise in national consciousness being created by the Governors at MIU and in Washington. All we need is group of 6,000 Sidhas. He himself needed such a group more than anything for the knowledge to come out. The purification of collective consciousness will lead to an upsurge of pure knowledge, he said. It's all there in the Vedic literature; it just needs to be brought out on the level of common sense. A large group, he was talking about 6,000, would form a laboratory for the unfoldment of knowledge. We are on the doorstep of Utopia, he said.

A Taste of Utopia

One afternoon shortly after this, Maharishi hooked up by telephone with Governors all over the world and David presented the findings of the research conducted in Israel. David spoke with such clarity and confidence as he explained how the number of

Sidhas changed the whole quality of life in that strife-filled region that Maharishi immediately took the whole thing global. We
would gather a group of at least 6,000 (this was changed to 7,000,
which was the square root of one percent of the world's population at that time) together at MIU and do a demonstration project
of how we can actually transform the world through our technology of the unified field. This would begin in a matter of weeks and
last for about three weeks. The course would be called the Taste of
Utopia assembly. Later on at one of David's birthday celebrations
Maharishi would say that David gave the world a taste of utopia.

This created a huge stir in the movement. Groups would be
moved to Fairfield from all over the world and Fairfield had to
get ready. Where would 7,000 people be housed? Fed? Where
would they do their Yogic Flying program? The Zimmerman family immediately ordered a large number of three-bedroom mobile
homes and they began to be assembled at the factory. Land was
taken over north of the frats and although it was winter, and the
ground would soon be frozen, it had to be prepared with electricity, water, and sewer lines. Roads had to be created between the
rows of the mobile homes as they went in. It was a huge operation.
Mobile homes started moving down the highways, nature cooperated, and they were placed and connected and filled with beds
and tables, sheets and towels. Truckloads of foam were ordered.
Where would they go? A huge assembly hall was designed on the
east side of campus and the walls began to rise. It was a miracle of
design, construction, labor, dedication, and support of nature, especially from the weather. Money and volunteer labor poured in,
buildings got finished and laid with foam, and soon people began
to arrive from all over the world.

Fred Gratzon, who had an ice cream company in Iowa, created a mango ice cream flavor he called Taste of Utopia and it was
handed out free to everyone who came to register. Young people
arrived from the Caribbean in light clothing and sweaters, totally
unprepared for an Iowa winter. All the local stores quickly sold

out of boots and parkas and more were ordered. People on campus were asked to open their homes to the visitors. Meditators in town set up dormitories in their basements and extra bedrooms. Food was ordered. It was an incredible task and somehow it happened. The Grand Assembly Hall had been finished, a stage set up for Maharishi, foam laid on the huge floor, and the dining rooms got ready to feed the masses. It was unbelievable. We were somewhat sheltered from all this activity in our little apartment, although we, too, doubled up and made a room available to a family.

The pressure was on for the scientists. They had to come up with data that would test the prediction of increased coherence, fast! They had to find sources and databases that would measure worldwide trends and, hopefully, show positive results! David, Skip, Michael, Ken Cavanaugh, Paul Gelderloos, Audri Lanford, and Tony Abou Nader had to work together to take the pulse of the whole world. They proposed studying a three-week period prior to the assembly, then the three weeks of the assembly, and then a three-week period after the assembly. That would give an idea of what happened during that unique period, different from the few weeks before, and then see what would happen when the group disbursed.

The papers they eventually wrote are published in Volume 4 of the *Collected Papers*. Who else would publish such research! See pp. 2715-2762. In brief, yes, there was a strong effect: statements and actions of heads of state worldwide took a positive turn during the assembly and reverted back to "normal" afterward; conflicts in trouble-spot countries and conflict in Lebanon improved; air traffic fatalities went down worldwide; and there were even effects on global health. The world stock index and other measures of economic success rose during the assembly and stayed high for a few weeks. We *could* change the world, but would anyone believe us? How frustrating to know you have the answer and no one will listen to it.

The course was over but the dynamics were clear. We needed a large group in one place in order to change the trends of time. MIU became that place and all the movement's energy began to be directed toward building up our group.

Assemblies and Celebrations

WE RARELY MISSED a chance to see Maharishi or be connected with him in any way. We were "in the ashram" at MIU, totally focused on his knowledge, his projects, and his goals. And he was well aware of us and our family on all levels. After the Taste of Utopia course in the winter of 1983-84, Maharishi called a series of big courses to influence world trends and to call attention to our ability to do so. In the spring of 1984 the national leaders for the TM movement in South Africa told David about a conference on the gifted child being held there in June. Could he propose a talk? The talk was accepted and we flew into Johannesburg in June, leaving the practically grown-up children on their own (Sara would turn 14 in a few weeks; Nate would be sixteen in October and had a very intense summer job so he could buy his dream bicycle). I don't know if Maharishi was told about our visit, but I suspect he was because he kept a close eye on that country and its apartheid issues, which were potentially explosive.

South Africa

Vicki and Richard Broome had set up a full agenda for us. David would give his talk (on how TM would make any child more gifted) at the University in Stellenbosch in the wine country; we would meet with the press, give talks to the meditators in

Durban and Johannesburg, and to university faculty, and speak at a residence course in the Drakensberg Mountains. Unfortunately they had set up an interview with the press immediately upon our arrival. David was jet-lagged and exhausted, but muddled through very well. He can talk about the research in his sleep. There we were in a beautiful country with horrific social problems. An early visit to a restaurant and past a beach showed us signs saying No Coloreds or Whites Only. I was remembering Frieda Adler. She was a tiny lady with a big personality. She had been raised in South Africa, an orphan sent there from Lithuania, and she hated apartheid. She had lifelong memories of a policeman beating a small black child for sitting on the bench that said Whites Only. The child couldn't read, she insisted!

As soon as she could, Frieda left South Africa for Palestine and eventually wound up in L.A., teaching Hebrew at a Jewish school and yoga in the evenings. She met Maharishi there in the '60s and was immediately swept up by his message and presence and traveled around with him in California in those early days. He called her "the mischievous one" and kept a close eye on her because she tended to be rebellious and very self-directed. Frieda took one of those early TTC courses in India and then Maharishi sent her back to Israel (no longer Palestine). She opened four TM centers there, the very first in the country. Later Maharishi sent her back to South Africa. She was ready and willing to go then, because she had something to give that would change the situation. She starting teaching TM to both blacks and whites, crossing the color line illegally. She could have gotten into serious trouble. While there she met an old beau. When she next went back to Maharishi, she told him that if he sent her back there, she would probably marry that man. Maharishi nodded and said that she had very good taste, and he sent her back.

Years later, when she was widowed, Frieda went to every rounding course she could. She often turned up in Switzerland while we were there, and I remember her hounding Maharishi for an advanced technique on one visit. He kept putting her off and she kept following him around and insisting. I am sure she finally got it. She came frequently to courses at MIU and she was always a very definite presence and a trial to the course office since she demanded extra attention and services. They used to joke that at course registration they had a housing table, a badge table, etc., and a Frieda table.

What would it be like to go into a foreign country, I wondered, and teach TM for the first time, to create a movement there? All by yourself. It must have taken a great deal of courage, energy, and self-confidence, as well as a total confidence in Maharishi and the knowledge and techniques. By the time we got to South Africa, the movement was well-established and Maharishi was directing its leaders in how to create coherence and peacefully change the situation. The residence course had a black TM teacher there, sitting and eating with everyone else. That was probably illegal, but everyone was comfortable with the situation. We had good press and TV interviews and I think we helped our movement there. I certainly had a new appreciation for Maharishi's long arm, reaching all the way into South Africa.

Later that summer of 1984 there was a political crisis in the Philippines and Maharishi sent a large contingent of Governors to round quietly in hotels in Manila as well as in the surrounding islands. There was even a prison project underway. The ground seemed fertile for a cosmic intervention.

The Philippines

Maharishi had the groups of Governors rounding in Manila and its surroundings in order to create a background of coherence for his activities. Maharishi was secretly ensconced in the Hotel Manila, directing his people, and creating newspaper pages of our message to be printed in Manila. Maharishi thought Marcos was an able statesman and with the right support he could lead the country into better times, not just drain its wealth for himself and his family. Revolt and conflict always killed thousands and destroyed infrastructure. A peaceful transition was in the interests of both the opposition and the government. Maharishi offered global programs that stretched their minds and imaginations. He was once again "drawing a bigger line"; offering something so beyond their quarrels with each other that they might be able to drop them for a moment and be distracted by new possibilities.

The VIPs (scientists, including David, Geoffrey, and John Hagelin, and top administrators) also stayed in the Hotel Manila; they were there to try to educate the government on how to both stay in power *and* create progress for the nation. David and the others had talks with the highest levels of the government and presented the research and theories to Parliament and to president Marcos himself, but he, his government, and the influential Cardinal Sin (I am not kidding) were deaf to what our scientists and movement leaders tried to tell them. Actually Cardinal Sin was supportive of our efforts at first, but pressure from anti-Marcos factions forced him to back off and even allow anti-TM statements to be issued in his name.

The Zimmerman family was prepared to buy the whole bankrupt University of the East and create a permanent coherence-creating group with the students. The students, however, were being manipulated by the opposition and demonstrated, on cue, whenever our people appeared. They surrounded one of our Governors in a hostile manner as he went through the building. "What would your mother think of you doing this?" he asked. The young men backed off.

As our groups quieted the violence by the coherence they were creating, we were seen as supporting the dictator and his family. The opposition saw that we were indeed having the effect we advertised; we tried to tell them that replacing one despot by another would not bring reforms to the people. Only a coherence creating group would raise the collective consciousness and set the stage for *any* government to begin to improve the quality of life for the country and thus to deserve better leadership. The opposition set fire to one of the hotels our Governors were occupying and Maharishi eventually pulled the whole group out of there. Marcos wanted the U.S. military bases out of the country and thus had garnered the enmity of the U.S. government. Maharishi told Marcos that the bases would go, and sure enough, a series of natural disasters forced the closure of all of them, just as he had told Marcos.

It is a very novel concept and therefore not easy to understand, and we had the same problem in Nicaragua and Venezuela during the World Peace Project. We would run into the same arguments from the opposition again during our project in Armenia in 1990. Somoza, Marcos, and all of their ilk, were destined to fall and be replaced by more progressive and evolutionary forces, although life often did not improve for the general populace without a coherence-creating group. Perhaps we should have pitched to the revolutionaries that if they all meditated they would win, but that might have been seen as promoting violence and might have increased the wrath of the U.S. government. Unfortunately, I was grappling with administration, teaching, and teenagers and missed this whole adventure.

College of Natural Law, January 12, 1985

In December 1984 Maharishi held a course of thousands in The Hague (Holland) to demonstrate in Europe what could be accomplished by group coherence. We faculty celebrated January 12 with Maharishi at the College of Natural Law, connected by satellite with everyone back at MIU and all the new Vedic Universities around the world, which Maharishi was inaugurating this year. He was very excited about inaugurating "a new gate to the beautiful new destiny of mankind." The Veda is not foreign knowledge, he explained; it has just been hidden from view. This is the first generation, he said, that has the opportunity to connect the intellectual understanding of consciousness with the intellectual understanding of the Vedas.

The next few days were filled with a conference on education. Being established in *samadhi*, the state of least excitation of consciousness, would be like a pilot having the control panel right in front of him, Maharishi said. One would learn how to channel specific laws to fulfill needs, like a lake opening up channels to various areas. And secondly, we wouldn't even have to be selective; just engage the total potential of natural law in a spontaneous manner, and we would get support of all its laws. And in the third stage, we wouldn't even need the support of nature. Nature would be acting for us. Whatever would be needed would just get done.

Maharishi gave the initial direction for the Vedic Science programs that would come along. First, learn Sanskrit. Then read all the syllables, words, sentences, paragraphs, chapters, all the books. Each book would have a different effect on the consciousness of the reader, even without meaning, simply on the level of sound and structure. The Vedas were not understood because the gaps, the *sandhi*, between letters and words, and other larger structures, were ignored. The processes which occur in the gaps reveal the mechanics of creation. Previous commentators focused on the intellectual meaning; it's like a spider web, he said. (The spider, the commentator, creates the web and then just hangs in it and nothing happens.) The Veda is hidden within the Self; it creates the universe and runs it from within itself. He spent the next few days going deeply into the mechanics of Vedic Science, clearly enjoying himself.

Maharishi also took time for some press conferences, an interview with the *New York Times*, and one with Philippine TV. He was still hoping to have a good effect there, but when Marcos finally ordered some of his police corps to learn TM, Maharishi commented that it was "too little, too late." Marcos had to flee the country for Hawaii the next year. Maharishi felt that the U.S. was on a very fragile platform, and was too dependent upon the whims of other governments. Only by creating coherence and raising collective consciousness would the U.S. be able to be a leader to other nations. He was promoting big groups around the world, especially in the U.S. and India.

World Assembly on Vedic Science, July 1985

David, Sara, and I attended the World Assembly on Vedic Science in D.C. in July 1985. The *Washington Post* ran a very good article on the Assembly called "Rising to the Occasion. 5,500 Meet to Meditate and Levitate." (Maharishi said 5,500 was as good as 7,000 since they were closer to the U.S. capital.) They explained what we were doing without ridicule or sarcasm. The Maharishi Effect, "say its partisans, wielding bar graphs and pie charts [that would be David], has been borne out scientifically by scores of controlled experiments and statistical studies." Maharishi gave a press conference by phone and he was asked by a reporter from *India Abroad* about the troubles in India, the *Post* reported. "The problems of India come from outside. Rest assured that the problems of India originate somewhere else," he said. Do you mean that India is contaminated by the West? he was asked. "That's exactly what I meant. If India is in the East, then the only thing left is the West."

The *Post* article closed by covering Mike Tompkins' report to the Assembly that after just the first day of our group practice, "there has been a very distinct softening of relations between the United States and the Soviet Union . . . from the Mideast, the vast majority of Palestinians favor talks with Israel . . . El Salvador has started talking with Honduran leaders . . . the food crisis has ended in eight African nations . . . and the world stock index is up 16 percent."

We stayed at the College of Natural Law, where we could hear the sounds of gunshots and sirens throughout the night. We met as a big group and did our meditation programs at the Washington Convention Center. Maharishi didn't come in person, but we watched tapes on Maharishi Vedic Science and a new one just made in India on July 13. He told us that the process of purification of world consciousness had been going on since he started going around the world teaching Transcendental Meditation and training teachers in 1958. It was the increasing purity in world consciousness that allowed him to bring out the TM-Sidhi program. And, he pointed out, conflicts between nations, like the one between Iran and Iraq, are seen to be local conflicts. Previously the superpowers would have taken sides and brought on a world war. World war is not happening, and the World Government can take credit for that.

David and the other scientists in his group did the research and eventually wrote a paper on the three largest assemblies, the Taste of Utopia in Fairfield, the Hague Vedic Science Conference in 1984-1985, and this World Assembly on Vedic Science in D.C. They were able to use a world index of daily stock prices and a database of international terrorism obtained from the Rand Corporation. From this they could do daily content-analysis ratings of international conflicts before, during, and after each assembly. They found a highly significant decrease in international conflict during each of the three assemblies (-36%, -24%, and -35%, respectively), and a drop in international terrorism immediately after the beginning of the three assemblies taken together (-72%). Think of the lives saved! They also found a significant increase in the stock prices during the three assemblies taken together. They presented their results at the Annual Meeting of the American Political Science Association and published a summary in *Collected Papers*, Vol. 5.

Yogic Flying Demonstrations

The summer of 1986 saw the first national and international Yogic Flying demonstrations. We started out in Washington, D.C. with another big assembly, "Maharishi's Program to Create World Peace," to run from July 4-13, 1986. There were 3,000 of us and we gathered on the Ellipse south of the White House for a group photo. Then we put on the biggest press event in the history of the Washington Press Corps that was not a presidential event. All the reporters, all the cameras from the networks, major and minor, were trained on the flyers. The reporters were all very sweet and serious. They felt something. There wasn't much to see; the flyers sat in the full lotus posture and hopped about on the foam, some of them quite high, all very silently. Some athletes who were in the audience got down on the foam and tried to do the same thing, but they couldn't. The atmosphere was very settled and respectful, and even a bit blissful.

The *Washington Post* covered the event with all due respect and seriousness. Reporter Victoria Dawson described the scene before her and the reason for it all, to create world peace. "On the escalator, in a haze of post-briefing bewilderment, a reporter tried to assimilate the TM argot. 'I don't suppose you know what a unified field is?' he asked meekly. If yesterday's competition was any indication," she wrote, "the road to world peace is paved with rubber mats . . . populated by would-be hoppers neutralizing their own and the world's stress." Ann McFeatters of the *Scripps Howard News Service* started her article by saying, "While Moscow witnesses the Goodwill Games, Washington hosted the North American Yogic Flying Competition," and then she went on to describe the events and winners in a neutral manner. Lucy Keyser of the *Washington Times* headlined her article, "3,000 meditators assemble, seeking peace, soft landing" and then went on to report all events, times, and winners, and she ended her piece with long quotes from a blissful meditator or two.

Alex Vanoss did a lovely piece on National Public Radio: "In Washington, D.C. this week—an unusual mind over matter athletic event. . . . I've always wanted to fly, on my own, without tickets or seat belts. And in my dreams I did fly. I would climb a tree, jump, and float back to ground and sometimes, with the right uplift to the chin, I would even rise up over the trees at the end of the yard and the fields beyond and on up into the hills far away. . . .

One Christmas, I asked for a Superman suit, and it came with a note attached saying that of course, only the real Superman suit with its red cape could make you fly." He then went on to describe the event, quoting Bevan and David explaining the EEG of flying and the coherence it generates, even in the whole group. "I don't know if you could feel that," David said. "I could feel the whole atmosphere becoming very settled and quiet." Alex concludes: "I came away satisfied with a thought that when thousands of people gather, if only to meditate, if only to hop together, how could this not help but improve humanity's collective disposition. As for flying itself, it is a fact that in a certain field in Maryland thirty years ago, there was a boy who dreamed of flying through the rows of corn. He wore a Superman suit, with a red cape, and he was happy."

I sat near David, who was doing the EEG demonstration off to the side and was showing his materials to the reporters. One radio reporter interviewed him and asked him to explain what he was doing and what the EEG was showing. David talked about coherence at the moment of lift-off and the interview was then played on the radio, perhaps NPR. David's brother, Bill, who was an MIT professor, called him up and berated him for talking about Yogic Flying on the radio. Bill was so embarrassed. He had learned to meditate years before, but never really understood what we were doing with our lives, until late in his life. Then he told David that he had gotten it right.

It was a lovely course. We stayed at the College of Natural Law and left the kids at home with a friend who moved in, not to take care of them, but to make sure no parties were spontaneously called. A large ladies group, Mother Divine, it was named, also stayed at the college. They were supposed to stay out of the tumult of the nation's capital and just round and be on the Self. For a joke and the entertainment of all, they plastered their dedicated elevator with large ads and posters showing clothes, jewelry, all kinds of items. It was a kind of fantasy Elevator Shopping Mall. Very funny.

We left Washington after the course ended on July 13 and flew to India for Guru Purnima and a big Yogic Flying demonstration in New Delhi. The event would be held at the Indira Gandhi Indoor Stadium and was announced with a full-page newspaper invitation with a picture of the Shankaracharya on one side of the page and Maharishi on the other. The page explained Maharishi's principle to create world peace and his practical program to do so. There was a big block with pictures of Yogic Flyers and the EEG research showing what happened during the practice. Another block explained the discovery of the unified field and its relevance to creating world peace. Everyone was invited to come and phone numbers were given for VIP seating.

I remember the rows of pandit boys lined up and hopping on the foam. They were students from the various schools Maharishi had established in order to train them to meditate and do the traditional chanting. Again, not very impressive to see, but a lovely atmosphere. David was once again demonstrating the EEG off to the side and talking with reporters. The Shankaracharya of Jyotir Math presided and blessed the event. Maharishi announced at the close of it that we would do this every year from now on. "Kiss of death," I whispered to David. This may never happen here again, I meant, and it was true. Maharishi was always in the moment, responding to the need of the time. He was never constrained by dates or promises of future events. Had it been worthwhile to hold another demonstration the next year, it would have happened. Obviously, other more important needs took precedence.

Along with the current big Yogic Flying event we met with Maharishi numerous times that summer in his ashram in Noida, just outside of Delhi. The heat and flies were unbelievable, unimaginable, but it was wonderful to be with Maharishi, especially in small group meetings with the MIU faculty. At one early meeting in the main hall Maharishi was entertaining ideas on what should be put there in the World Capital of the Age of Enlightenment. There would be representatives from each country, either individuals or couples. "Don't think of the living conditions," he said. That was all I could think of. These representatives would translate and dispatch the latest waves of knowledge.

Everyone began to throw out suggestions: How we would support 10,000 pandits on a permanent basis; offering people a chance to reserve future courses but paying now; some kind of tourism; exhibitions; a visitor's center; an Indian Vedaland; and Maharishi Yagyas® perpetually going on for world peace. There could be courses in Maharishi AyurVeda, Gandharva Veda, Maharishi Jyotish, and leadership training in all fields. There could be displays of all the glories of each country, perhaps a rotating Vedic University with 200-300 students visiting from other colleges; inviting all the Shankaracharyas to visit; courses in Vedic cooking; and satellite TV set up and broadcasting all over the world. A number of these suggestions became reality in the coming years.

When we weren't with Maharishi we met in small groups and studied either pulse diagnosis [vaidyas could assess a person's imbalances by feeling the various doshas in the pulse, and then recommend remedies] or jyotish from the scholars there. I chose jyotish; it was enormously complicated but fascinating to me. David came along with me. David, who could tell you the *p* value or the correlation on a TM study done years before, couldn't seem to hold onto planets, houses (bhavas), anything related to jyotish. Maharishi frequently invited the faculty to sit on the stage with him and discuss the Maharishi Vedic University (MVU) curriculum, ladies on one side, men on the other. He urged the faculty to present their connections to their professional organizations and colleagues. David and the psychologists had been doing research and publishing at conferences in journals and in *Collected Papers*. He wanted the others to do it also.

Maharishi much preferred delving into the Vedic literature; there was a lecture on the fourfold nature of the gap, and what happens when we listen to the Vedic pandits reciting the Vedic literature. The brain computes each syllable, the gaps between syllables, and the junction point. The gap contains the transformation of pure intelligence into the next word. The gap is the fountainhead of all the orderly evolution of nature. The Veda is in the junction points. You can count the gaps between the syllabi and see how many gaps are necessary to generate creation. Very abstract. Were some people actually experiencing this? I wasn't. So how do we know the Veda? We have to study the gaps, Maharishi said. How do we do that? Through the TM and TM-Sidhi program. I took pages of notes which are minimally clearer to me now, maybe through repetition and the frequent revisiting of these topics over the years. Fred Travis has recently done a study showing that brain coherence rises as one listens to the Vedic chanting.

In one faculty meeting Maharishi directed us to refer to the Self in each class, to the unified field within. Department heads should make it fashionable in their research papers to refer to the unified field. The first principle of nature's functioning is the rise of diversity from unity. No matter what we write we shouldn't go by the beaten paths of research papers. It is not research; it is too superficial, if it doesn't dig into the ultimate. Refer to the unified field and make it complete by referring to the technology of the unified field [TM and the TM-Sidhi program]. I want you to lead the educational world or you'll be running after scientists from Princeton, he said. Modern science is camping on the shores of my Vedic Science. Modern science can only watch from the shore, outside of the water. If it enters the water, it ceases to be "objective." We are the forerunners of the Age of Enlightenment. We are the only scientists who have a grip on natural law.

We also had discussions of Ayurveda. Maharishi was using these years in India to bring vaidyas and pandits together and develop herbs, treatments, and a deeper knowledge of nature's functioning. How did it relate to the DNA? To proteins? How could we develop immortality through balance rather than change? He went deeply into how we could dissolve stresses as a way to lead the mind and body to an immortal existence. Matter is just an expression of consciousness. When we experience thrills of happiness in the TM-Sidhi practice, when bliss is bubbling up, this is simultaneously culturing consciousness and the body. Consciousness and the physiology become more and more delicate and refined. A time will come, he said, when *real* self-interacting dynamics with be directly experienced in consciousness. Apparently what we were experiencing now, I deduced, was a mere shadow of things to come. Keep chipping away at all the stresses, he advised.

In one of the last meetings with the faculty that August, Maharishi again directed us to refer to the unified field and the technologies in our classes, our research, our writing, and our publishing. A person who has a little knowledge is always a nuisance, he said. We were educating our students at MIU in order to get them enlightened. Even if they don't understand everything about the unified field, he said, it doesn't matter. We take the conclusions of modern science, not the details. You may not know how to build a machine in order to know how to run it. Every student should be a walking, talking library of total knowledge, confident, soft, rising to higher states of consciousness.

MIU is going to come into the limelight, Maharishi promised. Put the unified field in your writings. If they don't publish it, it is their misfortune. Not publishing is not damaging to the sincerity of our findings. Feel restful; they'll catch up with us in due course. Everyone will adore you as being ahead of your time. We are producing heaven on earth; claim the credit for all good that is happening. Don't stoop down to convince others. We are on the level of the elephant. Education trains people to be the slaves of someone else's thoughts. You lose your own original creativity. Be a slave to Brahman, if you must be a slave. Finally he reminded us to round, at least one month a year, to go someplace like the World Capital. Take your students along with you, he advised.

January 12 Celebration in Maharishi Nagar, Noida 1987

We were invited to the celebrations the next January in Noida and we took Sara along. She was sixteen and was interested in going. We spent our first night in a hotel in Delhi and I remember the three of us sleeping in a king-sized bed. We were so exhausted from the trip that we could have slept on folding chairs. We saw elephants and monkeys in the streets. Quite colorful. We were moved out to Noida the next day and housed in one of the many partially finished buildings there and provided with mosquito netting, which David hung over our beds. There was very tight security that winter. Every bag and suitcase was carefully inspected whenever we entered or left the compound. I believe there were concerns for Maharishi's safety. There were reasons he was staying in India and not going to the U.S. or Europe, but nothing was said overtly. It was the thirteenth year of the Age of Enlightenment and we were celebrating our successes.

Maharishi was in an odd mixture of moods. On the one hand he was inaugurating the Year of World Peace, which had come about by the impulses of Vedic chanting reverberating throughout the world. He was projecting a year of peace, prosperity and happiness, the fulfillment of the desires of the Governors for all mankind. How would we know when we achieved world peace? When the world press could not find any negativity to report; when the Iran-Iraq war calmed down; when the terrorism in the Punjab and throughout the world calmed down; and when the rivalry between the nations calmed down and turned to friendliness. All the efforts of governments had failed to produce peace. It was up to us to do it. This year of peace is called for by nature, he said.

On the other hand, he once quietly admitted, "I can't tell you how much I didn't want to come out this morning." I think he was feeling discouraged. He was happy that Trigunaji and the other vaidyas had brought out their herbal formula, their rasayana suitable for everyone, which he called Amrit Kalash, the previous year, and he talked about the contributions of Maharishi AyurVeda for world peace. What more could we do? It all came down to our TM and TM-Sidhi program, along with our intellectual probing into the deeper dimensions of Vedic values. If peace is to be permanent it wouldn't be through any effort; it would have to be the byproduct of living unobstructed, unbounded awareness, living unity and diversity together. That's what the Puranas say. It all comes down to enlightenment; it is the only eternal antidote to war.

What more could we do? We could ask each head of state to send a representative there to the World Capital to be trained to enliven natural law in their country. The practice of Maharishi AyurVeda would save governments a lot of foreign exchange; we could introduce unified-field-based education, and train military wives and daughters to meditate so their husbands and fathers wouldn't have to fight. Might it look funny? he asked. One member of the couple is a fighter, the other is creating peace and harmony and softening the heart of the enemy. What might he think of the current state of the armed forces where women and mothers are sometimes the fighters and husbands are sometimes at home? We should do something in the prisons also, he said. We should free these stressed areas; there is such a gloomy, dim, dull feeling in their vicinity. Prisons are concentrated areas of stress. One mistake and a life was crushed. This was the first generation that could empty the prisons of all nations and create a crime-free, disease free-society.

Maharishi wouldn't dwell on these areas for long. His attention always moved to the Vedic literature. He was talking about the Veda Lila those days (the play of the Veda), showing in the medium of music and movement how diversity comes out of unity. He talked about the many different facets of Vedic knowledge, Yajur Veda, jyotish, yagya and *dharma*, all of which had no doubt been occupying his inner life and times when he wasn't dealing with all the nations and their difficulties. Politics is a very unreliable field, he insisted. "I was thinking of closing up shop," he said one day. We were startled. Shutting down the movement? Or, he went on, expanding Amrit Kalash, world peace, and watching how the world goes through unstressings as it purifies. We will continue to rejoice in good news. By doing least we will nourish the whole world consciousness as a byproduct of our own enlightenment, very neat, clean, comprehensive, effective, reliable, invincible, he said. I was relieved. Good, we were continuing, not closing up shop.

We had a few personal moments with Maharishi near the end of the visit. Sara wanted to leave a little early and Tom Egenes and Fred and Shelley Gratzon were heading back to Fairfield. Could she go with them? We would stay a little longer. Yes, that would be all right. Sara traveled with them to Frankfort and spent the night there, sharing a room with Shelley while Fred and Tom shared a room to make it work. Tom took Sara on a walk around Frankfort. They separated in Chicago as Tom went to visit family, and Shelley and Fred saw Sara back to MIU.

It turned out that we only stayed a few more days. It was time for us to return to MIU also and carry on with our work. Bevan brought us up to date on Maharishi's doings after we had returned from India. There had been a big celebration for Mahashivaratri on February 24. Maharishi had been closely monitoring the world news and was pleased to see favorable signs of peace breaking out in the Middle East and the Soviet Union. He said that mankind was on the doorstep of world peace so he wanted to lay out the divine government of nature.

Maharishi was staying there in Noida with the pandits working out the text and the moves of the Veda Lila, which would illustrate the emergence of creation from the self-interacting dynamics of the unified field in music, dance, and staging. He was enjoying the music that had already been written. John Hagelin would put together his "Play of the Unified Field" that autumn complete with music and costumes. It showed the levels of creation according to modern physics, including the atomic level, which was far above the level of the unified field. It was really charming. You could see one branch of the Veda emerging from another, peeking out behind one another, as the knower looked at the known, as *rishi* glanced at *chhandas*. Fun!

Maharishi also was absorbed in plans for Vedaland with Doug Henning. They were building models and discussing how the theme park would take the visitor through levels of creation, world cultures, and the new awakenings as heaven descended onto earth. Land was being looked at in South Florida and money was being raised. It all sounded very exciting. Maharishi also mentioned the beginnings of another stirring of the pot, music for world peace. We would fulfill our plans for creating an ideal society and for all the goals of the World Plan laid out in 1972.

'Always Choose Me'

ALWAYS CHOOSE ME, Maharishi advised us. What did he mean? Well, obviously, if you had a chance to be with him, to be in his presence and get his *darshan* and attention and guidance, you would choose to do that rather than some other thing that might seem important at the time. This meant dropping everything and going to the latest course, or wherever he might be, if you were invited, or could afford it, of course. Being "in the ashram" is a two-way street. If you are tuning yourself and your activity to the Master, to your guru, then he will guide and direct your evolution, even from afar. You are "in" the ashram. As you are to me, so I am to you, says the Gita (chapter 4, verse 11). "As men approach Me, so do I favour them," Krishna tells Arjuna. Maharishi comments that man, too, behaves to others as they behave to him. It is the nature of God, and of the guru, to give knowledge, to let the fullness of knowledge flow out. All we have to do is raise our cup to that level and it will fill to overflowing. We have to make the first move.

If you have taken the elevator up to a higher floor, glanced out of the door, and seen people having a lovely time there, and *stepped off* the elevator to enjoy yourself without reference to your evolutionary journey and its guide, then you are no longer "in" the ashram, but out somewhere on your own, at least until you wake up and get back on. I always think of Odysseus and the episode of the lotus eaters. On his journey home, at one of their stops, some of his men join a group who were blissfully eating the lotus and forgetting all about who they really were and about their journey home. Of course, everyone needs a break now and then, a little escape. At least I do.

Always choose me means, I believe, choosing your evolution above all other factors, being aware of the implications of what you were doing. As the Shankaracharya had told us in Jyotir Math in 1975, we needed to get enlightened ourselves first before we could effectively change the world. So choose rounding over some other project. We faculty got a month of that every summer and it was a delicious rest. Others often chose their work or their projects as being more important than rounding, but I believed they were of lesser importance and put rounding first. It inevitably produced major changes in my consciousness. I became a better person on all levels, and I needed that.

Next, I think he meant that one should work on a project that Maharishi had given you, not one imposed by someone else, to go by his advice and guidance first. It was sometimes not easy to discriminate among the many projects thrown at us. Maharishi's were always due yesterday, if not sooner, and for some specific event. Others, meant to be laid at his feet at the next Guru Purnima or January 12 celebration, were often someone else's idea of what might please him. Meditating in the dome was obviously what he wanted, which meant staying rested and able to get up early in the morning and go there. Or stopping work, however charming it might be, and heading off to join the community there.

In addition, there was the knowledge to be explored and absorbed. As the various waves or stirrings of the pot emerged, they were offered to the faculty and staff at MIU. I signed up for every course offered in Maharishi AyurVeda and Maharishi Jyotish, and became quite proficient in that knowledge, for a Westerner anyway. There was never enough money to attend the special courses and be trained as a jyotishi or Ayurvedic consultant, but

I learned what I could and applied it to our lives. I also studied Maharishi Gandharva Veda, the music for world peace that Maharishi was bringing out, and David and I even took a voice course which helped release some deep stresses in my throat that didn't allow me to scream or shout. And when Maharishi Vastu^{SM} came out, the science of architecture and directional placement of buildings, rooms and even furniture, I signed up for a course in that. The only things that didn't really interest me, I am reluctant to admit, were Sanskrit and Vedic Science. When it comes to them I have a slippery mind; everything slides off without making an impression.

Literature Conferences, Publications, and Grants

On the professional level, which meant making myself and MIU the best we could be academically, I was pretty busy. In 1983 the Literature Department got a grant from Title III (the U.S. government) to expand into minors in Spanish and French. Over the next few years we were able to buy four new little Macintosh computers for the faculty to use, seven Apple 2c's for the students in the language lab to use, twelve language lab booths for language learning, two Imagewriter printers, and software, films, filmstrips, books, and journals. It was a great help and it was Tim Ambrose who made it all happen. We all used those computers and printers to make our main point and unity charts, and the Spanish and French minors proved to be very popular. Every year Tim took a group of students to Mexico to refine their skills and have a fabulous time. The various French teachers took their students to France, including our future daughter-in-law Emily. They connected with the movements in those countries and there was much mutual fertilization. MIU was a wonderful place to be a student. We later got grants to expand the language program and later to offer an MA in Literature and one in Creative Writing. All this growth meant more teaching and administration.

Along with administration and teaching we were encouraged

to do research and publish, to popularize the unified field of consciousness among our academic peers. The archetypal criticism I had used in my doctoral dissertation had gone out of fashion and the whole area of literary theory or criticism became the dominant concern of teachers and scholars. It moved into increasingly intellectual areas, like deconstruction, and became less holistic as the years went by, with barely a nod to the emotions and senses. We were all supposed to connect modern science to Vedic Science, and for us in the Literature Department that meant connecting literature and literary criticism to Maharishi's knowledge as deeply as we could, and presenting these connections to our academic community. I had begun to work on a long paper, what would become "A Unified Field Theory of Literature" and be eventually published in our new journal *Modern Science and Vedic Science* in 1987.

As I developed my ideas I began to submit conference presentations to try them out on other people. In 1984 I presented a paper called "Unified Field Theory and the Theory of Literature" to the Iowa Council of Teachers of English (ICTE). It was a small pond and I could be a big fish. The conference was held at a different Iowa liberal arts college each year and I got to see what they were like. The next year I presented another one at ICTE called "Experiences of Expanded Consciousness and the Second Self in the Fiction of Willa Cather." I was teaching Willa Cather's novels and the students and I were enjoying her subtle writing and consciousness. The next year I broke into the Midwest Modern Language Association (MMLA), a bigger pond in which I was a very tiny fish, with a panel that I organized and was accepted by the organization. Our panel was entitled "Reading the Text in the Light of Unified Field Theory" and Silvine Marbury from our department and a Governor from Virginia Polytechnic Institute, Evelyn Toft spoke also. I also put together a group of (meditating) professors to comment on the papers, as was the custom. It went very well.

My big theoretical paper began to take shape. As well as reviewing recent critical issues, it brought out the seven states of consciousness, levels of the mind and the nature of language. It then presented our new theory of literature in three areas: the writer and the creative process; the Self-referral mechanics of reading; and the reader: Knowledge is structured in consciousness. I also approached the implications for the teaching of literature and the works of literature being read, anthologized, printed, and studied. As I look over this article some thirty years later I am impressed by how clear, intelligent, reasonable, and scholarly it sounds. I read it with amazement. I did that? I am so proud of all that work I did in my forties for and at MIU. At one time my paper was required reading for the literature majors. Check it out on the Academic page of my website RhodaTheWriter.com.

I continued to present papers at conferences. ICTE was always open. I gave another presentation there on Willa Cather in 1985 and "Transcending and the Creative Process: James Joyce's *Portrait of the Artist as Young Man*" in 1987. I gave a talk on Teaching Literature with Unified Field Charts there in 1989, and one on "Studying Feminist Utopian Fiction: Opening Students' Awareness to Change and Creating Heaven on Earth" in 1990. I refined the Joyce paper and presented it to the James Joyce Conference in 1989. There was a paper on "Vedic Psychology and the Understanding of Higher Stages of Consciousness Described in Modern Fiction" which I gave at a conference on literature and psychology at the University of Florida in Gainesville, also in 1989. I gave a paper on Willa Cather at the Third National Seminar on Willa Cather in Hastings, Nebraska. That was fun. I got to see all those places she wrote about and immerse myself in her Nebraska days.

Once I had broken into the MMLA with our panel on unified field theory as a theory of literary criticism, I kept going. I gave a paper on Willa Cather's novel *The Professor's House* at MMLA in 1987 at a Names Society session, and wound up chairing that session at the next MMLA meeting, putting together speakers and a panel discussion. I published that one, "The Use of Names in *The Professor's House*" in the *Willa Cather Yearbook* in 1991. I presented another Cather paper in 1989, and my last MMLA presentation on Fannie Hurst in 1991. I presented yet another Cather paper "From the *Aeneid* to *The Song of the Lark*: A Feminist Transformation of a Classical Myth" at the Fourth National Seminar on Willa Cather in Santa Fe, New Mexico, in 1990. That was really great, getting to see the places in the Southwest that informed her writing. These conferences and my papers on Willa Cather came out of the seminars I offered on her to the literature majors. David's mom came along to this last conference and got to see me in action. Looking back at all these conference presentations, I am amazed that I fitted them into my busy life. Do I still have copies of these papers? No, I don't. Ephemera.

Along with these scholarly presentations I was frequently asked to speak on conference calls to Visitors' Weekends and the TM centers, encouraging people to come to MIU and join our creating coherence groups in the domes. Over the years people would come up to me at MIU and tell me that they were there because they heard me speak on one of those conference calls. I was always running somewhere. Busy, busy time. I don't want to forget my students. I loved them and they were pretty fond of me. My birthday falls in July and they were never able to celebrate with me since that was during their summer vacation. They frequently dropped by the apartment and felt at home there.

One June (1985) my sister Adele was visiting with her two-year old son Michael. We had fun taking him around to the area farms. He was very interested in farm animals and in climbing on "trackers" (tractors) and we had plenty of them around. One evening David suggested we walk over to the Fairfield reservoir and show it to Adele and Mike. In the dark? I protested. Sure, why not. They persuaded me and we all went strolling over there. It was just a few minutes' walk from our frat. As we reached the grassy area leading down to the lake we saw a big celebration going on. There were lights and streamers, a table set with cake, and many students standing around. David walked confidently in that direction and we followed, wondering what was happening. At least, I wondered. They all knew what it was. It was a surprise birthday party for me!

But my birthday is a month away, I insisted. Yes, said Kenny Kolter and Patrick Pomfrey, our lit majors, but now is when we can celebrate it. I was really touched. Kenny was one of my favorite students and often dropped by the apartment. Adele was impressed by the warmth and spirit of our kids. We laughed and talked and ate cake. A memorable evening and a treasured memory.

And our helpers! We always had a devoted young woman administering our department and helping us with all our needs: Naomi Kleinman, Monica Grund from Germany, and many others whose names are not popping into this old brain. Thank you all.

While I was teaching the students and writing these papers, and working on the major theoretical article on unified field theory to be published in our new journal *Modern Science and Vedic Science*, I had to refer to the tapes that Maharishi had made over the years, either at SCI symposia or in response to visiting scholars. It was difficult to quote and cite these tapes. One had to listen to a long lecture and then try to take down his words in one particular area. The tapes could only be referred to as a whole, and they only existed in the MIU Tape Library, not accessible to other scholars or even to the students. I asked Maharishi at one of our personal meetings if I could transcribe these tapes, edit them, and print them as a volume so students and scholars could read and reference them. Yes, he said. Do it. At the time we were told not to take notes on his tapes so I had to proceed quietly. My colleague and co-author Susan Setzer and I put together a list of the most important tapes on literature and language and I began to transcribe them and pull out useful sentences for my articles and talks. This project went on for years, along with teaching, writing, administrating, traveling, and raising a family.

Nate

Once I heard a woman complain to Maharishi that her children were interfering with her meditation program. Maharishi quietly insisted, "Your children *are* your program." He said that the advantage of having children is that they are a twenty-four hour responsibility that you cannot shirk. Very evolutionary. He always sent people home to take care of needy parents or other close relatives. One needed to take care of one's spouse also, he always said. Protect their meditation. Promote their evolution. So life was quite a balancing act and sometimes it was difficult to see what would be best or how to compromise all these responsibilities.

Nate found his teenage years challenging. He had spent a few years in the Fairfield schools and was subjected to cruel discrimination. His two years at Lincoln Elementary weren't too bad, but the junior high years were miserable. The boys repeated their parents' hostility towards the 'Rus (short for gurus, what they called us meditators). Nate tried to remain unnoticed and sneak by the threats. It was a great relief to him when Maharishi School finally expanded into the high school years and he could transfer over. He loved sports and had fun with his friends. He had a paper route to earn his own spending money, making friends with all the old ladies he met along the way.

Nate became very interested in cycling with Brad Garso and wanted a top-of-the-line racing bicycle, a Specialized Sequoia with a chromoly frame. He worked hard the summer of 1984 as a dishwasher and earned enough money to buy himself that bike. Unfortunately, the narrow wheels often went out of alignment on our unpaved and gravel-strewn roads. While David and I were away in South Africa speaking for the movement there, some of the boys took that opportunity to have a big drinking party in our frat. We thought our kids were old and mature enough to stay by themselves. Perhaps they were, but their friends weren't. Sara cleaned up their mess before we returned home, but some of the stains in the carpet were indelible. We never left them again without having one of our middle-aged lady friends move in to prevent such a thing from happening.

That autumn, in eleventh grade, Nate worked on a science project to submit to the 26th Annual Science Fair in Des Moines that next spring, as did John and Julan White who lived upstairs in our frat, the children of our brilliant faculty member Douglass White, who had a PhD in Chinese and Japanese from Harvard and who taught Asian literature in my department. Doug's wife Bonnie was Chinese and quite a character. Keith's boys Gareth and Teddy also worked on projects. Nate was looking for something to do and David suggested he use a GSR machine, which David had used in his first TM study back in El Paso in 1971 (not the same machine! That one is still in a closet at UTEP, no doubt).

Nate wasn't interested in doing any research, TM or otherwise; he was having fun playing around with the machine and testing people's responses, to see how they responded emotionally. This is the basis of the lie detector test. David showed Nate how to operate the machine and hook people up. First Nate hooked up David and tried to ask him embarrassing questions. David remained calm and cool, a surprise to both of them. David was especially pleased to see he had some autonomic stability. Then Nate hooked up his friends, startled them and asked them about it. David helped him display his results graphically.

Nate's exhibit: "Exploring the Startle Response: The Correlation Between Certain Mental and Physiological Parameters as Derived Through a Startle Response Experiment" placed third in a group of 142 students in the senior biological division and won him a $200 college scholarship, a superior rating by the U.S. Air Force, and an embossed paperweight. Julan, who was in ninth grade, placed thirteen out of 210 entrants in her division and John placed 25 out of 195 in the eighth grade competition. The *Fairfield Ledger* sent a reporter and a photographer out to shoot the three of them standing in front of the old literature and art building, Foster Hall, dressed up in suits and ties, and looking very proud and happy.

This was just the beginning of Maharishi School winning the top awards at the state science fair and every other competition that could be found and entered.

Nate continued to experiment with everything he could, including marijuana. He and his friends got kicked out of Maharishi School at the end of that year. I taught him to drive (David was in the Philippines) and he tried taking some classes at Indian Hills Community College, but he wasn't ready or able to settle down. He got a GED instead of graduating from the school the next year and started MIU as a freshman that autumn. He threw himself into it: toga parties, parties, parties, parties with his new friends Steve Kelly and Kim Cottle and some of his old friends from high school and the Youth Invincibility Course courses. I have vivid pictures in my mind of him sitting in Yagyavalkya Hall in the old Learning Center with the freshman class, about three hundred of them, watching his mom up front trying to keep order and teach the literature core course to that rowdy group of eighteen-year-olds. He was proud of me, and all the kids seemed to think I was pretty cool *for a grownup*, but he was ever alert to any indication that I might embarrass him in front of his friends.

Nate in his soccer uniform

Nate became a literature major and minored in government and took some philosophy courses as well. He was in some of my literature classes and we managed that situation pretty well, I think. He was so brilliant, so verbal, so creative and mischievous that I couldn't help giving him an A each time. He was an A student even if he didn't always apply himself enough. He took courses with all the faculty: Bill Haney, Susan Setzer, Silvine Marbury,

Brian Aubrey. I don't know how they managed teaching and grading the son of their boss. I didn't ask.

He also was attracted to the international students who played soccer rather than football or baseball. He learned soccer and joined the team as goalie and played for years. He got bigger and more muscular and handsome.

The summer after his freshman year Nate took the flying block in Washington, D.C. and then took his place in the Dome, mostly sleeping off his late nights and busy student life. In January 1988 he had his turn at visiting Maharishi and India. He went on the Pioneers of Ayurveda course in Noida and learned pulse diagnosis, herbs, and a little jyotish, and he had a fun time. He and the guys even snuck out into the town to explore India a little bit. He was actually very good at pulse diagnosis, especially messenger pulse, where you think of another person and your pulse changes to reflect the physiology of that person. Nate also has good experiences meditating, but was his own man. He did not share our enthusiasm for our MIU lifestyle. He frequently reminded us that we could go out in the world and get good jobs and make real money. I answered, yes, but then we would just be saving up so we could come round at MIU during our vacations. During his college years he fell in love with a fellow student and when he graduated he got married in California. We had a big family wedding and reunion and Jean,

Nate graduating from MIU and taking his diploma and handshake from president Bevan Morris

David's mom, came to the wedding, along with her brother-in-law Kemper. She was the only grandparent left. The children loved her and Pop. (A jyotishi had told me that I had affectionate and loyal children. They are adopted, I said. No, no, he said. They are your children. They just came to you by a different route. It was all in my jyotish chart.) Nate would then live in California and later in the Philippines. It was the last family event for some time. We were on our own, David and I, but luckily we had our extended meditator family and our siblings and their children, and airplanes and telephones, and later email and texting and Skype. Every little text from those children gives my heart a warm stir.

After the marriage broke up he came back home and did an MA in Literature at MIU while he found his feet again.

Sara

Sara also had a rocky time as a teenager. It was not *all* difficult; we spent some wonderful Saturday afternoons driving to Iowa City and singing along to the latest popular music, of which I would have known nothing without Sara and Nate. They kept me connected to the world of the students, which made me a better teacher. We enjoyed shopping in Iowa City, sometimes with a best friend, often Adrienne, eating lunch out, and getting fantastic bargains, which was important because there was little money for frivolities and we loved to shop and buy clothes. We had good shopping luck together. We still do. We rarely argued and had a very good relationship. When Sara hit twelve I could no longer predict her taste in clothes. I would hold something up from a rack to see if she liked it. "For me or for you?" she would ask, giving me a look that answered my question.

Once when I was in Colorado giving a weekend seminar on literature and SCI, David came out of the Dome to find police cars outside our frat. Sara and one of her friends had taken our car (they were twelve!) and driven it around town and into a ditch. The car and the children were unharmed, but that friend was growing up too fast. She took Sara to meet some eighteen-year old boys in an abandoned bus. It was a relief when she and her father left MIU, an exit that we fostered along.

As she entered her teens Sara became increasingly restless. She often felt very sad, in the throes of some ancient grief. Sara admired the singer Madonna, who at the time was wearing her underwear on the outside of her clothes. All the young girls imitated her. Bevan was horrified; she was a disgrace instead of an example. Can't you control her? he asked David. David tried. At one point he nailed her bedroom window shut. Sara dutifully went to bed, slipped into the bathroom once we were all asleep, changed her clothes, and crept out the back door.

The summer of 1985 (when she had just turned 15) she came with us to the World Assembly on Vedic Science in D.C. and we all stayed at the College of Natural Law. One night Sara connected with another young girl staying at the College, Popi Bowman, a wild child, and the two of them disappeared. We were frantic. They eventually showed up. They had gone out to meet some older guy they knew, taking the subways around at night, two little blond children of fifteen in that dangerous city. Someone was watching over them. I just learned that Sara and Popi found a bar, showed their Maharishi School IDs, convinced the bartender that they were college students, and got served beer. Some military guys latched onto them and bought them more beer. They had a wonderful time being grownups at a bar, finally got on the subway late that night, and found their way back to the College, which, by the way, was located in one of the worst parts of the city, known then as the murder capital of the U.S. Sara says she has more to tell me about those years now that she is 46 and I am 76 and the danger is past. I am flinching in advance.

The next spring she was in a fever to leave Fairfield and Maharishi School. Her friend Laurel Hunter had moved to Denver and Sara wanted to do that, too. Our governor friend Rusty and his family took her in for a few months. She babysat for their kids a little, went to the public high school, worked at an afterschool job for spending money, and was pretty miserable. Would you like to come home? I asked on one phone call. Yes, she said, but she didn't think Maharishi School would take her back in the middle of the spring semester. I called Dennis Raimondi, who was the principal at the time, and he said she should come back. God bless you, Dennis, for being open, generous, and loving and not bound by rules and regulations. Sara came right home and appreciated home, school, Fairfield, and everything, at least for a while.

Sara turned sixteen the next summer. David taught her to drive, she got her license, and she bought herself a little VW for $500 from John Poole, one of Nate's friends. It had a blue body and one green door. She spray painted the whole car turquoise and when she went into her black period some time later, she painted it black. The car had a decent muffler but it was loose and needed to be welded to the frame. Have I said that money was always tight? That we only earned a few hundred dollars a month plus our room, board, car, gasoline, and personal expenses? David took Sara's car down to the motor pool on campus, borrowed their welding equipment, helmet and gloves, and set to work. He had learned to weld at his father's structural steel business in El Paso back in the sixties. During our stay in Maryland and his years in graduate school he had turned our garage into a studio and made sculptures out of old washing machine bodies using a small arc welder and an acetylene torch. Paul Gelderloos came looking for David that afternoon and I directed him to the motor pool. He was astounded to see David welding the muffler to Sara's car. How did you know how to do that? Paul asked.

Sara came to me one day that summer and said, Mom, I want a baby. *Or a cat.* I could relate. Right after I turned sixteen my mother gave birth to my sister Linda, an unplanned pregnancy, but a joy to the whole family. I loved that little baby. I thought she was the most beautiful creature in the whole world (her baby pictures do not bear that out), and I got a lot of happiness and

Sara, age 16, with her kitten and her car

fulfillment out of taking care of her for the next few years and taking her with me when I drove around Cleveland to see my friends. When I went off to college, she was the one I missed most. OK then, a cat, I capitulated. Sara wanted someone of her own to love. She found Catherine, the most adventurous one of her litter with a big voice and personality. The University administration often reminded me that pets were not allowed on campus. There were numerous hints and dark looks aimed my way. Catherine stayed and we installed a cat door in one of the frat windows. Catherine became an important member of our family and was until she died many years later.

Sara decided to apply to art schools her senior year so we went to look at a few of them. She and I flew down to Sarasota to look at the Ringling College of Art and Design and we stayed with a meditator in a funky, moldy-smelling old house. She decided on the California College of Arts and Crafts (CCAC), got accepted, and off we went late summer 1988 to get her set up. We stayed with my sister Adele who had her baby girl Leah right at that time. We had fun shopping for sheets and towels and everything she would need for her dorm room. That night her new roommate arrived, another little blond child, and the two of them bounced off into the night to explore Oakland (Oakland!!), giving me a hasty kiss good bye. Goodbye to my baby. Goodbye to that part of my life. I cried in the rental car all the way back across the bridge to my sister's house in San Francisco.

Sara even went to D.C. and took her Yogic Flying block the summer of 1989, after her freshman year. The course created a lot of purification in her, but she was happier in herself afterwards. After Sara graduated and worked in Berkeley for a while, she came back to Fairfield and did an MA in Art at MIU. It was wonderful to have her at home again. She is a major part of my evolutionary program, as is Nate. Mothering never ends; it is still going on, along with grandmothering, and is never in conflict with whatever else I must be doing.

I have to tell one jyotish story. When Sara was working in the Tahoe area after she graduated from CCAC she kept having accidents: falling off a roof at a party, a bicycle accident, and so forth. I looked in my jyotish books. Mars (male energy and sex, blood, accidents, violence) was stuck in one of her houses for months and was perhaps causing the problem. There is a remedy called an *upaya* where on a specific day you make a specific offering to a particular class of people. For Mars that meant giving red items to a celibate around noon on a Tuesday. I directed Sara to buy some red things (she got a red flowering plant and some red fruit) and to go find a celibate. That was a challenge. I asked her if there might be a Catholic church there in the Tahoe area where she was living.

Sara was nervous and uncertain about doing this really weird thing, but she was willing to try it. She found her way to the local Catholic church on the next Tuesday and knocked on a small door. A man in a white collar answered. Are you a celibate? she asked him. She wanted to get it right. Surprised, he answered, yes, he was.

She handed him her offerings and disappeared with no explanation. The accidents stopped occurring. I still smile, thinking of how that man might have stood there, astounded, having just been visited by a beautiful, blond, blue-eyed angel bearing gifts, and asking if he were a celibate. I am still wondering what it might have meant to his evolution at that moment. Nature works on all levels all at once.

David

Ah, my husband. We are like two oxen, yoked to the same plough for life. Is that too crude an analogy? A jyotishi told us we have been together for many spiritual past lives and here we are again. We had our issues (did I mention that money was one of them?), but we were and are committed to the same goal, enlightenment for ourselves and the world, and we are fortunate, blessed really, that we find ourselves to be compatible on numerous other levels as well. David had brilliant faculty working with him in the psychology department, a factory of researchers and writers, it seemed, and they turned out one great paper after another. They wrote chapters of *The Cosmic Psyche* and published them all in our journal *Modern Science and Vedic Science* and then David had the MIU Press print them all as a book he could give to Maharishi, to be published as he saw fit. But he did have difficulty with his secretarial help. He has an afflicted sixth house (according to jyotish) which meant he always has trouble with employees. He wanted me to work for him. No way!

I insisted that I had my own life and career and domain and would be miserable as his assistant and secretary. When I spoke before the faculty, gave papers, and showed my brilliance he was proud of me and had to agree that I could shine in my own area and contribute best that way. He always helped me in my work and I tried to help him with his. Maharishi said it is one's duty to protect your partner's rest so I also felt I had a responsibility to help him evolve, and that meant encouraging him to rest, to round, and occasionally to take a vacation, which he always resisted because he had so much to do, but which he needed and always enjoyed once he did. Often he even thanks me for dragging him out to a concert or off on a camping trip. Rather than ask him to go somewhere in those days, because he would always say no, he was too busy, I would say, the children and I are going to El Paso for Christmas, or to meet your parents in Rocky Mountain National Park. Would you like to come along? He was always hesitant, but he always came, and it was good for him.

I did always and still do read and edit his papers and help him with grammar, style, and spelling. I don't know what he knows and can't do what he does, so the only way I can help is by doing what I do best, writing and editing.

When Maharishi started talking about heaven on earth, David took it to heart. We fenced in a little yard off one wall of our frat,

David with his little sculpture of Mother Nature (a female figure made out of fish, birds, plants, holding frogs, etc.) which he found in Mexico. He plumbed her to have water coming out of her head and out of the frogs' mouths.

had some doors put in that wall to access it, and David plant-ed special arctic roses that would survive an Iowa winter. He fed them lovingly with manure tea of his own making. With Nate's help they poured concrete and built a little fountain in a pool with a submersible pump so it could circulate and spray water. He built a patio and a trellis over it and we grew morning glory vines on it and sat out there to enjoy it and invited friends over to eat with us. Maharishi had said that there were many things for householders to enjoy, many avenues for them to evolve. One didn't have to be a monk like him.

Of course, we were all working for Maharishi, but we all had lives to live as well. I remember once when David was in Interlaken with Maharishi and asked him if I might join him there. Maharishi thought about it and said, yes, if we are going to do something fun, something she would enjoy. Ha!

David also loved sailboats. When he was a boy, he and his broth-er built one and tried to sail it on a manmade lake his father had created as part of the Civilian Conservation Corps during World War II. He tried windsurfing in Iowa and one summer we drove around with a windsurfer attached to the top of our car, amaz-ing all our friends. He bought a daysailer and we got a hitch and

pulled the boat to Lake Darling and Lake Rathbun and camped out and sailed on those lakes, sometimes with Scott and Eva Herriot, sometimes with Lenny and Lesley Goldman. Not often enough, though.

One spring one of our for-mer art students (and quite an accomplished painter him-self), John Preston, offered a weekend watercolor course.

David had always painted in oils and loved painting, but hadn't done it in years. He had stopped painting and sculpture to pour himself full time into his work for Maharishi and the movement in 1971. When we were newly married and working in Cambridge the summer of 1963 before he started his graduate program at the University of Maryland we used to go painting together on Cape Cod. I painted with him for several years, more in Grandma Moses style, but eventually gave it up for literature, both reading and writing.

Watercolor would be a new medium for him, and is known to be one of the most difficult, but I was thinking more about balancing his brain. He was happiest doing art, and it seemed to do something for him, for his evolution. I signed us both up and we spent the weekend painting apples and pears, first in monotone and then in color. We still have some of those paintings that we both did. The watercolor course was a success. The genie was out of the bottle. He took up painting again and he hasn't stopped (www.orme-johnsonpaintings.com).

Our Parents

My mother and my sister Linda learned TM shortly after we did and they both enjoyed it. After a little while Mom expressed doubts about it. Was it consistent with her Jewish faith, she wondered. At the time there was a Rabbi Levine who had learned TM and loved it and he had made a couple of audio tapes explaining how good it was and how it aided his spiritual growth. We played these for my mother and she was satisfied. David has collected numerous letters from religious leaders saying basically the same things and posted them on his website www.TruthAboutTM.com. They are very inspiring. I recently saw a bumper sticker reading "God is too huge for just one religion," or something like that.

My mother was easily distracted, however, and rarely meditated. I would call her up and ask if she had meditated yet that day. Well, she would say, your Aunt Bernice called, and then I put in a load of wash, and she would go on like that. After my father died in 1956 she plunged into her first big depression and David and I had to take her and my little sister Linda, then aged ten, to Maryland with us for six months until Mom recovered enough to live on her own back in Cleveland. As I mentioned earlier she and at least one of her brothers were bipolar and her condition just seemed to get worse over the years. She stabilized somewhat with drugs but pretty much drove us all crazy when she was at either extreme. In 1986 she had finally decided to sell her little house and move into an apartment. She had the feeling she was going to die and she didn't want to stick us with a house full of stuff to get rid of. I tried to tell her we would have to dispose of it anyway if she moved, so why not just let us do it later and enjoy her house and garden in the meantime. I was afraid she would sell the house in a manic mood and then fall into a depression when it was time to move, which is exactly what happened. The house sold and then my brother Jay flew to Cleveland to help her find an apartment and she listlessly cooperated. When I went there in May to help her clean out the house and move into her apartment, she was deep into a depression.

When I got there she was lying on the couch, face to the back of it. I asked her to sit up and meditate. She reluctantly got into a sitting position and stared at me. I am only doing this, she said, because you have come all this way to help me. Yes, I insisted, working the Jewish guilt as best I could, I have come all this way. The least you can do is meditate with me. We closed our eyes. I cracked one eye open a minute or two later and there she was staring into space. Close your eyes, Mom, I said. She did. After twenty minutes or so when the meditation was over, I asked, Would you like to go out for lunch? All right, she said. Maybe you could get your hair done, I suggested. All right, she said. After the beauty shop and lunch (her nephew was working at the deli we visited and we chatted a bit with him), we dropped into a shop or two and then drove home. You had a pretty good afternoon, I said encouragingly. She looked over at me suspiciously. You think TM did that, don't you, she muttered.

She had saved every tulle bridesmaid gown I had ever worn and would never ever wear again. But you only wore it once, she moaned, thinking of the precious money spent on it. Fine, I said, let's let some other young girl enjoy it; I never will. There were old tires down in her rec room basement, and Linda's old paintings from art school, and boxes and boxes of useless things. When I had cleaned out the house and given an amazing amount of stuff to Goodwill and the Salvation Army, which would only take some of it after I screwed on loose legs and put missing parts back together, we were ready to move into the apartment.

Linda flew in from New York, and together we moved her into her apartment and unpacked everything. We couldn't persuade her to buy even a little plant. She used to garden and have plants all over her windowsills. No, she didn't want to take on the responsibility of even a small African violet. We went grocery shopping and she only bought tiny amounts of necessities. Linda flew back to New York and when my Aunt Dorothy came to drive me to the airport, Mom stood out in the parking lot and drank me in with her eyes, knowing, I think, she was seeing me for the last time. I was ignoring all the clues and was anxious to get back home. Sara was turning sixteen and was needing a lot of careful attention.

Later that summer as David and I attended those courses and Yogic Flying demonstrations in D.C. and New Delhi and Guru Purnima celebrations in Noida, India, I was worrying about her. Was she recovering from her depression and feeling better? Her sister and sisters-in-law all checked on each other every day, a little network of old ladies, almost all widows. Late one night when we returned to our hotel, I got a message to call my sister Adele. Aunt Dorothy was concerned that Mom hadn't answered the phone and got the manager to let her into the apartment. There she was sitting on her couch with Maharishi's Gita on the coffee table in front of her with her eyes closed. She was gone. The funeral would be in a few days.

We met with Maharishi to say goodbye and took a taxi to the airport. Our taxi broke down, had a flat or something, and we jumped out, hailed another one as we stood there by side of the road in the middle of the night, much to the unhappiness of our driver who not only had a cab to fix but had lost his airport fare, and we made our flights to Cleveland just in time. Nate and Sara borrowed a reliable car from the motor pool and drove to Cleveland to join us. My brother Jay and his wife Jenny came and Linda too. All of the other relatives, my father's remaining sisters and my mother's remaining brothers and their wives or widows already lived there. We cleared out Mom's apartment, had a funeral service, and went to the cemetery. She was to be buried next to Dad. On a nearby tombstone were a few lines from the following verses written by Mary Elizabeth Frye in 1932:

> *Do not stand at my grave and weep.*
> *I am not there; I do not sleep.*
> *I am a thousand winds that blow.*
> *I am the diamond glints on snow.*
> *I am the sunlight on ripened grain.*
> . . .
> *I am the soft stars that shine at night.*
> *Do not stand at my grave and cry;*
> *I am not there; I did not die.*

It was some small comfort, but I wept. My beloved mother was gone. My dad had asked me to look after the family. I would try.

David's dad had suffered a series of small strokes over the years leading up to the summer of 1988. They were detected by autopsy, but he acted as if he might have had something like Alzheimer disease, his short term memory going first, and he finally died just weeks before Sara's high school graduation. We had been making frequent trips to El Paso over the previous few years to visit him and to bolster up his mother who suddenly found herself in charge of the family finances and nursing home care. She sold their house and moved into an apartment where she cared for him until that became impossible and he no longer quite knew who we all were. He knew we were loved ones; he just wasn't sure about the details. It was traumatic for the family, but David and I weathered it pretty well. We were grateful for years of meditation and rounding. We could feel love and grief, but we were not overthrown by sadness of it all.

Over those years I also tried to get the rest of my family meditating. I taught my brother Jay and his wife Jenny and their daughter Elizabeth. When Raymonde Purcell, who was running the Cleveland TM center, would invite me to speak at one of her residence courses, I always accepted so I could visit my elderly relatives. My aunt Dorothy had learned TM earlier and was quite faithful while she had a job downtown as a legal secretary. She would meditate on the twenty-minute bus ride every day. When her blood pressure spiked suddenly I encouraged her to start her TM again. She came to a residence course with me one weekend and enjoyed the course and seeing me speak and entertain the CPs. I taught TM to my Aunt Adele, Dorothy's older sister, but it was too late. Her mind was gone and she couldn't even remember to close her eyes. My father's brother and my mother's extended family resisted, but I tried. Only my cousin Cindy took to TM. She had gotten breast cancer and was desperate to try anything. She liked it and became active in her local TM center for a while.

A Research Collaboration

David and I got the idea that we could test Maharishi's ideas about literature, that the experience of reading or listening to poetry, for example, would swing the reader's awareness from concrete details to more abstract emotions or broader concepts. And this swing would purify the reader's consciousness and develop it in the direction of higher states of consciousness. I made an audio tape of several poems that seemed to not only describe the process of transcending to unboundedness but to actually take the reader within as he or she listened. I made the tape so that part of the experiment would be standardized. Then we hooked up a couple of students to the EEG so we could see the effect of these moments on both their breathing and brain wave coherence, what we knew to be the hallmarks of the transcending experience. The results were amazingly clear.

Now, poetry (and probably fiction as well) gives the reader or listener frequent opportunities to go within. These occur in the gaps at the end of each line, in stanza breaks, in the sound or rhythm patterns, or in the meaning or sense that draws the reader inward. What we saw was that at the AHA moment of the poem, when the reader went inward, his or her breathing slowed down, and coherence increased. This process of going inward (we call it Self-referral) takes the awareness to a place where the brain is wide awake but undirected, what we now would call the Default Mode Network or DMN. This state is easily distinguished from focused thinking or any other kind of concentration or mindfulness technique and can readily be seen in TM practice as the meditator effortlessly transcends to subtler states within.

One of the poems I used was by the America poet James Wright. It is called Lying in a Hammock at William Duffy's Farm in Pine Island Minnesota. After sumptuously describing the sounds, colors, and emotions he experiences, taking the listener on a gorgeous sensual journey, he closes with "A chicken hawk floats over, looking for home. / I have wasted my life." Ahhh. The listener goes within. What does he mean? Does he mean he should have spent more time in the hammock and less time in the world? And what did we scientists see? As the poem ended with these lines, we saw a big drop in breath rate and a definite increase in coherence. The listener had gone within, had transcended to a more silent, comprehensive state of awareness. Then the listener came back, breathing increased, coherence dropped. And then, it happened a second time, because inevitably the listener thinks, "and, oooo, what about me? Have I wasted my life?" Another turning inward. Another drop in breath rate, another rise in coherence. So there were two self-referral loops in this poem and we could see them on the EEG. Fantastic. It was just a pilot study and we planned to have more subjects and expand it and publish it, but life intervened. The phone rang, and off we went to Russia.

Earthquake Relief

IN DECEMBER 1988 there were two huge, destructive earthquakes in the Soviet Union, in Spitak in the Socialist Republic of Armenia, or Armenian SSR. Over 60,000 people in that small country were reported killed, and probably there were many more who died because they were ill-equipped to handle the injuries. Over half a million buildings were destroyed, many of them schools which had pancaked on top of the children. The second largest city in Armenia, Leninakan, was particularly hard hit with over 80 percent of its buildings destroyed. The Soviets and their minions interfered with rescue operations and ordered foreigners out of the country. The whole country was impacted, either by a death in the family or by working to pull bodies out of the rubble. By the autumn of 1989 the country was flooded with relief workers and rebuilding efforts. A Russian man named Joseph Goldin came to MIU and told us about the disaster. He had a plan to simultaneously play a concert at several locations around the world and raise the collective consciousness that way. It was an idea you could run with.

Dr. Deepak Chopra had been talking about TM in Moscow and finding the doctors to be very interested, especially a Dr. Olganoff who ran a medical facility there. Perhaps we could send a team to Armenia for earthquake relief. We could build a dome in Leninaken as a TM center, instruct thousands of people, ease the suffering of the people, *and* have a remote effect on the Soviet Union, moving it in a more peaceful direction. David and Bob Wynne flew to Boston to try to inspire wealthy Armenians there to support such a project, but they thought we were a cult; they were wedded to the Christian Church and were very antagonistic to the project. David and Bob visited Deepak in his beautiful home outside Boston. Deepak was talking to Maharishi a lot in those days, and he told David and Bob that Maharishi said that they would be going to Moscow and then to Armenia, along with MIU architect Henry Clark, seasoned TM teachers Chris Crowell and Richie Quinn, American-Armenian TM teacher Greg Monokian, and Dr. Craig Perrinjaquet, along with medical supplies, just in case. Armenia had few anesthetics, fewer antibiotics, almost nothing in the way of medical supplies and equipment. Dentists did dental work without anesthetics.

David and Bob went to Washington, D.C. and met with a young man at the Soviet Embassy, Deputy Chief of Mission, Mr. Garnik Nanagoulian. They were approved for visas to go for earthquake relief under the auspices of the Sport Ministry (yoga, exercise, whatever). The Soviet Union was suddenly open to foreign visitors and outreach. Look up my father, Mr. Nanagoulian Senior, when you get to Yerevan, he suggested. The team left that autumn and landed in Moscow ready to teach TM. Doctors flocked to their talks and sent all their friends and relatives. They instructed hundreds and then moved on to the capital of Armenia, Yerevan, and began to move around and instruct many, many people without charge. A cadre of young teachers of English came to hear their American accents and test their language skills. They learned TM and stayed to help as translators, organizers, and friends. Some of Bob and David's first early contacts tried to limit their activities and even threatened them, but Mr. Nanagoulian Senior was welcoming and friendly. The Greek Orthodox priests begged them to give the meditators Christian mantras and send them back to the church. For the first time since the Soviet takeover the churches were allowed to open and resume their activities, but the people were not flocking back to them.

After a few months of intense teaching and the welcome disappearance of the Russian tanks that had been in the streets when they arrived, Dr. Perrinjaquet had to leave, and the guys asked if their wives could come over. That meant Linda Quinn, Maureen Wynne, Anne Dowe of the math department who knew some Russian, and me. Me!! International, meaning Maharishi, approved and visas and plane tickets were organized for us. We would bring a ton of much needed supplies, both for teaching TM and food for us. We didn't know how desperate the food situation was. Sara was home for Christmas and helped me to get ready.

I mentioned earlier that my mother was born in a small town in western Russia, in a *shtetl*, where she spoke Yiddish at home and studied German and Russian in a village school. When she was a youngster and bullets were flying through the village during the Revolution about 1913 my grandfather left for America and joined *landsmen* (countrymen) in Cleveland. He began to peddle produce from the farmers' market along the streets of East Cleveland until he had saved up enough money to buy a two-story house, put a renter upstairs, and send for the family, about ten years of hard work later, in the spring of 1923. I felt a strong affinity for the Russian culture, had read their great novels and taken a graduate course in Dostoevsky for my PhD. I had even studied the Russian language for two years at the University of Maryland. My mother was corresponding with cousins in Russia, in Yiddish and English. I didn't think in terms of the Soviet Union. It was Russia! I would be going home. I got out my Russian books, started to relearn the Cyrillic alphabet, and brush up my language skills.

Behind the Iron Curtain

I knew this would be an historic trip and as soon as I got to Moscow I bought a little notebook and started keeping a diary of our day to day goings and comings. Here are the first few entries

Here I am dressed in furs for the Russian winter saying goodbye to Sara. Wally DeVasier is ready to fly Maureen, Anne, and me to Chicago to catch our flights to New York, then Frankfort and on to Moscow!

(I had to fill in the two or three days before I got the notebook), which give the flavor of our teaching activities and our enthusiasm:

Tuesday, January 9, 1990, MIU—home sick with fever and chills. Packing with Sara's help: food, boots, Amrit, soap, toys, making little cloth bags to hold the puja pieces, grumpy. Lowell picked up the luggage around 9 to be driven to Chicago. We leave for Moscow tomorrow.

Wednesday, January 10, Fairfield Airport—beautiful clear cold day. Sara drove me to the Fairfield airport and we sat in the car talking until Brad came to drive us over to the plane. It was a joy and relief to see Wally the pilot there, and the joy and excitement grew as we all arrived and finally took off. As we rose into the air and circled the field I saw Sara and the others standing in the sunshine and snow waving to us. Was it true? Was I really going to initiate in Russia?!

Checking in with Pan Am, Russian being spoken around us. In

NY Maureen, Anne, and I stepped up to the gate and handed the young woman our boarding passes. "Are you a frequent flyer?" she asked me. "Yes," I answered. "I am upgrading you to Clipper Class," she said. "Is the upper deck all right?" I felt a wave of bliss, excitement—"Yes, yes," I answered, "and Maureen and Anne too." Linda was off somewhere so I couldn't include her. And so we flew to Frankfort with room and comfort and with our practically private bathroom. I read *Coping with Russia* and studied the Russian alphabet and wrote a letter to Sara to give to a traveler returning to the U.S. to mail. Anne studied and slept and Maureen worked all night on some MIU self-study materials. I meditated and took cough medicine but couldn't sleep. Still, I was the only one who had slept the night before we left so I was in charge of tickets, boarding passes and necessary information.

Thursday, January 11—flight delayed, everyone restless, exhausted. We four sat together and meditated and the waiting room in Frankfort quieted down around us, the plane arrived and we boarded a 3½ hour flight to Moscow. The plane was full of Soviets: broad, Slavic faces and a new flavor of collective consciousness. Arrival was hectic. Finally located our luggage. Kind strangers helped us get our heavy pieces off the conveyor belt, gave us a few rubles to rent carts (you can't change money until after you leave the cart area!), and warmly said "Welcome to Moscow." We got five carts for our twenty-five bags, boxes, trunks, computers, etc., and waited nervously in line for our turn. Should we sort out the stuff for each one of us? Strange trunks and boxes full of printed materials, pictures of Guru Dev, food, candles for initiating, incense, etc., all bore our names, one or another. Should we declare our tape players, jewelry, etc.? In the end the young man at customs scribbled over our forms where it said how many dollars we were bringing in and sent us through. He and the passport control fellow (so young and sweet looking) seemed genuinely friendly and delighted and amused when I stepped up to each one, organized my sleepy tongue, and said how are you? and good evening, and please and thank you in Russian, as appropriate, not all at once.

We pushed and pulled our five heavy carts toward the exit and finally spotted Bob and David. Bob greeted us in a loud, booming, joyful voice, "Welcome to Disneyland!" The guys had all been on a phone call to International [Maharishi] and told him we wives were coming. International said to welcome us warmly, so they left for the airport and arrived just as we were coming out, which was hours late, by the way. Karen [Malik-Simonian, our new Russian TM National Leader, pronounced Ka-ren, with the accent on the ren] was still on the phone with International, so Tatyana and Paulina [his wife and daughter] went along with them on a huge rented or borrowed Intourist bus, which then took us to the Hotel Mir and bed.

I didn't fully appreciate for days what an unlimited playground we had landed in. David looked happy and strong and very glad to see me in my big, furry coat [silver fox which Mom had given to Linda and she passed up to me]. Our two-room suite was very warm and cozy, too warm, in fact. The guys were full of news of their activities in Yerevan (7,000 initiations), their triumphs in Moscow (when they first arrived and 200 initiated already since they came to meet us), the conference they were attending as chief speakers at SEVA (the Slavic Economic Community) or maybe it's East European, which is attached to our hotel. We need passes to get in and out of the hotel, SEVA, etc. and no one speaks English. Very good feeling.

Friday, January 12, Hotel Mir, Moscow—slept half the day and lazily unpacked a bit since we didn't know if we would stay there [hotels were either on the ruble, cheap, or the dollar, inflated for tourists. Also restaurants had a ruble room and a dollar room. We invoked our mission of "earthquake relief" and usually got the ruble rate]. David and Bob attended another meeting at the conference. After a short meditation program [setting the pace for the entire rest of the trip], David returned and Anatoly came by to take him and Bob to a prep lecture at Olganoff's. Anatoly is a doctor and new meditator. He listened to my lungs. Seems I have bronchitis but will live. David will bring me home some herbal tablets later which will improve the cough.

Paulina came later and led us on the metro to Karen's where Tanya had fixed a great vegetarian meal, many courses served on tiny plates. I happily stuffed myself. After dinner Tanya presented us with traditional large round hand-painted and lacquered trays and dark brown, plushy fur hats. Mine is huge and would slide down right over my eyes if my glasses didn't keep it up, but it's warm and beautiful and David smiles and smiles at me and says I look like a real Russian in all my furs. And it's true—on the metro everyone is wearing hats just like ours and many women have fur coats, though few as nice as mine. Karen and Paulina see us home on the metro—we part minutes before it closes for the night and troop home through the fresh snow and subzero cold right past the American Embassy to our hotel—tired, happy, exhilarated. Joseph Goldin was supposed to try to tape Maharishi's January

On the Moscow Metro in our fur hats

12 talk. We didn't know if he had succeeded. But what a grand beginning!

The guys wouldn't let us catch our breath. They had already set up TM courses for all of us at Tanya's school, at Olganoff's medical facility, and then at the SEVA conference. Soon we would be rushing from one place to another with barely enough time to meditate or eat. They would sometimes teach with us or dash off to do some interview with the press or TV. Travel to Armenia had to be arranged, too. Linda wanted to go there directly to join Richie but Intourist, the official state tourist agency, said that was impossible. While I was recovering from my cold, I called around, speaking in German and French, and finally got a reservation for Linda. No one could believe it could have been that easy, but when they went to pick up the ticket it was there! We quickly organized getting her to the airport and getting us, with drivers and translators, to Tanya's school for our first course. Anatoly and his girlfriend Olga picked us up. When we got there and parked, Anatoly quickly removed the windshield wipers from his car. I was amazed! They will steal them, he explained, and in we went.

I was shown to a girls' sewing room, I had written in my journal, and a rug was put on the floor and there I was facing rows of sewing machines, brightly colored aprons and other projects on the wall and blackboard—an austere and long room. I drew a curtain over the blackboard, set out my gold-plated puja set and created an initiation room. It was getting lighter outside so I turned off the fluorescent lights and asked Olga to bring in the first group. They filed in quietly and respectfully carrying their piece of fruit, three flowers and handkerchief, men, women, and children, and we were off. Faces softened, eyes glowed—they became meditators before my eyes. During instruction they fell inward into their own silence at once, sitting perfectly still.

By the end of the day the room was warm, soaked with *sattva*, candle burning down, and the sweet smell of incense. During puja and instruction I was nervous at first and lacking confidence but as time went on I grew surer and more blissful and then felt a tingling at the back of my head on both sides. The people—the Russians—were so sweet, open—with their gratitude and friendliness, their feelings and doubts right up front—like Americans, not shadowed like many Europeans. As each one came up to me, I greeted them with pleasure and gratitude and delight myself. They came in with innocence, openness, appreciation and simplicity! I felt gushes of bliss. During one of the short meditations during instruction, I thought joyfully, "Is this heaven? No, it's Moscow!" We had been so conditioned to fear the Soviet Union, it didn't seem possible that we were actually there and teaching TM.

Olga didn't translate word for word; she would listen to me and would say everything in her own words. She was not easy to train to say exactly what I wanted her to say, the precise words of the TM instructions, but she was good—so deep in her own meditation sometimes she could hardly speak. While my sixth group was meditating she and I raced down six flights of stairs to the school dining room. Tanya's cooks brought out hot vegetable soup, a beet salad, some fried potatoes, bread and cheese and some green peppers in tomato sauce. It was about five o'clock and I hadn't eaten since breakfast at eight. Bob joined us and Tanya sat down with us. We ate gratefully and greedily in that huge, cold room sitting on long, wooden benches and then rushed back upstairs to bring the group out of their first meditation.

During my seventh and last group I could hardly speak. The words just didn't want to rise up. Some guy drove me and David home, both of us exhausted and happy. I especially remember one family with their eleven-year-old daughter. She turned from serious to joyful right before my eyes. The children breathe in the mantra; it naturally becomes them. The adults differ—some take to it right away, some need help. Olga was late returning once and I had to begin the initiation day interview form without her. Luckily one young girl spoke German so we began without her. I initiated seventy men, women, and children that day.

The next day David and Bob went down to the human ecology conference and then David left for a lecture at the Physical Chemistry Institute. Anne had a bad cold. Maybe she got it from me on the plane, although David didn't. Maybe she got it standing on the cold floor. My mother used to say, "Cold feet, runny nose." I think science is catching up with her. At Tanya's school I kept my socks and boots on instead of standing barefoot in front of the puja table, as we usually did. Maureen and I hurried off to Olganoff's to teach. We arrived late, and again the rooms were bare and unsuitable. Anatoly helped me move furniture and we created two nice environments. I had only one cloth for my table, but there was a big computer printer in the other room so I tore off a few sheets of white paper and voila! I taught three groups.

They were full of questions at the end. Is TM a religion? etc. I had to answer their questions and give them some slightly elaborated going-home instructions. One woman—young, dark haired, with a very tense, strained face—changed dramatically. She softened, relaxed, and became beautiful. I caught her eye and she nodded profoundly, as if to say, "this is it!" or "yes, yes, yes." I smiled and gestured. I'm communicating quite well with body language and my few words of Russian. I could, with some confidence and a decent accent, say close the eyes and good in Russian. By the time I had finished, it was dark and the office windows reflected the last flickers of the candles and the rooms felt warm and relaxed. It was good. Anatoly had seen the changes in their faces after their first meditation. These were his friends and colleagues, so he knew what they usually looked like. We were both very happy.

Maureen was just finishing up and we quickly left for the first night's checking of Tanya's group at the big school auditorium and arrived a little late. Sergei was already translating for Bob. Sergei was disappointed that David hadn't come yet from Olganoff's. He loved David, it seems. David's groupies were quite devoted to him. I offered to initiate a bunch who were waiting yesterday at the school, but they were waiting for him. The crowd cheered and applauded when Maureen and I walked in. The next day was even more hectic. We got into the SEVA Conference with our new passes and gave a preparatory lecture to a small group that David and Bob had already set up, interviewed them, and arranged to instruct them later that afternoon.

We had a quick bite in our room with some soup mix and vegetables we had brought from MIU and some black bread and cheese from the fifth floor buffet. Then Anatoly drove us to Olganoff's to do a first day check of the group we had instructed there the day before. Almost everyone came, 107 out of 111. We learned that not everyone came back for the three days of checking, which was too bad. They were missing very valuable knowledge, but the entropy was enormous. We were lucky to get what we could. Anyway, they welcomed us enthusiastically and after a brief interview with Good Evening Moscow (making a video for their TV show), we gave the lesson.

Immediately afterward, David and Bob went with Karen for a TV taping and Anatoly drove me and Maureen back to the Mir Hotel to teach our new group from the conference. They gave us two cramped, dirty little offices, but we spread out our table cloths and pictures of Guru Dev and created nice places in which to teach. We had hired an interpreter to help one of us and he learned TM along with my first group. I did my own TM with the first group and my Sidhis and Yogic Flying (piecemeal) with the second—great program, lots of bliss. They all sunk right in, hated to leave, lots of questions, very happy.

Afterwards, Paulina took us on the metro to her mother's school where we ladies led second night's checking with Paulina's help as a translator. The place was packed. My initiates kept smiling warmly at me. I gave a rousing checking meeting with funny stories about stress release. Maureen was still deep inside from the day's initiations and could hardly speak. One older woman gave me a tray and a lacquered spoon. She was frustrated at not being able to tell me what she had experienced. On initiation day she had pointed to Guru Dev in the picture and motioned up into the air. I take it she saw stuff in her meditation. One man wanted to us to go teach TM in Moldava. They would pay expenses and everything [we were teaching for free at that point since we had no way to process course fees—that would come later, much later]. I told him to talk to Karen. One of Maureen's initiates gave us tickets to the famous puppet theatre for Thursday night. Got home late. The guys had eaten at Karen's and had gone to their second night somewhere else—all we could get were two smaller halls that night and we had split the group of 435 in two. A great night, but again we hardly got to meditate or eat.

The next day was January 17, David's 49 birthday. Even busier than the day before. First day's checking of the SEVA Conference group, Anatoly took us to Olganoff's for a second day checking there, and we had a third night's checking at Tanya's school that evening. But first, one of our meditators, Maria Bobrova, who lived in Yerevan but was visiting in Moscow, insisted on taking me to meet some friends of hers. First we went to the Foreign Language Department at Moscow State University to meet her friend Larissa, then to the office of the Dean, Svetlana Grigorvna, where, over tea, cakes, bread, and cheese, I met some faculty, including one working on Willa Cather. I talked in English about TM, how we teach at MIU, Unified Field Charts (I had brought the one for literature), until Svetlana arrived—a very sharp woman—who quickly got the point and was open to lectures at the English club, TM courses for the teachers and students, lectures on literature, and she asked what fees I might charge. They all spoke incredibly good English. One of them had spent a year at Sarah Lawrence College. I saw them as future translators, TM teachers, Sidhas, the works. If only we had stayed in Moscow and not gone to Armenia, I sometimes thought when we got down there, I could have been with my peers and colleagues in Moscow!

Maria and I then hitched a ride with a friendly driver over to another friend's house for dinner (cold fatty slabs of meat and cold salads, oy!). One of her friends had a book of American folk songs and wanted to know what a paw paw was, and what was the translation for "de" (Southern for "the"), and they wanted to know the tune for "Down in the Valley." I can't carry a tune in the best of times, but I croaked it out as well as I could. Our host had just heard David speak at Physical Chemistry the other day. Small world, warm people, so gracious.

Maria and I tore out, caught a trolley and arrived at the school just in time for me to meet with my initiates after third night's checking. Maria helped me answer their questions and hear their results. I spoke pidgin Russian: you, meditation, two minutes, over there, good! Off we went to a big birthday celebration for David at Karen's. We had gotten a message from International; they had called earlier. "The whole world wishes David a happy birthday!" and we got our mission: "Go stop the civil war in Armenia!" We were all exalted and ready to leave (as soon as we finished up our other two courses). I loved Russia, felt at home in Moscow, but was willing, even eager, to move on. Karen asked us whether we would we go to Baku (the capital of Azerbaijan, their mortal enemy, the people who had been killing Armenians and sending them fleeing for their lives). Well, if Maharishi said to go, we would. Surely he would not do so unless it were safe and that he would do whatever necessary to keep us safe, we answered. We took the metro back to our hotel all by ourselves. We were feeling quite at home in Moscow and could easily read the Russian names and recognize our Metro stops.

A word on Communism. Karen and his family had a one-bedroom apartment. Paulina and her grandmother slept in that bedroom; Karen and Tanya opened up the sleeper sofa and slept on that in the living room. There was a toilet room, a small bathroom, a little kitchen, and a little dining room. All was very nice and beautifully decorated in the apartment, but the entry to the whole building was dirty and bare and smelled of urine; the corridors were dirty and bare; most of the overhead lights weren't working. People had bought beautiful front doors for their own apartments, but there was absolutely no communal spirit to take care of the rest of the building. Everyone was on his or her own. Is that Communism? Seemed like a failure to me.

The next day we raced off with Anatoly to Olganoff's for third day's checking. A great success, if smaller numbers. I couldn't seem to find that lady who had changed so dramatically, but there she was, smiling and laughing, almost unrecognizable, she had changed so much. We had interviews with *Trud* (a labor magazine) and some Medical Gazette, which made us late for our second day checking with the conference. Dmitri, our hired interpreter, had moved it to later, so that was okay, but some Chinese herbalist had usurped the room. David had another interview with some newspaper from the Academy of Science while we waited. David looked at our initiates, people he had been seeing every day at the conference and he couldn't believe how changed they were, how much light was in their faces. We hung out for a while with our initiates waiting to see if a room would materialize, and finally postponed the meeting until the next day. This kind of difficulty with rooms, halls, times, and schedules would follow us to Armenia, but get even worse, much worse. Both countries were very entropic.

We finished up the conference group the next day. Several of the older men kissed my hand. One serious young daughter was full of smiles. Lovely. After the meeting David and I were interviewed by a reporter for the *Young Communist*. He was very intelligent and asked good questions. At one point he told us that many people try to come to Russia and organize things but don't succeed as well as we do. Who was doing the organizing for us? We spontaneously and simultaneously said, "the unified field" and we laughed and laughed, amused by what we had both thought and simultaneously said.

Bob and Maureen went over to Intourist and got our plane tickets for Yerevan. A coup! Someone wanted us to go there.

Nature? The Party? Who knows?! Karen and his organizers, we called them the two Yuris, wanted to talk about organizing the movement, course fees, and so forth. There were more interviews, Radio Moscow—Youth Channel. Dmitri, our hired interpreter, came with us on his own time. He was now one of us. We had a very warm goodbye and he kissed my hand. We packed, decided to leave a bunch of stuff with Karen, but we still wound up with two full suitcases and carry-ons.

Before we left, Karen took us to Gum's Department Store. First you pick out what you want to buy and they give you a ticket. Then you go over to the cash register and pay. Then you carry your paid ticket back to the original counter and get your stuff. I bought some wool hats for David and three beautiful traditional Russian tablecloths for $1 each. It was shopper heaven, except there was hardly anything to buy. Then we stopped at a lookout near Red Square near some ski jumps. A bride and groom were there drinking champagne together. So beautiful, looking down at the scene at night, the colorful domes on Red Square all lit up. Life could be lived anywere with love and beauty.

On January 21 we went to the airport to catch our plane. We had been in Moscow only eleven days and so much had happened, so many profound experiences. We got to the airport on time and then waited and waited. Our 6:50 am flight had been postponed until two, so we had a leisurely brunch in the Intourist lounge. Suddenly one of the other passengers, who must have figured out why we were there, told us the plane was boarding, last call! We dashed out of there at 12:15. There was a huge crush on our bus out to the plane on the tarmac. Then we had to climb up stairs into the hold, stash our luggage ourselves, and then climb up more stairs into the passenger section. Bob was amazed that the flight cost less than the fuel must have cost. The whole thing was sub-sidized. There was no attempt to make things pay for themselves. He would learn again and again in Armenia how ignorant of basic business principles these people were after years of Soviet rule.

Yerevan

Once we settled down, the flight was quite pleasant. We all meditated or napped. David tried out his new chart talk on us. I love it, he said, flying around the Soviet Union on Aeroflot, their national airline. When we landed and got off the plane, we were in a vastly different collective consciousness. Lots of dark men, few women, dark eyes, dark clothes and hair. Yerevan was smoggy and poor looking. I felt very uncomfortable, terribly tired, and I was "resting." We were taken to the Hotel Ani and given a simple dinner of beans, rice, bread and cheese. I didn't realize it, but that would pretty much be every lunch and dinner until spring came along with some greens and vegetables and fruits. The dining room was freezing cold, but it seemed warmer when Chris Crowell and Greg Monokian joined us. Then we all went to a party up in Richie and Linda's warm room with Sveta Galstyan, Bob's helper and translator, and got filled in on the progress, problems, and challenges.

The Armenian hotel, the Armenian culture, all took some getting used to. First of all, to use today's terminology, the whole country had PTSD, Post Traumatic Stress Disorder. Nearly everyone had lost someone in the earthquake; nearly everyone had spent gruesome hours digging victims out of the rubble; many were still quartered in public hotels, waiting for housing to be built. Many were often too terrified to leave the building, watching anxiously for new tremors; many were refugees from the holocaust in Azerbaijan. Some of the men were fighting a war on one of their borders, and the fighters came and went; the country was blockaded by the Soviets so very little gasoline, produce, or supplies could enter. And yet, *and yet*, these people had energy and spirit and warmth. Our interpreters gave themselves over to our activities, often neglecting their families or jobs, like Rouzanna Vardanyan. Many were English teachers at the colleges or schools. They loved us and we loved them. I think we gave them hope.

Daily life in the Ani could be quite pleasant, especially when the electricity was on or warm water was available for bathing, not frequently but often enough. We made a little haven of our room with an electric samovar between our beds, our Mac, and our books and papers scattered everywhere. Our friends were just down the hall on the seventh floor. We got a little heater with a grill you could cook on, make a soup or a hot cereal, and since we had food in the room, we had mice. They were bold and one night I awoke feeling little claws on my arm. Yuck.

A word about the key ladies. There was very tight security in our hotel. You had to pass by some watchman at the front door, who seemed to know all of us. Once they wouldn't let my interpreter come upstairs. I had to make a fuss at the front desk before they would let her into the elevator. Then each floor had some key ladies sitting in desks just across from the elevator. You had to pass by their scrutiny as you went to your room. They were loud and seemed to be always arguing, just about to break into a physical fight. No, we were told, they were just normally conversing. A different culture, it seems. They were a Stalinesque hangover, these key ladies, and we ran into the phenomenon again and again, at the Physics Institute, and many other places. Sleazy guys hung out around the front door of the hotel and once when David escorted Anne Dow downstairs for a late dinner, some guy in the elevator asked him how much he would take for her. It eventually improved over the weeks we were there.

Early on we were taped for a TV interview in the lobby of our seventh floor at the hotel, which impressed our key ladies. It played the next night on the nine o'clock news that everyone watches. We watched it from our lobby. Nina Dadayan, a physicist and one of our enthusiastic interpreters, called to tell us it was great. She was very excited. From then on service improved in the dining rooms, people knew who we were, the key ladies became very deferential and helpful, and lectures and initiations really took off. We taught at the Physics Institute and at the University of Yerevan, in most of the separate departments. We also taught at the Physiology institute, the micro-electronics group of the Physics Institute, Ani, and many others. With his helper, Emma, Henry Clark, our architect from MIU, taught a whole theatre group and went back often to give them advanced lectures. Building the dome for Armenia was not happening very quickly so Henry threw himself into teaching. He was a real hero. He also ran a frequent headache clinic. If you concentrated on the mantra and didn't understand what it meant to be effortless, you could give yourself a headache. Since these people had so little control over the big things in life, they could over-control the small ones. A little checking and the problem could be solved.

The Ani group was especially fun. They started off really badly on initiation day. No rooms were ready, the halls were noisy, and phones kept ringing in the initiation rooms. People kept walking in and out, my interpreter got sick and left me during the first group, Nina and David left at two, and I had lots of problem ladies who couldn't seem to close their eyes, but the first day's checking was another story. One of my initiates, a man named Villen, wrote on his form that nothing had happened and that he wasn't satisfied so far. I needed him to translate so he came up to the front and translated my first day's checking. At the end, a couple came up to the stage and asked if I could tell if someone was meditating. I told them that when David and I gave the intro their faces were tense and tired and grey but today they were bright and relaxed and happy.

Villen said, yes, he saw it, too. He knew these people. They had changed. He was very happy and joyful and thanked me for the chance to practice his English and walked me to the car and made sure I knew his name: Villen, Bill! At the end of the course the new meditators thanked us and gave us gifts and were very sweet. And so it went from the intro to the end of each course. Not everyone meditated; not everyone came back; but those who did changed profoundly in just a couple of days, and they knew it. Word spread and our classes grew and grew. No one trusted the papers or official TV; word of mouth was the only reliable way to know what was good, where items had arrived suddenly for sale, anything important.

One night in the large dining room there was a big party going on at a long table. As we ate our dinner at a small table off to the side we couldn't help but notice that there was something unusual about the group. First of all, they weren't making any sound. Second of all, they were gesticulating extravagantly, arms and shoulders all over the place, standing and waving at each other. Finally we got it. They were deaf and were speaking in sign language, but typically Armenian, with large effect. When we got back to our room that night, the mice were particularly active. There were two up on a shelf. I yelled at them to get out. They yelled right back, sitting up on their hind feet and squeaking loudly and not going anywhere. I collapsed in laughter on the bed. Armenian mice!!

The dining room often gave us a kind of vegetable soup along with the usual lobi (red beans) and rice. Once David noticed a big meat ball in the soup. He called the waiter over. It was supposed to vegetarian. We were told it was vegetarian. Oh, yes. The waiter grabbed a spoon and flicked out the meat ball. Vegetarian! he proclaimed. For a treat we all visited the Mushroom Palace a couple of times and ate ourselves into a stupor: cheese puffs, mushroom puffs, French fries, sautéed mushrooms, cheese melted on julienne mushrooms, fresh bread, lemonade, and some great nut pastries for dessert. We tried some other hotels too, but until spring we had to do with beans and rice, bread and cheese. Henry always had a little chicken. Very good, he said. Natural. No pesticides or chemicals since they couldn't afford them. Sometimes we had chicken too. Chris and Henry were always being romanced by the girls; everyone wanted to get to America somehow. Henry's girls always brought him food, usually a chicken.

The shortcomings of our domestic life seemed inconsequential once we were caught up the ceaseless round of introductory lectures, long initiation days every Saturday and Sunday and sometimes during the week, three nights checking, often several groups in the same night, advanced lectures, and checking meetings, as well as administrative meetings with our "directors," mostly women, who would establish the movement there, later become Sidhas and teachers and take the knowledge all over the region and beyond. Heroes all, they worked tirelessly and enthusiastically to help us.

We mainly taught at Yerevan University (EU), the Physics Institute, and the Polytechnic and all within walking distance. Bob was jubilant to acquire a van and driver who could take us to these places and bring us home, a wonderful thing while it lasted, because we were in the middle of a late winter inversion, trapped in a bowl of intense smog and air pollution. Everyone said Mt. Ararat was just over there, and pointed vaguely in some direction, but we hadn't yet glimpsed it through the poisonous soup. I remember one day of initiating at the Polytechnic when the electricity went out just as I was finishing up. I had to give the last parts of instruction without the first day interview form; we couldn't see to fill out any forms. In the flickering light of my last candles on the puja table, I packed up the supplies from my two rooms, sacks of apples and carnations from the initiates and papers from teaching, and carefully and cautiously walked several flights of stairs in total darkness down to the relief and joy of the van waiting below. I hadn't eaten since breakfast and I was dehydrated from not drinking all day (if you drank, you had to pee, and that was a problem!). When I got back to our room, it was warm, but there was no hot water so I had to warm up water in the samovar in order to wash my hair. But the room was full of flowers and I was blissful from a day of teaching. It was all right.

There were several young woman over the weeks who confessed to me that they had tried to commit suicide. After a few days of meditating, light and joy came into their eyes and faces; they could handle their grieving and life could go on. One young woman thanked me profusely and as she was leaving, I called out in Russian, until tomorrow, and blew her a kiss. She blew one right back. What a relief! One young man came with his loving and protective mother. He could barely speak. She told me he had not been able to work, to do anything, was just lying around the house, grey and empty. David said he was schizophrenic. He seemed to do all right during instruction and the three days checking. I told his mother to meditate with him, see that he did it twice a day.

He showed up the next week at the Polytechnic looking for "Mees Rhoda." He was smiling and his face looked natural and relaxed. He talked to me through Vahagn, a young student who had latched on to me because he could understand my English and soon got good enough to interpret for me. He told me that he had had suicidal thoughts and he asked if meditation could help. As he spoke to Vahagn he gestured and showed feeling and looked natural and coordinated. I told him he looked much better. I gave him hope, told him to be sure to meditate twice a day and get a good night's sleep (these people didn't sleep; they lived on coffee; they socialized way into the night and got up for work the next day; they had no appreciation for the value of rest!). He lit up and smiled. What a relief! What a transformation. He had been totally frozen, intense, and miserable when he first sat in the initiation room. He came back often, looking for me, asking me out for coffee (David said "no way"), and smiling and smiling at me if there wasn't a translator around.

It wasn't all teaching. One morning Chris, Anne, and I hitched a ride over to Maria's mother's apartment, my friend who took me around in Moscow. She was also helping me learn more Russian. The driver had just returned from fighting at the front and was very talkative. People would give rides to earn a little money, kind of like Uber, except you had to flag them down on the street like a taxi. When they heard we were American they would never take any money. president Wilson, *shat lov* (very good), they said. It seems that Wilson stood up for the Armenians during the aftermath of World War I, drafting a treaty to guarantee their borders, and although it was never ratified, they never forgot it. Besides they all had at least one relative in America, usually Fresno, California, and they all knew about Disneyland. Many had Disney artifacts on their dashboards.

Maria's mom served us a lovely lunch—very Russian. First we had a salad course: bread, mutton, cheese, red peppers and an eggplant dish (from her own canned eggplant), potato salad, and two carrot salads. Very good! Then a course of grape leaves stuffed with some grain, lentils and garbanzos. Then came preserved peaches, then little dishes of stewed apricots, stewed rose petals, and then tea and English biscuits. During the meal we drank her homemade peach water and cherry cordial. I toasted her and her delicious cooking. Maria translated for us and Anne and I added compliments in our basic Russian. Chris had learned a little Armenian and cracked everybody up every time. "It happened or maybe it didn't happen," he would begin, which was the Armenian version of "once upon a time," and everyone was totally charmed. He had learned fairy tales from his interpreter Rouzanna's children and talked about rabbits. Everyone loved him.

Anne wasn't feeling very well so Maria put a mustard plaster on her chest. It was like the old days in America when everyone used home remedies and canned produce from their summer gardens, which many had in the surrounding countryside, and lived off the fruits and vegetables the whole winter. Initiates often gave us jars of their canned food as thank you presents. Maria showed us her art books and family photographs, and helped us hitch a ride back to the hotel. Again the driver wouldn't take any money. Back at the hotel, I was feeling sleepy. Too much good food? The cherry cordial? The previous day? Even the cup of tea I drank didn't keep me awake. I nodded off during program and slept a little afterward. We seemed to need more sleep in Armenia. All that stress!

When I initiated I always begged people to take the apples home with them. Two, four, etc. were unlucky numbers there, so they always brought three pieces of fruit (or flowers) to initiation and took just one each home, as is the tradition. After instructing all day I had sacks of apples left over. *Please* take them, I said. If you really want to please me, take them all and make me a compote. One night a lady brought me a large bottle of canned apricots, apples, and juice. I recognized her as a lady who had stood forlornly in the aisle of the crowed hall a few nights earlier until I got a young girl to give her a seat. I brought her jar back to the hotel and we had the fruit the next morning with yogurt (*ma-zoon*). Heavenly. They often gave David art books. I got food and cakes, and sometimes rings for my fingers. They wanted to thank us somehow. They knew we were volunteering our time and that we missed our families at home.

One day at the Polytechnic a young man came to David's instruction room and brought his brother. Instruction went well as usual, but afterward, the man asked about his brother. How did he do? David was a little surprised. The brother had answered when asked the usual questions and seemed responsive enough. The man explained that since his brother had returned from the front he hadn't been able to speak. David turned to the brother. How do you feel? he asked. The brother said he felt okay. The man was amazed. They were now bringing us their worst cases. Those two came back to see David again. The brother was talking more, but he was now dealing with the stress of his recent experiences. We had to tell them all it would take time; they needed to meditate regularly, every day, and things would get better and better. Another good experience. One fifteen-year old girl who stuttered changed from serious to joyful. She wrote on her form that during meditation she saw Guru Dev and he was all blue and was saying her mantra along with her.

One Saturday as I walked toward my instruction room at the Polytechnic, Nina said, there was a strange man in there. I don't think he has been to a lecture. Maybe he just wandered in here. I recognized him from the last intro lecture. He was a long-haired Persian, grumpy and very unhappy and constantly working his worry beads. He didn't have any fruit; he just had some dried little wisps of flowers, but he did have his interview form, so I went ahead. He sank right in. Afterward, when I went to collect the forms, he asked if he could help, smiling and transformed! Wow.

Teaching at the Polytechnic was always a challenge. Sometimes we couldn't get in. Often the rooms had broken windows with glass on the floor. The ones on the street side were too noisy to use. And the bathrooms! No running water, no anything. To be avoided at all costs. And we were usually thrown out at nine, at least until the watchman learned to meditate. Then he would let us finish up and stay later. Once the lights went out in the middle of a checking meeting. We quickly lit some candles, placed them around the hall, and spoke more loudly. The Armenians were used to coping and they sat unusually quietly so everyone could hear. We never knew if the hall or rooms would be available to us on any day since we were competing with student activities and we had no way of knowing what was going on.

One night there was a huge crowd waiting outside at the door for the intro. We were finishing up our checking group, so we led them out a side door, and let the crowd in. They filled all the seats and were standing in the aisles. We tried to move part of the group to the Disco (one room for Russian translation, one for Armenian— usually we had to do both, but the Disco wasn't open so they all came back). It was a little worrisome. We lectured and afterwards they started to mob the stage. What was going on? Ah, we found out, they knew the drill; they were eager to get their paper and fill out the interview form. We ran out of paper, tore sheets in half, and made everybody sit back down. I went up the aisle along the rows and pointed, nine thirty, ten o'clock, ten thirty. No time for choices. No personal questions. Take no prisoners, Larry used to say. The next day we initiated all day long and into the evening.

One day Richie called from Leninakan, where he and Linda and Greg were teaching, to tell us that a group of American TM teachers had arrived in Moscow: Ken and Wendy Cavanaugh, and some others, and would begin teaching. He also told us that their local Supreme Soviet lady, Ludmilla, told them that the First Secretary of the Party for all Armenia was well-informed about our activities and was very pleased. How about that! We got the uplink working in our office building and Bob was able to talk to the team in Moscow. I was then able to call the kids and hear their sweet voices; well, at least Nate's. Sara had moved and I still didn't have her phone number. Chris talked to Karen. They had an intro in Moscow for 150 people and they all signed up to learn. They were going to charge a fee for the first time and no one objected. The team had moved to a hotel near to the Kremlin and would begin teaching that weekend.

Maria had set up a series of lectures for Bob at a business institute. Bob was thinking it would be an advanced business course and he and Sveta spent hours drawing up main point charts for his lessons. He came back from the first talk looking rather shell-shocked. They don't know the basics, he said. They don't understand profit and loss. They don't know that banks make money from their activities. I have to start *before* Business 101.

Sveta set up a lecture for me at EU to the English faculty. It was kind of fun to speak in English without a translator and show them my Unified Field Chart for literature. They were interested, but only mildly. One of them was studying some English writer I had never heard of. I checked on it later. He was probably some Russian writing in English and passing himself off as an English writer. Nothing much came of this.

It was a rare and pleasant morning when we could do a full meditation program, and not have to rush off somewhere, and have a jolly breakfast in the warm dining room. They always tried to lead us to the large cold one, but I eventually went to the front desk of our hotel and, in Russian, and with a little help insisted that we be able to eat in the smaller, warm one with the other foreigners. Joseph taught me how to say fried eggs and I insisted on them every day and almost always got them, even though I was told they were not on the morning menu and they wanted to give me their national breakfast, a kind of oatmeal with chicken in it and chicken fat floating on the surface. And I always asked for hot chocolate! Sometimes it happened. Sometimes the power was out and we could only get a cold breakfast. Once there was a group of surly French people there working on some relief project. I chatted with them in French but they were very suspicious of us and of meditation in general.

David and I sometimes gave presentations together, but we were usually all split up because there were so many places to go and talk and teach. It was really nice when we could all get together and do something fun. One Sunday we packed up the last of Richie's room and took the van up there to visit. Leninakan had had the most damage and there were many building projects going on there. Above the pollution of Yerevan, Leninakan was sunny and warm. The town square had once been lined with old stone churches and public buildings. The Soviets had built modern highrises in front of them but they had all crumbled. The rubble was now nearly all removed, and the old stone churches and public buildings still stood there as they had for hundreds of years, which amused the locals.

There was construction and reconstruction everywhere. The Austrians had built a little village of bungalows, which were very cute, and we learned from one British contractor that one of the reasons there had been so much damage was that the cement had been stolen and sold off, so the concrete they poured didn't have the right proportions of cement to gravel and sand. Every time they brought him a mixer full of concrete he would stick his rod into it, he said. He could tell from that poke if there was enough cement in it and send it back if there wasn't. We were supposed to build our dome there, but Henry and Joseph were having delays getting permits and permissions.

We had lunch at Hotel Leninakan, which had withstood the quake and was where the three of them were staying. It had once been very elegant, with high ceilings and wide corridors, like one of the old Swiss grand hotels. Bathrooms were simple, just a toilet, no shower or bath, and a drain hole in the floor, but there were pieces of lovely old wooden furniture, large arches, and curtains on the tall windows. A good feeling, really. The guys were initiating that day at the cultural center. Beautiful children, a wonderful settled happy feeling. As we descended back into Yerevan we caught a glimpse of Mt. Ararat through the smog. Then burning eyes, burning lungs, back to the Hotel Ani.

Soon the tire factory closed and the air improved. Spring was coming. Along with carnations we started to get tulips, snow drops, hyacinths, and freesia. Their perfume filled our rooms. Our groups seemed to be more open to the knowledge; they settled in more quickly, a higher percentage came back for the three nights checking, their experiences improved, and everyone seemed happier. One lady wrote on her form: I love you. You are a very exciting and beautiful woman. Ha! Me! It seemed as if a notable change in collective consciousness had occurred. Or maybe it was the cleaner air and warmer weather.

March 1 was Maureen's birthday. We picked up Sveta and then went to the Poly for Bob and Chris. They had just had a fabulous meeting with the Rector, the Director of Facilities, and the Trade Union. They want to give us permanent places, have teacher training, advanced lectures, etc. They had bought eight TV's for the TM Club and wanted tapes to play. We sent off some faxes and then we all drove to a church near the border with a great view of Mt. Ararat. It was the place where Gregory the Illuminator was put in a cave underground for fourteen years. We climbed down a ladder through a narrow hole to see the cave. First, as we usually did whenever we went into a church, we lit some candles and prayed for our success in Armenia and world peace. Couldn't hurt.

Then we drove to Sveta's uncle's place and his neighbors loaded us up with bread, their home-canned veggies and fruit and we went to a restaurant in Artashat and had a jolly lunch and a birthday cake that I had bought at the bakery. The bakery lady now knew me and would always pull a loaf of bread out from under the counter to sell me. The shelves were always empty, of course.

Mid-March we finally got to teach at a school, #67. We had set it up with the principal ahead of time and explained everything we needed, but when we arrived it was chaos as usual. We gave an intro to about two hundred kids with lots of talking and rustling about. We tried to give them the interview questionnaire. It was a failure. When we asked the question, married or single, they broke up laughing and it went downhill from there. Of course, we were also interviewing the teachers who would learn, so the question was relevant for them, but hysterical to the young students.

My first group of students had no fruit, flowers, or handkerchiefs (no one had told them about the ceremony, it seems) and many of them had an incomplete form or no form at all. I had to start at the beginning. Classes only last thirty-five minutes and then they change rooms, and bells keep ringing. So as my first group (9C) and four teachers sat there, bells rang, other students kept banging at the door trying to get in. Somehow we got through it. The second group (8B) was better. They were prepared and most of them seemed to settle in at least for a few minutes. The next day I checked those first two groups and taught another one (7D), this time in a room that wasn't a regular classroom, as well as a group of teachers. The principal was happy and the kids loved missing classes. What a zoo! The others didn't do much better. What an experience!

Then after an evening teaching refugees at the Physiological Institute, we did a third night check at Poly, and so the days went on. Checked 7D, 9C, 8B and the teachers. If you cracked an eye to check on them while they were meditating, you would see that half of them had moved to some other chair, and many didn't even have their eyes closed! 9C and 8B were hellions, but once we got them separated, boys from girls, they settled down and into a full ten-minute meditation. 7D was great. One little girl brought her mother to Poly to hear a lecture and said she would bring her Sunday to learn. The teachers had actually meditated at home and were very happy with the results. I was full of admiration for Richie and Linda and Greg who had taught thousands of children in Leninakan. We should have gotten their help. On a pleasant note, the refugees at Physiology had turned into meditators: warm, happy, friendly. Groups of refugees were particularly difficult to teach because they were the ones who had failed to integrate and settle in and they were especially entropic.

We heard that Maharishi was sending an English team to relieve us but they were having difficulty getting visas. The Soviet Union had shut down again and was only letting in a few people. Just as we had slipped into the Himalayas on our Jyotir Math trip in 1975, so had we snuck behind the Iron Curtain when it briefly opened. I had initiated close to one thousand people by that time and David had taught nearly two thousand. We were tired. On March 5 we got a fax. We were all to go home. We had gotten Gorbachev elected and a new era was dawning in Cold War politics. We had prevented the civil war. We would turn everything over to Geoffrey Clements' group. I was ready to go home, and I wasn't the only one.

Concerts and Museums

When we had been in Yerevan only about two weeks Nina, our physicist translator, took me to the Opera House for the first time to get tickets for the weekly Friday evening concert of classical music. The lady at the box office said there weren't any tickets. Nina insisted that we were American professors and the concert had been announced in English in the newspaper. She found some tickets. Three rubles each, at the new devalued rate, about thirty cents a ticket. We got all dressed up and gathered our friends and went to the Opera House. Maria was there, Nina and her children, Henry brought Joseph Goldin along and Emma, his translator, and Anne brought her interpreter Nooneh. Bob and Maureen weren't interested in going to the concert so they went off to give the introductory lecture at Poly.

The Opera House was very beautiful, ornate, plush, and warm. Even the ceilings and the balconies were elegant in rose and white. They played Beethoven's Egmont Overture, a Mozart violin concerto, Brahms' Second Symphony and, for an encore, Grieg's Peer Gynt Suite. The conductor was an American-Armenian, a man named Tcheknavorian, and he was really good. We led a standing ovation, MIU fashion. They began and ended with the national hymn of Armenia which was very rousing and moving. I felt for the first time, emotionally not intellectually, that Armenia is another limb of the world's refined cultures, another member of the family.

From then on we tried to go to every Friday night concert. The ticket lady now knew me and I could say in Russian, ten tickets, concert, Friday, and she would hand them over. Bob and Maureen would lecture at Poly, but Henry, Chris, Anne, and our friends were eager to go and we treated them. The concerts were really nourishing and inspiring. David and I felt that they kept us going, refreshed us, and gave us a needed break from the constant pressure of initiating, checking several different groups each day, and having interviews and writing articles.

Another concert a few weeks later featured an eleven-year old boy who had won a Soviet competition. He played the solo part for a Haydn piece very well, with a lot of feeling. The audience went wild over their native son. They also did a Shostakovich piece which had the violins whispering back and forth to the rest of the orchestra, very subtle. The crowd was so enthusiastic that night that the orchestra did several encores including the overture to La Traviata and some Armenian songs. I was especially moved by the traditional Armenian hymn they usually played. I felt the deep life of the people, their emotions and love of their country, and tears came to my eyes as I looked around the hall at all those beautiful Armenian faces. It was at one of those concerts that one of our initiates from the Physics department at EU came over and invited us to visit their Observatory in the mountains. She would see when we could get rooms at the hotel and would call Liliana, one of our English teacher interpreters, to make arrangements.

Over the following weeks we also went to other concerts in other venues and visited art museums. The Armenian State Art Museum was beautiful with many good Armenian and Russian paintings, but they were hard to see because there was no interior lighting, just a lot of reflected light from the big windows. We finally made it to the Saryan Museum. He is one of Armenia's best and well-known modern painters and the small museum housed his works and his studio. He is like an Armenian Bonnard, full of light and Mediterranean color. When we walked in, the woman in charge lit up. She was "my guy." We used to call our initiates our "guys" and we would run into them all over town and at the least likely places, and they would grab us for a mantra check. She rose up and came forward and greeted me, "Mees Rhoda." She had been studying English. She looked full of inner happiness and I told her so. She was very pleased and offered to show us Saryan's studio, which was not open to the public and had some really fine paintings in it from his private collection. What a day!

Stargazing

Spring had come. Sveta brought over the traditional dish welcoming spring, greens sautéed and folded in between pieces of Armenian flatbread. Heavenly. The air was getting much warmer. When the power went off and we couldn't use our computer, we would go stroll through the parks or visit an artist's studio. In the middle of March it was finally arranged that we would teach the astronomers and a refugee group in Byurakan, a village high up on the slopes of Mt. Aragats. Just before we left I had taught a total of 1,022 people. Yes! The observatory, operated by the Armenian Academy of Sciences, was one of the main astronomy centers of the USSR. Due to the clear air and devoted scientists it has discovered special star clusters, more than 1,000 flare stars, dozens of supernovae, many nebulae, and hundreds of galaxies. We took along David's interpreter Sam Simonian, a physicist. David had taught his whole family to meditate and he and his wife and his mother-in-law had invited us over for several meals. They were all quite devoted to David. I took Liliana, who was a very intelligent and mature English teacher, as were all of our translators, all exceptional people, and so generous with their time and resources.

We got a ride up there and dropped our luggage at the main hotel (old, clean, charming; our room had blue walls and a pale green ceiling). The air up there was pure and clear and the night sky was full of bright stars. We began with the refugee group assembled in their cantina, a poor shabby place. Mostly old people, some young women, and some children. We had dinner that night with an artist Sam told us was the greatest living painter in Armenia, Organik Zardarian. His paintings were full of light and color—really, really beautiful. He had some fantastic paintings of Greece, quite celestial. David would later teach him and his whole family TM. We also met with the physics club and gave a course at the high school: students, teachers, and a few astronomers, including the school director and his wife, a very sweet couple, and then raced back down the mountain for our evening checking meeting at the Polytechnic. We joyfully rejoined our gang and found out we were booked to fly out of Yerevan in eight days. What a shock. So much to do!

The next day we caught the 8 a.m. bus to Byurakan, seeing some of our guys on the very same bus! Teaching the refugees was really difficult; they were so distracted and unfocused. Some were mentally defective. One lady lent us a chair from her room and was very intense about getting it back. One refugee lady from Sumgayit told us that she had lost her whole family in that massacre in Azerbaijan but stayed on there because she had a four-room flat and foreign furniture, not running away until she had to in order to save her life. Now when she thinks of the furniture, she cries. Not when she thinks of her family, she said. Probably she could not even contemplate the loss of her family, too deep a stress.

We stayed overnight a few times, dining and breakfasting with our initiates. One evening after our checking meetings, we walked across the observatory grounds in the dark over uneven paths, over a bridge spanning a chasm with a river and waterfall and torches and up the hill to a small optical observatory. Toma and Anahit, our initiates, led us there and Toma, a tiny thing in blue jeans with pale skin from sleeping days and working nights, jumped onto the huge scope and pulled it around with her body weight. She showed us Jupiter and a nebula, and we looked through the open slot onto the starry night. Afterwards we walked back in the dark to Anna Raphaelovna's and she fed us again, a great vegetarian meal and a great lemon cake. We were ravenous.

We ate heartily and talked with her and a lady astronomer who had lived up there for forty years looking for nebulae. We talked generally of life and language and customs. Her husband came in. They had a one-room flat in Byurakan and also a nice four-room flat in Yerevan. They used to have a two-room flat in Byurakan, they said, but they exchanged it with a family with kids. Now they are building a house with a garden on the hill. Their three children are grown, and they have grandchildren. The husband is maybe 70, I think. But life is the same everywhere, I had been thinking, or so I wrote in my journal. It doesn't matter if the shops are empty, the flat is small or large, the principal things in life—family, friends, meaningful work, art, music, nature—are the same everywhere. One could be happy or miserable anywhere. David and I felt very comfortable among these artists and intellectuals.

When we finished all of our groups and checking meetings, everyone helped us onto the bus and gave us books and flowers and kisses and preserves. A group of children, including a ten-year-old I

Enjoying our last concert in Yerevan. David and I are joined by Henry Clark (between us) and Vahagn Petrosyan, my interpreter. Vahagn later made it to MIU, graduated in the literature major, and became a fine interpreter back in Yerevan.

had taught, ran alongside the bus and waved to me as I blew kisses back to her. When we arrived back in Yerevan, Henry knocked to say we had tickets for the concert that night, so we got ourselves together in a hurry. It had been my desire to go to one last concert. It was fun to have the English team here and we all stayed up quite late talking and laughing. One of them thought we Yerevan teachers looked radiant but the Moscow group that had replaced us looked very tired. Thinking about it now, I suspect that we had changed the situation in Yerevan, that it was much less stressed than it had been, and we were able to exist there fairly easily. Moscow, on the other hand, was much larger, more stressed, and they were taking on a huge negative collective consciousness.

Leavetaking

Our last few days were filled with meetings with our interpreters, now the directors of the Armenian movement. On one walk through Saryan Park we bought two little landscapes with Mt. Ararat in the distance. Very sweet. One of them now hangs in our house in Florida. We were now eating with the new group, Geoffrey Clements, Guy Hatchard, Nigel and Dori Kahn, and others, sharing our apricot juice from Sveta's cousin and the halva and cherry preserves we got in Byurakan. They had spinach they had cooked with some beans. We discussed Armenian and Russian phrases that would come in handy while initiating and had a jolly time. Our initiator/interpreter meeting was very inspiring. We introduced Geoffrey and his group and they gave lovely, inspiring talks. They had brought jyotish materials, planned to offer the TM-Sidhi program and to take the movement to a great new level. We introduced our beloved friends/interpreters and Bob was so moved to tears, he couldn't speak. I took over until he recovered. We all meditated together and gratefully went to bed.

The next day Sam took us to see an artist whose meditation David needed to check. No time for lunch so we grabbed our puja stuff and headed off to Poly. When we got there the building was closed to us. The guy at the door said he had no orders to admit us. We "coherenced" him, I have in my notes, and he folded. We got the British group set up and David and I each taught a room full of small kids their childrens' technique. Really fun. Loved it. I shook their hands. They kept smiling at me and they worked on drawing their pictures and doing their childrens' technique and in the end were very radiant and happy. Our last course! It was time to go.

That evening we had a lovely program in our rooms and a huge celebration at Poly. The room was full of flowers and streamers and looked terrific. Geoffrey's talk evoked lots of applause and appreciation. Maharishi had told him to tell them how intelligent the Armenians are, how creative, what a great culture they have. They loved the idea of his founding Maharishi Vedic University there. Some of my guys from the Saryan Art Museum gave me a big bunch of pink roses. Lots of love and appreciation on all sides.

We walked home in the spring night. A rock and roll band had waited patiently for us to leave so they could rehearse and they began carrying their equipment inside as we left. Seems they have a concert there tomorrow night. Hmm. Where would first night's checking be for the Brits? Where would we check our little kids? We told them we would be there at 7:30. There is that saying, "Sufficient to the day are the troubles thereof" (Matthew 6:34). One day at a time. We went to bed.

At lunch Guy Hatchard looked at my jyotish chart, which I always carried with me just to see what might be coming down the road, and he told us that jyotish-wise, the planets were signaling the end of our trip, some delays in travel, but also wisdom and new responsibilities and higher status for my husband. Our friends helped us pack the paintings we had bought and the rest of our stuff; Maureen was packing art books for us all to send to the MIU library. We would keep only one beautiful Saryan book. We went off to Poly, found our kids, and checked them, walking them around a statue of Karl Marx to make sure they were meditating properly. The Brits were holding forth in the video bar. One more day to go in Yerevan.

Sam came by after breakfast and took us over to Anahit Zardarian's studio. She is a very, very good painter. She mainly paints portraits but she gave us a small oil painting she had done in the dark night, looking at the lit up windows of her father's studio in Byurakan. It is rich and full of light and intense feeling for the beauty of the scene and her father and everything. When I first saw it, I loved it, and I was surprised and delighted that she chose that one to give to us. I have it in my bedroom in Florida. She took us downstairs to see the flat where her father used to live and where her brother lives now. It was like a museum, full of art, including two original Saryans.

Sam was also helping us get ready to go. David said he wanted to go say goodbye to Mr. Nanagoulian. Sam was stunned. Mr. Nanagoulian! Do you know who he is? If you look at the pictures of Brezhnev visiting the U.S., there is Mr. Nanagoulian, head of the KGB, right behind him. Now he was heading Intourist, watching everyone coming and going into the Soviet Union. Our men had been reporting to him weekly. Maybe that's why we got cars, uplinks, offices, cooperation. Hmmm. Fran Clark, Henry's wife, says she was later told that the Soviet government was in favor of our project because they thought TM would make the people passive. We did bring peace and less violence, but Armenia won its independence shortly after our group left and was anything but passive in those years.

Anne and David and I were booked to fly to Moscow the next day so we caught a car and paid for our tickets at Intourist. David transferred stuff on his computer to Guy and we went to our final goodbye party at Nina's. Henry and Emma were there, Aida and my Gayaneh Zargaryan, who had recently joined me as an interpreter, and Vahagn, as well as Henry's new guy, and Rouzanna, and Anahit. We had a lovely, jolly meal. Nina's mom came in (she is a world-famous physicist!) and then Sveta and Bob and Maureen and the British. Anahit sang and David played the harmonica and we gave away books and wrote inscriptions in them. Back at the hotel we gave away everything we could; puja supplies, heaters, pots, rose petal jam, compotes. Got to bed very, very late.

Last day: We got up early, packed frantically, stuffing things in everywhere. Friends arrived with more gifts. David and I had a quick breakfast downstairs. Nina said a van was coming from Physics but it didn't show up. Sveta hailed an Intourist bus and we all climbed aboard along with all our interpreters: Sam, Vahagn, Rouzanna, Sveta, Nina, Mariam. Sam got the agents at the airport to overlook our overweight luggage. Lots of hugs and tears and off we went with Anne for Moscow. We were actually feeling very joyful, but we stifled it because our friends were so sad to see us go.

Sergei met our flight, David's guy! The baggage lady said she loves Americans and hugged me. Sergei drove us to Karen's past birch trees in the sunlight. Very fine! Paulina fed us and eventually we got to our rooms in the Hotel Rossia, right down the hall from Ken and Wendy Cavanaugh and their group. We were glad to be going home, but we were also caught up in the excitement of the growth of the movement in Moscow.

The next day our friends took us to Gum's for a final shopping trip and then to Olganoff's to speak to about thirty-five people. One lady I recognized. She asked me to check her mantra and told me that TM had really helped her health. Back at the hotel Bob and Maureen and Chris and Henry had arrived from Yerevan. They said their farewell was very weepy and Geoffrey gave a very moving talk on the bus to the airport. Henry said that he and Bob could barely contain their glee at leaving. Back to Gum's for more souvenirs. Lunch at that fabulous Indian restaurant we had visited before. At one point Bob refused more food saying he had curvature of the tie. We laughed and laughed. David, Henry, and I caught a car to the Pushkin Museum. They had a great Greek room; we loved the modern French stuff, a fabulous Bonnard of a mother and kids in a garden at sunset, Picasso, Matisse, Van Gogh. We were admiring a copy of Rodin's "Kiss" when Chris walked up to us. What's going on here, he demanded sternly. "Earthquake relief!" Henry said. We all laughed joyfully. Finally I was too tired to look at another painting. We walked home along the Kremlin, things turning green, spring in the air, people eating ice cream, school kids on holiday.

Our goodbye dinner with Karen and the Yuris was that night and the next day we gathered everything up and assembled our group. I had gotten us into four suitcases and two carry-ons and off we went. We got to the airport late but breezed through customs, check in, passport control, etc. Chris went off to the dollar shop and the Pan Am lady freaked out. She was trying to get us all on board before the door closed. We huddled together in the only seats available, in the smoking section (the bad old days of smoking on airplanes), and there we sat in the smoky haze for ten hours: some sleep, a couple of meditations, two movies and two meals. We were already back in America. Once we cleared customs in Moscow everyone, the pilots, the stewardesses, were all American. American milk in our tea.

Although the collective consciousness in Moscow felt much lighter than it had in January, New York amazed us. Clean air, clean streets, light feeling, fruit and vegetables pouring out of the shops on every street. You may not think of New York City as clean and light feeling, but the contrast with Moscow and Yerevan was striking. We had been in the third world. We were now back in the land of plenty.

Life Magazine

In New York City, we took a few days to rest up and visit with my sister Linda before we got our flight to Chicago and on to MIU. We met with a reporter doing a big story for *Life* magazine on Maharishi to be published that November (1990). I have no memory of who organized that. The reporter had visited Maharishi in India and then got to see him again, just after he had left India and reestablished himself in Vlodrop, Holland. The article he wrote was sometimes irreverent, sometimes faithfully observant, a mixture of respect and disrespect. David told him about collective consciousness and showed him the research on Yogic Flying and its effects on crime and global terrorism. I piped up from time to time, saying things Maharishi had said, and my zingers got quoted twice: "According to Karen Melik-Simonian, Maharishi's disciple-designate in the U.S.S.R., Group Meditation is practiced 200 meters from the Kremlin, affecting positively Gorbachev. Says Rhoda Orme-Johnson, part of a team that claims to have taught TM to 35,000 earthquake survivors and pogrom victims in Armenia: Maharishi told us, 'Go to Armenia and prevent the civil war.'"

The article also says: "According to the movement, more than three million people currently practice TM, and Maharishi's disciples claim that the massed brain waves of all those meditators have generated a mighty wave of peace and freedom now rolling around the globe. Rhoda Orme-Johnson of Maharishi International University insists that Maharishi 'has kept South Africa from flying apart.' TM spokesmen give him credit for unifying Germany . . . and physicist John Hagelin, a TM specialist, says the seer's lasting impact 'will be far greater than that of Einstein or Gandhi.'" So I wasn't the only one making these colorful statements.

Postscript on Armenia and the Soviet Union

In August, a few months after we left, the Armenia SSR was re-named the Republic of Armenia but it remained in the Soviet Union until its official proclamation of independence on September 21, 1991. One of the British team, Guy Hatchard, shared the follow-ing story with us about what happened after Armenia regained its independence: "There were democratic elections and inevitably a section of the population was disappointed by the result. Because of the history of the struggle for independence, the group who lost the election was heavily armed and there was a confronta-tion between two armed groups outside Parliament who swore to fight to the death for power. At just that time, the very first group of Armenians to learn the TM-Sidhi program were begin-ning their instruction nearby to the Parliament. As the instruction began, there was a clap of thunder and it began to pour with rain. Armenia is similar to southern California where it seldom rains; the combatants rushed home to escape the downpour and the very next day they unexpectedly decided to hand in all their weapons and the opposing groups became reconciled."

Within a few years the TM movement was established through-out the Republics of the former Soviet Union and our Cold War enemy had been transformed into our often difficult and some-times adversarial colleague in the global community.

Life at MIU

THAT AUTUMN SARA took a semester off from CCAC in order to do a semester at MIU in the art department, and we did program together in the dome, very blissful and loving, cuddled up together in our down puffs and walking back and forth from our frat to the Dome. She transferred her credits back to CCAC and returned there the spring of 1991 with her new boyfriend. Sara and I took a ceramics course together and brought home all our amateurish little pieces and showed them to David. At that time we were regularly watching the Cosby show and on one episode right at that time, Claire and one of her daughters took a ceramics course and showed their funny little pieces to the whole family, just like us. We laughed and laughed.

I had realized in Armenia that I had been wasting my time trying to learn any more of the Russian language and had turned my attention to editing some of the tapes I had transcribed for my proposed volume of Maharishi's lectures on literature and language (I had brought some of them with me). Once back at MIU I continued to transcribe and edit them in between teaching and administration during the following years. I felt a kind of familiar subtle urgency, as I had with my doctoral dissertation. Nature wanted this finished and there was a constant gentle push from behind. The project was always in my awareness. I did lack one tape, the July 6, 1976 conversation between Maharishi and Peter Malekin, the one made on my birthday while I was playing around on Lake Lucerne. There was a tape freeze at the time. No tapes were coming to MIU, no matter who requested them, even Geoffrey Wells, the chair of the SCI Department. I thought I knew how to get that done.

When we lived in Seelisberg I had observed that whenever anyone asked Maharishi for something, like a tape, he would always say yes, but somehow it might never happen. There was a German couple in charge of the tape library in those days, Alfred and Gertrude Birke. It was their responsibility to keep those precious tapes safe and secure. It was Alfred who would ask Maharishi in private if some course or some individual could have a certain tape, and they would only go out after Maharishi himself had chosen and approved them. They had to be signed out and returned without fail. I wrote a letter to Alfred in Seelisberg, told him that Maharishi had said that I might have that tape, which he *had* said, and asked if he could please check. The tape arrived a week or two later. Everyone was astounded. Geoffrey Wells looked at me in amazement. How did you do that? I never said. It was not public knowledge.

January 12, 1991, Maastricht, Holland

We got invited to the January 12 celebration the following winter, and we were eager to go. We hadn't seen the Maharishi since our last visit to Noida with Sara in January 1987, four years earlier. Now that he was back in Europe it would be easier to see him. The celebration was to be held in a big convention center in Maastricht with no group program or housing arranged for us all. We had to do that ourselves. We rented a car and a little holiday A-frame bungalow with Claude and Susan Setzer and drove back and forth through the picturesque little Dutch villages to the convention center. Maharishi was very concerned about the tension in the Middle East. When war broke out on David's birthday Maharishi didn't want to come out of his room. David felt terrible, that we had all failed somehow to prevent that war. I think Maharishi was staying inward to assess and mitigate the damage. He eventually did emerge and speak to us, see people, and accept flowers. My friends remember that Frieda Adler gave him one and Maharishi smiled lovingly at her and told everyone that she used to be a yoga teacher in California.

After we got home from Maastricht, we travelled to Pacific Palisades so David could speak there and we had fun seeing both kids again, who were living in California, and my sister and her kids in San Francisco, and we had a lovely spring and summer in our garden and camping and boating on the lakes close to Fairfield, Lake Darling, Lake Rathbun, and Lake MacBride.

David built this arbor as well. Here we are entertaining Vernon Katz, Ken Chandler, Tom Egenes, and Susan Humphrey (from left to right). I think David is holding Catherine in his arms. She always joined every celebration and often sat on top of the trellis.

The Natural Law Party

Later that year Maharishi called David on the phone in our frat at MIU. If you got such a call, when you answered the ring, there would be a thrumming silence on the other end, then an Indian voice asking who you were. If you gave a satisfactory answer, then the voice would request the party desired. By then you knew, of course, who was calling. David got on the phone and said, Jai Guru Dev. Maharishi told him that we were going to get into politics and present the knowledge directly to the people. We would create the Natural Law Party in England and it was going to stand for elections that winter. Could David come to Vlodrop and help make posters and handouts for the campaigns? David headed off and wound up touring England early in 1992 with Keith, Bevan, Geoffrey Clements, Steven Benson, Doug Henning, and even Deepak Chopra.

Everyone enthusiastically campaigned all over England. There was quite a bit of press coverage, some of it very amusing. One ad (not by us) featured a small monk bouncing up and down. No text, just bouncing. The banner streaming across the bottom of the ad said this is a paid political announcement. Another TV ad featured two puppets representing the man from the Conservative Party and his wife driving along together and commenting inanely on trivial details and saying nothing of any substance or interest, again, not by us.

One of the highlights of the tour was a concert set up by George Harrison at the Royal Albert Hall in London in order to raise money for the Natural Law Party campaign. George was semi-retired at that time, so he borrowed Eric Clapton's band and performed many of his more spiritual songs to an audience of 10,000. Ringo was sitting in the box next to David's, as was Mike Love of the Beach Boys. Ringo couldn't stand being left out. He joined the set after the break and played joyfully away. David got to meet George at a little private get-together afterwards. Maharishi seemed sincerely surprised when the results came in that none of our people had won, especially since everyone seemed so unhappy with the two other alternatives being offered. I hope someone else tells this story in all its fullness. I was home at MIU.

Breast Cancer

Just before Sara was due to graduate from CCAC that May in 1992, I discovered a lump in my breast, a hard little thing like a garbanzo bean under the skin. I couldn't do anything about it until we returned from the graduation trip, which David's mom had treated us to, including a week or so traveling around the Lake Tahoe area and then setting Sara up in her new apartment in Oakland, all very joyful and fun, but overshadowed by the need to find out what was going on. The night before the biopsy was scheduled up in Iowa City at the University of Iowa teaching hospital, David and I camped at Lake MacBride, just north of the city, so we could easily make our dawn appointment at the surgery center. It was a beautiful evening out on the lake under the stars and as we went to sleep in our tent, I thought, this is the last time that I will *not* know that I have cancer.

The biopsy brought the definite bad news. I was terrified, sure I was going to die. I hadn't known anyone who had had breast

Sara in her graduation robes and hat in Oakland, May 1992

cancer, let alone survived it, and none of our young friends had had any health challenges like this. We called Deepak Chopra. We were friends; he and David often sat on stage together speaking at various TM organization functions around the world. Do whatever they tell you to do, he said very sympathetically, and then we'll clean you up afterward with Ayurveda. We set a surgery date for July and waited for the biopsy incision to heal up.

At that time the faculty and top administrators at MIU were getting yearly birthday Maharishi Yagyas. These were not for any specific purpose; they were just to give you a boost for the coming year. I went to see Maggie Schneider who was the young woman scheduling these yagyas. My birthday is coming, I reminded her, but I would like you to ask if the yagya could be for heath, explaining my situation. Oh, no, they never do that, she replied. Patiently I said, Maggie, I am not asking *you*. I am asking you to ask *them*. She did, and the answer came back that I would be getting a three-day yagya, brief but very powerful, and the intention of the yagya was to change the outcome. What did that mean? Did they see a negative outcome in my jyotish chart? They soon notified me of the day and the approximate hours of the yagya. It was being performed during the day in India, which would mean during the night in Fairfield. At the time of the yagya I felt suddenly awake and alert inside, like someone was looking at me, even though it was the middle of night. I sat up in bed. What was that?

When the surgery was over, with no lymph nodes involved, meaning it hadn't spread, we went back home to rest up. It was summer time, so no one knew anything about it. Maharishi had said that people should *see* you as healthy. I was a very well-known and public figure in our community. I didn't want strangers or casual acquaintances coming up to me, looking very sorry for me and asking how I was. It would be torture. I told Lenny and Lesley the results and we arranged that I would be on sabbatical the following autumn in order to work on the book of lectures. I would round in the Dome every morning with the Creating Coherence

Program (those people who came to round, sometimes for months at a time, some for years of their lives) and in the afternoons, once my six weeks of radiation were over, I would work on my book. Had they told Maharishi? Did this schedule come from him? Of course. It must have.

A few weeks later I got a call from the campus clinic. All the faculty and staff were given a week or two of Panchakarma (PK) every year, an Ayurvedic spa treatment, consisting of two-person massages, steam baths, and all kinds of treatments, e.g., for the eyes or for the sinuses, whatever one's pulse revealed would be necessary, along with recommended herbs, diets, and behavioral rasayanas. It was a lovely perk, one we all treasured. It was purifying, rejuvenating, refreshing, detoxing. The caller was wanting to schedule me, but it wasn't even close to my time. Yes, I was assured. I was to have PK for a week every three months, indefinitely. Who had ordered that? You guess. When I started doing these weeks in the clinic, I often ran into Charlotte Cain of the art department. She had a medical condition and she too was offered PK every three months. We were known; we were being cared for.

After radiation I was deeply fatigued and slept away hours in the Dome for week after week. David's mom came to visit and to drive me to my appointments in Ottumwa; so did Sara. Sometimes my faculty friends pitched in. I hadn't told them anything, but they had no doubt guessed what was going on. David was as emotionally exhausted as I was. It is very difficult to stand by your loved one and not be able to do much to help. I was having very severe hot flashes as well, and David installed little fans all over the house, next to my bed, in my reading corner, everywhere. If I got hit with a flash during a meal, I would stand in front of an air conditioner, or if it was winter, I would step out the back door into our snow-filled garden and stand in the freezing cold until it passed while the family shivered inside. I had taken hormones for the hot flashes the spring before and that is no doubt what triggered the cancer. I didn't realize the connection until it happened again fifteen years later.

Buying Land in Paradise

In February of '93 David surprised me by coming home one day and suggesting we take a vacation, go south for a few weeks, get out of the cold. He never proposed vacations, always went along unwillingly, at least at first, not wanting to be away from the Dome and from his important work. Our friends Prudy and Albert lived in a place called Seagrove Beach in northwest Florida and next door was Albert's mother's house, often empty for the winter. Prudy had previously invited us to visit and stay there. That would make it affordable. I called, but the house was not available; it was being rented by a snowbird. "Oh, that's all right," I said. "We will take our tent and camp somewhere." "That's different," Albert said. "If you are campers maybe you would like to stay in the unfinished bottom of our house. There are beds in one room, a screened-in porch with a table and benches, and a toilet. You can come upstairs for showers." Perfect. We packed up and got ready to leave. A blizzard was coming, and we should have left early, but David had quite a few things to finish up before we could go, so we set out late in the day, and soon we were driving through heavy snow and sleet. We could hardly see where we were going. We finally made it to our friends in St. Louis, Susan Koppelman and her husband Dennis. We sat in their warm kitchen while the storm raged outside.

When we awoke the next morning and looked out of the windows, we saw that our car was buried in snow, just a hump of white in the snow-filled street, but it was delightfully clear and sunny and cold. We felt relaxed and free. We had made it through the threshold guardians. Joseph Campbell describes these as forces that try to prevent you from beginning your evolutionary quest. We were now in the gap and enjoyed tromping around the neighborhood, passing the time very sweetly with our friends as we waited for the plows to make it to our little side street.

After we left, as we drove south we saw spring in all its stages, early spring with just a thickening of buds and flowers, then warmer and warmer with more and more greenery, until, when we arrived at the sign that said Welcome to Florida, it was fully green and leafy. We were remembering those winter trips to Florida that we took when we were graduate students at the University of Maryland.

In those days in the early 1960s, we had a Volkswagen camper and Maryland had a long break between semesters in January: exam period, intersession, and then registration. We were graduate students, so we had no exams, just papers and lab reports, and we had signed up for our seminars in advance, so we didn't have to wait around while forty thousand undergraduates waited in line to register for their classes. We had about three weeks and we took off for Florida, sleeping in our camper, and as we drove south, we watched as the snow disappeared and the Spanish moss began appearing on the southern trees. The air would become warmer and moister, until one day we would cross some invisible line and be in the tropical zone. We stayed in Army Corps of Engineer parks, community parks, and state parks. We bought fresh fish (right out of the water) from fishermen along the Florida Keys and cooked it at the next pull-over on our Coleman stove. Gas was only thirty-five cents a gallon and we had to pay for food wherever we lived so the whole trip was affordable. When we got back, tanned and rested, David's graduate advisor would look at us and shake his head. What is wrong with this picture? I am the professor and these students are living a better life!

We loved those trips to Florida in our graduate school days, but this time I was in a different state of mind. It wasn't just rest and relaxation I was seeking. Having cancer and recovering from it, or rather waiting anxiously for X-ray and lab results every three months, had changed something. Like other breast cancer survivors I had read about, my priorities had been rearranged. I was thinking, who am I and what do I want to do with my precious life now? As we drove down to Florida and listened to the radio I especially resonated with a new song by Mary Chapin Carpenter called Passionate Kisses. "Is it too much to ask / I want a comfortable bed that won't hurt my back / Food to fill me up / And warm clothes and all that stuff. . . . Shouldn't I have all this, and . . . passionate kisses from you . . .Pens that won't run out of ink / And cool quiet and time to think . . . Give me what I deserve, 'cause it's my right! / Shouldn't I have all this?" I sang along whenever it came on. It made me happy just to sing these words. What did I want? No matter, I would have it!

At Prudy and Albert's we set up our little stove and cooked our meals, David shaved in the back yard, and we walked the winter beaches; it was in the sixties, sometimes in the seventies. David painted watercolors and I read. One day I was looking at my jyotish chart and noticed that it was a good day to buy land. Imagine having a piece of land in this beautiful area! Prudy knew a realtor she had initiated, her whole family actually, and that woman, Sandy Nichols, took us to see the best lot she knew of, one her company was listing. It was full of pine trees, south of the little road that ran along the beach, on a sandy street that led to the emerald waters and white sands of the Gulf of Mexico, a seven-minute walk. It was only nine thousand dollars. The area was just coming out of a recession and lots were cheap. We fell in love with it. Remembering how Maharishi always said to get three bids we insisted she take us to see some other lots. She was right. This was the one for us, and the owners would finance it, so we would pay it off as we could. We gave her a check for $1,000 and asked her not to cash it until we got home to move the money around to cover it.

This was something I had always wanted, a home at the beach. I love being near water, swimming in lakes and oceans, and soaking in vistas, like sunrise and sunset across the water. David loved the water, too. Could we have a little beach house in Florida and maybe escape the brutal winters on the plains? It was a totally charming idea and it seemed so easy to accomplish. I felt the hand of nature leading me along here. Not that we wanted to leave

MIU. No. But a little beach house of our dreams somewhere? Why not? Prudy told us about a builder called Jim Walter Homes who would build you a home with the land you owned as the down payment. We went to see their affordable homes and house plans and I started to dream.

That spring, back in Fairfield, four women at MIU had formed a group called Mother Design and they were offering a Maharishi Vastu course in building. This was another great stirring of the pot that Maharishi was bringing out, how to build a house so it would be in tune with all the laws of nature and be most evolutionary to live in. Their name was a play on Mother Divine, one of the meditation groups around Maharishi. He hadn't yet formalized his version of this ancient science of architecture, but he was starting to emphasize that our lives would be better if we lived in the correct location and room placement (*vastu*). This course was an early version of what was later developed in its fullness. Our lot faced east, the preferred direction. It was long and narrow, unfortunately. Wide and narrow would have been better, but no matter, that was what we had. I learned about room placement (kitchen in the southeast corner, etc.) and started drawing up plans modifying one of the Jim Walter plans. We would start paying off the lot and then, sometime in the future, we could build our little beach house there.

The National Demonstration Project: Crime in D.C.

That summer of 1993 the movement was once again going to try to convince governments that our Governors doing the TM-Sidhi program together in a group could affect the quality of life, especially crime. John Hagelin took on the responsibility of mounting a course of about 4,000 in the nation's capital on short notice. It would run from June 7 to July 30 and Governors would come and go for as many weeks as they could manage, just as on the Israel project. Housing was set up in college and university dormitories all over the city; flying halls on each campus had to be found and filled with foam; dining halls had to be arranged. It was a huge task and there were many minor miracles as it was accomplished. Having the group broken up in so many locations was not ideal. David, Skip, and the other faculty put together a twenty-seven member Project Review Board of independent scientists and local citizens, including the D.C. police department, and proposed *in advance* to show a decrease in crime during the assembly as well as other factors. Rachel Goodman, one of David's doctoral students, was looking for data, daily if possible, on other indicators of quality of life. The pressure was on to be able to know what was happening and seeing if it was happening in a positive direction.

David and I moved into a movement building we called the Senate. It had been an old folks' home in its former life but had been completely renovated and was quite comfortable. I spent those weeks sitting in front of the window air conditioner; my hot

David and Skip Alexander going over the police reports and data from the many sources they had located. The floor of our room of the Senate was the only surface big enough to spread out their papers.

flashes were severe and came on every twenty minutes. In between hot flashes I worked on my book, editing and summarizing the papers to be included in the volume. All around me David, Skip and the others were hunched over daily crime statistics and flying numbers, just as they had been in Israel.

From our room we could hear ambulance and police sirens blasting night and day. Homicides were being reported daily; it seemed to be business as usual in the crime capital of the nation. Were there more or less than usual? The statistics finally started to tell the story. When David and his team looked at similar periods in other summers (heat predicts violence quite definitively) and at the weeks before and after our assembly, the numbers showed a definite decrease in violent crime (assaults, rape, and homicides). If the group could be maintained, they could predict that violent crime would drop by about 48% (*Collected Papers*, Vol. 7, paper 578).

Rachel was able to get data and statistical results showing fewer emergency psychiatric calls ($p=.009$), fewer hospital trauma cases ($p=.02$), fewer complaints against the police ($p=.01$), and fewer accidental deaths ($p=.05$). What do those p values mean? In the first case, this meant that the likelihood of this result happening by chance was nine in a thousand. Taking these four together, the chance of them all decreasing together was 3.22 x ten to the minus 5, or three in one hundred thousand. Wow. She also was able to evaluate the approval ratings for president Clinton and media positivity toward him, which were highly significant as well (*Collected Papers*, Vol. 7, paper 579).

Congress was getting along better in the weeks we were there, and the whole air of the nation's capital had changed. Sally Quinn commented on this change in the press on July 18: "Well, in case anyone hasn't noticed, Washington at the moment is in a lull—at least from the vantage point of the inmates. After months of terrifying, near-death experiences, things have settled down. Put another way, having completed the first eighth of a presidential term . . . the Clinton administration appears to have revived. You know this must be so because columns of newsprint have proclaimed it to be so. Suddenly, all you read about is that David Gergen saved the day, that Clinton 'captivates Japan,' that he is being tough with Saddam Hussein, that he is bringing relief to the flood states in the Midwest. Boring human interest stories ramble on. Washington has relaxed. But such a swift reversal of political fortune is not easy to account for. The inmates may logically wonder whether Clinton really turned things around or if something else is going on . . . almost mysteriously and almost overnight, in the face of government distress, the press seemed to be transformed from a hostile, angry mob to a pack of fawning pussycats. . ." (To the couch, Mr. Clinton. The *Washington Post*, p. C1).

Reporters also noted that there seemed to be a new trend in the capital's restaurants; people were asking for water without ice and it was becoming commonplace. They were baffled. We all knew that Maharishi AyurVeda says that ice puts out the digestive fire. It is not good to have iced drinks with a meal. Simple! I guess our group was eating out a lot, enjoying all the fine restaurants in D.C. I know we were.

John Hagelin held a big press conference at the end of the project and Maharishi phoned in. David was supposed to tell them what would happen once the group left. Violent crime had gone down 23% from what it normally would have been given the usual summer and past week trends. He predicted, of course, that things would return to normal after the group disbanded, that is, violence as usual. There actually were a few weeks after we left when violent crime continued to feel the effects we created in those last two weeks when the numbers had peaked and then it rose again to the usual levels. Did anyone believe us? No, of course not. Why? There is certainly enough research (there are now over 50 studies on the Maharishi Effect); there have certainly been enough demonstration projects in prisons and cities and other institutions. It is the collective consciousness of the nation that is determining how the national press and government would respond. We were the "washing machine" for the nation's stresses, Maharishi would say, and only when the collective consciousness of the U.S. became cleaner and purer would people be able to see the truth.

The most memorable moment of the whole Assembly was when Maharishi came on the huge screen over our heads at our first meeting of the whole group, a full color, frontal face view, and we all just gasped. He was there. We were incredibly moved and emotional. It was a high, I think, for all of us. If you were there, you will remember that. My eyes filled with tears. My heart was bursting with love.

Another Cosmic Push

While we were in D.C. David asked me why we were waiting to build our Florida house on our new lot. I thought we should pay off the lot first. He insisted we begin and he was right. I set about finalizing the plans along with working on my book of Maharishi's talks. I, too, began feeling an urgency to build that house. We had enough money from my mother's estate for half the house. David's mother said she would lend us the rest against our future inheritance and we could pay her interest on the loan. It was a plan. I had two major projects in front of me, finishing my book and building that house, and both seemed very important. Once again, nature was leading us in a certain direction, but also gently pushing me from behind, right to the edges of my comfort zone.

When the course ended we drove a car that a Governor had lent to the movement for the duration of the course back to his dealership in Philadelphia and David and I had a chance to visit my brother and his family who lived there. My cousin Shelley, the one who got us Nate, also lived there and he and his wife Jill invited us to spend a little time in their beautiful beach house on the Jersey shore. We studied the house and I took note of several things we might work into our beach house plans, like their open master bedroom and bathroom. We got to relax and rest a bit after the hectic schedule of the D.C. course, and David got to paint some watercolors of the beach. We returned to MIU for a lovely autumn and managed to take a month off between teaching our one-month courses and to drive down to Seagrove Beach to meet with our new builder. We had found a better one, thanks to our neighbor down the street, and he could give us a turn-key house (that means completely finished and ready to move in) for less than the Jim Walter shell which required us to do all the finishing work, which could easily be half the cost of the house.

We met with our builder in DeFuniak Springs, just north of the beach, and had the joy of selecting cabinet style, countertops, flooring, and paint colors, and discussing the final plans. We chose Saltillo tile for the great room floor, just as we had often seen in El Paso and Mexico. It reminded us of the Southwest, our old home. I felt once again that as we planned and thought about the beach house that nature was pushing us in that direction, not leading but pushing. The whole thing seemed to be very important and even evolutionary, although we might have felt quite the opposite— that it was pulling us away from MIU. Perhaps it was.

We also made several trips to El Paso later that autumn and winter to visit David's mom, who was having lung problems and symptoms of lung cancer. She had lived with David's dad, a life-long smoker, for over fifty years, and the air in their neighborhood was polluted pretty badly by ASARCO, a nearby copper refinery. She went onto hospice care that winter. We took Nate along on one trip and Sara on another to say goodbye to Nana. That was when Nate's marriage was ending, and he was grieving.

As winter came and wore on and we were surrounded by snow and ice and unbelievable wind-chill readings, we were buoyed up by the arrival of little Polaroid pictures showing the pilings going in, the framing, and the roofing. On Albert's day off, he and Prudy would go check on the house. The workers thought they were the owners and that they were being watched. They reported the progress of the house to us. It would be finished in March. That little house was a very happy place in my mind that I kept going toward while winter was ravaging Fairfield. I bought bedding and packed up anything extra we had in the kitchen and anything we could use to furnish this empty house and we took off. When we arrived, the builder, Kirby Rushing, and his wife were waiting on the porch for us in order to give us the keys and get their final payment. I took in the whole presence of that house with joy and amazement, and I just loved it; I wanted to hold the whole thing in my arms. I had to make do with hugging the pilings underneath the upper floor. We walked all over the house, admiring the floors, the screened-in porch, all the windows, the piney woods all around the house, everything. We took pictures and videos to send to the family.

We borrowed a couple of mattresses from Prudy and Albert, put them on the bedroom floor, and set about turning on the utilities and furnishing the house. We didn't have a refrigerator yet, but we did have a cooler, so we made our first granola breakfast and ate it sitting on our front steps and looking out over the undeveloped area around our house. Then we set about buying whatever we could find at the used furniture places in the neighboring towns, horrifying our children, especially Nate, who thought we should put the best of everything into our new house. We didn't want to go into debt, however, and we had a very limited amount of money, *and* we were going to rent it out for the summer and who knows what renters might do to really nice things. We did find some renters for the summer and returned to MIU for the rest of the spring semester.

Family Matters

David's mother was fading quickly. She had hoped to visit us in Florida and see the new house, but she was too weak to travel. She was being taken care of by David's sister Jeanie. We spent a lot of time with her that summer talking about the OJ Simpson trial and trying to entertain her as she lay in bed. Theresa Olson had told us what Maharishi had told her about how to conduct a loved one's final hours and we followed her instructions. One of them was to speak to her about God in language she would understand. Jean had taken a course in typesetting and printing at UTEP and she had a framed copy on the wall of one Psalm she liked and had printed herself. David took it down and read it to her. Then he got out the Bible, found the 23rd Psalm and began reading that one. She was lying there quietly and nonresponsively with her eyes closed but she reached out and took his hand when he began.

> *The Lord is my shepherd; I shall not want.*
>
> *He maketh me to lie down in green pastures: he leadeth me beside the still waters.*
>
> *He restoreth my soul: he leadeth me in the paths of righteousness for his name's sake.*
>
> *Yea, though I walk through the valley of the shadow of death, I will fear no evil: for Thou art with me; thy rod and thy staff they comfort me.*
>
> *Thou preparest a table before me in the presence of mine enemies: Thou anointest my head with oil; my cup runneth over.*
>
> *Surely goodness and mercy shall follow me all the days of my life: and I will dwell in the house of the Lord forever.*

He finished and then began again. I entered the room during his reading and recited the lines from memory along with him. In the middle of the second time through, her breath stopped. David felt overwhelmed with grief and sobbed and suddenly her hand twitched in his direction, as if to comfort him. He told her it was all right and she let go. David then did a puja and saw in his mind that she was greeted by his father and they were joyfully together again. We were sad but accepting of the cycles of life and death. David's brother and sister were out of the apartment when it happened, which perhaps contributed to the peacefulness of it all. They were both very upset with grief and unsettled issues. Jean had wanted us to be there; she had sent for us when she felt near the end. We felt blessed and grateful that we had our perspective and our program and our knowledge of the nature of life.

We returned to MIU after the funeral to our work and our projects. My book was coming along well. Susan Setzer was working on the Language section while I worked on the Literature section, and we were making good progress. David was writing up the D.C. project and many other things, including publishing the chapters of the Cosmic Psyche in *Modern Science and Vedic Science*. As for me, my mind went frequently to the beach house. I saw myself sitting on the porch among the trees, quietly reading or working. It created happiness in my mind and I tried to imagine how we might actually be able to live there. We couldn't leave MIU. That was impossible.

A New Beginning

One day that winter I came home from the Dome after morning program with an impulse to write something. I sat at my computer and out came a poem. I was amazed. I am a novel reader, a story teller. I never thought of myself as a poet. I am not drawn to reading poetry. I usually do not care for other peoples' poetry. Yet here I was writing poems, one after another. Here is the very first one. I wanted to describe and recapture that magical moment of our first breakfast in our new beach house.

Breakfast in Seagrove

We sit on our deck in Seagrove Beach
 and eat breakfast with the rising sun.
The warm spring light shines on our granola
 and charms me out of my robe and slippers.

We feast on the blue sky, long needles of the slash pine,
     taste the salty air, hear the hum of the rumbling surf.
We savor the glow on each other's faces, radiant
     from meditation and lit by love.

Happiness alone stops Time and makes him pause.
     He smiles at our joy, and forgets to tilt
The hourglass and hurry the rushing sands.
     He marks the moment with streamers of taste and touch.

We are awake to the present and awake to each other.
     Only Timelessness can stop time, halt the tumbling seas,
Give the flavor of eternity to a morning meal.
     We breakfast in the hands of God and live forever.

Where did this come from? It was inspired by that first breakfast in our new house, for sure, but the God part? There is a part of me that speaks that is not well-known to the rest of me. Familiar, somehow. Who is she? I kept writing (it was very blissful) and I sent my poems off to the yearly volumes of *Lyrical Iowa*. My second poem was published there, and another one the following year. If our life hadn't changed and we had stayed in Fairfield I might have published many more in that series. It did change, but I kept writing poetry over the years. Another new door had opened, quietly, all by itself. Perhaps I will put these poems in a volume one day.

A Year of Major Life Changes

THE FACULTY WERE INVITED to Vlodrop in January of 1995 and this time we shared a little place in the Bungalow Park with Kim Sands and her two little girls. We were like a family and it was fun. We took walks all around the area and around the big old building where Maharishi and the staff lived. That was creepy. It was a well-known national landmark, but full of endless dark corridors and strange feelings. Maharishi preferred to meet with people and groups outside in the garden or in big tents. The movement wanted to tear the place down and build something beautiful and evolutionary, something according to the principles of Maharishi Vastu, but the local and national governments were resisting the idea.

We found a month to slip away to the beach that spring. We drove there with Sara and her new boyfriend Jeremy, a very talented artist. They focused their energies on painting wooden chairs with an eye to selling them and having a little craft business. My sister Adele and her family came for a visit during that month also and her kids Mike and Leah loved the beach and the house and so did I. It was difficult to leave and go back to Fairfield.

A Message from Maharishi

In early May or about that time, Bevan gave David a message from Maharishi that turned our lives upside down. "We've reached that time in life when what we do should bring us joy," he had said. We were to leave MIU and set ourselves up somewhere else. We would have a year or so to make the transition. Bevan suggested El Paso as one possibility, or perhaps we could find some project to do that would explain to our friends and fans in the movement why we were moving along. He told us that Maharishi was reinventing the movement yet again, sweeping off many of the people who had been with him for years and years, and taking on a new group and a new direction. We would be surprised, he said, to hear who was going off "to bless the field," many of the staff and national leaders we had known for years. It was time for them to pursue their path to enlightenment in other venues.

We had to think deeply about Maharishi's words. It was true that some of our joy and enthusiasm for MIU had given way to more jaded and dutiful behavior. David would go to his office in the morning with his shoulders slumped. I am going off to do my grim duty, he had said one day. It was his responsibility to address all the negative attacks on the research and the movement. It was emotionally exhausting, depressing, and his workload was huge. At committee meetings, when some new program for attracting students would be broached, we would roll our eyes. We had already tried that and it hadn't worked. The move had to be for our evolution, we were sure, whatever that might mean. It was exciting, and yet it would tear us away from almost everything dear to us: our children, our friends, our community, our place in the sun. We were disoriented, to say the least.

The next day we got the news that our dear friends Lenny and Lesley Goldman had gotten a similar message and had disappeared within a day. Lenny's elderly mother needed companionship and they would go to Long Island and move in with her at once. Another lawyer and administrative team would take over their activities. They also had been under tremendous pressure and this would give them some relief from the burdens they had carried for so long. Some reason was given as the motivation for the move, but it was essentially the same as ours: it was time in our evolutionary path to leave MIU and go out into the world to accomplish there what we could not accomplish here. It became apparent to us that we had a place to go, loving hands opening up to catch us, our beach house in Florida. Was this the reason that building and furnishing that house seemed so urgent and joyful to us? Nature had been preparing our next home. It was part of the cosmic design.

That spring MIU would change its focus and get a new name. The small liberal arts college we had founded and nurtured would give way to something more timely and necessary to the world, a center for business and computer degree programs. Developing countries were lacking both those areas of knowledge and skills, as we saw firsthand in Armenia. As Maharishi University of Management (MUM) we could provide them both through distance education and programs on campus. All the signs were changed, and there was an air of excitement, but David and I felt somehow that MIU hadn't lived up to Maharishi's hopes and expectations and that we hadn't fulfilled our mission. We were depressed about it, not as enthusiastic as we might be. Was this part of the same sweep going on in the movement all over the world?

Skip would take over the Psychology Department, Michael Dillbeck would take over collecting and publishing all the research and many of David's other responsibilities, and Susan Setzer would take over the Literature Department. Neither of us would teach any courses in the '95-'96 school year. There was plenty of time for both our departments to set up their new schedules without us, but we were committed to far too many things that summer and the following year to just pick up and go. One of these commitments was to finish my book and have it printed. Another was to collect all the *Cosmic Psyche* chapters into a volume and print that. And we had a wedding to put on. Sara and Jeremy were getting married that summer out of our frat.

The summer wedding was lovely. Sara designed an area outside

of our frat to be surrounded by tall torches and an arch with flowers woven into it. All our brothers and sisters came and Jeremy's
parents. One of Sara's friends catered the event and we had a lovely time. I officiated. I had become a member of the Universal Life
Church, sent in my $20 and was ordained. I performed at a couple
of weddings that last year, but Sara's was the sweetest. The newly-
weds would be living close by in Fairfield. Nate had fallen in love
with Emily Skopin and she was already a member of the family. I
had stayed with her family in Columbus once when I was deliv-
ering a paper on Willa Cather at an MMLA Conference there in
1987. Emily was seventeen and was working on a high school project with her father. Her sisters had attended MIU and so had she.

Nate and Emily Skopin in our frat living room, July 1995

We were enjoying a wonderful family wholeness. The only sad
thing was that David's brother Bill, who was a brilliant biochemist
at MIT, was obviously not himself. We had noticed, when David's
mom had died the summer before, that Bill could not focus on
what had to be done to close up the apartment and the estate.

He showed obvious short-term memory loss but he and his wife Carol were in denial about the whole thing. He did tell David that he hadn't been able to write any successful grants for some time. Now, a year later, he seemed even more disoriented and forgetful. As a biochemist he had had a lot of exposure to benzene and other toxic chemicals in the lab, and in those days they were unaware of the necessity of ventilating the lab areas. He would decline further and further into an Alzheimer-like state, at first thinking it was depression over his mother's death, but finally forced to see a neurologist, who would order a brain scan, and give him a vague diagnosis of some indeterminate kind of dementia.

We had to postpone our autumn departure for Florida until David returned from Washington, D.C. He had been invited by NIH to a Technology Assessment Conference on the effects of alternative and complementary medicine in the areas of pain and insomnia. He was charged with presenting research in all types of meditation on pain and insomnia. Others would present on relaxation, acupuncture, and yoga. Dr. Herbert Benson was there, strongly lobbying to have his Relaxation Response get a positive review. He had a history of presenting all the TM research at his public lectures and then claiming that his Relaxation Response did the same thing. There was no scientific research to bear out that claim. David vigilantly countered his appeals and presented research on other meditation techniques that did affect pain and insomnia, as well as related issues.

By the end of the conference the panels concluded that meditation did have good research showing its effectiveness in these areas, but when the report was finally published in JAMA, the journal of the American Medical Association, the Relaxation Response had been bundled with other meditation techniques and recommended, although there was no research on it to justify that recommendation. The medical establishment closed up ranks with their own Dr. Benson and sought once again to diminish the uniqueness of TM's benefits.

While David was in Washington, Hurricane Opal hit our part

of the Florida panhandle and made landfall nearby. Neighbors told us it had miraculously skipped our street, although there was serious damage all around us. We heard that horrific storm surges had pushed the contents of ground floor condo units lining the beach up onto the road behind them. Sofas, dishwashers, and all sorts of debris littered the area. We fearfully gathered up our work and packed up our car to head south. David was in the middle of writing several papers and I had my book to finish. No more classes to prepare for, but a new life to bring into being. It was especially hard to leave Fairfield when both the children were settled there with Catherine, but off we went, worried about the devastation we would see.

Our street and house were just fine, although a number of trees from our vacant lot to the south were leaning on the house and our gutters had blown off. The insurance adjuster gave us a good sum of money to have those trees removed, to replace a screen door that had been ruined, and to replace some of the screening on our porch which was blown out or had holes in it from the flying debris. We fixed everything up and used the cash to get a new TV and VCR and settled in to enjoy the winter. Prudy was already teaching TM in our small rural area so I began to explore teaching further afield: Birmingham, Alabama; Pensacola and Gulf Breeze to the west; and Panama City to the east. The plan was to set up a little TM center and try to earn enough to support ourselves when our faculty salaries came to an end. A jyotish pandit had told me years before that in the autumn of 2001 I would do something different. Oh, no, I had said. I will always work for the movement. Anyway, that was six years in the future.

During that whole winter of 1995-1996 David was intensely focused on writing a big health insurance paper, a follow-up on his earlier study of Blue Cross statistics on meditators. This time he was comparing MIU/MUM faculty and staff with the faculty and staff of other small colleges in Iowa: same profession, same kind of people, same challenging climate. The MIU/MUM group not only did TM, but they also were doing panchakarma and taking rasayanas. The use of archival data from Blue Cross ensured objectivity and accuracy and provided a 100% response rate. The findings were impressive. Whereas TM alone had reduced patient days/1,000 by 68% in the older group (45+ years), TM plus Maharishi AyurVeda had reduced them by 91%. Similar reductions were seen in costs and disease categories. Bob Herron helped David a little with the study from his position in Fairfield. The paper got accepted for publication and came out the following fall in the *American Journal of Managed Care*. A great accomplishment.

MIU had set up a number of tours for us to raise money for University projects, to spread Maharishi's knowledge, and to inspire the Governors and meditators in the field, so we returned to our frat at MUM in the early spring of 1996 and traveled out from there. Later in the spring of 1996 we did a tour of Washington, D.C., Philadelphia, New York, and Boston, and fitted in some visits to family and friends in those areas. In May they sent us to San Francisco and the Tahoe area, so we got to visit Adele and be there for her son Michael's Bar Mitzvah. In the early summer we taught a residence course at the movement's Cobb Mountain facility, and once we were back at MUM we turned our attention to finishing up some of our projects. For David there was an endless stream of them. He likened them to jets sitting on a runway, gunning their motors, waiting in line to take off. By the time we left MUM, David had published sixty-eight papers and edited three books on the effects of TM on various areas of life. He had many more in the works and had to pack up numerous files, books, data, and everything he needed to carry on his work in Florida. Without teaching and administration, he would be able to do even more. My life was much simpler.

The Flow of Consciousness

I had already written a long introduction to the volume introducing Maharishi and the movement to any reader who might be beginning their acquaintance with Maharishi's thinking with this book. Susan and I had both written summaries of Maharishi's ideas on literature and language, the two major sections of the book. We had written summaries for each talk; we had written call-outs to go along with the text in the margins, highlighting the main ideas. I had written several appendices: one on the TM and TM-Sidhi program; one on higher states of consciousness (taken from my long theoretical paper, "A Unified Field Theory of Literature"); and a third one on the scientific research in general followed by a bibliography of all published papers. We had both referred to the research on creativity and other results in our explanations and summaries, or as footnotes to Maharishi's lectures where he introduced or referred to them.

What remained to do was to bring it together in one document, and I spent endless hours proofing and typesetting. I spent days, weeks, in the Press at one of their computers going over the book and bringing it to completion. Shepley Hansen had designed a lovely format for the whole book and a beautiful cover. The Press printed ten preview copies. Susan and I couldn't just print the book and begin to promote and distribute it without Maharishi's approval, but we could do a limited run in order to give him a copy and give copies to all the literature faculty and the department to have for their own research and teaching. I handed the disks over to the Press so they would have them should the permission come to publish the volume. Big mistake, as it turned out.

Moving to Florida

Actually packing up and moving proved to be more painful than I had anticipated. We would be leaving all our friends, our community, the Domes, a life where we had status, and most important, our children. Sara was pregnant, Nate and Emily were planning a wedding, and we were leaving! It seemed cruel and badly timed, and I found myself feeling angry and resentful. Our families were horrified that we were being pushed out after so many years of dedicated service. Cousin Shelly thought we should sue the movement. We held fast to our belief that the move would prove to be evolutionary and was really in our best interests. We and our friends couldn't see how it could possibly be in MUM's best interests, but it had to be. It had to be right on all levels; it was just not obviously apparent.

I decided to sell all my literature books and just to keep a few favorites. I took the rest to bookstores in Iowa City and got rid of them. I wouldn't be needing them anymore. I was perhaps being short-sighted, but I was in a snit. I sold off most of my sarees. I wouldn't be needing them anymore. David's psychology department gave us a big send-off party at Theresa Olson's house, and then gave us a picture book full of all the photos from the party. Lots of candle lighting, cake cutting, and loving wishes. The University as a whole turned a quiet shoulder to our departure and I felt hurt. There was no pension, and there would be very little Social Security after all those years of volunteering and getting tiny stipends. We were fifty-six years old, and we would be starting fresh.

We sold off most of our furniture, gave away a huge amount of stuff, and rented a small U-Haul van. Ron Khare and Paul Frank, both David's graduate students, had some moving and packing experience and they helped to pack that little van with as much stuff as they could. The kids helped us pack, too and gave us a loving farewell. We would see them soon in Columbus for Nate and Emily's wedding. Goodbye and off we went into the ever-changing relative. We were leaving the physical ashram of MIU/MUM. How would we stay connected with Maharishi out in the field? At least we knew where we were going—to our beautiful little beach house on the emerald coast of Florida.

Oil painting of Maharishi by David Orme-Johnson from a photo by Victor Raymond (c. 1975). Completed in 2009.

Part Four
Blessing the Field

The Emerald Coast TM Center

WHEN WE ARRIVED at our house in Florida, we put most of the contents of the van into storage and tried to settle into our new life. We felt that we would ultimately appreciate the move as evolutionary, but it certainly was difficult to see that up close and in the present. We felt isolated, lonely, without a clear direction, and not very joyful. I was pretty grumpy.

TM Teachers Once Again

Soon after we arrived David and I looked into teaching in our academic fields at the local colleges and universities and branches of the state universities. The atmosphere in their buildings was so depressing and the pay so low, we quickly abandoned any thought of that. David continued to work on his writing projects. He felt that was his primary focus, bringing out the knowledge and spreading the information on the benefits of the research. I was concerned about money. Our MUM salary had stopped with our departure and we had to figure out how to survive. We set about expanding our own little TM center. We also started to make plans to enclose the bottom of the house into a rental unit. We had built the house on pilings, as people often do in Florida, because then the house is cooler and dryer. I had another motive. I wanted to have a rental unit so we would have income from that, and if we got elderly and couldn't go up the stairs to our level, then we could rent out the top and move into the ground-floor level. I began to draw up plans, which was especially challenging because there were pilings about eight feet apart to somehow fit into the walls so they didn't clutter up the living spaces. Then we would need to get the plans approved and learn how to enclose our downstairs by being the general contractors ourselves.

While planning and working on the addition, we expanded our TM teaching in all directions. We found we had a sympathetic Sidha in the Pensacola area, a cardiologist named Steve Teague. He helped us out by giving us keys to his cardiology offices and by recommending heart patients to us. His offices were very nice and clean and we could go in there after their working hours, meditate and then host an introductory lecture that evening. We could instruct on Saturday and Sunday and then come back for three nights checking. It meant a lot of driving, about one a half to two hours each way each evening, but we had a nice, professional looking center, even if it had no sign or posters or displays. We had another enthusiastic Sidha living there too, Debra Bagenholm, and she and her family sometimes hosted us overnight so we could cut down on some of the driving.

We found ourselves once again foot soldiers in the movement, trying to get press coverage and putting up posters at health food stores and on college campuses. We had lost our status and were starting all over again. No one knew who we were. We were working hard and still not having much success. We also felt discouraged and depressed to see how little TM was known and appreciated and how many competing new-age technologies were out there. When we learned TM in El Paso, there was nothing else. It was a tribute to the rise in collective consciousness that there was a big and growing interest in yoga, other meditation techniques, and various complementary health programs, but why didn't they see that TM was superior to all of these? We plugged along. David, I have to say, was not enthusiastic about being dragged all over the place and having to drive hours and hours along Highway 98. It was exhausting and I felt that it was not the best way to approach teaching supreme knowledge with the worry that we needed people to sign up in order to pay the bills.

We expanded to Birmingham, Alabama. Dr. Ed Taub was there. He had done an excellent study on skid-row alcoholics showing how TM helped them. Many of them got off alcohol and got back into productive lives. We found supportive and congenial Sidhas to stay with, David and Vendla Weber. They were musicians and had started a business making and selling oboe and English horn reeds as well as manuals and videos on how to make them yourself. They opened their home to us and we could stay there during a whole course, and teach TM out of their offices and extra bedrooms. It was very kind of them to allow us to hold advanced lectures there and generally turn their house and business into a TM center for a week each spring and autumn. It was a five-hour drive to Birmingham so we couldn't commute. I wrote articles and ads for the student newspaper of the University of Birmingham and we had a nice group of meditators to keep active. Sean and Kaeli Ferguson were there taking care of his mother, and one time they came down to the beach to get an advanced technique and stayed with us.

On one trip to Birmingham David gave a talk about TM's effects on heart health to the Cardiology Department at the University of Alabama to all the faculty and medical students. The department chair was a woman named Suzanne Oparil. She was also president of the American Heart Association at the time. She had done one of the pioneering studies on TM and blood pressure when she was at the University of Chicago in 1974, over twenty-years before. The students loved the talk and gobbled up the handouts David had made. The rep from the drug company that had sponsored the lunch and event came up to us afterward. That was pretty amazing, he admitted. You will be putting us out of business, he laughed. Somehow we always got up a good group of students and others and conducted some very nice courses. This lasted for a few years until the Webers moved to Arizona.

We also taught in Panama City and Fort Walton Beach, again lots of driving back and forth. Towards the end of our time running the center, early summer 2001, we got a Continuing Legal Education course approved for several CE units for stress reduction, including TM instruction, and the movement provided some money for advertising. I had a huge mailing printed and sent to all the lawyers in Pensacola, but only one lawyer responded, a prosecutor. It was his job to see if people were telling the truth or not. He could see we were honest and sincere and signed up, but the collective consciousness was not going our way. It was very discouraging. And when I did the math, all of that TM teaching barely, only barely, covered expenses (gas, meals, advertising, etc.).

Our most successful events from the beginning were the ones offered to our meditators and Sidhas.

TM Residence Courses

We had loved residence courses when we were meditators, and, as TM teachers, we had found they really stabilized experiences and commitment to the practice. Prudy was too busy to organize or host these courses, even though the other Florida teachers and the meditators were very eager to have them, so we explored how we could do it locally. We had no facility nearby like the Holy Cross Retreat we had used when we taught TM in El Paso. We were surrounded by a lot of resort housing so I had the idea of renting condos over long weekends (minimum of three nights got the best rates) and putting a couple in the master bedroom and then two others could be in each of the other two bedrooms with a shared bath. Two of the condo complexes had party rooms with little kitchens. We could rent those to show tapes, have group meetings and meditations and serve the meals. We bought a lot of foam to put down in several condos for a men's program room and a women's program room.

Prudy had given the Maharishi Yoga^{SM} course the year before and we had tried using a professional caterer for that. Pretty much a disaster and expensive too. I wanted to keep the course costs low so more people could take advantage of them. I thought I could do the cooking myself. I wrote out menus, figured out how much food to buy to do the cooking, bought paper plates and large pots, pans, and bowls from a restaurant supply house, figured out a few shortcuts, like desserts from Sam's Club and a last pizza lunch when we had to clean up and leave. We had accumulated lots of video tapes from other centers and the Maharishi Channel on TV. We had all we needed.

I got lists of meditators and Sidhas and announced our courses from Atlanta to New Orleans. Somehow between twenty to thirty people showed up every time, especially a very faithful group from the New Orleans and Baton Rouge areas. Sometimes people came from as far away at North Carolina or New York, but not often. We chose the long weekends when people would have an extra workday off, and kept adding more until we could select the best five: Martin Luther King, Memorial Day, Labor Day, and Columbus Day, Veteran's Day, and later I even added Thanksgiving weekend. I kept the prices low, but even so we could make several thousand dollars per weekend. With five or so courses we could make enough to live on. It was very hard physical work though: the planning and organizing, shopping, cooking, moving foam and chairs and tables, setting up, registering everyone, and then cleaning up and moving everything back the way it had been. Gail and Dave Seager, the TM teachers for New Orleans, became friends and helpers, bringing their meditators and Sidhas and coming themselves for each course, staying with us, and helping with the cooking and teaching for a couple of years.

Our TM activities were keeping us busy, but I was missing the children and our life at MUM. Sara sent us pictures of her growing tummy and we couldn't wait to see her at Nate and Emily's wedding in Columbus just before Christmas. My brother and sisters came with their families to the wedding and we got to see my cousin Susan and my favorite Aunt Dorothy. She was now quite elderly and living with Susan not too far away. Emily's family was warm and wonderful. Nate had a bad cold but somehow managed to stand up for the ceremony and enjoy all the gift opening and family fun. When it was over we drove to Fairfield with Sara and Jeremy, spent Christmas with them, and then returned home to Florida.

The Brahmasthan Project

During the winter of '95–'96, our first year at the beach while we were still officially with MUM, Maharishi had begun talking about each country and each state or province finding and occupying its geographical center, the central point of silence and Being, its Brahmasthan, and creating an influence of *sattva* from that place. We worked with the Governors in the Tampa area, Hugh McFarlane and his family, to locate that point on a couple of plots of vacant land (no water to the south or west, and other requirements), and they had enthusiastically embraced the project. We had travelled to the Tampa area and had picnicked on the land and meditated together there. I remember sweet-smelling, yellow blossoms all over the forest floor. It seemed like an omen that we were in a celestial place. Later I learned that they were Carolina Jasmine. We have a vine of it blooming now on our porch and spreading into the neighboring trees on the lot to the north of us.

Over the summer of 1996, before our permanent move down to Florida the following October, we had visited Heavenly Mountain in North Carolina, a new movement project. David Kaplan was spearheading the Brahmasthan project and we were there representing Florida, along with the MacFarlane family. We spent a few blissful weeks in the area. I remember floating in the pool at the Kaplan house and writing two poems there. The Kaplan house did not seem to me to be accurately attuned to the principles of Maharishi Vastu, however. The main entrance was on the west side, not the east side, so you had to voluntarily not enter that way but walk all the way around the house to the east side and enter from there through some minor entrance. From the east side you could see the pool and a lovely view of the mountains. David Kaplan was developing the whole site as a future home for the Purusha and Mother Divine groups (two special rounding groups that Maharishi had set up) as well as with lots and houses for couples and families. Building was underway in every direction and Governors were buying lots and having them prepared for building.

Right after we returned from Christmas in Fairfield with Sara and Jeremy, we were able to travel to Vlodrop as part of the Brahmasthan group for the January 12 celebration (1997). We were not specifically "invited" as we had been on all our previous trips to see Maharishi, and that made all the difference. It was not a pleasant occasion for us. We were not included in some of the meetings with Maharishi, Bob Herron got to present the fabulous health paper David had written, and the one meeting we were allowed to attend with Maharishi in person was uncomfortably aimed at all the wealthy people who were expected to support the project, obviously not us.

It wasn't totally Bob Herron's fault that he got to give the results to Maharishi; John Hagelin had introduced him and the paper and didn't mention David as first author. Bob later apologized to David for the slight, but David told him that it was all right. Bob hadn't gotten much recognition or appreciation for a major health paper he had published earlier analyzing health statistics from the Canadian government showing that TM had decreased health care costs year by year, until they dropped about 50%, which was what David's original Blue Cross paper had shown.

David had brought a number of his watercolor paintings along on the trip as well as a large drawing he had done of Guru Dev. In order to feel close to Maharishi while we were living in Florida he put his attention on Maharishi's beloved Master and had created a detailed pencil drawing of him. He showed the drawing and some of his watercolors to our friend Paul Gelderloos, who had earlier been on David's psychology team at MIU and who was now high up in the TM movement in the Netherlands. Paul loved the drawing and bought it, as well as a number of paintings. He later gave that drawing to Maharishi, who was surprised and delighted to hear that David was an artist. Maharishi kept that drawing in his puja room and after his passing it appeared one day on one of the movement websites as the gateway button to videos of Guru Dev, with no credit given to David. We have no idea how it got there.

We also gave our now printed books to Maharishi's secretary. David handed over the beautiful blue volume, *The Cosmic Psyche*, that he and Skip and Michael and the others had put together, published first as papers in *Modern Science and Vedic Science* and then collected in this volume. I gave the secretary *The Flow of Consciousness* and we waited around until quite late at night to see Maharishi in the hopes of meeting privately or semi-privately with him and getting some feedback on our books and maybe some direction for our lives in Florida. Finally we had to leave because we had a flight the next morning back to Florida. We had a residence course scheduled that weekend with thirty people coming, which meant food to buy, cooking to start, furniture to move, people to register and show to their rooms, the whole operation, with us jet-lagged and sleep deprived from the trip. We were disappointed, but not too surprised. Our personal time with Maharishi was clearly over for now, and we were expected to thrive and support the movement on our own. We felt orphaned, but at least we had an evolutionary direction for our lives.

A year or two later we heard from our friend and fellow faculty member, John Fagan, who was later to head up the movement against genetically modified crops and foods, that he had been to see Maharishi in Holland and had to wait for hours and hours. They put him in Maharishi's puja room, and after he had

David's drawing of Guru Dev

meditated a long time and then gotten a bit restless, he moved about a little, exploring the room, and then he saw our volumes sitting on Maharishi's own puja table. We were thrilled to hear that. We were still in his awareness. It might not be the time to publish either volume, but they were not filed away and forgotten.

They were sitting right there close to him, vibrating with our love and consciousness. We were connected.

Our First Grandchild

After the Martin Luther King Residence Course we held that January 1997, I wanted to go to Fairfield. Sara's baby was due in mid-March and I wanted to be with her. I didn't have any reason to worry; she and the baby inside were perfectly healthy, but for some reason (lifetimes of worrisome births and deaths perhaps) I was feeling very panicked. Tom and Linda Egenes lent us their apartment while they were away enjoying some warmer weather down south, and we settled in to wait. Sara and I took long walks together and the baby eventually dropped down. We got a call from Jeremy that he had taken her off to a hospital and birthing center in a nearby town. There would be time to meditate and have dinner, and pray a lot, before she would actually deliver.

We stayed in the room with her while she labored. They don't call it labor for nothing. I kept putting cold cloths on her overheated brow and cheeks, but she remembers nothing of that. David sat in the corner thinking that this was a life and death event and it was maybe a good idea to keep men out of it. He meditated over all that time, hoping to have a good influence on the birth process. Jeremy stayed right with Sara, supporting her, rubbing her back, and encouraging her. The doctor was wonderful too. Suddenly she said, here comes the baby. Cleo's head popped through, and then the rest of her, and the nurse lifted her up and away to get her cleaned up. It seemed to me as I saw her in the nurse's arms, that I sensed an enormous presence, a huge Being filling the entire room. This dazzling view only lasted a couple of seconds and then there was little Cleo being put in a warmer and gently washed.

A baby. A grandchild. It was a profound and joyful new reality. If you have one, you know just what I mean. We could all spend hours just holding her, looking at her, watching her sleep. We gave Jeremy our movie camera and he sent us videos of just that. While

Jeremy was off on a business trip, Nate, Emily and Sara came down to the beach for a few weeks and we all passed baby Cleo back and forth. We went up to Fairfield again that summer and stayed with Nate and Emily in their new little house just around the corner from Sara and Jeremy's and we all played with Cleo. We had helped both kids with down payments so they could have their own homes and gardens. Jeremy was working with Bovard Studio in Fairfield at that time and had designed and created a big semicircular panel of flowers for Nate and Emily's arched bedroom window. He was a really good artist, in many different media.

That autumn (1998) we worked very hard finishing up our downstairs apartment. The kids all came down for Christmas, as well as the rest of the Bonovitz clan, and it turned out to be the

Sara and infant Cleo, Fairfield 1998

coldest holiday season we had ever had there. They were soured on our part of Florida for quite some time. We found some renters for the apartment and our finances stabilized a bit. With the rental income, TM teaching, and our residence courses, we were managing quite well for the time being. There was even enough money to travel back and forth to Fairfield and later to the Lake Tahoe area when the children moved up there.

Visiting Heavenly Mountain

During those years of teaching TM we were often invited to Heavenly Mountain, David to lead the January 12 or Guru Purnima Purusha residence courses for Sidhas in July, and me to lead the parallel courses for Mother Divine. One January 12 Mother Divine invited Lesley Goldman and me to lead their course, which basically meant putting on tapes, and answering complaints and requests for this and that. Those January 12 courses occurred over the times when Maharishi was in silence and the courses kept silence, too. Lesley and I managed all right out in the meeting rooms and dining rooms, but once we closed the door behind us, speech would burst out. Neither of us could keep from talking. We had so much to say to each other, comparing notes on our exiles from MIU/MUM and trying to figure out what had happened and what it meant. Is it natural for women to keep silence? I know some nuns seem to do it, but it just didn't work for us. The men were better at keeping silent, but they wrote copious notes complaining that the tapes were too loud, the tapes were too soft, etc. It was certainly not in the spirit of silence. David posted them all on the bulletin board so they could see their opposing unstressing and he didn't have to do much more than that.

In the summer times, the time of the Guru Purnima courses, David and I could take "walk and talks" along the paths on the mountain and sometimes see each other. These were part of the course routine and an opportunity to enjoy the fabulous woods around the buildings. I was also invited to entertain the guests at the new Ayurvedic clinic set up there on Heavenly Mountain and run by Stuart Rothenberg. They were supposed to pay me in clinic time, but that didn't happen until long after that particular clinic had closed.

One time the Purusha guys were telling David that they had heard about our Florida residence courses, how big and popular and successful they were, as big as theirs and *they* had the whole country to recruit from, and they had heard how good the food was. Who advertises and collects the group? they asked. Rhoda, David told them. Who organizes the event and arranges the housing? they asked David (they had a guy for each task, and they had a kitchen and dormitories to use). Rhoda, David replied. Well, who does all the cooking and serving? they asked. Rhoda, David answered. What do you do? they asked. I put on the tapes, David laughed. He actually did much, much more; prepping vegetables, moving furniture, helping me with the big shop for ingredients for six or more meals for thirty people, etc.

Sometimes we stayed on in North Carolina for a week or two afterwards so David could paint and we could just enjoy the cool mountain air and have a break from the intense heat and humidity of Florida summers. Jim and Audri Lanford invited us to stay in their guesthouse one summer. Audri had been part of the Psychology Department years before, and once they had stayed in our apartment during one of the big courses. Unfortunately Catherine's cat door was in their room and I think she disturbed them. Sorry!

Around this time we worked with Prudy to set up an Ayurvedic clinic in nearby Seaside, the set for the movie *The Truman Show* with Jim Carey. Seaside is a wealthy resort community and we thought a clinic would do well there. Robert and Dale Davis, who had founded Seaside, were meditators and they were interested. This idea was developed at a time when the movement had been buying quite a few facilities and setting them up as clinics or for other purposes. Then the time came to pull back and sell quite a few, at excellent prices, I might add. So our clinic plan did not come at the right time. Bevan did bring it up to Maharishi, he told us, and that when Maharishi heard that we were settled there in northwest Florida, teaching TM and proposing a clinic, he laughed happily but didn't say why. Bevan passed this along, but he didn't understand why Maharishi was so happy and laughing. I think Maharishi had seen that we would end up there and when it happened, all by itself, through the workings of nature, he was delighted. And the report made us feel good, that he knew and approved of where we were and what we were doing.

We also stayed connected with Maharishi through video courses. All centers were encouraged to get satellite dishes and watch the new Maharishi Channel. We signed up for all the courses they offered in order to keep up with the latest knowedge and directions from Maharishi.

Maharishi Jyotish Tours

Over the years, Prudy hosted tours of Indian teachers coming to our area to give advanced techniques and Maharishi Jyotish readings. We had a spacious house so we saved the movement money by hosting the teams who traveled through. We enjoyed the advanced technique tours especially because the Indian couple was always very sweet. They enjoyed their rest at our house and at the beach after they finished teaching and before they moved on to their next center. They insisted on doing all the cooking, although they would allow us to help them. We learned how to make chai, chapattis, and all kinds of things. But the jyotish tours quickly became my favorite ones. A couple of pandits stand out in my mind. In the spring of 1996, we hosted our first jyotish team. That team was headed by pandit Pandey who had been Maharishi's jyotishi and was now travelling for the movement to TM centers in America.

Like all the teams, pandit Pandey traveled with a translator and cook. He spoke some English but not enough to explain things to the person whose chart he was reading. His translator was also a professional jyotishi, Dr. Dixit. He seemed unhappy with merely translating. Initially they moved in with us. We had recently enclosed part of our long screened-in porch into a third bedroom and we slept in that room on a sleep sofa. Pandit Pandey had the master bedroom, and Dr. Dixit and the cook shared our meditation room. Dr. Dixit felt the arrangement was below his dignity and appealed to the movement organizers to give him a private room. Prudy quickly moved them into a nearby condo.

I was still studying jyotish and David had made two blocks of wood, one for each of us, with indentations in them and he had marked off the houses. In the indentations we put little stones representing the lord of the house, something clear and diamond-like for Venus, something red for Mars, and so forth. Then we had some larger stones representing the planets and these we could arrange on the boards. When we showed pandit Pandey our boards

From left to right, Prudy, Dr. Dixit, David, Pandit Pandey, and their cook

with the planets on them, his whole attitude changed. He had been polite and distant towards us at first; suddenly he became warm and friendly. "You are one of us," he said. My chart showed that I could be a jyotishi, and from then on he let me sit in with him in his readings and after the person left he would answer my questions and confirm my guesses.

Pandit Pandey told us that our location, with its white sands and the emerald waters of the Gulf just down our little sandy street, was very special, celestial in fact. He approved our plans to build another unit under our house, although he looked dubiously at the rows of pilings, and he said he hoped he could come back and live there. He told me and David that we had been together for many lifetimes, some of them together with a great guru. It was very uplifting for us and made us feel better about leaving MUM.

The other pandit I remember well was pandit Mishra, who came in May of 1999. He actually did a formal reading for both David and me, courtesy of the movement for hosting all the teams. As I read over my notes, which I annotated over the years with events to see if he was accurate or not (which he generally was), I see the one phrase which had stuck in my mind. He said that around November 2001 there was a possibility of change in work; I might do other things. Oh, no, I told him. I will always work for the movement. I couldn't imagine doing anything else.

Welcoming a Grandson

In June of 1998 Sara and Jeremy moved back to the Lake Tahoe area. Jeremy loved that mountain country, those beautiful Sierra Nevada mountains. He skied and was a very good snowboarder. Sara had imprinted on the Alps and snow from her months in Arosa and all the other Swiss villages we lived in. She felt at home there, and has lived in that area ever since. She skied too, and learned to snowboard. We visited them that summer in their little rented guesthouse close to Lake Tahoe and enjoyed our baby

Cleo. They had heard about a man looking for a couple to live in his guest house in exchange for taking care of the main house and grounds right on the lake. There were thirty applicants for the job. Sara and Jeremy wanted it so badly that they both starting meditating regularly, and since we were there meditating too they hoped our combined consciousness would help them get the position. They got it and moved over there in August. Nate and Emily visited and we came back and we all spent Christmas together in the big guest house. It was not insulated and quite cold. We had fires going constantly, but it was beautiful and wonderful to all be together as a family.

Nate and Emily eventually decided to leave Fairfield and move there too. They packed up everything, including Catherine, and moved up there. They stayed with Sara and Jeremy for a few months until they found a house to rent in nearby Incline Village. When we visited all of them that winter even I tried to ski. Jeremy got us all discounts on cross country ski equipment at the place where he did snow grooming and I tried it out. I slipped and slithered on the ice and snow and fell down laughing. Was I hopeless? Probably, although if I lived there and took some lessons, maybe I could do it. I loved the mountains, didn't mind the cold, but I am basically a water person and the beach was home. We never considered moving there to be with all of them.

The summer of 1999 we held a big Bonovitz family reunion up in Tahoe. We loved being together and could talk and laugh continuously. Adele's husband Robert had some kind of interstitial lung cancer which was inoperable. He was having trouble breathing. He came up for a few days and we all met him at the train. He was surprised and pleased, but was too uncomfortable to stay. It was a great reunion but Jeremy seemed stressed out and unhappy and Sara seemed uncomfortable, too.

Sara and Jeremy separated the next spring, and I rushed out there to help her get settled into a new apartment, acquire a car, and get financially set up with a shared custody agreement. I was very fearful that she could lose custody of Cleo, and that would be a terrible thing for both of them and for her whole karmic history and future. It was unspoken but I felt it deeply. Emily had become pregnant (!!), and Nate and Emily moved back to Fairfield that summer. Nate got a new job at Aeron Lifestyles in Fairfield and they would be near Emily's parents and sisters.

We went off to North Carolina that summer as we usually did in those years, David to Purusha and me to speak at the Ayurvedic clinic and then we moved into Richard and Andrea Beall's place near Heavenly Mountain for a week or two while they were away. We were enjoying the whole area and David was painting water-colors. While we were there, we drove over to the Eastern Music Festival in Greensboro, North Carolina. Our little Michael of the "trackers" was now an accomplished bass player with the San Francisco Youth Symphony. He was attending the Festival and was giving a recital with the other students there. His father Robert was going and so was his Aunt Cathy. It was very good to see him and support him and spend some time with Robert who was getting quite weak but still had all his mental faculties. David made a video of the event and gave it to Adele.

Then suddenly we got a phone call. Emily was going into labor. We packed up the car and drove like mad to Fairfield. On August 11, the little boy arrived and they named him after David. He was deeply touched and we hovered over the little guy. He had Nate's little hooked nose. We were melting, remembering our first days with little Nate.

We hated to leave them and return to Florida. We visited them again over Christmas, and Sara and Cleo came too. Family whole-ness! A great thing. I remember one incident when we were getting ready to take Sara and Cleo to the airport at the end of their stay. Cleo was sitting on the couch playing with her dolls and Sara and David and I were in and out of the house packing the car. I came back in to get a suitcase, and Cleo looked at me accusingly. "How could you leave me all by myself?" she accused me. "I am just a little child." I collapsed in laughter. She was obviously channeling my mother.

By the summer of 2001 with income from our rental unit and our various TM activities, we were managing, but we had to be very careful with our expenditures, and it was a lot of hard work, especially for me. I stood for hours cooking while David conducted the residence course meetings. We had a little extra income from jyotish tours, advanced technique tours, and sending people to the TM-Sidhi courses. We had been able to do this for about five years. When the TM course fee was raised from $575 to $1,500 that summer and we were no longer to get any commission from the other TM activities, it was over. Time to move on.

Even with all the TM teaching and the tours and the residence

Nate, Emily, and baby David, August 2000

courses David had managed to publish seventeen papers and edit two books during those years since we left MUM, on a wide variety of topics. He was always having to learn and master a new area. He could think of more and more projects so there was never an end in sight. But, as it says in the Bhagavad Gita, happy is the Kshatriya (warrior) who finds such a battle unsought, an open door to heaven. He would continue doing research and writing. But what would I do and where would the money come from?

Rhoda the Realtor

WHILE WE WERE VISITING Fairfield in the summer of 2001 we heard about a famous jyotish pandit who was visiting named Surendra Pandya whom everyone called Shastriji. I needed a little direction now that the TM activities were dying down, so we went to see him. The reading was very long. It covered my lifetime (I was 61 at the time so there was a lot of lifetime to cover) and he accurately described my family, the various difficulties I had gone through, when I met David, when Nate was born, and when I learned TM. I was speedily dragged into a spiritual path, he said. It was interesting that he used the word dragged. I was dragged; David dragged me along, protesting and complaining, but going. What subtlety was there in the planets that he could see that? Then he described those years with Maharishi: unconditional love, surrender to the guru, accepted as devotee, endless journey with guru and work, no money, supporting the guru with work and intellect, along with husband; guru loved me, both of us, personally knew us, high regard, total personal attention; he looked in your eyes and said, "I am there, I will be there forever."

Shastriji also told me that after 1990 some ambitious people didn't want me at MIU but they couldn't touch me. He then alluded to my first bout of breast cancer, and to our uncomfortable move to the beach. That was good, he said. Florida was a good place, the best place. He told me I have an *upper kala sarp yoga* (I knew that; it is when all the planets fall above a line drawn from one shadowy planet to the other, Rahu to Ketu). This meant, he said, that I would make money only in my sixties. He said prosperity was there, and that we might buy another property for the purpose of doing courses. We misinterpreted this, thinking he meant that we might buy some building for the movement to hold courses. Now we realize it meant buying a building so that we could attend courses (see below). He also warned against some shaky investments we might make in the next few years. Unfortunately, we forgot that advice; some of the lots we bought then have greatly gone down in value and we may lose money on them, whenever we sell them.

Shastriji also told me that David and I had been together three times with Maharishi, once in Shankara's time, once when Guru Dev was young, and now. Unprovable but interesting, eh? What to do now? I asked. Providing services, he said. My main dharma is educational, providing services. Doing what? I could sell insurance, life insurance, mortgages, he suggested. Yuck, I replied. Well, then, real estate would be best, he said, but there would hurdles, obstacles. No problem, I thought, obstacles can be overecome. And he cautioned, my Mars is debilitated (weak, because it lies in the house of an enemy planet), so I shouldn't act independently. I should work for a big group, a big company; I should work under someone else's umbrella.

There was much more, of course, but this was just what I needed to hear at that moment. I remembered jyotish Pandit Mishra saying I would do some different activity, just at this time. We needed money. *I* needed money, not just for living expenses, but for ease, and for financial security. I didn't see the movement building any old Yogi homes; we were on our own and we had almost no Social Security because we had been volunteers at MIU with small stipends, and they didn't take any contribution out of our salaries most of the years we were there for various reasons. Worry over financial instability was a major stress for me. It wasn't so for David; he rarely thinks about money. He has more important things in his dharmic list of things to do.

Ah, Real Estate!

Even before Shastriji, whenever I would consult a jyotishi, he would open my chart, glance at it, and say, "Ah, real estate!" No, I would say, I am teaching at MIU. Yes, all right, he would answer, that is there, too. As soon as we returned to the beach, I found that a class to get a real estate license was beginning shortly and I signed up. It met four days one week and three days the next, culminating in a final exam. The large class had some young people, some middle-aged people, and some older ones like me, retired and contemplating a new career. Classes went from 8:30 to 5, which was difficult for me. I had to get up early, do my whole TM-Sidhi program, eat breakfast, and drive the 45 minutes to Panama City. I wouldn't get home until nearly six. After meditation and dinner, I was pretty tired and ready to go to bed. There was just enough time to flip through the pages of the huge manuals they gave us, but no real time to study. The instructors went over much of the material in class so I managed to pass the final exam pretty well. The class covered material on licensing laws, dealing with the consumer and the consumer's funds, some of the aspects of investing in real estate, and other topics were touched upon. There didn't seem to be much on how to practice real estate. That was still a mystery.

The pandit had said there would be obstacles and there were. I had sent in my application and fingerprints to the state, but didn't hear back for weeks that I was approved to take the Florida state exam. It was too late by then to study hard and get ready for the exam because the holidays were upon us and we had planned some trips: David was going up to North Carolina to lead the Purusha silence course and since Mother Divine was no longer giving courses, I had planned to fly out to California to visit Sara and Cleo. It was a delay but a good delay. I also spent some time with my sister Adele and she treated me to an outfit to wear in my new profession. Sara was worried about me starting a whole new career at age 61½, but her friends reassured her that I would do just fine.

When I got back home from California it was time to get ready for our annual Martin Luther King Weekend residence course, another delay. I had to plan and shop and cook for a large group of people. Finally that was over and I got down to studying in earnest. I made my appointment at the state testing center in Pensacola, and David and I spent the night out there since I had to be there really early. I passed on the first try and we drove home to begin the next stage, looking for a company under which I would put my license and begin working. David reassured me, saying that cream always rises to the top. I didn't have much self-confidence, but I was determined. I dressed up in the outfit Adele had given me and interviewed with three places.

The first two faced south, not a good direction for success according to Maharishi Vastu. The third one was Pelican Real Estate. I had an appointment with Jeannie Carter, the new co-owner, in their Seagrove Beach office, just a few blocks from our house, but when I got there I found out she was busy and I was to be interviewed by the founder and owner Bill Smith. He was very warm and personable, qualities common to most realtors. They are sales people, people people, and generally very friendly and outgoing. He told me about his time in Vietnam flying a helicopter. He said that no matter how stressful the business got, at least no one was shooting at him. He offered me a place in the company, saying that my experience teaching was what it took to be successful because you have to educate your customers on how to buy or sell real estate, get financing, and all of that. He was sure I would succeed.

And, in addition, the doorway to the office building faced north, the Maharishi Vastu direction for wealth. Also, Bill and Jeannie had just reorganized and I would get in on the old commission structure for experienced agents: 60% of my side of the deal if it was involved with another agency and 70% if it was a Pelican listing or sale. Usually agents start out 50/50, then move up to 60/40, so this was a jump to 70/30. Pretty darn good! After me the new agents would be getting less. A good sign that I was on the right path.

I went into the office the next day to sign papers putting my license with Pelican. While I was there I pointed out to the other agents and to Bill, that most of their desks were facing south or west. Both the agents and the company had sustained some pretty major losses in recent months. I told them about Maharishi Vastu and how they should face north or east when they sat at their desks. They listened politely to the new girl, the new aging hippie-looking girl, but seemed to be quite interested and friendly. When I returned the next day, I was astounded to see that all the desks, upstairs and down, had been reoriented, even Bill's. Realtors are nothing if not practical. They were always eager to try anything to improve their business, and this was a simple thing to do, so they did it! Would that the rest of the world was so open. And, I might add, the company took off. Within months, Bill and Jeannie had added dozens of new offices along the Emerald Coast to their company and taken on over a hundred new agents. Pelican soon became a billion-dollar company, the largest local (not franchise) company along the Emerald Coast. Everyone was making money!

David was quite busy by then also. In addition to writing his research papers and books, he had been offered a consulting job by Robert Schneider at MUM, writing up papers that his grant had funded and that no one had yet managed to analyze and submit for publication. Robert, flush with NIH money, offered David wages commensurate to those of a small college in Mt. Pleasant, near Fairfield. David was thinking he was worth more, given his research status and experience, and held out for a better offer. Robert relented and finally gave him a very good hourly rate, quarter time. Keith thought half time would be better since there was so much to do, so in February David was working half time and making $2,215 per month. This was plenty to live on with our rent from the downstairs unit and the residence courses, so any real estate income was going to be a bonus. We could invest it! We could think about setting up a secure future and old age.

The office manager, Donna, was supposed to orient me and show me the procedures, but she was too busy. I drove around Seagrove on all the back streets, discovering subdivisions I never knew existed. I had to learn the market and what was for sale and be able to find houses and subdivisions. I had a lot to learn. Finally, I asked Jeannie Carter for help and she directed me to Tee Daniel. She promised that Tee would mentor me. I didn't want to enter into an official mentoring situation in which I would work for someone and give her a certain percentage of my sales. Anyway, Tee was too busy. The office was really humming.

Tee suggested that I take the post-license course now. A new realtor has to take that course by time of license renewal (in two years) and she said by that time I would be really busy and would not want to give up the time. So I took her advice and signed up for the upcoming March course. Another agent in the office, Ann Mosely, helped me list my first lot, to put it on the MLS, and to get a sign on it. Then David and I went off to Fairfield to visit the kids. While I was there Nancy Turman, another experienced agent from our office, called me on my new cell phone. She had a buyer for my lot and pretty much did the whole thing for me. She even faxed stuff to my sellers. All I did was present the deal to them, and since an earlier offer hadn't worked out, they were ready to go. When I got back, the deal was in the works and just waiting to close. It was seeming very easy. Support of nature?

One day our friend Connie Carlberg from MIU days, who had moved to our area and had also become a Realtor (that's the official designation for members of the National Association of Realtors), took us out to see a subdivision her company was selling in Panama City Beach. It was called Tapestry Park. We had a plat map, but there were no roads or landmarks, so we walked the empty fields to see where the lots might be located. It was a warm sunny day and the property felt good. The whole venture felt good. We decided to reserve a couple of lots and Connie would reserve one. It only took $1,000 (refundable) to reserve a lot and hold it until the developer was ready to go to hard contract and then we would have to put down a total of 10%. Since the lots were only $36,300, it seemed like a good idea.

Panama City Beach was growing and this place was close to the newly planned Pier Park, which would be a huge shopping mall with restaurants, right next to a Pelican condo development called Calypso Towers, which the agents in my office were peddling to their investors. Connie was a little nervous showing the property to us because her boss, Larry Davis, was hoping to sell the whole thing in-house, but Larry didn't mind, and I split most of the commissions with Connie so we all benefitted, including Larry. We signed the reservation agreements and wrote the checks. We had become real estate investors. Or so we thought. We were actually becoming real estate speculators. Undeveloped land is one of the riskiest investments you can make, but we didn't know that.

As Tee suggested, I took the post-license course, again over two long weekends. It turned out to be a good move because about 50% of the material was a review of the course I had just finished, so it was pretty easy. And one just had to pass the course exam, not a state exam. Next I signed up for a class at our Emerald Coast Association of Realtors (ECAR) called Stairway to Success. It met two afternoons a week for the month of April. It covered what I needed to know about getting into real estate. There were classes on how to list a property, how to write a sales contract, how to brand oneself, how to start one's own business, how to make goals, how to negotiate, etc. Pelican just gave me an umbrella under which I could work—no office, no health insurance, no training. I could make phone calls, use their fax and copy machines, use their office supplies, and they made my first set of business cards for me. For everything else I was on my own.

The lesson on how to get started suggested 1) sitting in open houses (houses for sale and open to visitors) and meeting people; 2) doing floor duty (sitting in the office when your turn came and meeting people who called or walked in off the street); and 3) working your sphere of influence, telling everyone you know or would meet that you were in the business, so I set about these three with a vengeance. I felt a kind of pressure that I recognized. Nature was pushing me again, urging me onward. I didn't really have much of a sphere in Seagrove, but I did have the meditators. My first listing and sale had actually been from one of them.

On our annual Memorial Day residence course, I let everyone know I was doing real estate and told them about Tapestry Park. Some of them jumped on. It seemed pretty risk free to take the option and wait and see. By the time the developer put in the infrastructure (roads, sewer lines, water, telephone, etc., one would have an idea of what the property might resell for). I sold two that weekend, and another one a year later to meditator friends, and we all made money on them. My first lot deal closed in early April and I got $1,365. Very encouraging. My first commission. Almost what I made on a small weekend residence course for a fraction of the time and work.

Then one of our Sidha friends from Pensacola said she wanted to invest in a condo in nearby Destin. I didn't know anything about buying condos or about the Destin market or Pelican offerings there, so I invited a Destin Pelican to partner with me and he took off running. We sold her a three-bedroom condo across from the beach, in a place called Emerald Waters, for $310,000. We got a contract in April and it closed later in the summer when it got finished. I sold it for her for $610,000 in 2005, three years later, just as the market was peaking and before it started sliding down. I made a nice commission on both transactions and she made a huge profit, impressing her doctor husband and me, too!

Next: open houses. Just a few blocks from our house there was a new Pelican development called Summer's Edge and my fellow agents had homes there for sale. They had sold the lots to their builder clients. Then they got to list (sell) the houses the builders built on those lots. It was obvious that I needed some builder clients badly. My fellow agents were too busy and had too many houses to sell to service them all, so they welcomed me to sit in them. I would take some materials to hand out (map of the subdivision, data on all the houses for sale there, my business cards, something to read if I got bored) and I would set up shop. Usually there was some furniture there for showing how the house could be decorated. David would bring lunch and a tablecloth and we would picnic over lunchtime. People wandered in and I went into high gear, charming them, being helpful, pointing out the good features of the house and the neighborhood. I tried to help them with whatever they were looking for. In my enthusiasm I often forgot to get their contact information! A huge oversight, but I was learning.

Pelican had hired an IT director named Cindy Tant. She had a PhD and was helping us set up websites and to make the most of the new opportunities on the internet (this was fourteen years ago, so this field was just getting going). There is a concept in real estate called farming. The idea is that you select an area or a neighborhood and then you farm it; you knock on doors, leave pumpkins on Halloween, and keep up with all the folks. Then when they are ready to sell or buy, they know you so they call you. That idea wouldn't work on the beach. Most of the property is owned by people in Atlanta and Birmingham and Nashville and Montgomery, all over the southeast, but *email* farming was a concept I could use.

Cindy taught us to elaborate our email signatures so they were like little advertisements, told us to collect lists of prospective customers, and to keep in touch with them by giving them information. I jumped on this idea. Every time I interacted with a customer I told them that I sent out an occasional newsletter with new preconstruction projects and news and asked if they might like to get it. Most people who are reluctant to give you a phone number or address will easily surrender an email address. Soon I had a sizeable list of people I had met and I started feeding them with deals. I called my e-letters "News from the Beach" and they became very popular. My people forwarded them to their friends and I would get requests from people I didn't know to be added to my list. Whenever Pelican had a project I would send it out to everyone and over the next few years, I got quite a lot of business from these emails and from referrals from them.

My first big break that spring came when a young couple pushing a baby in a stroller came in to one of my fellow agent Rosie Baird's houses in Summer's Edge. Lynne and Susan were looking for an investment and a beach house combined. I strolled the baby up and down the street while they looked in every house. I visited them in their rental house a few blocks over and brought them listings and materials. Finally, they decided to make an offer on one of the houses that was still under construction. Tee had a prospective customer for that house who was ready to go and my ladies were still indecisive. I couldn't push them to make up their minds more quickly. I could have lost the deal, but Tee told her guy the house was under contract and steered him elsewhere in order to help me out. She and Rosie gave me advice and help and urged me onward, and Ann Mosely was always there for me, to check over a listing or sales contract. My palms would be sweaty with nervousness. This house deal was my first real financial contract and I had to get it right.

Finally, the deal from hell got underway. We negotiated a good price and then we had to make sure the girls would get the finishes they wanted for that price. A sharp young woman named Deborah Irby, another Pelican agent, was the agent for the builder and his backers. Lynne and Susan had already signed up with a rental company and had renters coming in June and the house wasn't getting finished fast enough. They were in Birmingham ordering furniture and trying to get the house moved along. The builder was new to the area and didn't have much clout with the subcontractors, and those guys called the shots. They were in demand, too much in demand, and if they had something better to do, they didn't show up. There were many, many builders buying lots and building spec homes on them and they all needed subs. I remember one guy who had a banner plastered on his windshield saying, "I show up," to advertise himself as being exceptional.

We did walk through after walk through with the builder and Lynne's brother Charlie, who was a builder in Birmingham, and with Deborah, who promised that everything would get done on time, and even with Bill, my broker. Finally, we got to closing day and went to the title company to close. The house wasn't finished by a long shot, but the girls wanted to close and start decorating, so they planned to escrow some money to cover the remaining work. Normally, in our area the buyers go first, sign off, and then the sellers come in, sign off, get their money and go. Deborah brought the sellers in first. We arrived to find it was too late to escrow any money. Lynne was a lawyer and wanted to sue. She was in tears. I told the title agent that we would not close. Simple as that. We would not close. I didn't really know what I was doing, but I knew what was happening wasn't right. We sat in the conference room and waited. The title agent called the sellers. They called Bill. Bill called the title office.

Bill was in tight with the builders' backers and he wanted to get the deal back on track. We explained the situation, I held firm, and we asked him to go see for himself. He did and he called us back and agreed that the house was not ready and suggested we hold back the whole commission (mine, Deborah's, and his) as escrow ($28,000) and he would make the builder finish up. He had called the guy in and told him that if he ever lied to him again, he wouldn't work in the 30-A area ever again. Deborah was furious. She wanted her money. I wasn't too happy with her machinations, but I kept my cool. Eventually the builder made good, and I got my check from Pelican. It was for \$11,000. Oh, man, a check for \$11,000 made out to me. I had earned \$4,800 per year at MIU (along with room and board, etc.). Here was a check for more than twice that for just one deal. David and I were incredulous. We built a car port and pavered our driveway with colorful concrete blocks, a huge step up in our quality of life, to have our Saturn out of the sun.

When the kids visited us, I worked the beach instead of the office. Lynne brought her brother Charlie to see me one day on my beach blanket and I sold him a lot in the new section of Summer's Edge (and one the next year in Heritage Dunes, a non-rental subdivision nearby). He wanted to get started as a spec builder in Florida. At last, I thought, my first builder! I also made friends with a young couple vacationing with their five little girls and sold them a lot on a nearby street. My sister Linda heard that I was working the beach and sent me a classy bathing suit with a pareo, a kind of wrap around skirt, so I would look good. David was working the beach too. He was painting and attracting an audience. Sometimes they followed him home and bought paintings off the walls. Sometimes they commissioned paintings of the whole family on the beach. My fellow agents asked him to paint pictures of the houses they sold as gifts for the buyers.

On floor duty in August, I got an email floor call from a guy who wanted a lot in Panama City Beach and that was a challenge for me since I didn't know that area very well. He was coming down over Labor Day weekend and I had a residence course planned. I mapped out all the lots in Panama City Beach in his price range and David and I drove from one to the other. I wanted to look as if I knew my way around. He came down with his wife and three boys and I got in their car and we drove from lot to lot. Finally they picked one. They were coming to our house on Sunday afternoon to write up the contract. I had checked the new listings on the computer that morning and another lot had popped up, even better than all the ones we looked at. They went to look at it, found friends of their parents across the street, and decided that was the one. They came over and we wrote it up. The stove was covered with pots on all burners and here I was sitting at the dining room table writing up an offer. I never even saw the lot. I had to wonder, why was I still doing residence courses? I went through with the residence course over Columbus Day weekend that I had already announced, but I resolved not to hold the courses I normally would over Veterans Day Weekend or Thanksgiving Weekend. I was feeling too divided.

By then I was also working in a subdivision called Seacrest Beach. I had bugged fellow Pelican agent Jan Freeman all spring and summer to let me have floor time out there. She and Deborah Irby were the queens of Seacrest Beach and they were camping out in a temporary Pelican Branch office in a house owned by one of Bill's friends. Deb and Jan were so busy they needed more agents to take floor time while they worked their customers, so they reluctantly let me in. I watched and learned. Deborah would never just sit in the office; she would go out on the Pelican electric cart and drive around and corral people who were walking around, so I did the same. I went out walking the subdivision, learning the houses and lots, meeting customers and adding them to my list. I even started a separate newsletter just for Seacrest Beach, and I sent out monthly or quarterly or year-end reports with sales statistics, offerings, bargains, etc.

The annual Pelican Christmas party came up the first weekend in December on a very chilly night. We ate and danced and I introduced David to the few people I knew in that big company. The whole thing was rather boring for him. It was exciting for me. This was my new family and my new profession and I wanted to mix and mingle and be one of the guys. As soon as it was over I already had it in the back of my mind that I needed an outfit for next year's party. Then we drove south and took Sara and Cleo to Disneyworld. Sara pulled Cleo out of school for a week and we bought them tickets to fly into Orlando. Cleo was in her princess phase and was wide-eyed at seeing the Little Mermaid, Cinderella's castle, and having her picture taken with all her Disney heroines. She wanted a medieval peaked hat with a veil which she wore everywhere. She would only eat peanut butter and jelly and occasionally got tired, but she was a great trooper. Sara put dinner together while we meditated and we spent quiet evenings in our little rental condo with Cleo doing a little homework. We had gotten up really early to meditate so we could hit the parks when they opened and we were wiped out by evening. Really fun and very special to see the whole thing through a child's eyes.

It had been a very busy first year. I was driven, obsessed you might say. I talked, walked, ate, and slept real estate. My cell phone seemed to be permanently attached to my head. It was the time, I felt deeply. It was the time and I had to make the most of it. David was equally busy writing papers and getting two volumes he was editing ready to go to press. I would get home from floor duty at the office or some other location, usually after 5 p.m. and exhausted, we would do a late program, and then during our rest period after Yogic Flying, he would ask, what are we having for dinner? I would say, "Cereal?" He would say, "I'll cook something," and he did, something good. He took over the shopping and cooking, and did a great job of it. He worked all day alone in the house most of the time, but he didn't complain and supported me emotionally and with my work, even though he was bored to death hearing me talk about real estate *all the time.*

All in all, even with visits from the kids and trips to Fairfield, North Carolina, Disneyworld, and all the TM activities taking up my time, I earned nearly $34,000 that first year in real estate and had another $11,600 in deals in the works which would close the next year or two as things got built. Fairly typical for a first year in real estate, I was told, but I ended in the top 33% of the realtors on the Emerald Coast that year, so I guess it was impressive for a first year. It made me wonder how the other two thirds of realtors were making a living. It was not all that much money in absolute terms, but for me and David, it was dazzling. I had made nearly ten times my MIU salary my first year. Very encouraging, and as we were living on David's consulting salary, all my income was a bonus and could be put toward investing, which to us financially illiterate ex-college professors unfortunately meant speculation. I felt a strong need to think about our future and inevitable retirement since we were already 62 years old. I became deeply involved in the business of making money and drew back from any TM activities. It felt right, however. It felt evolutionary and easy. It felt very right.

The Gold Rush

David and I were determined to understand what goes on with finances and money. We read Robert Kiyosaki's *Rich Dad/Poor Dad* and it was an eye-opener for us. He doesn't give any specific financial advice; rather he emphasizes the need to get financially literate, to understand the way the rich look at money, and to look for opportunities. We definitely fell into the Poor Dad category. We were used to getting salaries, benefits, hoping for raises, and not using our money to invest wisely. When David had gotten some grant money back at MIU, we had bought a new TV and VCR. We should have bought a rental house in Fairfield. We had some money in stocks and we helplessly watched about half the value of it evaporate in the tech bubble and bust of 2000. We did invest nearly $30,000 in an oil exploration partnership called Harvest Drilling on the advice of Ken and Sheila Ross, Fairfield friends. This, of course, would be considered wild speculation and risky investment by anybody in the investment field. What did we know? As it happens, that partnership turned out to be a cash cow for years and years, and still is. Subsequent partnerships were not as lucrative, but nature was successfully setting us up.

Kiyosaki's basic point is that being rich doesn't mean a certain amount of income, but rather that one's income exceeds one's expenses. Now, our expenses were always pretty moderate, so that seemed doable. And he redefines an asset. Not our house. Not our car. No. An asset is something that throws off money, something that doesn't cost you money, something that works *for* you. If you have enough assets generating income, not costing you money to hold but covering your living expenses, then you *are* rich; you don't have to work, or you can work at what you like. We realized that we did have one little business like that: our downstairs rental unit. We had built it in 1997 and even with taxes, utilities, insurance, and maintenance, it was netting enough to even pay our share of the house expenses and much more. This was definitely in the arena that he recommends: real estate. So armed with software and instructions on how to calculate the viability of a real estate investment, we started searching the MLS and the surrounding area.

Prices had already risen in our area, and even in nearby Panama City Beach, to the point that nothing worked. We didn't figure on the rapid appreciation that was going to take place, but were following his guideline that you make money when you buy. That is, something has to make sense financially when you buy it. Future appreciation is frosting. We pretty much gave up on finding a rental unit, but we were now actively looking for something that would throw off cash. Kiyosaki's book had changed the way we saw things. The agents in my office bought fancy cars and houses—doodads or toys, Kiyosaki would have said. Bill was teasing me about the old Saturn, so we got on a waiting list for a Prius. And we kept our eyes open. Kiyosaki said your dollars are your employees. Are they working for you or just sitting around idly?

On one of our residence courses, David was chatting with a Sidha from Atlanta and uncharacteristically asked him what he did for a living, something he never would have done earlier. Ed told David that he operated a small alternative banking business. He and his brothers would take an armored car to a plant on payday and cash the checks of the people who didn't have regular bank accounts. We knew all about those people. David's sister

Jeanie could never manage a bank account. Ed had the permission of the plant. He charged a fee. I think it was $1 per hundred, but they recycled their money week after week and did well. He was expanding and needed more cash and was paying 16%. We decided to "invest" $25,000 with him, and checks for $333.33 began coming in every month. We now had another asset and it was throwing off cash at a nice rate. These dollar employees were all out working for us.

I went on to read everything Kiyosaki had written and especially liked *The Cash Flow Quadrant* because it led to self-examination and self-knowledge. David and I are constitutionally self-employed kind of people. We like to be our own bosses; we don't like working for others. We work hard and are self-starters. We are not employee types because we don't like being under some arbitrary authority. We are not business types. And, Lord knows, we didn't fit the investor profile. Kiyosaki's point is that you can be whoever you are, you just need to learn to operate in a way that builds assets that cash flow. We had our rental unit. Our oil partnership was hitting a few wells and the cash flow would soon start. We had money with Ed. We had a few stocks that paid dividends. We were on a roll.

I had observed from reading how Kiyosaki's own story had unfolded, that he had actually made quite a lot of money trading real estate, not just renting it out. He had bought and sold properties and then used the profit to buy good rentals. Shastriji had told me that I should invest in something like IPOs, companies that were not yet on the market, and I should favor gas, oil, things hidden from view, and resort properties. A bell went off in our heads. Our area was beginning to be rampant with development and developers used the pre-construction model to fund their projects. Take our Pelican project Magnolia Cottages, for example. In order to finance the expense of putting in the infrastructure (clearing the land, putting in roads, platting the lots, putting in the amenities, etc.) they offered the houses for sale as pre-construction contracts.

A buyer would put down reservation money to hold the unit, often only $5,000 or $10,000, fully refundable. Then when the developer had the development platted and approved by the county and was ready to go to the bank for the infrastructure money, he would go into the hard contract phase, showing the bank that the project was viable. Then the buyer would have to put down hard money (non-refundable), usually 20%, and get a contract on the unit.

Now, if the property increased in value before hard contract time came, which became pretty common those days, the buyer was encouraged to go ahead. And once you had the hard contract, you could resell the property or flip it, as the terminology went, if the developer would agree, and they usually did, because as the market rose, and the value of the property rose, the increased sales suggested the whole project (including the unsold units) was worth more and more. Since our area was in a period of rapidly rising values, sort of catching up with South Florida, a lot of money was going to change hands in this way over the next few years. This seemed to fit our profile: Resort property not yet made public, a real estate IPO.

I had gotten involved with Magnolia Cottages that year. Roxanne Costello, another Pelican agent, was in charge of the project and she was working with a developer from Atlanta. It was promising to be a really cute subdivision, just across the street from the beach and with a very nice pool planned. The cottages were going to be finished with granite countertops and gorgeous cabinets. Bill set up a sales trailer on the front of the land and one of the rooms held displays of all the choices a buyer could make: hardwood flooring, cabinet doors, carpet samples, tile, and granite. It looked very classy. Roxanne had an office there and so did the construction manager. I got to know the project and the developer, but Roxanne wanted to sell it all herself and wouldn't give me floor time. She was very intense and had a temper and was somewhat emotional and difficult to work with, but that was just another obstacle I could overcome. I was so used to meditators being easy and flexible that I could only shake my head when someone was rough, and wait patiently for the unstressing to finish. These non-meditators, I thought, are taking everything so hard, getting so upset. The mind needs a mantra, Maharishi used to say. I mentioned meditation to them, but few were interested, or had the time to spare.

Roxanne hadn't really wanted to give me any houses to sell, but the developer liked me because I took an interest in and tried to improve the project. When I saw the cabinet design for the kitchen in one of the first cottages under construction, I called him in and pointed out how the pantry cabinet was sitting on the counter top blocking the view of the dining room area. I showed him how if I were washing dishes or getting a meal ready, I couldn't even see my table, my guests. He called in the kitchen designer and they re-did the whole thing. Soon I had sold two Magnolia Cottages, one of them to a couple from Ohio I had met trolling Seacrest during the Christmas holidays. I had one more reluctantly allotted to me by Roxanne.

I couldn't find a customer for that third cottage and then I thought, why not us? Jan, Roxanne, and Rita Montgomery (and maybe others) had bought one for themselves. Jan planned to move into hers, keep it for a few years, and then sell it. We put down the reservation money and waited to see what happened. If it was worth a lot more when we had to go to hard contract, then we might buy it. Pre-construction became a fever and everyone wanted to get in on it. Prices were rising and customers reselling their contracts would soon be making more money than the developers. Magnolia wasn't ready to go to hard contract, but it would be ready someday soon and we would have to decide if we were going to do that and try to sell it. We would have to come up with a lot of money if we didn't sell it to someone else and we had to buy it ourselves, and we would have to get a huge loan from the bank. I was starting to lose a little sleep over this, but it was what everyone was doing and property values were rising fast.

Big money was starting to come in from my deals. I was doing floor in my Seagrove office one spring day and a very nice couple walked in. It was my lucky day! The husband was a big guy, but very gentle and soft spoken. He was a sheriff in the Birmingham area and he and his wife owned a lot not far from the office, just north of 30-A, in an area close to the beach, but full of trailers. I remembered those lots had cost $3,000 when we bought our Dalton lot in 1994. I listed that lot for them and soon it sold for an unheard of $112,500. Even Rosie was impressed! Then they wanted to 1031 the money, which means a tax-deferred purchase. The government gives you a chance to roll your investment into a similar one and keep deferring the capital gains taxes. Then you can leave it to your kids, they get it at face value, and no one ever pays the taxes on the gain. This is one way the wealthy have structured the tax code to game the system for themselves.

Soon this couple was looking for another piece of land, one on the water, with the thought of maybe building on it. They found one on a bayou off the Choctawhatchee Bay, bought it, then decided to sell it and get one closer to the beach. Even though their prospective buyer had gone directly to them, they asked me to handle the deal. Then they wanted to 1031 the profit and we found a nice house in the Cassine Gardens subdivision, just north of 30-A, with two pools, tennis courts, beach access, and good rental potential. They bought it, fixed it up really nicely, and enjoyed it themselves. They listed two more residential lots with me and we sold those. They bought a beach house on Dauphin Island (off Mobile Bay) with that money and when one of those 2004 hurricanes washed it into the sea, they were ready to sell that now empty lot and buy something in our area, from me again, which they did in early 2008. We became friends over the years. I met their son, his wife, their new baby, and when I was recovering from surgery in the spring of 2007, they brought me food and flowers. I sometimes asked Jan to cover for me when we went out of town to visit the kids, and she always commented that I had the nicest customers (unlike some of hers), and I have to agree. God sent me good people.

One day a young woman and her teenage daughter walked into my office and they wanted a home at the beach. Teresa was a commercial developer from Atlanta and very warm and direct. We became friends as I drove her and her daughter Sadie around Seacrest Beach in the Pelican electric cart. They bought a great corner house with balconies all around it and a carriage house to boot. She called me the day they were on the way down to the beach from Atlanta to close on the house, and she asked me to get them some beds to sleep on that night in their new house (Realtors find themselves doing all kinds of things not part of the process of buying and selling!).

I went into a frenzy of phone calls. I found a place in Panama City that would deliver frames and mattresses, but they couldn't do it until the next day. David and I loaded up a couple of sheets of foam that we had for our courses and took them over to the house so they could manage for that first night. I left David there with Sadie unloading the foam and drove over to the title company to be there for the closing. Teresa's credit had some problems and it was touch and go for weeks. If it hadn't been for TM I would have gotten an ulcer for sure. David painted a picture of the new house and I gave it to Teresa as a closing present. She loved that house and cried when she had to sell it in late 2004 because she needed the money. We sold it for $1,200,000, almost twice what she paid for it, so, not all bad.

Then the Seacrest Beach house we were using as an office sold and Deborah found another one, rented it with Jan and shut the rest of us out. I never lost my temper like some of the other agents, but I wasn't about to be shut out either. I started sitting other houses there, one Nancy Turman had listed springs to mind, and I met people there and I walked the streets, hailed prospective buyers, and sold lot after lot. Deborah objected. She dropped hints at our weekly sales meetings that no other agents should be out there competing with the Pelican Seacrest office, that it wasn't fair to the agents on floor there. Tough! I ignored her and looked the other way. Bill wasn't about to argue with success and his cut of my commissions. I knew Seacrest was the hot place to be and I hung in there.

I was also working Seagrove, where we lived, and Magnolia. Roxanne had finally gotten overburdened keeping up with the developer and the buyers and she offered me floor time and I took it. One afternoon a very sweet guy from Alabama wandered in. His father-in-law was a major builder in Dothan, Alabama, and he wanted to break into the resort market. I gave him lists of lots and directed him to them by phone and later drove around with him all over Seacrest and Watercolor, one of the most elegant and expensive subdivisions going in. They eventually bought four Watercolor lots adding up to a million and half. Big commissions!

Then Centex, a national builder, built a model home in Seacrest Beach. It got a prize and they wanted to keep it open so agents would sell their custom homes. Deborah wasn't interested. She was stretched too thin. I volunteered and got friends Ann and Darlene and some others to take turns. Starting the summer of 2003 I sat in that house for many, many days, over a long rainy fall and winter, and I sold lot after lot and eventually even one of their houses.

I still managed to take a little time out and enjoy life, but every time I left town some deal slipped through my fingers. Too bad. One has to live. In June Jay's daughter Liz got married and we all went up to Philadelphia for the wedding. It was a grand family reunion. Linda and her husband Lloyd came, Adele and Mike came. Nate came. Sara and Cleo came, with Sara's fiancé Ted. We liked him very much. A real *mensch* (Yiddish for rectitude, character, dignity, a sense of what is right, responsible, decorous—according to Leo Rosten's *The Joys of Yiddish*). He had been the mayor of Truckee and they were planning a fall wedding in Hawaii. He had also been on the Truckee city council for years and if they got married locally, they would have had to invite the whole town. By getting married in Hawaii and combining the wedding and honeymoon they were limiting the guests to those who would fly to Hawaii and rent themselves a place. We rented a condo for a week with Nate, Emily, and David and had a grand time. My friend Tracey came over for a few days from Oahu. Ted's father Ralph and his wife Lenna gave Sara and Ted a weekend at the Grand Wailea for a few nights around the wedding day. Cleo would stay with us.

The day of the wedding Sara and I spent the morning at the Wailea's elegant spa, moving from Jacuzzi to pool, to waterfall, to massage. It was delicious and very cleansing and meditative. Sara and Ted were getting married on the grounds just up from the beach. The weather was fabulous. We all wore leis and Sara and Cleo came across the grass to join Ted in a ring of flowers. The ceremony was sweet and very moving and the sun was setting across the waters. The wedding planner had done a great job.

When we got home, deals were still happening even though it was fall and hence the slow season, and I kept selling properties from the Seacrest and Magnolia offices. I ended up finishing in the top 20% of realtors my second year! We hosted our last Indian couple doing advanced techniques in January of 2003 and gave our last residence course over Labor Day 2003. I got a local restaurant to make the dinners, since I just couldn't spare the time anymore and I had no help. That era was over! We stopped giving residence courses. There wasn't any TM teaching to speak of, so David focused on his writing projects and I continued to throw myself into real estate, emphasis on throw.

The year 2004 proved to be even more successful. I was back in the Seacrest office by then. Deborah and Jan had gotten too busy with development and they needed more help and let me back into the group in the fall of 2003 so I was there for the gold rush of 2004 and early 2005. On my allotted floor days I sat in the living room of the condo and greeted those who walked in and led them through the French doors out to the 12,000 square foot resort pool, a selling point if ever there was one. I had floor time there several times a week, and it was always busy. I met many people and added them to my email lists.

We also sold our Magnolia contract, our first flip. We would make $95,000 when it closed the following year. I had sold a number of preconstruction lots in a place called Forest Lakes the summer before and they suddenly started flipping. I got more and more customers who bought and resold, and by the time they all closed in August I made about $75,000 in commissions, just on those little lots. My friends in the office were calling me the Queen of Forest Lakes. We closed on our Tapestry lots that spring too, as well as the ones I had sold to friends and other customers, and I started selling those too. We held our two, hoping to get the lower capital gains rate if we held them at least a year.

One day my client Teresa brought me a great deal. She and her partner Paul wanted to develop something on 30-A. I found them a large piece of land with a house on it near Gulf Place a bit west of Seagrove and then talked a neighbor behind it into selling her house and lot to enlarge their parcel. They bought the two lots and then they decided to flip the whole parcel. They made over a million dollars on the deal, and I made about $100,000 on all the commissions combined, so everyone was happy. Everyone was making money, but I do believe nature had steered me into this situation and supported me throughout. Like the buying of our beach house, nature was preparing a soft landing for us when it was all over.

I encouraged my sister to buy a lot on Brown Street near our house for about $30,000. I got an engineer to divide it into two lots and sold them both. This is no longer possible in our area, but at the time we could do it. The first went for $475,000 and I got both sides of the deal. The second sold for $450,000. Adele was thrilled. Her current boyfriend, who was a Realtor and property manager in the Bay area, was really impressed. He just couldn't believe her luck and he called her the poster child for real estate.

Ann was promoting a project called Hidden Grove, lots north of 98 just west of the 30-A corridor, and we bought one of those lots, and I also sold a couple to my other customers. They resold for higher prices, but I was thinking of capital gains again and wanted to hold ours for a year. Bad decision. This was a case of the tail (taxes) wagging the dog (making money). Shastriji had warned us about shakey investments in these years, but we had forgotten. These definitely fell into that category.

By August I had sold over $12,000,000 in property and that meant I could go to a higher level of commission. Ann and I added up our sales and applied and both of us were raised to 75% for our side of a sale or listing with another Pelican agent and 65% of one with an outside agent. This was a substantial raise and it applied to my deals from then on, even when the market slowed down.

I was still the mainstay of keeping the Centex house open for sales, and although it was often quiet, I didn't mind being there. I worked on my deals, communicated with my customers, and read a little. It was worth it because I continued to meet people and sell properties. The day after Thanksgiving a young woman from Smyrna, Georgia, walked in, looked around, and wanted to know about other Seacrest houses. I felt I shouldn't leave the house un-attended, so I gave her lists and tips and off she went. Cindy came back and had decided on the house she wanted, but she wanted me to represent her because I had been so helpful. She wanted to be in the house for Christmas. We worked very hard to make that happen. I called it the Christmas house because that's how I identified it to David ("I'm running off to meet the inspector at the Christmas house" or "I have to go now to meet the appraiser at the Christmas house."). There is a lot more to real estate than just getting the contracts signed, a lot more. This house was the site for my most embarrassing moment in real estate.

Cindy came down to see the house again with her son and his friend. I was at the front door opening the lock box with my Realtor Suprakey and had just gotten the key out of the box when my cell phone rang. I was juggling the lock box, the key, and my phone, and I dropped the key. It bounced on the deck of the front porch and disappeared between the boards. Cindy didn't miss a beat. While I stood there horrified (the seller was in Tennessee and this was the only key), she offered a steak dinner to whichever boy retrieved that key. Her son's friend whipped around the back of the house, found an opening in the skirt, and crawled on the sand under the decking to the front of the house, found the key in the sand, and pushed it up between the boards. Cindy's son grabbed it. They weren't going to let me near it again! I got them into the house by Christmas and later they bought a Watersound lot from me and then a Watersound house, and sent various friends and acquaintances my way. Watersound was another elegant, very expensive subdivision along the beach. High prices, big commissions.

By the end of 2004 I had sold over $33,000,000 in contracts and reservations that year, $20,000,000 of which actually closed by the end of the year. That amounted to 58 transactions: 38 sales and 22 sold listings. Are you getting bored? I am still finding it exciting, just writing and reading about it. There were days when I could hardly sit down. I just stood between my computer and the fax machine in my home office, printing out and faxing contracts, talking on the house phone and my cell phone at the same time, and then running out the door to the office or to meet someone at a property or at my office. We were paying more in taxes than we had earned in both our entire working lives. I ended the year in the top 2½% of the realtors on the Emerald Coast, and 2005 was already guaranteed to be a success since I had millions in sales yet to close. It had been an unbelievable two years.

There were several interesting side effects of having all this money flowing through our hands. We were able to donate money to MUM and to various other movement projects. We could be generous to Maharishi School where our little David was a student. I was also attracted to charities and gave quite a bit to the Native American educational funds and to the Smile Train. I was very moved by those little children with cleft palates being given a whole new life by a $250 operation. I loved conservation and Sierra Club projects, including one group called Earthjustice which sues the government into doing for conservation what it promised to do. It was a joy to give. It had always been a big pinch before, and I had felt that I needed to hold tight to our resources because it was uncertain that we would survive financially. Generosity was one of the behavioral rasayanas that we had heard about but we never could give in to it before. Now we could.

The second side effect was that I felt more deeply settled than I ever had before. I had proved that I could go out, learn, and succeed at a new profession. I had much more self-confidence. My earnings had put us on a platform of self-sufficiency, a modest self-sufficiency to be sure, but I began to think I didn't need to worry about money anymore. Most of our wealth was in property, of course, which would soon evaporate, but some of it was in cash-flowing investments. Something inside me relaxed. I had reached some life goal I didn't really know I had had, and it changed me inside and out. I began to dress better and to feel like a queen, in fact. We joked about that, calling me the queen of the family.

We didn't change our spending habits. We still lived quite modestly and frugally, but the attitude change was profound. David and I didn't have to agonize over how much food and other essential items cost. We didn't have to start reading the price column of a menu before deciding what to order. We could eat at a nice restaurant without comparing the price of the tab to other things we needed. We could be generous to the waitstaff, who were working very hard for very little money. I might not do it, but I could buy anything I wanted. It was liberating, very liberating. The whole experience had been evolutionary on so many levels. I understood now the urgency I felt while doing it, the pressure to do it while that window of opportunity was open. Shastriji had said I would earn money only in my sixties, and he was right. Big money, anyway.

The Music Stops

The year 2005 began with Magnolia closings and the first five months were pretty active with sales and closings, but we managed to slip away quite often for little trips. In February we flew out to visit Sara and Ted in the new house that Ted had built. We all went dog sledding. The concession was at the edge of the national forest, and the owner had a couple of trucks with little cubicles, one for each dog. They were very excited and he had to anchor the sled as he hooked them up or they would have run away with it. We got into one sled, sitting on a padded bottom with a blanket over us and the driver standing behind us on the runners. Sara, Ted and Cleo were in another one. When the drivers released the brakes, the dogs enthusiastically rushed onward and we swooshed off into the forest, riding along through the silence and snow and tall trees, bumping our bottoms occasionally, but warm and comfortable. The dogs' feet threw up little ice crystals, and they later told us the dogs just peed and pooped as they ran so the ice crystals may not have been pure water! It was exhilarating and lovely and quiet.

Then we took Cleo down to Oakland on Amtrak to Adele's house. The ride went from the snow-covered trees of the mountains down into the blooming spring of the lowlands. We watched the scenery fly by and ate in the dining car and enjoyed the ride immensely. We took Cleo to Chinatown and Fisherman's Wharf and the Museum under the Sea. She was very adventurous and even did a bungee jumping ride. Sara and Ted drove down over the weekend to pick her up and we all went out to eat in San Francisco and to the wharf. It was a great week with Cleo. We walked and took the subway everywhere, and I kept talking on my cell phone, doing deals. Deborah's developer friend Jerry released his project in Freeport called Riverwalk. In or out of town, I sold about 10 reservations to people eager to flip and make money. David took many photos of me talking on my cell phone wherever we were, everywhere we were. I was well-known for actually answering my phone; it made me valued by my clients.

In March David's sister Jeanie died suddenly of hypoxia. She had sleep apnea and didn't like to wear her mask. We flew out there and held a memorial service for her. Jeanie wanted her ashes sprinkled on Mt. Franklin, like her mom's, so we took Mary Jane, her Mom's best friend, and her daughter Marta (Jeanie's best friend in her school days), and we walked into the park at the foothills and found a lovely place to do it. Desert flowers were blooming everywhere. Then we flew on to Tucson to visit my old high school friend Susan Koppelman, her husband Dennis, and her mother Fran. Susan and Dennis had moved there from St. Louis. We stayed in a cute little trailer on their land with beautiful views of the mountains. We enjoyed the visit and it reawakened our love of the Southwest, so we went back in the fall for two weeks and David painted some beautiful watercolors of the views around their house and from a nearby park. While he painted I walked about two hours every day to build my bones.

That spring of 2005 my Aunt Dorothy died, the last of the Bonovitz aunts and uncles, and we flew to Cleveland to be with everyone. We were really glad we had gone to visit her in Lexington and spent some time with her and Susan in the fall of 2003. She had said at the time that if we were going to visit her, now was the time. She was right. After our visit she deteriorated and had to go into assisted living. Susan found her a nice place and she settled in, but she had a tendency to get emotionally upset and I think it was hard on Susan and her son Franklin. Franklin visited her often, and both of them were grateful that we had gone there too. The family all gathered for the funeral and it was really good to be together and see everyone, even if it was for a funeral.

David kept asking all spring how we would know if the market was in a bubble and how we would know when to get out. He kept saying, it's like musical chairs. You don't want to be sitting in a big chair when the music stops. You don't want to be holding a very expensive property when demand ends and prices begin to fall. In May he observed that my phone had stopped ringing. That was one sign. Then we lost the Seacrest condo where we held floor duty, so we had lost our Seacrest base. Another sign was that although Freeport had gotten hot (even though it was 20 minutes away from the beach), and my new developer offered a beautiful project there in June, which I promoted to all my customers, to all Pelican agents, and to the whole market, I got only one bite. Not the usual feeding frenzy. He wisely dropped the project.

Looking back it is now obvious that prices had gone way beyond values and that the market had peaked that spring. Prices started to drop and the smart people were getting out of things. Some of these price drops I sold as bargains. Deborah kept insisting that we weren't in a bubble and she continued to work on developments with her partners. She offered me a chance to sell both their projects. I had earlier gotten a few reservations for her project Water Oaks, but I couldn't get any interest in Jerry's project called Osprey Creek, which was on the north side of 98 near Rosemary Beach. The signs were there, but Deborah was planning her wedding in the Bahamas that July and she was wearing blinders.

I wanted to go to the wedding so I dropped a hint and soon I got an invitation. It came inside a clear bottle filled with sand and seashells. We had never been to the Bahamas so I was eager to go. We caught a small plane over to Marsh Harbour, and we got in early in the day so David painted a couple of boat scenes from the harbor restaurant, and he took a photo of Deb and her fiancé Harry in their boat Tough Catch, which he later made into a watercolor and gave to them as a wedding present. We were to spend the night in Marsh Harbour so that evening we took a taxi to the local Goombay festival. There was music, food and dancing, and almost everyone was black, pure black. They promised T-shirts to those who would get up and dance so we got up and danced and got T-shirts that advertised the festival.

The next morning, David painted another harbor scene, we shopped for groceries to take to our place in Guana Key, and caught the afternoon ferry. We stayed at a cute little place called Seashore Villas overlooking its pool and the harbor. We rented a little electric cart to drive around the island and we were just around the corner from the famous Nippers and the eastern ocean beaches and could just walk over. The sand was white and the waters were a gorgeous shade of blue green. It was really a paradise.

David painted the views from our balcony and from Nippers' top deck while I checked my email at the bar. They had wireless and my little computer worked just fine. Deborah had given us noodles, a map of the island, a whole welcome package, and we went from party to party. Jan was there, and Roxanne and many other Realtors, as well as Deb's whole family. We all enjoyed the Sunday buffet and music at Nippers and ate at the country club. Deb organized a boat tour of the nearby islands. The wedding finally came and it was out in a pavilion on the beach. Then there was a dinner dance at a local restaurant and the music at both events was provided by a Bahamian named Stone McEwan and his band.

One day I was checking my email at the country club to keep up with my real estate customers (very few at that moment), and I told Jerry that it was over. The big run on real estate was over. He argued with me, saying that ReMax said they were having their biggest year ever. Yes, I agreed, but they are seeing the momentum and closings from 2004 and that now it was over. Depressing news, to be sure, and he couldn't accept it. He had too much invested in projects. He kept trying to promote Riverwalk and Osprey Creek, but neither project survived the downturn. Roxanne liked Guana so much she and her husband Barry bought a house there and put it on a rental program. Unfortunately, I couldn't accept the news either and David and I went ahead with several deals we should have dropped; losing our deposits would have been far better than losing the whole sale price, or close to it. A friend who had his own investment fund and clientele told us about a year later that the real estate market was getting soft. Ha, David told him, you are way behind the news on the street, or in this case, on the beaches of Florida.

In August we flew out to Tahoe to visit Sara and Cleo and Ted. It was really beautiful and cool there and I took the girls shopping in Reno and David painted views from their porch. My real estate business had become so slow that it was easy to think about traveling. I sold one lot I had listed to one of my customers in August, so I got both sides of the deal and that made me the agent of the month for September. Agent of the month for just one deal! That means everyone else did worse. Really pathetic for our office, which had been Pelican's top producer. I sold only one house and two lots after August. No one was looking for property any more, no one was buying things sight unseen just to get something.

We Realtors took comfort in each other. We had formed a core group we called Girls Night Out. We went out about once a month for dinner and drinking and laughing, usually celebrating one of our birthdays, or for no reason at all. There was Deb, her sister Rebecca, her cousin Dana, Jan, Stephanie (who was our title attorney and a good friend of Deb's), Lisa (an old friend of everyone from Panama City Beach), and Roxanne. We would go to a really nice restaurant, usually a different one each month, and not talk real estate, just relax and enjoy. (This went on for a full year ending with my birthday in the summer of 2006. I chose Canopies on the Bay in Panama City. Our group was so uproarious that some people sitting near us left. Lisa ordered every kind of dessert on the menu and we passed them all around, taking bites out of everything. We had a grand time. After my birthday party in 2006, we stopped the regular meetings. We just had the occasional dinner out.)

Later that fall of 2005 we got a call that the movement was prepared to offer me a week of PK at their Lancaster, Massachusetts, clinic in exchange for those weeks entertaining the North Carolina guests with talks of literature and higher states of consciousness years earlier. It was surprising to hear from them and a wonderful reward from nature just when I needed it. We signed David up for a few days of treatment too, and we had a wonderful week of massages and oil treatments and walks in the woods through the turning leaves. We picked apples from a local orchard and got a lovely rest. David and I were both pretty tired from the constant pace of work. I was totally vata deranged (Ayurvedically speaking for being overexcited and stretched too thin). No one seemed to know or could tell me how the offer had originated and from whom after so long, but it came at a really good time. I suspect that Maharishi was quietly behind it, he of the long arm.

Our last trip of the year was to take Nate, Emily and David to Disneyworld. Little David found the parks too noisy and irritating, and he had the most fun buying stuffed animals and toys and then playing with them and with us in the condo. A Realtor friend had set us up with his three-bedroom condo near the park. It was very luxurious and we enjoyed a comfortable home base from which to visit all the parks.

TruthAboutTM.com

On the drive back home from Disneyworld David and I were having lunch one day at a restaurant and David's phone rang. It was Bob Roth. People were going on the internet, he said, and seeing negative stuff about TM. The movement had always ignored these things; Maharishi called them mosquitos. We didn't want to publish our responses and rebuttals because most people didn't know about these things in the first place, so why publicize them? But now everything was out in public, on the internet, and it was time to take out the files and show that these negative attacks were baseless. Bob wanted David to put up a website and put these issues into the public forum. David groaned. These mosquitos were horrible to investigate; they were hard on the heart and emotions. Also, he had so many projects to finish, so many papers he wanted to write, and so many emails requesting TM research. Oh, no, he told Bobby. I don't have the time or website expertise to do this. Let me talk to Rhoda, Bobby said.

I had to agree. This was the most important thing for David to do. It would reach the widest audience possible and be far more effective than any scientific paper. When we got home, David set up his first website. Our friend Paul Stokstad helped David design it and take it to a more professional level. David called it Truth About TM, hoping that title would attract viewers looking for the inside story. His pages grew in subject matter and importance. Here was a place to put letters from people of all religions and faiths endorsing TM; here was a place to put posts by other researchers, bibliographies of all the TM research, and materials supporting the movement's claims that TM was the answer to problems in society, prisons, education, everything. Now he gets about five hundred visitors per day, as well as messages from non-meditators. It is a great resource for the Governors and for the movement as a whole. It has been a huge contribution, but it does require upkeep and attention, another jumbo jet on David's crowded runway.

At the end of 2005 the first of our personal Tapestry lots sold, thank God. I finished the year with over $34,000,000 in sales. Again I was in the top 2½% of the Realtors in ECAR. Those were the gold rush years, the peak of the market. I was driven. I would say to people that the salmon were running and I would be a fool not to be out there with my net. Unfortunately, we wound up sitting in a few pricy chairs when the music stopped. Still, it could have been worse, and it was worse for a lot of people, including my Realtor friends. Sales and prices continued to drop. I made very little money in the next few years, and many Realtors did much worse and dropped out of the business altogether. They owed mortgages on property they had bought on speculation at very high prices and many went bankrupt, as did their customers. It was time to think about moving on. But where? To what?

The Invincible America Assembly

AS REAL ESTATE TOOK less and less of my time and energy, we turned our attention to other things. We went on a little trip to St. Augustine, the family came here to the beach, Cleo came all by herself to visit us for two weeks in the summer of 2006, and inevitably we got more involved with the movement. I had accomplished quite a lot with my career in real estate: more self-confidence, a secure financial platform for our lives, and a finer way of living and enjoying our lives. In that time of supporting me (and doing the cooking) while I sold real estate David had published fourteen papers in scholarly journals, as well as the two volumes he had been editing, one on rehabilitation research and one honoring Skip Alexander. They finally got printed, and he had been working hard setting up his new website. Was this one of the reasons why Maharishi had sent us out into the field? To accomplish what he couldn't do at MIU? We had worked very hard to do all this and we hadn't rounded in a long time. We both were tired, deeply tired. Happy, but tired.

The Best Rounding Course Ever

Later that summer Maharishi asked John Hagelin to put on an Invincible America Assembly (IAA) to raise the coherence in the country. Governors were gathered in two places, various locations at and around MUM and in Washington, D.C. The highlight of the course, the real draw that brought everyone together again, was Maharishi's daily conference call hearing experiences and commenting on them. We had reached new areas of subtlety and we needed Maharishi's guidance and direction. He heard the experiences and interpreted them and was very pleased with what the Governors were reporting. The rounding program was another enticement. To do long meditations with a large group of our fellow long-time Sidhas meant that experiences and knowledge would be at their highest level. Yes, we would affect the consciousness of the nation and head off whatever threat Maharishi saw coming, but that would be a side effect. We wouldn't go into that. We would focus on our own growth toward enlightenment.

David and I were ready for this. We chose the Washington, D.C., course for four weeks of the new rounding program. The two families who put on the course did an amazing job: the families of Bob LoPinto and Dean Dodrill. They used the D.C. TM capital that Jeffrey and Rona Abramson had developed out on the outskirts of the city. They expanded into neighboring houses and lots and set up program rooms and dining halls in them and in temporary tents. They found housing for us all at nearby hotels and organized buses to bring us back and forth. They subsidized most of the costs so many people could afford to come and stay on. They had no cooking facilities so they catered the whole course with neighboring restaurants. We had professional Indian cooking one day, Italian the next, Thai the next. I was very happy with that. They even put out big containers full of large umbrellas we could use if it rained, and they gave us ice cream and cookie snacks every afternoon.

The program areas were clean and cool, and I meditated and slept and meditated and slept (and flew, so to speak), and slept some more. This led to quite a bit of purification, I am embarrassed to admit, but so it was. I found myself to be very delicate and easily upset and my friends sat around me and created a foil to protect me. It was fun to see old friends, like Tim Ambrose, but mostly I kept to myself. One of our friends commented to David that I looked vulnerable and uncomfortable until he joined me in the dining room after the long mornings and afternoons of rounding. Maharishi said that married life gives security to the heart; it gives stability. What is most necessary, he said, is security, a man's security as much as a wife's. Very true of us. We both flourish with the quiet (or noisy) support of the other at our backs.

In the afternoon we gathered in the meeting hall/dining room tent and connected by conference call with the various groups at MUM and with Maharishi in Holland. Bevan was master of ceremonies. Governors would get on the mike and give their experiences. Maharishi would validate them, interpret them, explain them as high stepping stones toward enlightenment. I could barely sit through these sessions, especially when he would invite John or Bevan to comment. I wanted to lie down. David had some subtle experiences and presented an experience of the gap on the mike one afternoon. When he finished there was a long, long silence. Bevan began to get nervous. He was wondering if Maharishi was still on the line. Finally, Maharishi spoke. He had been looking us over, I believe, checking us out, assessing where we were in our evolution. He gave an encouraging little talk, not personal, and Bevan moved along to the next experience. It was okay, we felt. We were okay.

When the four weeks ended David wanted to stay on, but we had arranged earlier, before the IAA course had been announced, to take some Elderhostel (now called Road Scholar) courses at the Arrowmont School of Arts and Crafts in Gatlinburg, Tennessee, in the Smoky Mountains, and I was ready to air out after all that rounding. We had rented a condo for a few days so we could explore Dollywood (Dolly Parton's theme park) and that beautiful area for a few days before the art courses started. David took what was supposed to be a watercolor landscape course, but the teacher was not a landscape painter and she made them do ugly still-life arrangements and only took them outdoors on the last day or two. I took pottery, and I threw some pots and made some slab plates. My fingers and hands remembered what to do, even though it had been sixteen years since Sara and I had done this at MIU and about thirty years since I had done it in Santa Barbara when we founded MIU there. Was I a potter in a previous life? So fulfilling and nourishing.

From Gatlinburg we drove to Fairfield and rounded some more on the IAA, staying with Nate and Emily. On that course, now the only one in session since the D.C. course had ended, Maharishi continued to connect with us, now in the mornings, and the experiences were incredible. It was very encouraging to all of us. As one of my favorite authors has his character say, "Even the scouts are part of the wagon train." We got a lot of rest and really enjoyed the more relaxed atmosphere of the course there at MUM. Fairfield never felt better. We had fun with little David who was blossoming in Maharishi School. He learned to meditate and began to grow in confidence, strength, and social abilities. We had dropped quite a lot of fatigue and stress and were feeling much better. From then on we would manage to get ourselves to Fairfield and onto the IAA every year, at least for a month.

Creating a Little More Heaven on Earth

After years of selling fancy houses I had a desire to live in something larger and more elegant. We had flirted with the idea of building a Maharishi Vastu house on our next door lot during the gold rush years, but we couldn't find a design that was in harmony with the principles and still give us what we wanted. (No, you can't put a door there; no, you can't put a wall there; no, you have to do it this way; no, no, no). And then the market slowed down; the new house would have cost about half a million dollars, which we no longer had to spend, and it would have raised our property taxes and all that. We dropped the idea. Then it occurred to me that we could just add on to the back of our house, and we designed an addition that fulfilled all our desires. With these plans I would have the foyer I had wanted. David would have a huge studio/office. I would get the master bath I wanted with marble countertops, a bidet, double vanities, an extra-large soaking tub, and a separate shower. You can see by all the details that this was something I longed for. I would have a separate office and a walk-in closet as well. We also would redo some of the floors, move some doors, and make quite a few improvements. In the end we did such a good job insulating that our heating and cooling bills did not go up at all even though we added about 600 square feet and a lot of windows.

We were ready to start construction in January of 2007. Then David's brother Bill died on January 1 and we flew to Boston for the memorial service. David gave a wonderful tribute to his life and told of their humorous times as boys, blowing things up and experimenting with parachutes. When they were boys they made parachutes and decided their cat would be the lucky one to have the first flight off the roof. Much to their surprise the cat was not honored or even pleased. David's mom was surprisingly not supportive of the whole parachute idea. Who knew? She put a stop to all that. Our nieces, Dolly, Maggie, and Ruth, spoke beautifully and sang, and Bill's wife Carol and their church put on a lovely meal for everyone. Our niece Liz and her husband Tom came (both families had become friends when Liz helped Bill's oldest daughter settle into Bryn Mawr) and we got to see them and bond with the whole family.

Once back home we began to build our addition. The renovation process was exhausting. We had to move into the front bedroom, a tiny room which would also double as David's office during the building. I set up my office in the living room and we carried on. We had sheets of plastic covering all the other openings while they tore off the back wall of the house and framed in the new part with its new roof. The crews would arrive at 7 a.m. so we had to wake up early to do program so we could be finished before the tumult started and the dust began to fly. Weekends were a relief, but we spent most of them at Home Depot or Lowe's buying doors, hardware, paint, etc. Sara and Cleo came for Cleo's ski/skate week in February and they were to stay in a little rental condo we had foolishly bought. On the first night none of our slide keys would work to open the condo door and they wound up sleeping on our living room floor. We had put all the foam into storage and were sleeping on one piece in the front room, so we made a mattress from all our blankets and towels, and we all survived. Then they used our car to drive back and forth from the condo to the house once we got a working key.

We also slipped away from the construction for a family re-union in Savannah. It was Adele's suggestion, but I was the one to locate B&B's, restaurants, things to do, and set up a whole itinerary. My aunt Dorothy's kids, Susan, Frank, and his wife, Jeanne, came too. We had all grown up together, first in a two-sto-ry two-family house in East Cleveland and then in a side-by-side duplex in Cleveland Heights. It was wonderful to be with Nate and his family and with Linda and Lloyd and Jay and Jenny. Jay was enjoying a manic phase and Jenny kept trying to quiet him down, but we were all loving it. He was so outgoing and jolly and friendly and eager to do anything. I look back on that now and am grateful we did it. It would be the last time we would be with our Linda, the very last time.

Right in the middle of the chaos, when I didn't think I had the energy to survive another day, I had an abnormal mammogram. It turned out to be cancer in the other breast, which partly explained the deep fatigue I had been feeling. I went out with my real es-tate friends, on one of our girls' nights out, and everyone wished me well and asked what they could do. I asked them to cook for me. Jan Freeman organized them, and for the week after I got home from surgery, one of my Realtor friends showed up every night with food: Linda Lee and her daughter, Ann Mosely, Jan, all those loved and lovely faces showing up with comfort food and caring. Instead of keeping it secret as I had done in Fairfield, I let everyone know and I enjoyed their love and support. Pelican sent flowers; Jay and Jenny sent flowers; people visited and helped out. Somehow we finished the renovation and just loved everything about it. It had raised our whole quality of life. Even now, I look about me and love, love, love it all.

While I was recovering from the radiation following the surgery, Jay called to say that our little sister Linda had died suddenly just a few days before her birthday. I felt like I was down and got kicked again. We went to New York for the funeral. It was very painful. Jenny and I held each other and wept. I threw my handful of dirt onto the coffin in the hole and could hardly stand up. Linda had damaged her heart by being obese and using that Fen-Phen drug to lose weight (it was discovered that drug was associated with primary pulmonary hypertension, a heart and drug related condition). She had the Bonovitz heart, it seems, like my dear father, Uncle Harry, his brother (who survived his heart attack), and like my grandfather Frank. She would have been only fifty-one in a few days. I would miss her forever. That was a painful item in my suitcase of karma, and only a few weeks on the IAA could begin to lift my energy and spirits.

Another of my desires, beside money, money, money, and a great bathroom, was travel. All my life I wanted to see the world, any of it, all of it. You have to fulfill all your desires to get enlightened, some say. By August I was feeling strong enough to fly to Fairfield for little David's seventh birthday and do some necessary rounding on the IAA, and then on to Tahoe to visit Sara and her family. We all drove from Truckee to Bodie, Ted's favorite ghost town, and on to Convict Lake and Mammoth Lake and had a great time. David and I joined a travel club called Evergreen for people over fifty. You host them, they host you, with breakfast, advice on where to go, what to see, sharing travel memories and trips, about $20/night. My real estate friend Carolyn's mother and father belonged and they had had some wonderful experiences.

David was dubious. Strangers in our home, staying with strangers, did we really want to do this? Why not? We could use the club as we traveled back and forth to Fairfield and we could host a few snowbirds over the winter. No big deal. I was also flirting with the idea of becoming a travel writer.

Maharishi Drops the Body

Real estate was still slow so I planned some more trips. We flew to California the next February to Adele's and we were about to leave for Yelapa in Mexico when we heard that Maharishi had died. He had removed himself from the administration of the movement in January and handed everything over to his teams from various countries, set up an international organization, and he had retired into almost complete silence. I was in denial. I thought he was just pulling back to see how everyone would handle their new responsibilities. I was wrong. He was ready to drop the body, as we say, and move into another sphere of activity. A guru can choose his moment to go and his future path.

We were shocked and grieved and briefly considered going to India for the last rites, but decided that we were already launched on the trip to Mexico and that going to India without visas and planning and places to stay could be a nightmare. Some of our friends had great luck and great experiences. Others couldn't find a place to sleep, and some got very sick. It seemed strange not to have Maharishi in our physical world and sad not to have resolved the issues we still had with our relationships with him. Somehow I felt he was still there, still in my consciousness, still looking over me. He had weaned us away from his personal presence over the past thirty years and had moved into our internal realities. Yet, it was sad to think that never again would the phone ring summoning us into his presence. We would see how we felt about it as time went on. It boggled our minds to think of the movement in the hands of the people we knew. We hoped for the best. If he had organized it and felt fulfilled about it then it would be all right.

Over the next few years we spent a month or more on the IAA each summer and traveled, sometimes with my sister Adele, sometimes just the two of us or with other friends, to Ireland, Iceland, Scotland, the Santa Fe area, the Caribbean on a long cruise, Alaska and the Pacific northwest (where we stayed with a few Evergreeners), Playa del Carmen (and Tulum and Coba and Chichen Itza), and even a short trip to neighboring Mobile and New Orleans, again staying with Evergreeners, and hosting them too. I did write a travel article about it and published it in the *Iowa Source* under a pen name. There's a link to it on my Rhoda The Writer website travel-writer page (rhodathewriter.com).

A New Fairfield Home

During the summer of 2010 while we were visiting Nate and his family and rounding on the IAA, the big oil spill created by British Petroleum happened about two hundred miles west of our little place in Seagrove Beach. It sounded horrible, but it seemed that our area wasn't particularly affected. No one was reporting oil on the beaches. We were making plans to return home when we had lunch with Ken Walton, a biochemist, one of our old friends from faculty days. You can't go back, he said. When oil breaks down, and it is spread out all over the Gulf right now, it creates benzene, a very powerful carcinogen, and, when it is burned, hydrogen sulfide, another one. You don't want to breathe that in, he advised. We called our neighbor Alice and our Realtor friends. It smells like lighter fluid here, they said. Benzene! It smells like burning tires here, they said. Not encouraging. We decided to stay for a while longer.

We rented a little condo near the railroad tracks from our friends Christer and Margareta Cederroth and settled in for the summer months. We decided to get recertified while we were there. Maharishi wanted all the TM teachers to go through a process of reregistering with the movement, bringing their skills and knowledge up to date, and recommitting to the organization. We had no plans to teach TM since Prudy was running the center in our area, and we were not really interested in going on another big project like Armenia, even if it should arise, but we wanted to do the latest thing that Maharishi had instigated only a few years before, not long before he died. Our course was full of old friends and familiar faces and was really a lot of fun and very inspiring. It almost made me want to teach again. We were formed into small groups to study together and practice our skills on each other: lecturing, checking, everything, the basics.

David's small group had Jerry Jarvis in it, whom everyone loved, had worked for, and wanted to see. It also had Bob Daniels, who was helping to run the U.S. movement at the time, a semi-retired businessman; Fred Gratzon, our old friend who started Great Midwestern Ice Cream Company and the Telegroup Company, where Nate got his start in Fairfield businesses; Bob Boyer, another old friend and fellow psychologist; and Frank Wintroub, a new

From left to right, Bob Daniels, David, Jerry Jarvis, Bob Boyer, Fred Gratzon, and Frank Wintroub

friend, TM teacher and MUM supporter. The guys had a great time laughing together and making Jerry perform for them, he, the master of TM teaching and mainstay of our U.S. movement for years and years. My group contained Fred's wife, Shelley, who was writing an Ayurvedic cookbook at the time, Prudy, our dear Prudy, and some new friends, all TM teachers, Mary Roché, Marji Wintroub, and Heather Hartnett, whose father had been and is a great supporter of the movement and Heavenly Mountain.

They played some beautiful, old lectures of Maharishi on how to teach various aspects of the teaching process. I wish I had heard them earlier, but they weren't made until years after I became a teacher. It was like being in his presence again, in his knowledge, in his worldview. He said before he left that wherever his knowledge was, there he would be. I take that very literally. I remember one tape in particular. A young woman was gushing at him and telling him how he came to her (in a dream) and told her certain

From left to right, Heather Hartnett, Shelley Gratzon, Mary Roche, Marji Wintroub, Prudy Farrow Bruns, and me

things. No, he said sternly. I do not do that. If I want to tell you something, I will send you a Telex. This was good to hear, because people were sometimes saying that Maharishi came to them and told them to do something. Bogus! Bring in the stretchers, as Dr. Elliot Abravanel used to say.

We got to round on the IAA and, as usual, I wanted some time and space to air out afterwards, so we took a couple of weeks to tour South Dakota, the Badlands, Mt. Rushmore, Crazy Horse, Custer, the works. We saw herds of buffalo and I felt connected to my Midwestern roots. Back in Fairfield we had what David's parents would call "an endless round of gaiety." One highlight was the yearly Italian Festival put on by the local meditating Italians, with opera sung in the cupola of our town square. It was celestial to sit out there in the warm summer evenings and hear the music of Puccini filling the air. There were concerts in the park, plays, and other musical events at the Sondheim. Hardly a week went by without some birthday party, lunches out with friends who lived there or were just passing through, and Irish music at Café Paradiso. We had become very fond of that music since our time in Ireland. David found a congenial art community and began taking weekly watercolor classes with John Preston. Fairfield was the college town par excellence! How could we leave?

That was an intriguing thought. If we could stay in Fairfield for the summers, where would we live? We would still go home to Florida for the winters. A jyotishi had told David that he could not live in the extreme cold; he has a chest weakness and when he gets a chest cold it can be a bad one. We explored various options, went to look at some condos for sale and some little houses. We wanted something affordable, something in line with Maharishi Vastu (David wanted the real thing!), and something we could rent out in the wintertime when we were in Florida. This narrowed the search to the University Manor, two buildings that had been built over forty years before. It wasn't Vastu (newly, perfectly built), but it had been rectified, that is, renovated under Henry Clark's direction, so it was more or less in tune with the principles of Maharishi Vastu. They were the classiest apartments on campus in their day but there was nothing for sale there.

Then one day I fell into conversation with a friend, Elaine Reding, and told her what I was looking for. She perked right up. I live in the Manor, she said, and there is a unit just below mine that might be perfect for you two: two bedrooms, washer and dryer, dishwasher, lots of closets, plenty of space to be our little summer cave, and very affordable. We drew up an offer and the sellers accepted it! We now had a second home in order to do courses, as Shastriji had seen. We did not remember the prediction until years later when I was reviewing my notes. We found a lawyer to handle the transaction, got a rental inspection, and put it on the rental market, partially furnished. We found a tenant right away. Perfect. Support of nature, eh?

While this was going on we traveled to Vermont to see the changing leaves. Poor David. He just wants to stay home and work (at the most beautiful beach in America), stay home and paint, stay home and round, just stay home. He has visited over 50 countries and thinks there is nowhere better to go or be than our beach or Fairfield. He loves me, packs his suitcase and his paints, and off we go, this time visiting my cousin Frank again and Clint Lee, David's old high school buddy who had first told him about TM. Vermont was beautiful. The hillsides and villages were blazing with the reds and golds of maple trees that I grew up with in Cleveland, but better. When we got back to Fairfield we were ready to pack up and head home to Florida except for one thing that hadn't been finished. Actually there are usually about ten things, David's important projects, papers, whatever, that have to be finished right now before we can leave town. This was different.

Book Signing

About six months after Maharishi left us I had mentioned to John Hagelin that Susan and I had done this book on Maharishi's talks on literature and language and maybe now might be a good time to bring it out. He enthusiastically agreed. MUM Press had lost my disks so they scanned in the copy I had with me. I thought I was ready to get it approved and printed. Easier said than done. Craig Pearson, MUM's executive vice president, thought I should bring the introduction up to date. I had written it nearly thirty years before and there was a lot more movement history to include in it. My coverage of Maharishi's ideas and contributions should be complete. He envisioned the book as the first in a series of volumes of Maharishi's talks in various fields, so he wanted the introduction not to focus particularly on literature and language but to stand alone as the introduction to each subsequent volume. Okay, I could do that. That made sense.

It should have an index, Craig thought. I once did one for a book when I was at Maryland in graduate school. I could do that. And there was the section on scientific research (and all the footnotes referring to it) that needed to be brought up to date. Quite a bit of research had been published in the last thirty years. I was living with the expert. He could help me with that, expanding the bibliography of published papers on TM, picking the best ones to mention in the footnotes, changing all the numbers so they matched. Oy. We could that. When I looked at the scan, I found it was full of errors, large and small, from misspellings and typos to dropped lines. It would take many hours of work, many hours. There wasn't anything more important happening in my life; real estate was still very slow, so all through 2009 I had worked on the book and had gotten it to the level where it could go through the approval process.

Halfway through the approval process, the process changed, and I had to start over. A few sensitive lines had to be removed, which was a bit ridiculous since they are in a tape that everyone plays at the TM centers and they are still there in that tape. There were some Sanskrit words and terms to check. Tom Egenes helped me with those. It was joyous work, and I didn't mind any of it. I love having a project and doing something meaningful. This would be my legacy. Occasionally I did a real estate deal, but mainly I worked on the book. All that summer Dara Llewellyn and her team had helped me proof and correct the final copy once we put it all into the program that Shepley Hansen had designed for it. The book went off to MUM Press that fall of 2010 and then to the bindery. We waited for it to be finished. I wanted to be there for the launch and to sign the printed copies. We turned the condo over to our new tenant and moved back in with Nate and Emily and waited and waited and the weather got colder and colder. Finally, in early November we had the hard copies, all golden and radiant, with a glorious cover designed by Shepley (see RhodaTheWriter.com, the Academic page, for a look at the cover and some videos I made on the book).

Harry Bright, the head of the Press, made some large posters announcing the book signings. Susan Andersen (this was now her

Signing Susan Humphrey Tracy's copy of *The Flow of Consciousness* in the bookstore on MUM campus, November 2010

name, no longer Setzer), my co-author, was in California with her son, so I met my public and signed copies. All my old friends turned up and celebrated with me: Susan Humphrey, Cathy Gorini, all my faculty friends and MIU family. Very fulfilling. I signed, David took pictures, and we finally left for Florida. We would come back the next summer and spend it on the IAA and enjoying Nate's family, Sara's visits, all our friends, and all the summer events and parties. It was the beginning of our new life, half time in Florida, half time in Fairfield. My sixties were over; I had made big money; we were financially, if modestly, self-sufficient, and a new phase of life was beginning.

Reconnecting with Maharishi

OCCASIONALLY, OKAY NOT SO OCCASIONALLY, I dragged David off to see the world (a family wedding in Philadelphia, another one in Idaho for Jay and Jenny's son Nathaniel, visits to Sara in California, a winter trip to Hawaii to stay with Tracey on Oahu and Stuart and Moki Zimmerman on Kauai, another trip to Vermont

Marie-France and I at one of the events at the 50th reunion of our Vassar class of '62. Here we are at a garden party at the beautiful home of one of our classmates. It originally belonged to a painter from the Hudson River school. You can see the river in the background.

after my 50th Vassar reunion, with an extension to Quebec, where I gave some talks on my book *in French*, and a fabulous one-month trip to the Dordogne region of France to visit my friend, filmmaker Marie-France Siegler-Lathrop. Marie-France and I had reconnected at the Vassar reunion but hadn't seen each other in years, maybe since I taught her TM in Paris in 1974.

From Marie-France's chateau in the Dordogne we went on to Provence and the Côte d'Azur, and once again, I totally loved France and was already thinking about how we could go back. There aren't many Evergreeners in Europe so we joined the Affordable Travel Club, too, and stayed with a great couple in Marseille and with a lady in Nice who lived right near the water and told us how to take buses all over town, to the Matisse Museum, to the Chagall Museum, and even to neighboring Monaco and the towns along the coast, all for one euro. We stayed with her five nights, with a French breakfast, all for under $150. Heaven on earth, at least for me.

Then there were visits to and with friends and family: to Tucson to help our friend Susan Koppelman downsize, to Universal Studios

Overlooking the harbor in Antibes. We drove there from Nice to visit the Picasso museum.

(Cleo is big Harry Potter fan), and to David's 50th Columbia college reunion in New York City. He reconnected with some old friends and roommates, and we went in search of the slum building where we first met and courted in the early sixties. We wandered the streets looking for familiar landmarks and couldn't find it. Susan, who had introduced us to each other in the basement of that horror of a building, went online and discovered that it had been bought by Columbia University, torn down, and was now the site of a small international center and a public park for children. We found it and sat around under the trees (trees had had time to grow up!), watching the children play, remembering our reckless youth and falling in love. It seemed so remote, almost like a past life. It was good to see the whole, where we had come from and where we were now.

While we were in Fairfield the summer of 2013, after the Columbia reunion, we celebrated our 50th wedding anniversary (Nate and Emily made us a lovely party), and I helped host a reunion of our literature faculty and students that Susan Andersen and Nynke Passi had inspired and set up. I remember Nynke coming from Holland to MIU as very young student years ago. She has matured into a beautiful young woman, an excellent poet, and now a teacher of creative writing at MUM.

David went that same weekend to Chicago to give away one of his brother Bill's daughters' hand in marriage, Ruth Orme-Johnson. That summer we heard about MUM's Rotating University plan to once again lead a five-week trip around India, visiting many of the places that were important to Maharishi and the movement, including Allahabad, the winter seat of the Shankaracharya, as well as some rounding at the movement facility at the center of India, the Brahmasthan. We hadn't been to India since we took Sara there the winter of 1987, about twenty-six years before. We had missed Maharishi's last rites and a chance to connect with him in that way. It was tempting. India is always a challenge to the physiology: the long flight there, the twelve-hour time change, the food, the poverty, the air pollution, and the list goes on. We were seventy-three years old. Hmm.

Bob and Carol Markowitz were leading the group, as they had several times before, and they assured us that our Indian guide Ranjan would make it clean and comfortable for all of us: elegant four-star hotels, good, safe food, our own buses, as well as flights and trains from south to north, everything smooth and arranged in advance. The group was going to be a mix of students, young and not so young, and old yogis like us from Fairfield, D.C., other parts of the U.S., and even South Africa. We got our visas, no small feat, and I started to look for flights. Most of the group got cheap flights from Chicago, but we would be leaving from Florida. My travel brain woke up and got creative. Perhaps I could be a travel writer and describe all the places we would visit and write a series of articles to publish. I was looking for some new purposeful activity since real estate had died down and no longer captured my interest. What about starting with trips and travel writing?

The best flight to Thiruvananthapuram (it used to be called Trivandrum), where we would meet up with our group, stopped in Dubai to change planes. Dubai is the capital of one of the five United Arab Emirates. An Affordable Travel member lived there!

Dubai and the Arab World

You have probably guessed where I am going with this. Why not see Dubai on the way? Our prospective hostess, Donna, was open to the visit. We could stay with her for three nights and she would show us around. She was an American Phys. Ed. teacher teaching in one of the Arab schools and had been living in Dubai for some years. Twenty dollars a night with breakfast! We had heard about the high prices there but this could work. I organized an unofficial stopover by jiggling with the departure date and it only added about $50 or so to our tickets. I jiggled with the departure date from India, too, and arranged a stopover in Amsterdam on the way home for another small amount, but more about that later. David says I am a force of nature. One pandit told me that when I say something, it becomes a mantra and it gets carried out! Whoopee! If you are just interested in Maharishi, skip ahead, but I have to say the whole adventure was mind-expanding, evolutionary, and had the support of nature that told us we were on a good dharmic path, learning and growing.

Donna took us to buy a few exotic fruits for breakfast and we saw our first woman completely covered from head to foot in black robes with only a little window for her eyes. This was unusual for Dubai, Donna told us. The Emirates allow women to show their hands and faces, as they like. At her cute little apartment we fell drop dead asleep and were awakened at dawn by the call to morning prayers from a nearby mosque, and then a dense wall of bird song and chatter. It was as if they were greeting the day and exchanging news and their daily plans. After breakfast Donna took us to a flamingo sanctuary and we admired the Dubai skyline.

Dubai was very impressive: modern, beautiful, spacious, and clean. There was construction going on everywhere, preparing for Expo 2020. There was even a Disneyland under consideration. Local joke: what is the national bird of Dubai? Answer: the crane (meaning all those huge cranes used in building the skyscrapers and hotels). We spent a day at the Dubai Mall touring an aquarium several stories high. You can walk along the see-through plastic walls right next to huge fish. There was also an underwater zoo and a tunnel through the aquarium, so you were surrounded on all sides by the fish-filled water. We had a really delicious and unusual Middle Eastern lunch out on a patio overlooking a huge water display with dancing fountains and accompanying music. There were shops of all sorts, every international boutique you could imagine, all the major brand names. We learned that most of the labor and menial jobs are filled by Indians and Arabs from other countries who send money back home. The ten percent or so of native Dubai residents are wealthy and they employ workers of all kinds. They were walking along the mall dressed in their traditional costumes, different for each tribe, and there are numerous ones in the five Emirates. They were pushing baby carriages and shopping in the Western shops.

After tea and a patisserie at a French café (a little oasis of a familiar culture in the middle of this very modern yet foreign place), we took elevator after elevator up the tallest building in the world, the adjoining Burj Khalifa. At each station where we got off our elevator and walked to a new one, we saw floor to ceiling displays illustrating the building of the tower and showing all the international teams of scientists and engineers that made it happen, names and countries of origin given. Very few Arabian faces. The view from the (almost) top was expansive, dusty, impressive, but not beautiful. We were hustled along from elevator to elevator both up and down. The whole thing took a long time because of the waits and the lines of tourists. What was most striking was the interest and ability of the leaders of Dubai to create world landmarks, the tallest building, the tallest hotel, the best of everything.

As we toured around, we talked to all our drivers, asking them about their lives. One was a 68 year old man from Jordan. He had three wives, twenty-one children, and 52 grandchildren. Muslims can have more than one wife, one in each country they may live and work in, and they can only have sex with a wife. Another driver was from Kovalam, the southern part of India, to which we were next headed. He was a Christian, which is a sizable minority in Kovalam. He lived in Dubai in a kind of dormitory, got two months paid home visit to India each year, and he told us that someone from each household in his home area worked in Dubai and sent money home. We had no idea.

The next day we visited the Jumeirah mosque. It is open to the public for tours, so we tourists donned the black robes and head gear, the shayla, and had an educational morning. First we were taught about how the visitor cleanses him or herself at some designated area before going in, mouth, ears, face, head, arms, legs, and feet. Cleanliness and purification are very important. The inside of the mosque was beautifully inlaid with colored stones or ceramic pieces in the shape of calligraphy, words from the Qu'ran, or flowers, no human representations. Normally, the men would line up in rows, shoulder to shoulder, showing that all men are equal in the eyes of the Lord. Women pray in an adjoining room. Simply, it would be uncomfortable and distracting to be all mixed up and that close together. Made sense. Like in our Domes.

Women can pray at home, but men should go to the mosques (five times a day). They get ten rewards for that versus one for praying at home. These rewards add up and dictate where you go in the seven levels of paradise. The prayer times change according to the sunrise. Now there's an App for that! Then we were shown the postures for praying: standing, bending, kneeling forward, standing, etc., a whole ritualized progression of postures. You look to the right and left, "peace be with you" in all directions. They are coming together to praise the Lord. The five pillars of Islam: declare your faith before two witnesses, that there is no god but the one God; prayer; charity (tithing 2.5% of savings yearly to the needy and the community; fasting (no eating or drinking until sundown during the month of Ramadan); and pilgrimage, one time in a lifetime, if you can afford it, to Mecca for forgiveness and purification. The lifestyle is also very pure: no alcohol, drugs, or pork. One doesn't judge others; one hopes that all are saved. I hope I am getting this all right. A word about predestination. The Lord knows what will happen in our life, so it is comforting to think after some sorrow or loss, "It was written."

All in all, it seemed to us to be very rigorous and religious, distinctly but not completely different from the Judaism, Christianity, and Hinduism that we knew, but very different from what was displayed in the popular press.

On our last evening Donna drove us outside of the city to the Bab al Shams Desert Resort. On the way we saw trainers taking their little groups of camels out for exercise in preparation for the weekly camel races. Camel races! Wish we could have stayed for that. We also saw horses from the breeding farms being exercised. The resort was laid out with pools, guest rooms, dining areas, all outside in the open air, very elegant. The dinner was lovely. First we had hot chocolate or mulled wine, then warm and cold mezzas, kind of like tapas, mostly vegetarian, some meats. As we sat at low tables and leisurely ate the many courses, the sun gradually set and the sky filled up with bright stars, so bright you felt you could reach up and touch them, no light pollution there. Arab guests strolled around in their long white robes. While we ate, several musicians played lilting desert music. It was heavenly, a taste of how tribes might have lived among their tents in the desert, maybe even my Jewish ancestors. We came away with admiration for all that is going on in the Arab world, but my dominant impression was that it is a very male and masculine world and is desperately in need of the feminine to balance it and nourish it.

The MUM Rotating University Tour

The MUM tour took us to many temples, a few days at a tiger preserve, the Taj Mahal, shopping, river cruises, and much more, but the highlight for me and David was seeing how Maharishi had impacted Indian culture and feeling his presence there in his homeland. That is why we joined the tour. Each day ended at an elegant, clean, luxurious hotel with really good food, a very necessary respite from days traveling through the impoverished countryside without proper rest stops, bathrooms, and other conveniences. The tour was fun and the company was very congenial: we made new friends, deepened our relationships with old ones, and really enjoyed the boisterous company of the young students. *Karma bhoomi Bharat*. India, the land of karma. Not everyone can make it to India; not everyone in India can visit its holy sites even in a lifetime; and nearly everyone who visits is there for an evolutionary purpose, if only to burst some boil of stress and come away purer and clearer.

The Library in Trivandrum

On David's birthday we had a full day of events to make it memorable, not exactly like being with Maharishi, as we had so many times in the past, but close. We were planning to visit the library where Maharishi first spoke to the public about Guru Dev and the wisdom of the Veda, but it was tucked behind some buildings and we couldn't locate it at first. While Bob and Carol searched for the correct address, we all visited our first Indian temple of the trip, Padmanabhaswami temple. This huge Vishnu temple is closed to all but Hindus, but we had been told we could enter. It would not be the first time we would be told what we wanted to hear, but not necessarily the truth.

The men in our group were dressed traditionally for this visit: *lunghis* (a wrap around sheet of cloth from the waist down), bare chests, bare feet. We women were all in sarees, of course, and we walked along a rough, sandy road to the entrance. The Indian ladies around the entrance smiled happily at us. We became a tourist attraction. They took pictures of us. We were an oddity to them, and several ladies wanted their picture taken standing among us so they could show their friends Westerners dressed in sarees. As we found everywhere, the lavishly carved and decorated temple was closely boxed in by shabby buildings and could not be fully seen and appreciated. In the end, we could not enter. We could only admire the entranceway and go back to our bus.

We were dropped at a narrow opening between two buildings which then led to a courtyard behind them and another small building. The library was a small, neat, and clean little building with an office and a meeting room, which was a jumble of wooden chairs and a stage upon which Maharishi may have sat when he gave his first series of talks. We meditated together. Very sweet feeling. Then we pulled the chairs together and took a group picture. It was humbling to imagine Maharishi beginning the movement in such a modest little place. If someone hadn't stopped him on the street and asked him if he was a monk from the Himalayas and organized his talks for him, where would we be now? Where would the world be now? Perhaps "it was written." We felt grateful and deeply moved.

Mother Divine

After we rested and swam and ate at glorious buffets for breakfast, lunch, and dinner for a few days at a resort in Kovalam, we then climbed onto our bus to go see a Mother Divine temple at the southernmost tip of the Indian peninsula. This was the place where Maharishi said he received inspiration from Devi, Mother Divine, to spread Vedic knowledge to the west. In the Devi Upanishad, and you remember that the Upanishads are about the Absolute, absolute reality, it says that all the gods waited upon the Goddess Devi and asked her: "Great Goddess, who art Thou?" She replies, and this is my rendering of the language: "I am essentially Brahman. From Me has proceeded the world, made of the Absolute and the relative, Nothingness and Fullness. I am all forms of bliss and non-bliss. Knowledge and ignorance are Myself. I am the five elements and also what is different from them. I am the entire world. I am the Veda as well as what is different from it. I am the unborn; I am the born. Below and above and around am I."

Earlier on I quoted the prayer that Maharishi offered up when he was inaugurating the Dawn of the Age of Enlightenment on the Flagship Gotthard on Lake Lucerne in Switzerland in 1975: "Mother Divine! Now on Thine own, think of bringing the dawn of enlightenment to the whole world and destroying the fear of all that is not good. Do not wait for our prayers to reach Thine altar. Ma! Thine immeasurable influence and strength is beyond the reach of prayers even from the Lord Almighty, the Lord of Creation, and the Lord of Dissolution." What this means to me is that Devi, Mother Divine, is the One God, beyond and subsuming all the other intelligences and laws of nature that govern all aspects of creation. Devi takes many forms and aspects and each temple to her recognizes that aspect as well as the wholeness. I felt very comfortable with this understanding of the One God; She is the One. I was hoping to feel something of that power and wholeness as we visited temple after temple.

When we reached Kanyakumari, the pilgrimage site at the southernmost tip of India, many of the group bathed in the waters where three oceans come together: the Indian Ocean, the Arabian Sea, and the Bay of Bengal. David went into the sea with all the students and most of the older men; I could not even contemplate it. Then we walked through an alley to the temple entrance. We had hoped to meditate inside, to get a feeling for the spiritual aspect of the place, but Indian temples don't work that way. They hustle the pilgrims quickly through the place, giving you only a moment to nod at the various stone deities dressed in flowers and silks (and set behind grates or they would be lovingly vandalized). Then you are literally shoved away by the other pilgrims, and pushed along. We did a little sit-in in a vacant corner and we did meditate for a few minutes, but it was not memorable for me. Even so, I did feel something deep and ancient, some presence of a force beyond and underlying the tumult and the noise. You don't get silence in an Indian temple these days, but maybe when our own pandits grow up and take over the running of these temples, the atmosphere and procedures will change.

During the five-week trip we would visit a number of temples, most to Mother Divine in some aspect or other. My favorite one was the temple at Vindhyachal, which we visited on the way from Allahabad to Varanasi. Again we walked though long narrow alleys lined with shops selling offerings, temple souvenirs, and bangles. We were met by our own Maharishi pandits from a nearby ashram. They were tall, good-looking young men. They told us to chant *Jai Mataji Vindhyavisini* (Hail Mother Vindhyavasini, which means she who resides in Vindhya) as they ushered us along to view the deity within. We made offerings, got big red dots put on our foreheads, and were each given a scarf/shawl in red and gold and white (David's is partly green). Vindhyavasini is the name of a benevolent aspect of Devi Amba or Durga. Mother Divine has three three major aspects: Lakshmi, Saraswati, and Durga, the destroyer of the negative. This temple is one of the most revered Shakti Peethas in India. Google all that if you want to know more and see a picture of the deity.

On the way out I bought a little souvenir, a tiny enameled picture of a small black stone wrapped in flowers and silks and it sits on my dining room table. I hemmed the ragged edges of both of our shawls and we wrap ourselves in them when we meditate in the dome. How can I explain this? I was taught as a Jew not to worship idols, just the one true God. The shawl, the little enameled picture, both remind me of something fundamental and sweet; they evoke some feeling I can't really describe or recognize. I just know it is there. I wrap myself in it, and it brings some comfort and bliss. Life is mysterious and must be embraced in all its aspects, knowable and unknowable. I am not going to worry about the meaning of it; I am just going to enjoy it.

The Brahmasthan

From the Jabalpur airport we were driven to the remote area where the movement had developed a large campus for pandits, Purusha, and visitors like us. It was a thrill to walk outside the little airport after our two-hour dawn flight and see a big bus with a banner saying Maharishi Mahesh Yogi Vedic University. Our people! David and I and Bob and Carol and Sue Brown (who was leading the course for the students) and a couple of others were led to the VIP van, given bags of sandwiches and snacks and driven for over three hours on dusty, rough roads to the campus. David and I were told we were movement royalty and we were given a huge suite in the best building right next door to Bob and Carol, all marble and beautiful hangings; very, very nice.

We were oriented to our daily routine: meals, rounding, two afternoon visits to the pandit campus for big yagyas, and afternoon and evening meetings, with smaller yagyas right there in our meeting room on the other afternoons, and tapes of Maharishi. We were ready for a week of rest and rounding here at the center of India. We had heard that meditations there were very deep, and so they were. The major yagyas, the Maha Durga Saptashati, to give the nourishing value of Mother Divine, and the Atirudrabhishek, for world peace, were extremely powerful and moving. In the Atirudrabhishek, which is done with at least 1,331 pandits, the pandits are structuring silence, we were told, and reverberating within it. This was, without doubt, the most spiritual place in India. Raja Harris Kaplan, the Raja of India for the TM movement, explained why this place was chosen and described its history in the movement.

In the *Mahabharata*, the epic of Mighty India, the sage Agasthya tells the Pandava brothers that they should go to the Brahmasthan of India, the geographical center of that vast country and meditate there before they go on with their lives. As a very young man, Guru Dev asked his Master's permission to meditate in the forests of the Brahmasthan. He took silence in the remote areas there and visited Jabalpur, where Maharishi met him. As early as 1985 Maharishi had sent various people to scout for land in this area, which was barely accessible. Starting around 1995 a man named Sant Ji began to acquire land for the movement and Maharishi called him every night to hear the progress. It took over a year to gather the first 150 acres. It was very difficult because each landowner had about one quarter of an acre and not many were willing to sell them, but many would trade them for another. So buying, swapping, trying to get enough adjacent parcels to begin to build something was a long and tedious task, one on which Maharishi kept his attention year after year.

Sant Ji happened to be visiting the Brahmasthan just then and he told us his story. He first met Maharishi in Amherst in 1971; he was a new meditator from the D.C. area. Later, Maharishi asked him what he was doing. He was working for IBM at the time. "You are wasting your life," Maharishi told him. "You should come and join me and just be around me." And so he did and was in Majorca and later other places, full time. At one point Maharishi directed Sant Ji to go to India and find land for an ashram in Uttar Kashi, up in the Himalayas, and he told the story about finding a suitably remote area and then trying to get heavy equipment and building supplies up there on the backs of sherpas. All this was going on in the background (the background for us) while we were living around Maharishi and developing our little corner of the movement. From the very beginning it was in Maharishi's mind to build this place in the center of India and the places in Uttar Kashi for Purusha and Mother Divine, and to restore the pandit culture.

Now there are about 1,770 acres there at the Brahmasthan with three different campuses: the Bijouri or international one where we were and the Purusha buildings were located, which we could see over the trees; the Karoundi or pandit campus, where over one thousand pandits were housed, where they studied, and where they did their daily yagyas; and the Banhara campus where the Rajas, the leaders of the various branches of the movement, have their winter homes. We visited there and had lunch with some old friends, Chris Crowell, our buddy from the Armenia project, and his wife Ann, and saw the houses of some others we knew. It was an ambitious project, one with miraculous support of nature, and it was so thrilling to see it being carried out as Maharishi had wished.

One afternoon we all drove over to the official Brahmasthan, a small monument built by the government of India, with statues of lions pointing in the four cardinal directions. According to our surveyors it is just a little off center. The true center is on the movement land, we were told. We all sat on the monument and meditated for a little while the workers there looked on us with amusement and amazement, I think. I wrote a poem about the experience. All of us students on the course (the India trip) were supposed to create something. I actually wrote quite a few poems as we went along.

Brahmasthan

Beyond the howling of the dogs,
Beyond the screeching of the crows,
Beyond the beeping, beeping, beeping of the horns,
Lies Veda Bhoomi Bharat
India, the land of the Veda.

Since the beginning of time and place,
Saints have settled quietly
Near the center of India,
The Brahmasthan, where Brahma, the Creator,
Establishes himself.

They meditate there,
Live simply,
Know *that from the Center,*
Beyond the business of daily life,
A Silence radiates throughout the land.

When the Pandavas were exiled to the forest,
The sage Agasthya counseled them:
"Go to the Brahmasthan. Meditate there.
Accrue karma equal to 1,000 cows given to holy men,
A gateway into Heaven.

"Know yourselves to be
One with the One Reality.
Bathe in the River of Being
That transcends this relative world,
Flow with the bliss of the gods."

And so we pilgrims venture there, and
Pose for photos with stone lions
Who guard the monument.
We face east and meditate,
While government workers stop and stare.

We will come again to India's heart,
Establish ourselves at the Center,
Float in that River of Being,
Bask in that golden silence,
And illuminate ourselves and our lands.

The Maharishi School

Back in Jabalpur we settled into the Narmada Jackson Hotel and then visited a Maharishi School the next morning. First we went to the principal's office and got a brief introduction to the school and its programs. She took us to the puja room where eleven pandits do daily *rudrabhisheks* and other yagyas all day long. We sat with them for a while and enjoyed the deep silence they were creating for the school and the whole area. Imagine having that in your school! The school was on holiday so the 2,000 students were not there, just a small group of them who had been asked to perform music and dancing for us. Small groups of beautiful young people sang welcoming songs and performed a classical Indian dance, their original composition, undulating and swaying, which was paying tribute to the holy Narmada River that runs through that part of central India. There were large pictures of Maharishi looking benevolently down on the central open area where we were seated, and banners with familiar movement slogans were all over the walls: Knowledge is Structured in Consciousness, and so forth.

Was it the chanting? Was it the singing and dancing? I don't know, but the whole experience moved me deeply. My travel journal reminds me that my emotions were overwhelming me as I sat there that morning. Tears started rolling down my cheeks. I felt gratitude for Maharishi; I felt a profound realization of his greatness; I felt awed that his vision was being realized. Reservations and resentments I had harbored knowingly and unknowingly over the years just melted away, leaving love in their place. It was all very humbling. I felt a very great expansion of my heart. It seemed to be pushing against the walls of my chest. I told the physics teacher and the head lady that I had been a teacher all my life and that this was the fulfillment of it all.

The principal showed us trophies and awards that the school had won; it takes all the prizes, just as Maharishi School in Fairfield does, and it is the envy of all the other private schools in Jabalpur. In her office were pictures of visitors, our friends Alarik and Cynthia Arenander, David Lynch, and Raja Harris, of course. The school even had a vaidya available and a little Ayurvedic herb store. We stocked up at bargain basement prices on my favorite throat syrup, and a few other things. There are now over a hundred of these schools throughout India, with more than 100,000 meditating students and teachers, we were told. There should be more, and hopefully there will be.

After lunch we drove outside of town to see the Narmada River and falls, but the highlight of the afternoon was a stop at a little roadside cluster of temples and alcoves right by the river with a ghat leading down to its banks. We were told that Maharishi had stayed here for some period of time as a young man, meditating in the various little shrines and probably bathing in the river, which was said to be a purifying thing to do. The pandit in the little Shiva temple closest to the road where our bus was parked claimed to remember him. We wandered from shrine to shrine, all very silent and meditative. No noise, no hustling, no pushing. Just our little group walking about and stopping to soak up the vibes here and there. There were little alcove shrines to Surya, the Sun god, and to Hanuman, the monkey who helped Ram conquer the demon Ravana (described in the other major Indian epic, the *Ramayana*), with pictures of Ram and his consort Sita and his brother Lakshman. There was a little alcove with an orange-red Hanuman in it and a small temple to the planet and deity Saturn that held a black idol and had all black walls, very Saturn-like.

We all wandered down the steps of the ghat to the river and

cupped the water in our hands and anointed our heads and offered the water back to the River Narmada. It was now early evening, and behind us cows and buffalos were being led back to their stalls and were lowing softly. Some of the guys got into the water. I waded in a bit. Whatever tradition told us to do: walk around the Saturn temple three times, sprinkle water on our heads three times, whatever, I did it. Why not? Couldn't hurt. Might help. I am an equal opportunity devotee. It was sweet to imagine Maharishi as a young man living here, soaking himself in the rural silence, perhaps thinking and planning how to carry out Guru Dev's instructions to take the knowledge to householders in the West, pulling back the arrow and getting ready to shoot forth. It made us feel closer to him, closer to Guru Dev. It was humanizing, personal, immediate, not remote and abstract. Very nice.

Shankaracharya Ashram

We traveled to Allahabad (named the place of Allah by the Muslims, the home of God). The Shankaracharya, Swami Vasudevananda Saraswati Maharaj, was not in his ashram when we arrived, but we were able to visit it. We all had a nice meditation outside and then were taken inside to see the renovations and reconstructions going on with marble, carved stone, and beautiful arches and stairways. In the central recessed area there were paintings of Adi Shankara (the first Shankara), Krishna and his consort Radha, and Guru Dev. They were flanked by a large orange Hanuman on the left and a Ganesh on the right. A huge marble dais was being built there for the Shankaracharya to sit upon and lecture to his audience. Maharishi was responsible for all this, for turning this humble little ashram into something that would reflect the glory of the knowledge. I suspect he was behind having Guru Dev's picture there along with that of Adi Shankara.

Just outside this inner sanctum a group of eleven pandit boys and their teacher were performing the *rudrabhishek* and then a celebratory *aarti* afterwards. We sat or stood in the open air around them, sang and clapped along, and enjoyed the whole thing. As they were finishing, a large orange van drove up. The Shankaracharya had returned. The van had been given to him by the movement, as well as a big orange bus. Why orange? The Shankaracharya wears orange dhotis, the traditional dress of the sanyasis. We waited until he climbed the steps to his temporary little reception area on a porch overlooking the courtyard, and then we went up too. He knew who we were and smiled very kindly at us. David and I and Sue Brown and Bob and Carol presented him with elaborate garlands of roses and everyone else had bouquets of marigolds to offer. Bob told him who we were, mostly in Hindi, which he loved, and Ranjan translated for us.

Bob told him what we were doing to support Maharishi's movement and the spread of the knowledge and then introduced David and me as founding faculty of MUM. Raja Harris had asked David to speak and David told him how grateful we were that Maharishi had brought the knowledge to the West and he offered forty years of research from 200 research institutions in over 30 countries, over 700 studies on TM, to his feet. Swami Vasudevananda smiled very sweetly and benevolently at us. Then there were subtle indications that our audience was over and we all descended the little stairway. After I got my shoes back on I glanced back up at him. He was watching. I smiled at him and made the Namaste gesture and he looked back lovingly and nodded to me.

The Maharishi Smarak

We drove across the river to the memorial to Maharishi that was under construction near one of our pandit campuses (with over 1,000 pandits). It was largely unfinished but already had large sculpted columns, lots of white marble, pieces of which were scattered about outside. There were panels of text, which had been done in Fairfield at Creative Edge Mastershop and filled in with gold by MUM staff. One of them said that scientific research had established the validity of the Vedic knowledge. David was very pleased and we took some pictures of us standing there pointing at those words. Our group had gathered together outside and we did a brief meditation together.

In the Maharishi Smarak, pointing at the words engraved and gold filled: The scientific validation of this most ancient value of human knowledge is established.

Inside, in the middle of the open space, was a raised kind of altar with a large picture of Maharishi, and people had offered flowers, so there were some dried old ones and the recent remains of some fresh ones in front of his picture. Many of us climbed up the few steps and bent our heads there. As it turned out it was February 5, the anniversary of the day that Maharishi had dropped the body six years earlier. I wasn't thinking of that, however. I was overwhelmed with a very emotional and tearful outpouring of love and gratitude. I felt his presence. He was there! He came to be with our group. It was very powerful. I couldn't doubt it; I could only enjoy it and try to get myself back together and climb down.

The only thing left was to take little boats out into the middle of Ma Ganga, the Ganges River, at the *sangam*, or confluence, where the Ganges meets the Yamuna River, and the underground or transcendental Saraswati River. It is said that a bath there flushes away all one's sins and frees one from the cycle of rebirth. Ah, would that it were so easy. There is a huge sandbar in the middle of the river and many small boats tie up there and you can step out and walk around and dip and play and pray, which we all did. You cup the water in your hands and pray, for your guru, for your family, for your self, for the whole world. You dip your offerings in the water: bangles, red cloth (red for Mother Divine), flowers. It was warm and sunny and the air was clear. It was a lovely afternoon, much easier and more enjoyable than I thought it might be. I was remembering the ice-cold water of the Ganges up in Rishikesh when we visited the ashram there in 1975. Here it was warmer and milder.

Varanasi and Sarnath

Formerly known as Benares, and way before that, in ancient times, as Kashi, this is the city on the Ganges famous for its burning ghats where people are cremated and their ashes set afloat in the water. We took boats upriver from our hotel area to visit the Kashi Vishwanat Temple. Again, a crowded, dirty, noisy, unspiritual experience. I was most impressed with a story Ranjan told me. It seems that when the Mughal emperor Auranzeb destroyed the Hindu temples and built his mosque there during the seventeenth century, one of the temple priests put the Shiva lingam, the principal stone representative of the god Shiva, down a well for safekeeping, and during all the murders and destruction, the knowledge of its location got lost. When the time was right for rebuilding the temple, Ahilaya'bai, Queen of Mandu in the province of Madya Pradesh, had a dream locating the lingam in a well. She got it recovered and helped to relocate and build the new temple. I bought a little memento with her in it, as well as Shiva, Parvati (Shiva's consort), and the Goddess Annapurna, the goddess of food. My guy! As we headed downstream in the dusk we were struck with the ancient beauty of all the buildings and their ghats lining the river.

The next day we went on a day trip to nearby Sarnath, the place where Buddha first expounded his teaching in the Deer Park. The place was very silent and sweet. We could see the ruins of

old buildings and our guide pointed out the various stupas that
had once stood there. No animals or vendors were allowed on
the grounds, so it was all very clean and quiet, and it felt familiar,
very old and very familiar. Had we been there before in a past life?
Why not? In preparation for the visit, I had learned that when
the Buddha got there he was approached by the ascetics who had
been his former companions when he was doing his austerities
and was challenged by them. Buddha had gotten enlightened and
it changed his perspective. "Austerities only confuse the mind,"
he had said. "In the exhaustion and mental stupor to which they
lead, one can no longer understand the ordinary things of life, still
less the truth that lies beyond the senses. I have given up extremes
of either luxury or asceticism. I have discovered the Middle Way."
His former colleagues were convinced and became his disciples at
that moment.

Buddha preached the four Noble Truths and the eight-fold
path as the way out of suffering. The problem with the eight-fold
path is that you cannot practice those activities naturally and easily until you have *already reached enlightenment.* If you transcend
and grow in consciousness, those behaviors will spontaneously
develop. They are a description of enlightenment, not a path to it,
Maharishi explains. The most effective path is through transcending and purification. We visited the museum there, with its elegant
sculptures and very intelligent guides, and found what was supposedly the descendent of the original Bodhi tree and meditated
near it. A nice afternoon.

That evening we were invited to attend the nightly aarti to Ma
Ganga. This ritual is performed all along the Ganges, at every
town and city, but this one was spectacular. Our twilight boat ride
took us to the Dashashwamedha (ten horses) ghat, where special
platforms had been set up for our group and areas were marked
off for pandit boys from Maharishi's local pandit school. Their
parents were sitting near us, very proud of their boys. The man in
charge was a devotee of Maharishi and he had organized a very

theatrical performance. Five men stood at platforms facing the river, and they were dressed in elegant kurtas of dark red, white, and gold. There were loudspeakers, bells, tabla playing, and the evening was very noisy and smoky due to the huge smudge pots and fistfuls of incense used. At a certain part in the performance we honored guests were invited to go down to the banks of the river with the pandits and to make offerings to the River Ganga: sandalwood, flowers, water. We set little paper boats alight with tiny fires to float down the river into the night. People were watching the performance behind us right up the steps leading up to the buildings, as well as in front of us, sitting in many little boats upon the water. Twinkling lights and little fires everywhere.

When it came time to leave and we walked toward our waiting boats, the pandit boys gathered around us and chanted away, giving us a glorious send off. Quite a night. It was thrilling to see that Maharishi's influence was everywhere, restoring the pandit performances. We still had some little paper boats we could light and float off into the night from our boats as we slowly made our way back to ghat closest to where our bus was parked and back to our hotel.

We went to one more aarti on the river, this one in Rishikesh during our stay there. It was a much smaller and local affair, very low key and nice. Our group ran into some Mother Divine ladies there, some old friends. I dipped the necklaces David and I had bought in the river to purify them in its clear waters. We had bought some nine-gem (one for each planet) necklaces for me and our daughters and granddaughter, and a crystal and pearl one for me. We offered little flower-filled boats again and set them afloat. One of our group said he saw Ma Ganga, huge and recumbent, swooping by our aarti and smiling at all of us benevolently. A very sweet evening and lovely end to the trip.

On our last day some of us went to another Mother Divine temple, the Kamakshi Devi Temple in the Om Karananda Ashram in Rishikesh. Nothing official was going on so we could just sit in front of Devi and meditate in the silence. An old Purusha friend turned up there too. It is so sweet to be in a totally foreign place far from home and bump into a familiar friend. It makes the world seem like a small homey place, doesn't it? Some of our group visited Maharishi's old academy in Rishikesh down the river, now overgrown and given back to the forest. There is talk of restoring it because, after all, the Beatles met Maharishi there. We shake our heads. Oh, boy, as my father would say.

Panchakarma

While we were in Rishikesh David and I were getting over a cold, so Ranjan took us to a Maharishi vaidya at a small clinic he ran there. Some Purusha friends were staying there as well. The vaidya took our pulses and looked us over and prescribed some herbs and potions and said we both needed an abyanga, an oil massage. I needed two. I was especially vata deranged (frazzled by all the movement and travel). Okay, we agreed. That seemed like a good idea. He indicated a door and when we walked that way we discovered we were to have the treatment right now! It had been a long time since our last ones. When I smelled the fragrant oil and felt the warm hands of the technicians I was delirious with joy. So, so wonderful. The next day David went with the others to visit Vasistha's Cave; I went back to the clinic for a second abyanga, grateful for the precious knowledge Maharishi had brought out of India and made available. I was feeling very fortunate. It seemed as if we had been given a gift directly from Maharishi.

I have left out all the shopping and tourist visits, the many temples, the long bus and train rides. They were fun, but beside the point. A visit to Lelystad, the Ideal Village outside of Amsterdam, on the way back to the U.S. showed us again how wonderful it is to live in a meditating community, to stroll past friends' houses, as you walk to the meditation program. We gave a talk to the group there and told them about our trip, and we got to see a wonderful museum not too far from Lelystad, the Kröller-Müller museum with its big Van Gogh collection. In Amsterdam we were able to visit the newly renovated and just opened Van Gogh and Rijksmuseums. Paul Gelderloos' daughter Padmini lent us her apartment and we could walk all over the old town and directly to the museums. That was very inspiring and enjoyable, of course, but the real effects of the trip would become more and more evident in the following months.

I now felt Maharishi in my heart and mind, as I used to feel him, as a distant but quiet presence. I felt part of the whole spiritual enterprise again, after all those years of separation. I felt that his hand had been in everything we had done over all those years, that his guidance had subtly directed our lives, perhaps spontaneously through the workings of nature. Same thing. A boil had burst in David's and my relationship as well, and when we returned home and finally got over the flu and fatigue we were at a new level in our marriage. Maharishi had done it again!

Epilogue

THE ANCIENT GREEK WORD for the good life is *eudaimonia*. It means a life not necessarily easy, but one filled with meaning and striving toward a goal. *Eu* means good, and *daimon* denotes divine forces or powers. So a good life is one in harmony with the laws of nature, we could say, or with the will of God, as some might have it. And there is a dharmic element to it also. One's life and actions would be in accord with one's evolutionary life path, best for the individual and best for the environment, and that would result in happiness, which is the common translation of the word.

The last few years have brought the balance of six months on the IAA in Fairfield (with some travel) and six months at our winter home in northwest Florida (again with some travel). David has written or co-authored another fifteen publications since we began the IAA in 2006, and continues to explore entirely new areas of research, as he has done his whole career (from prison rehabilitation to collective consciousness), and he is now exploring the uses of big data. He was recently appointed to be the Research Desk for the Maharishi Foundation so he is now getting a salary for what he has been doing *pro bono* for the movement for the last twenty years. He was also given a Lifetime Achievement Award by the movement which deeply touched his heart.

After basically amusing myself and wondering what to do next after the trip to India, in the fall of 2015 I suddenly conceived the idea of writing my memoirs, not as an autobiographical story, which I had begun some years before and abandoned, but with the angle of my connection to Maharishi and my involvement with the TM movement. This spurred a joyous project of self-discovery, reconnecting to my past and to some old and dear friends, and resulted in this volume. David pulled out all my course notebooks, which he had lovingly saved. Some friends volunteered to design the book, scan in and tweak the photos, and help me upload it and print it. Support of nature. The old, familiar feeling of being on a dharmic path set in, along with the usual loving push from nature. Here I was again, onto something good.

In addition, when we returned to Fairfield for the summer, we got the opportunity to build a Maharishi Vastu, a new townhome in North Campus Village, just north of our old condo (see www.FortuneCreatingBuildings.com). David always claimed he could feel the vastu effect when we visited a friend in their new home. I thought, vastu shmastu (Yiddish for big deal!). Of course it felt good. A new home, lovely furniture, why not? However, as we bought the house and made the move it became apparent, even to me, that there was a profound difference between the two dwellings. I am happier, it seems, more creative, more settled. It became the perfect base for finishing this book.

Now, as we walk the forest trail, through the biodiversity of trees, wildflowers, chipmunks, and rabbits, on our way to the Dome each morning and evening, we feel very fortunate. Maharishi had always emphasized the need to get into a proper Maharishi Vastu in order to have the happiest and most evolutionary life, another gift of knowledge from him. The time had finally been right to do so. The two-way street was open and flowing. After this book? Perhaps a reworking of my dissertation on transcending in myth and literature into a more popular, less scholarly format. Maybe a book of poetry, mine and others more spiritual.

What will happen next? I'm waiting for the next cosmic nudge.

Acknowledgments

FIRST, I HAVE TO THANK my husband David for profoundly enlivening and structuring my life in a spiritual direction, not that I had any choice once we found each other and recognized that fact. I have to also thank him for always supporting my rest and my evolutionary activity, and that meant strongly encouraging and helping me with this volume. Love is not always easy, but it is the most important thing in life, is it not? Without love, where is the background upon which to live, where is the joy of sharing?

Takoma Park, Maryland, 1963

I must also thank my beloved family, who sometimes felt that they were taking second place to my movement activities. I hope that reading this volume shows them that was not the case. I love them very much and they repaid my love many times and in many ways, because they were my evolutionary path and made me into a better person.

To all the dear friends who shared this wonderful journey and helped me recall it and relive it once again: Lesley Goldman, Susan Humphrey Tracy, Emily Levin, Rachel Parry, Vesey Crichton, Nadine Oliver, Susan Seifert, Jenny Rothenberg Gritz, and so many, many more. Please forgive me if I left out your name. Thank you, thank you, thank you.

A profound thank you to new friends Janice Prescott and Warren Simons who have designed and built this book and made the whole project easy and joyful. And many thanks to Linda Egenes, Fran Clark, Jan Thatcher, and Bob and Carol Markowitz. And thank you to Debbie Thompson who showed me how to compose the legend on the inside cover and place all the various copyright marks. If there are any mistakes, it is their fault. Ha ha. Just kidding. If you find any typos or errors, please let me know.

I also have to thank Vassar College. My experience there, often uncomfortable, always challenging, profoundly evolutionary, made me into who I am, a Vassar Girl forever.

And finally, I have to acknowledge and thank Google and Facebook. How did we ever live without them? When I wanted to know where someone was or how to contact them or had a question about something from the movement past, I posted it on Facebook, and an answer always came, and sometimes a very lively discussion followed.

To Maharishi and Guru Dev, this volume is my acknowledgment of their grace.

Jai Guru Dev